DATE			

Ⓢ THE BAKER & TAYLOR CO.

Labor Unions and Autocracy in Iran

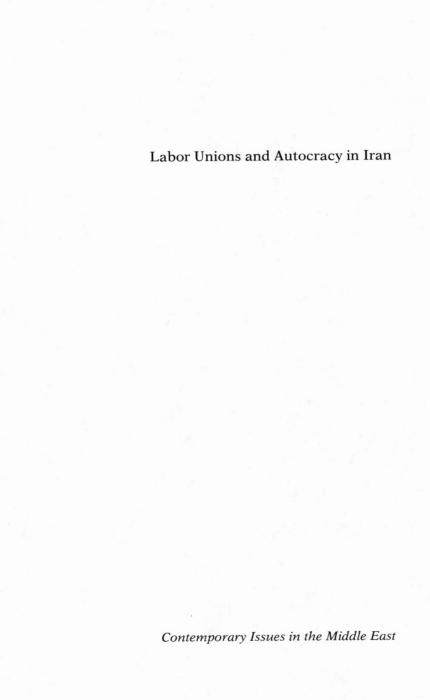

Contemporary Issues in the Middle East

Labor Unions and Autocracy in Iran

HABIB LADJEVARDI

SYRACUSE UNIVERSITY PRESS

1985

The paper used in this publication meets the minimum requirements of American National Standard for Information Sciences—Permanence of Paper for Printed Library Materials, ANSI Z39.48–1984. ∞˜

Library of Congress Cataloging-in-Publication Data

Ladjevardi, Habib.
    Labor unions and autocracy in Iran.

    (Contemporary issues in the Middle East)
    Bibliography: p.
    Includes index.
    1. Trade-unions—Government policy—Iran—History.
2. Trade-unions—Iran—History. I. Title. II. Series.
HD6805.2.L33 1985   331.88'0955   85–17300
ISBN 0–8156–2343–7 (alk. paper)

Manufactured in the United States of America

For Goli
Who enabled me
To discover
My own capacity
To love.

Habib Ladjevardi is Director of the Iranian Oral History Project, Harvard University. Born in Tehran, he grew up in Scarsdale, New York, and was educated at the Yale Engineering School and the Harvard Business School. Dr. Ladjevardi returned to Iran in 1963 and began work as personnel manager in his family's business. Subsequently he was responsible for founding the Iran Center for Management Studies in Tehran, where he taught until 1976. He also served on a number of boards and councils in the private and public sectors. Dr. Ladjevardi received his Ph.D. from the University of Oxford in 1981.

Contents

Tables

Acknowledgments

I AM INDEBTED to a number of friends and colleagues who have made the completion of this work possible: Reza Alavi urged me to go to his alma mater, St. Antony's College, Oxford, and continue my studies. Gregor Melikian and Professor Louis B. Barnes, my two closest colleagues in Iran, accepted additional responsibilities in order to allow me to pursue my new interest. I wish to thank Professor J. Alan Brown, who introduced me to the University of Oxford and British hospitality; Robert Mabro, who guided my initial work, and Alan Angell, who supervised the preparation of the doctoral dissertation that served as the heart of this book. John Gurney offered much valuable advice. The late Habib Naficy and William J. Handley directed me to primary source materials and to individuals with valuable information. Dorothy Kegg and Laura Serafin carried out the difficult task of typing parts of the manuscript, and Kathleen Ahern did a superb job of editing. I am grateful also to Nadav and Anita Safran, who encouraged me to publish the manuscript. Barkev Kassarjian listened to various drafts with enthusiasm and patience.

Cambridge, Massachusetts
Spring 1985   HL

Introduction

$\mathcal{T}$HE IRAN of 1978 was in many respects dramatically different from the Iran of half a century earlier. During the intervening years major economic and social changes had taken place, especially in the urban areas. These changes included the establishment of a strong central government, creation of an educational system that enabled millions of children to become literate, legislation of greater rights for women, and construction of roads and factories. In sum, impressive economic and social gains had been made since the 1920s. However, when one looks at the third leg of the triangle of development—namely, the political—the picture is entirely negative. Not only did "political maturity" not emerge after decades of social and economic development, but the political experience gained, beginning with the constitututional revolution of 1906 and continuing erratically until the mid-1920s, was forfeited during the autocratic rule of Reza Shah (1925–1941).

The invasion of Iran by the Anglo-Soviet forces in August 1941 led to the restoration of constitutional monarchy and a second chance for Iran to develop politically as well as socially and economically. However, this second opportunity for Iranians to learn to live under the rule of law did not last very long. The young Mohammad-Reza Shah, who replaced his father, Reza Shah, in 1941, gradually succeeded in reestablishing an autocratic monarchy, apparently believing that social and economic gains could not be made under a democratic form of government. As early as 1944, the young Shah had made his views clear—not to the Iranian public but to Western diplomats. For example in December of that year he told the visiting American diplomat, Averell Harriman, that "the country could not be truly democratic, which he [the Shah] desired, until the people had acquired sufficient education to understand the principles of democratic government and be able to form intelligent individual opinion." In fact, the more the autocratic regime succeeded in removing the vestiges of constitutional government, the more it attempted to justify and legitimize its existence on the basis of its socioeconomic achievements.

This work aims to follow the ebb and flow of political development in Iran from 1906 to 1963 by looking at one aspect of political growth, namely, the emergence of labor unions—an excellent barometer of political development. In periods of political freedom in Iran, labor unions were the first institutions to appear; when political repression reemerged, unions were the first to be suppressed. Then came the turn of the press, the legislative branch, political parties, professional associations, the judiciary, and other independent power centers.

I first became interested in the question of labor unions when, as a graduate student, I studied the subject of trade unions in developing countries. I remember in particular that George Lodge, author of *Spearheads of Democracy: Labor in Developing Countries*, made the compelling argument that encouragement and promotion of independent labor unions in developing countries was an effective means of countering Communist influence. This contention was supported by a discussion of the role of unions in a wide variety of third world countries ranging from India to Tunisia.

The question that puzzled me at the time was the following: If independent labor unions diminish the influence of communism by providing a more attractive alternative to the workers, why is it that many developing countries, such as Iran, do not promote or at least allow the formation of labor organizations—even though the governments of these nations exhibit a deep fear of communism? This question remained unanswered for me, although periodically I reconsidered it while living and working in Iran from 1963 to 1976—initially working in a family business as a personnel manager and later in a school of management as an administrator and teacher.

In September 1976 I decided to go to England to study the problems of labor unions in Iran. The diplomatic dispatches and periodic labor reports of the British and American embassies in Tehran, which had become open to the public, turned out to be the major sources for this study, since almost no useful documents were available from the Iranian government or labor unions. However, Iranian newspapers, banned for many years, as well as pamphlets published by different opposition groups, many of them dispersed in various libraries outside of Iran, were also of value. I was also able, through the Freedom of Information Act, to read additional reports prepared by the United States embassy in Tehran and thus to carry on the research through the year 1963. Finally, interviews with key participants (whose names are listed in Appendix A) in the events of the period provided me with both information and insight.

In the early stages of the research I was struck by a number of findings. Although as a primary school student in Tehran, I had lived through the politically exciting period of the 1940s, I had never compared the great differences between the political atmosphere of those years with the Iran I came to know as an adult in the 1960s and 1970s. In the earlier period, I recalled, even school children were aware of the major political issues of the day. They read and discussed speeches by their favorite deputy in the Majles (the parliament) and argued the pros and cons of the crucial issues. School teachers had a particularly important influence on their students as they encouraged and participated in these political discussions both inside and outside the classroom.

Suffice it to say that in the 1970s, newspapers were forbidden to publish the speeches of deputies who had been hand-picked by the regime itself. On the rare occasion when a deputy's statement was published in the press or read on the radio, he was referred to by his electoral district but not by his own name—the regime apparently believing that even the mere mention of the deputy's name might eventually lead to the emergence of a popular political figure.

As I began to analyze the data I had collected, I realized that the difficulty faced by the Iranian workers since the 1940s in trying to organize unions and to choose their own leaders was shared by such diverse groups as businessmen, lawyers, writers, doctors, engineers, journalists, and even the alumni of universities, who were also prevented by the government from forming and controlling their own associations. The autocracy's attitude had its own internal logic: If workers were allowed to form their own organizations and elect their own leaders, how could the government continue to prevent the general public from electing their own representatives to the national legislature?

The government's dilemma in trying to prevent the erosion of its unconstitutional powers was reminiscent of an old Persian proverb about a child who refused to recite the alphabet. In response to his teacher's insistence that he should at least repeat the first letter, the child replied: "If I agree to say 'A,' then I'll have to say 'B,' 'C,' and 'D'!" Thus, the political rights of the workers were an integral part of the political rights of the Iranian population as a whole.

Returning to the question of labor unions and communism, I came to the tentative conclusion that independent trade unions do indeed offer an attractive alternative to communism; but only a country that is proceeding on the path of political development, as well as that of social and economic advancement—i.e., a democratic country—allows the formation of unions. An autocratic regime perceives a greater threat to its stability in independent labor unions than in a Communist movement. The "Communist threat" can always be used by the local authorities as a pretext for greater political control of the population and as a basis for obtaining additional military and political aid from the United States and its allies. Labor unions, on the other hand, *are* a threat, for they *can* shake the pillars of an autocratic regime.

Independent trade unions, therefore, cannot coexist with an autocratic government. Yet even though Great Britain and the United States, in the late 1940s, adopted the basic policy of supporting Iran's movement toward autocracy, they nevertheless appeared interested throughout the two following decades in assisting the development of Iranian trade unions: Both nations assigned labor attaches to their embassies in Tehran and invited potential Iranian labor leaders for study tours to their respective countries. They also conducted seminars on trade unionism and showed films illustrating how British and American workers organized and bargained collectively, and at times went on strike.

My study of the labor movement turned out to be a window through which the political system of Iran could be scrutinized. A similar study of the legislature, the press, or political parties could have achieved the same objective: Each could have served as a window through which a country's political development or regression could be viewed.

Iran's experience dispels the notion that a nation can develop socially and economically without at the same time developing politically. It has been declared all too often that a country has to be *prepared* for democracy; that a strong, determined government must first be given unquestioned power to carry out social and economic reforms, and only then should grant political freedoms. This study questions the proposition that the problems of socioeconomic and political development can be approached sequentially. The history of the labor movement in Iran proves that, to achieve meaningful change in the lives of the people, political progress must go forward simultaneously with social and economic development.

Another common assumption that I hope this book will dispel is that strong men rule in certain developing countries because few competent and patriotic citizens are available to participate in their nation's governance. It is also assumed that labor unions are not formed because workers lack leaders. This study shows that, at least in the case of Iran, there were capable and public-spirited men who did attempt to influence the course of events in their country. Their efforts failed to bear fruit, however, because they were removed by the autocracy from participation in political life. Those with exceptional strength of character were imprisoned or exiled. Political leaders of lesser conviction were harassed, their privileges abolished; or they were co-opted by appeals to their self-interest.

Another impression common among upper-class Iranians and foreigners is that Iranians, especially those of the "lower classes," are like sheep who can be swayed in any direction by the demagogue of the day. They are ridiculed as members of Hezb-e Bad (Party of the Wind). It would appear, on the contrary, that Iranians, especially the common people, distinguish between leaders with strong convictions and those without. Iranian workers frequently followed to the end those leaders in whom they believed—suffering hardship, imprisonment, and in some cases, loss of life. Yet time and again they refused to acknowledge the leadership of men who had been imposed on them from above, or to participate in government-sponsored organizations, or read government-controlled newspapers. These acts of passive resistance were interpreted by many observers as evidence that Iranian workers were politically apathetic.

Many well-meaning individuals with reformist intentions but without the steadfast convictions required—those who thought that perhaps the end justified the means—and who served the autocratic regime in order, as they said, "to do the best we could under the circumstances," lived to regret their choice. In many instances they were used to strengthen the pillars of autocracy and were discarded as soon as they were no longer "useful."

For many years the workers of Iran and, for that matter, most of the politically informed population demonstrated an extraordinary capacity for patience and tolerance toward their political circumstances. However, after witnessing countless contradictions between words and deeds, they became cynical about constitutional government, parliamentary elections, the promises of the ruling elite, and the friendship of the United States and Great Britain. This account of the labor movement in Iran should leave little doubt as to why Iranian workers turned against the monarchy, against "Western democracy," and against the West. The fact that they did not all take refuge in communism is the question to ponder—*not* why they rebelled.

Labor Unions and Autocracy in Iran

1

Genesis of the
Labor Movement

The Formative Years: 1906–1921

ON 5 AUGUST 1906, the ailing Mozaffar-ed-Din Shah of the
Qajar Dynasty signed the decree making Iran a constitutional monarchy. The decree was followed by the first session of the
Majles (the parliament) on 6 October, and the promulgation of Iran's
constitution on 30 December of the same year.

Briefly, the constitution of 1906 established legislative, judicial,
and executive branches of government. The shah was merely the
symbolic head of state, reigning without executive responsibilities.
The legislative branch, chosen by popular vote, approved the bills
proposed by the prime minister and his cabinet and then supervised
their implementation. The ministers were to be accountable to the
legislative branch and could be tried and discharged by majority vote
of the Majles. The constitution enunciated the principles of free
speech, free association, and free assembly. It further stipulated that
anyone accused of committing political offenses be tried by jury.

Unfortunately for the proponents of constitutionalism, Mozaffar-
ed-Din Shah died on 8 January 1907 and was replaced in the same
month by his strong-willed son, the Crown Prince Mohammad-Ali.
Displeased with his father's acquiescence to the constitutionalists,

1

Mohammad-Ali Shah from the beginning of his reign endeavored to restore to the monarchy its absolute powers. Within eighteen months of his accession to the throne, the tug-of-war between the shah and the Majles forced the legislative body to suspend its work. It did so on 23 June 1908. The Majles was bombarded by the shah's forces on 22 July as martial law was declared in Tehran and civil war broke out between the supporters of constitutionalism and absolutism.

By early summer of the following year, the constitutionalists recaptured Tehran, forcing Mohammad-Ali Shah to flee to Czarist Russia. On 26 June 1909, they placed his thirteen-year-old son, Crown Prince Ahmad, on the throne, with Nasser-ol-Molk serving as regent.

Following the expulsion of Mohammad-Ali Shah, Iran returned to its experiment with constitutional monarchy. The second session of the Majles was inaugurated on 16 November 1909 and sat until 25 December 1911. For the next three years (1911–1914), however, the Majles was not convened by Nasser-ol-Molk. As regent, he governed the country without the participation of the legislative branch. In 1914 Ahmad Shah reached the legal age of eighteen. The regent was dismissed, and elections were held for the Majles.

The third session of the Majles began its work on 6 December 1914, but lasted no more than a year. After the occupation of Iran by Russian, Turkish, and British forces, the work of the third session was suspended on 14 December 1915. For the next 5½ years, the country once again lacked a functioning legislative branch.

Iran's labor movement followed on the heels of constitutional government. In 1906, Mohammad Parvaneh and a group of fellow workers organized the country's first trade union in the Koucheki print shop on Nasserieh Avenue in Tehran.[1] The constitution, with its guarantees of the rights of association and assembly, provided the necessary political context in which a labor union could germinate and grow. Moreover, by transferring considerable power from the absolute monarch to the Majles, the constitution prevented the executive branch from suppressing the activities of independent power centers as easily as it had done before 1906.

The return of the absolutists in 1908 made the predictable impact on the Koucheki printers: their trade union ceased to function. However, with the triumph of the constitutionalists over the supporters of Mohammad-Ali Shah and the reopening of the Majles, the situation was briefly reversed. By 1910 the printers of Tehran had organized an industry-wide trade union,[2] published their own newspaper, *Ettehad-e Kargaran* (Unity of Labor),[3] and in June 1910 carried out a successful strike,[4] referred to by the Iranian scholar Tarbiyat as "the first manifestation in Persia of a collectivist or socialistic movement."[5] The trade union and its newspaper ceased to appear shortly thereafter when the British and the Russians on the one hand, and domestic supporters of despotism on the other, prevented the proper functioning of the constitution during most of the 1910s.

Russia and Great Britain also influenced the political development of Iran and hence the formation of trade unions. Prior to 1917 the two countries had been competing for commercial as well as strategic advantages, and in pursuit of their goals had exerted great influence over Iran's domestic affairs. The October Revolution of 1917 radically changed the role of these two powers in Iran. Henceforth Russia, which had previously identified with the most reactionary elements in Iranian society, became the ally for the working class, with the long-term aim of converting Iran into a Communist state. On the other hand Great Britain, heretofore identified with Iran's constitutional revolution but now apprehensive of Communist influence in Iran, cooperated with the privileged classes to establish and support an autocratic monarchy.

Britain's fears were not entirely unfounded. In support of his allegation that Russia, as early as 1918, planned to annex Iran, Polish-born historian George Lenczowski, who worked at the British embassy in Tehran in the 1940s, quotes the following statement attributed to the Communist writer, K. Troyanovsky:

> Revolutionary Russia is the sincere and disinterested inspiration of Persia, a precious counselor, a guide worthy of confidence to orient her toward democracy.
>
> Our policy with regard to Persia must be simply a revolutionary democratic policy. Hence, our interests coincide perfectly with those of the Persian people. . . .
>
> India is our principal objective. Persia is the only path open to India. . . . For the success of the oriental revolution, Persia is the first nation that must be conquered by the Soviets . . . cost what it may.[6]

To such statements may be added others, such as that made by Joseph Stalin, a number of years later: "It is impossible to win over the vast proletarian masses unless the trade unions are won over."[7] Such statements led many observers to conclude that Communist-led trade unions were an instrument of Soviet foreign policy. This was certainly the view of the British government, which continued to look upon trade unionism in Iran as another manifestation of Soviet designs upon Iran that were inimical to British interests in the region.

The Russian revolution had great impact on the political development of Iran in general and on the growth and nature of Iran's labor movement in particular. While the Iranian constitution provided the necessary political setting for the development of trade unions, the emergence of the Communist movement in Russia molded the character of Iran's labor movement and increased the pace at which it developed. After all, trade unions had played important roles prior to the triumph of revolutions. In the words of Lenin: "The development of the proletariat did not, and could not, anywhere in the world, proceed otherwise than through the trade unions, through their interaction with the party of the working class."[8]

Conversely, the trade unions had to be developed in close collaboration with the Communist Party and could not limit themselves to economic issues. According to Lenin, the proper course of action was to combine the economic struggle with the political and to make them both revolutionary.[9] This tradition was continued in Iran, as we shall see, into the 1940s.

Even before the triumph of the October Revolution in Russia, the ideas of the Russian Social Democratic Labor Party had reached Iran. As a matter of fact, the first chapters of the Social Democratic Party in Mashhad, Tabriz, and Tehran were established as early as 1904 by representatives of an Iranian political group named Hemmat, which was based in Baku, capital of what is now Soviet Azerbaijan. These local party chapters, which were to become intermediaries between the Russian bolsheviks and the working class of Iran, were referred to in Iran by a number of names, including Ejetma'iyoun-e Amiyoun (Social Democrats), and Mojahedin.[10]

Because of their ideology, the Social Democrats, led mainly by middle-class intellectuals, paid particular attention to the status of the working class. For example, in a manifesto published on 10 September 1907, the Mashhad branch of the Social Democratic Party called for recognition of the workers' right to strike for political as well as economic objectives. The Social Democrats also protested against attempts to force striking workers back to work. Finally, the party urged the government to institute free and compulsory education for all classes of society[11] and called for the enactment of an eight-hour work day[12]—a demand that went unheeded for the next forty years.

The Social Democrats were also active in the northwestern city of Tabriz, a city in close proximity to revolutionary Russia. On 28 October 1908, under the party's leadership, about 150 workers in three local tanneries went on strike. They elected representatives to negotiate with the employers on the following nine demands: piece rates to be increased by 1½ *shahi* (one-twentieth of a *rial*); employment and discharge of workers to be approved by their representatives; hygienic conditions to be improved; half wages to be paid during illness; overtime hours to be reduced; overtime work to be compensated by twice regular pay; strike pay to be granted; striking workers to be retained; and striking workers not to be replaced. The strike was settled three days later, when the employers agreed to increase the piece rate and to refrain from discharging the striking workers.[13]

Thus, as early as the 1900s, political parties in Iran were championing workers' rights, urging them to make political demands, and leading them through industrial action. During the next decade, while the Communist movement was triumphing in Russia, the collaboration in Iran between political parties and trade unions became closer and more apparent.

By the time the Soviet Union was firmly established and the Soviet policy of promoting revolutionary movements in other countries had begun, there already existed a large number of Iranians fully schooled and dedicated to Communist ideology. For a number of years after the turn of the century, thousands of Iranian workers had left the stagnant Iranian economy in pursuit of employment in Russia's relatively prosperous industry. Soviet historian Z. Z. Abdullaev gives us an idea of the extent of this movement when he states that, in the year 1911, about 193,000 workers left Iran to work in the southern regions of Russia, while 160,000 returned to Iran from Russia the same year. He believes that in Transcaucasia there was a constant Iranian population of "some hundreds of thousands," who in certain branches of enterprises constituted the mass of workers. For example, in 1915, 13,500 Iranians comprised 29.1 percent of the workers employed in the Baku oil industry. In 1912, in the copper-smelting plant of Kedabek, Iranian migrants accounted for 27.5 percent of permanent workers.[14] It was from this vast pool of Iranian migrants that the future leaders of the Communist and labor movements in Iran emerged.

Revolutionary ideology did not simply rub off on Iranian immigrants in Russia. The Russian Social Democrats made a special effort to indoctrinate their guests, and urged them to spread the ideas of social democracy among their fellow workers upon their return to Iran.[15] Many of the Iranian workers and intellectuals residing in Russia were already fully receptive to revolutionary ideas. One reason for this receptivity was the failure of the constitutional revolution in Iran to satisfy their expectations. Although the Iran of 1910 had become somewhat less autocratic than the Iran of 1905, the benefits of constitutionalism had not bettered life for the working class; and the position of those groups that had enjoyed social and economic privileges prior to 1906 continued as before.[16]

It is not difficult, therefore, to comprehend the dismay of the more politically aware members of the working class who witnessed the events taking place in Iran. According to one participant in these events, the immigrants had lost faith in the constitutional movement in their country. They had seen the tribal chiefs, the large landowners, the senior religious leaders, and the rest of the privileged classes become the real beneficiaries of the constitutional revolution. The immigrants wanted to return to Iran and this time take steps to ensure that the same old cliques would not once again regain control of the government merely "by changing their clothes and labels."[17] So a large number of Iranians residing in Russia came to regard a Communist revolution as the means of solving Iran's problems.

The revolutionary environment in Russia during the late 1910s and the desire of the Iranian immigrants to bring about a major change in Iran's political life encouraged them to form and join political organizations. As a result the Edalat Committee was established in Baku in 1916. Iranian teachers, journalists, and oil workers employed in Baku made up the bulk of its membership. Mirza-Asadollah Ghaffarzadeh was elected as its first chairman.[18] Other leaders of Edalat included revolutionaries such as Mir-Ja'far Pishevari, Ahmad Soltanzadeh, Dr. Salamollah Javid, and Heidar-Khan Amoghli, all of whom had spent considerable time in Russia.[19]

The date 23 June 1920 is an important one in the history of political parties in Iran. The Edalat Committee held its first congress in Anzali (a seaport on the Iranian side of the Caspian Sea), calling

itself the Persian Communist Party (PCP). It endorsed the rights of
the toilers (*ranjbaran*), in both government and private organizations,
to establish trade unions.[20]

In a document seized in Tabriz in February 1921, signed by
Heidar-Khan and stamped with the seal of the "Central Committee
of the Communist Party of Persia, Edalat," the local branches of the
PCP were urged to "make propaganda immediately to reorganize the
guilds created by the workers of the same trade, the importance of
which is considerable for the grouping of workers; awake class feeling
among the workers and spread agitation among them in the country."[21]

Although the thread connecting the Soviet Union, the Iranian
Communists, and the trade unions was rarely visible in the 1940s,
this was not so in the 1920s. In a report describing the work of the
PCP, Soltanzadeh wrote in a July 1921 issue of *Pravda:* "The
Communist Party tries to rally round it the most advanced elements
among the peasants and the workers, to organize them, to elevate
them under the inspiration of the Third Communist International,
and to create simultaneously trade unions in all cities and the unions
of agrarian workers in the villages."[22]

The work of organizing the trade unions began in earnest in 1918
when demands were being made for the reopening of the Majles,
closed since 1915. The printers once again took the lead. In that same
year their union was reorganized under the leadership of Seyyed-
Mohammad Dehgan, a newspaper editor and an avowed Communist
who had studied in Russia.[23] Soon after its formation, the printers'
union waged a fourteen-day strike and succeeded in reaching a
collective agreement with its employers. The printers' working day
was reduced to eight hours, overtime pay was instituted,[24] medical
care was provided, and arbitrary dismissal of workers abandoned. [25]

The victory of the printers encouraged other trades to organize.
In 1919 the bakers and the textile-shop clerks formed their own trade
unions.[26] Their leading organizer was Dehgan, who also assisted the
textile workers (*parchehbafan*). After observing their working conditions, Dehgan provided all three unions with membership cards in
the union. A week later, members of the new union were invited to
a private home where elections were conducted, and Shokrollah Mani
was chosen as union leader.[27]

One of the first acts of the textile workers was to call a strike.
Having requested and received part of their wages in advance, they
were able to establish a fund which helped them to prolong the strike

and eventually achieve their demands. Their piece-rate was increased by 33 percent to 4 *abbasi* (one-fifth of a *rial*) per *zar'* (41 inches).[28]

Having seen the benefits of united action, the textile workers joined the General Trade Union (GTU) of the Workers of Tehran (Ettehadieh-e Omoumieh Kargaran-e Tehran),[29] which was formed in October 1921.[30]

According to Dehgan, by 1922 the GTU had succeeded in organizing eight thousand of Tehran's thirty thousand workers. The membership of the eight trade unions that were affiliated with the GTU in 1922 was as follows:[31]

TABLE 1
Membership of General Trade Union of Tehran in 1922

Trade	Number of Members
Bakery workers	3,000
Textile workers	2,000
Shoemakers	1,800
Postal & telegraph workers	90–350
Confectionery workers	90–350
Printers	90–350
Retail clerks	90–350
Trading house clerks	90–350

Tehran was not the only center of trade unionism. Other cities in close proximity to Russia also developed labor organizations, including Tabriz,[32] Rasht, and the port of Anzali—each with approximately three thousand members.[33] The major reason that trade unionism developed more rapidly in the north and northwestern tier of Iran was, as Lenczowski has noted, "their greater knowledge of the workers' movement in Russia."[34]

Dehgan became a labor leader after he had been a journalist[35] and a translator of important Communist literature. His political-journalistic background had its impact on the character of the Iranian labor movement. On 30 December 1921, only two months after the formation of the GTU, Dehgan founded the newspaper *Haghighat* (Truth).[36] Identifying itself as socialist (*ejtema'i*) and a supporter of both the toilers (*ranjbaran*) and the trade unions, the first issue of

Haghighat left no doubt as to its Marxist orientation. Moreover, on the top right-hand corner of the paper appeared the slogan "Workers of the World, Unite"; on the opposite corner were the following lines: "You who are drunk with the power of wealth, beware. There is a fall past the heights. If workers today become satisfied with you, tomorrow you will be saved from revenge."[37]

With the publication of *Haghighat*, the link between the GTU and Marxism became a matter of public knowledge. The pro-Soviet, anti-British, and anti-upper-class views of the newspaper were made strikingly clear in every issue.

The Years of Confrontation: 1922–1925

Prior to 1917, the British and Russians enjoyed separate spheres of influence in Iran, fixed by their treaty of 1907. As a consequence of the October Revolution, the Russian forces evacuated Iran (although they returned temporarily in June 1920), leaving Great Britain the sole imperial power in the country. To consolidate this position, Great Britain, in August 1919, secured the Iranian government's approval of a treaty making Britain responsible for Iran's financial and military affairs. This treaty, however, was nullified by widespread opposition in Iran and by Britain's decision to reduce its armed forces stationed abroad. The British decided instead to sponsor a "stable and strong" government in Iran rather than intervene directly in the country's affairs.

On 21 February 1921, Reza-Khan (commander of the Cossacks), professing allegiance to Ahmad Shah, marched into Tehran and, together with Seyyed-Zia Tabataba'i, an allegedly pro-British journalist, took control of the government. He dismissed the cabinet, arrested a large number of officials, and appointed Seyyed-Zia prime minister. Within a few months Reza-Khan himself became minister of war. Although it has not yet been conclusively established that Great Britain did in fact stage-manage this coup d'etat, it can be stated with certainty that soon thereafter the British government did support Reza-Khan's subsequent rise to greater power.[38] The British rationale for this policy was fairly clear. British public opinion no longer supported the employment of force "equally for a right as for a wrong cause."[39] Iran, as a gateway to India and as the source of crude oil, had to be protected. Thus Lord Curzon, the British Foreign

Secretary, instructed the newly appointed British minister to Iran, Sir Percy Loraine, "to find out, where you can, any sensible discerning and patriotic Persians whom you can find, and work through them."[40]

Loraine, believing, in his words, that "the cohesion of the Persian Empire as a whole is far more important to British interests generally and in the long run than the local supremacy of any of our particular proteges,"[41] began to implement the new British policy of strengthening the executive branch of the Iranian government. He sought a man who could maintain "the cohesion of the Persian Empire" and so safeguard British interests. As time went by, it became increasingly evident that from Britain's point of view Reza-Khan was the right man for this task.

By the end of 1922, Reza-Khan had demonstrated his capabilities as an army officer by providing Iran with two years of unprecedented internal security. This was the view of the chairman of the British-owned Imperial Bank of Persia who, in December 1922, stated that, for the first time in seven years, not one of the bank's branches had been closed because of disturbances.[42] On 8 May 1923, Loraine wrote to the British Foreign Office, that "if he [Reza-Khan] accepts the responsibility for the security of the oil fields, it will be very difficult for us to oppose him."[43] After central government authority was extended over the southwestern province of Khouzestan, Loraine concluded that "the APOC [Anglo-Persian Oil Company] had not suffered, and might even have benefited." T. L. Jacks, the oil company's general manager in the south, concurred: "As far as the Company is concerned, we are experiencing no misunderstandings or difficulties with the new regime."[44]

When Reza-Khan was elected prime minister on 25 October 1923, the British did not object, but became even more convinced of the benefits to be gained from supporting him. More than a year earlier, Reza-Khan had allegedly told Loraine that "he would do with Persian hands that which the British had wished to do with British hands, i.e., create a strong army, restore order."[45]

In return for Reza-Khan's promise to provide them with "security," the British gave him a free hand in establishing his supremacy over Iran's fledgling political institutions, including the Majles. The gradual supremacy of the executive over the legislative branch greatly weakened the position of the trade unions, for, although the independent deputies in the Majles gave little verbal support to the labor unions, their constant concern for the preservation of political freedom and the prerogatives of the Majles lent indirect encouragement to the labor movement. The first encounter between Reza-Khan and a Majles deputy had occurred in October 1922 when Reza-Khan was the minister of war. The deputy, Mo'tamed-od-Tojjar of Tabriz, accused Reza-Khan of violating the constitution. He also criticized his Majles colleagues for remaining silent while the government shut down newspapers without legal authority and arrested, imprisoned, and beat their editors, who had criticized wrongs committed by various ministries and military authorities.[46] During the subsequent debate, Seyyed-Hasan Modarres, the leading religious figure in the Majles, reminded his colleagues of the superior authority of the legislative over the executive branch: "We are not afraid of Reza-Khan. We have the power to dismiss the monarch, to install, question, and dismiss prime ministers. And also to question and dismiss Reza-Khan."[47]

Although Modarres concluded by expressing the belief that Reza-Khan's assets outweighed his liabilities, the minister of war was not satisfied. On 7 October he gathered his military officers together and accused his opponents, to whom he referred as a "handful of individuals under foreign influences," of not desiring prosperity for Iran. After recounting his own services to his country, Reza-Khan announced that he had tendered his resignation to Ahmad Shah.[48]

The line was being drawn between those who supported constitutional government and those who desired a "strong and stable" government, holding lightly the provisions of the constitution. Supporting the constitution were a number of Majles deputies, the GTU, and a segment of the press. Supporting autocratic government were the army, the privileged classes, and the British.

While the army commanders were organizing demonstrations in various cities in support of Reza-Khan, a number of newspapers took him to task. For instance, *Toufan* (Storm), a vocal opposition paper, replying to charges that the Majles was unresponsive to the people's needs, expressed a preference for a parliamentary dictatorship of 140 deputies to the one-man dictatorship of Reza-Khan. Behind-the-scenes efforts at achieving reconciliation between Reza-Khan and the Majles succeeded in bringing him to the parliament where, on 16 October 1922, he affirmed his loyalty to the constitution and announced an end to martial law[49] which he himself had imposed at the time of the coup in February 1921. The Majles had clearly reached the zenith of its independence from the executive branch. Henceforth, Reza-Khan and the executive branch which he controlled would determine policy, for only he could stave off chaos, using the army as a national police force.

Within a year from the date of his pledge before the Majles, Reza-Khan was making it abundantly clear that he intended to ignore the constitution and to establish one-man rule. A short time after becoming prime minister in October 1923, he said: "The long history of Iran demonstrates that the people of Iran prefer a strong, just government more than any other kind."[50] In case there was any question of who was to provide this "strong, just government," Reza-Khan announced, "At this time when thanks to the will of the Almighty God . . . the reins of government have been entrusted into my hands, I am obliged to look after the oppressed and to liberate them from the oppressors. I will permit all my countrymen to bring their complaints directly to me and to request redress directly from me."[51]

As we have seen, the British and the increasingly powerful Iranian army clearly favored Reza-Khan's consolidation of power, whereas a number of Majles deputies and newspapers were strongly opposed. On this issue, the positions of the PCP and the GTU were somewhat ambivalent. As for the Soviets, they were covertly working to promote an Iranian revolution while overtly supporting Reza-Khan. As early as April 1921, when Theodore Rothstein, the new Russian envoy in Tehran, presented his credentials to Ahmad Shah, Russia had resumed its interference in Iran's domestic affairs. The Iranian historian, N. Seifpour-Fatemi, who served in the fourteenth session of the Majles, writes that Rothstein, soon after his arrival, established a propaganda machine for Russian purposes: a previously closed Russian school was reopened and staffed with Communist teachers.[52] With a staff of one hundred, the Soviet minister directed his attention toward the Iranian press, especially *Toufan, Haghighat,* and *Enghelab-e Sorkh* (Red Revolution). Seifpour-Fatemi claims that material for these three papers was furnished by the Soviet legation.[53]

Opponents of the Soviets accused them not only of waging a propaganda campaign in Iran, but—what was worse—of taking active, militant steps to destabilize the Iranian regime. In a note of protest to his Soviet counterpart in Moscow, dated May 1923, Lord Curzon stated:

> The Russian Minister at Tehran has been the most tireless, though not always the most successful, operator in this field. . . . That these

activities are well known to, and have been authorized by, the
Soviet Government at Moscow is demonstrated by a report in
February 1923, from M. Shumiatsky, the Russian representative
at Tehran, to the Commissariat for Foreign Affairs, which contains
the following interesting paragraph: "Our mission, in carrying out
the instructions which your telegram amplifies, had decided on
this political line of action, especially in North Persia and Tehran:
a good group of workers has been organized who can act in an
anti-British direction with real activity. . . . If the Commissary
for Foreign Affairs will agree to the plan of the mission 300,000
tomans will be necessary for the first expenditure as a credit to
enable us to work."[54]

While the Soviets were attempting to subvert the political system
through the press and the trade unions, they were expressing a high
regard for Reza-Khan "as the representative of a national liberation
movement of anti-imperialist tinge."[55] Soleiman-Mirza, who was
a Qajar prince and a leading socialist in the Majles,[56] and the Marxist
newspaper *Haghighat* agreed with this public Soviet position.[57]
Soleiman-Mirza endorsed Reza-Khan by accepting the post of
minister of education in his first cabinet,[58] and the newspaper
Haghighat defended Reza-Khan "because he is not from their class
and owns no peasants or estates or titles."[59]

As long as their favorable attitude toward him continued,
Reza-Khan was able to consolidate by skillful management of
opposing forces. Such expressions of admiration for Reza-Khan
ceased, however, when it became evident that he was the chief
instigator of the campaign against the press and the unions. A series
of strikes in the public sector and continuing attacks by the press
against the British and the government brought Reza-Khan's true
intentions out in the open. It is within this context of autocratic rule,
emerging but not yet fully established, that the development of the
GTU must be seen.

As noted earlier, the GTU, led by the Communist, Seyyed-
Mohammad Dehgan, was formed by about eight trade unions in
October 1921. Prior to its formation, labor conflicts with employers
did not involve the government, as the disputes occurred in the
privately owned printing and textile industries. After formation of the
GTU, however, a number of strikes did occur in the public sector.

One such dispute involved the telegraphic workers, whose union
was temporarily dissolved by the Swedish director of the telegraphic

service. This action led to a strike by the postal workers, who protested this anti-union move against their fellow telegraphic workers.[60] In this dispute, Prime Minister Ahmad Qavam (Qavam-os-Saltaneh), who later played a prominent role in the 1940s,[61] sided with the Swedish director and tried to bar, by executive order, all civil servants from joining unions.[62]

The inconclusive strike of the postal workers was followed in January 1922 by that of the Tehran school teachers. Like these earlier disputes, the teachers' strike began over economic issues; teachers' wages were six months in arrears. Since the strike was against the government, it inevitably entered the political arena. The government, with an empty treasury, was unable to meet its payroll. The strike lasted for three weeks, and in its final days the teachers were joined by sympathetic students. The cabinet of Qavam fell before the end of the month.

Although these strikes may not have played a major role in the change of prime ministers,[63] as Dehgan and Soltanzadeh have suggested, the public sector strikes did bring the GTU into confrontation with the executive branch, not only as the governing authority but also as the country's chief employer.

Another important strike that must be considered along with the disputes in the public sector was that of oil workers against the Anglo-Persian Oil Company (APOC) in Abadan in 1922. This action, taken against a company owned by the British government, reaffirmed the British decision to support a strong, autocratic regime as a means of eliminating Communist influence in Iran.

There are a number of indications that the 1922 strike of Abadan oil workers was supported, if not initiated, by the GTU. According to Hossein Jowdat, a veteran Communist who later became a leader of the Tudeh Party, the GTU had taken steps in that year to organize the forty-seven thousand workers in the oil industry.[64] Although Ossertov, a Soviet writer, has reported that this effort did not succeed,[65] nevertheless, an important strike did take place in Abadan that same year. This strike of Iranian workers for a one hundred percent increase in wages was supported by most of the Indian employees, but was broken by British troops. Not only were the strike leaders arrested, but two thousand Indian workers were dismissed and repatriated to India. According to L. P. Elwell-Sutton, who was employed by the APOC in the 1930s and served in the British embassy in Tehran in the 1940s, "By way of conscience money, a 75 percent increase was granted" to the workers who remained.[66]

Ahmad Qavam was out of office for only six months before he was reappointed prime minister in June 1922. Once again he responded to political turmoil and opposition by asserting executive authority. At this time the main thrust of the opposition against the British and the government was through the press. *Haghighat*, having printed clearly pro-Soviet, anti-British, and anti-government editorials, was inevitably one of the fourteen[67] newspapers to be suspended. An editorial appearing in June 1922 dealt with foreign policy and left no doubt about *Haghighat*'s pro-Soviet position: "Because we are familiar with the true nature of the Russian revolution and do not harbor the slightest suspicion in regard to Russia and consider the Russian revolution the savior and the means to progress from the grips of the oppressive nations, for the whole world and Iran, we therefore consider the support and defense of the Soviet Union to be the duty of every one."[68]

As usual, an independent Majles was the first to voice its protest against the suspension of the fourteen opposition newspapers by Prime Minister Qavam. Soleiman-Mirza was among the first deputies to speak out. The Soviets, through their minister in Tehran, joined the protest and offered refuge to Mohammad Farrokhi, editor of the liberal *Toufan*.[69] The printers' union, claiming that the suspension had left five hundred workers unemployed, offered the most concrete form of opposition to the government's actions by calling a strike, thereby preventing publication of the pro-government papers. Ali Dashti and Zein-ol-Abedin Rahnama, publishers of two pro-government papers (*Shafagh-e Sorkh* and *Rahnama*), took their complaint to Qavam, who ordered the arrest and imprisonment of union leaders. He also ordered the roundup of the striking printers from their homes at night and their forced return to work. Consequently, Dehgan, as editor of *Haghighat* and head of the GTU, convened a meeting of the labor organization, which approved a call for a general strike. Armed with this threat, a number of trade unionists and *Toufan*'s editor, Mohammad Farrokhi, met with the Majles president, Mo'tamen-ol-Molk (later known as Hossein Pirnia). As a result of the latter's intervention, the imprisoned union leaders were released,[70] and the suspension of newspapers was lifted by Qavam as of 9 September 1922.[71]

The working class had almost no influential allies within the political system of Iran. The only exceptions were a few independent deputies in the Majles, such as Soleiman-Mirza, who discussed the needs of the workers on several occasions and called for legislation that would respond to those needs. One such occasion was in January

1922 when Soleiman-Mirza called for the enactment of a labor law.[72] Responding to the socialist leader's proposal, the conservative deputy from Shiraz, Seyyed-Ya'ghoub Anvar-Shirazi, voiced his opposition: "We do not yet have workers in Iran. Everyone is an employer. If God so desires, and our country becomes important, and trade and agriculture commence, and factories are founded, at that time a labor-employer law will be enacted. However, at the moment we have neither workers nor factories nor railroads for which to have workers. All my attention is focused on extension of security throughout Iran. What the people want is physical and financial security."[73]

Soleiman-Mirza responded to Seyyed-Ya'ghoub's preoccupation with security with a question that is still asked today: What is the value of security and who pays the price? Soleiman-Mirza defined security as a situation in which the people's rights are protected in accordance with the constitution. Otherwise, he said, security is meaningless. An unjust government, he declared, must be overthrown by force and replaced by one that is just—one that will abide by the constitution.[74]

In spite of its suspension in September 1922, *Haghighat* resumed its aggressive stance against the British, the upper classes, and the government, and was again suspended in November of that year, never to resume publication.[75] Thus *Haghighat* became the first casualty of the confrontation between the government—allied with the British, the army, and the privileged classes—and its uncompromising opponents, which included the GTU, the PCP, a few independent deputies of the Majles, and a segment of the press. In this process of removing obstacles from his path, one at a time, Reza-Khan would next eliminate the GTU, and finally subjugate the Majles.

The suppression of the GTU soon after the silencing of *Haghighat* was to be expected. Dehgan, as editor of *Haghighat* and chairman of GTU, had forged a link between the two organizations, and the GTU had become associated with editorial positions adopted by *Haghighat*. Abdossamad Kambakhsh, a leading Communist in the 1930s and a Majles deputy in the Fourteenth Majles (1944–1946), clearly associated the GTU and *Haghighat* with the PCP when he asserted that the suppression of *Haghighat* was a blow to the PCP. However, in a short time a new publication named *Kar* (Labor) replaced *Haghighat*, and the publisher of *Peikar*, another journal of the Left, placed some space in his paper at the disposal of the party to disseminate Marxist ideas.[76]

At about the time that *Haghighat* was closed down, the GTU received another damaging blow: Dehgan left Iran for the Soviet Union to attend the Fourth World Congress of the Third International, held in Moscow in November and December 1922. In his absence, his fellow Communist, Mohammad Akhoundzadeh, was unable to lead the GTU through the maze of government persecution.[77] By the time Dehgan returned to Tehran in early 1923, the union had been seriously weakened. Although Dehgan temporarily cheered his colleagues by his report that the GTU had been recognized by the Fourth World Congress,[78] the fate of the union seemed to be sealed. Every effort to call a strike was met with the arrest of the strike leaders. For example, in 1923 the important trade union of port workers at Anzali was closed by police. Many union members, including Akhoundzadeh himself, were arrested and exiled, charged with being Communists.[79] Under these circumstances Dehgan retired from the GTU to a cotton farm in the northern province of Mazandaran, permanently depriving the union of its main driving force. Thus, by 1925 the period of confrontation ended and the period of repression began.

Autocracy and Labor under Reza Shah: 1926–1941

On 30 October 1925, the Qajar dynasty, which had ruled Iran since the eighteenth century, was deposed; and on 12 December, Reza-Khan, formerly the prime minister, became the founder of the Pahlavi dynasty. Only a handful of Majles deputies, including Dr. Mohammad Mossadegh,[80] Seyyed-Hasan Taghizadeh, Hossein Ala, and Seyyed-Hasan Modarres, opposed the change of dynasties. The rest of the deputies, along with the landowners, important merchants, and high civil servants, joined hands with the army to point Iran once again toward an absolute monarchy.

Predictably, as Reza-Khan came to the throne in 1925, the liberties of independent institutions such as the Majles, the press, and the trade unions were dealt a damaging blow.[81] The Communist author Kambakhsh writes that as soon as Reza-Khan attained the necessary powers, he began suppressing the leftist organizations. Just a few days before the change in dynasties, the last Communist paper, *Nassihat*, was shut down.[82] During the last years of the Qajar dynasty, Reza-Khan's government had attacked its opponents subsequent to their actions, i.e. strikes; however, once he became shah, Reza Shah's antagonists were pursued because of their beliefs. Late in 1925, an unrelenting attack commenced against the PCP and the remnants of the GTU, forcing members of the two organizations to carry on their activities under cover. May Day celebrations, for example, had been held publicly for two years prior to 1925; from that date, participation became a serious political offense, and the event was celebrated semi-secretly until 1929, when celebrations took place for the last time during the rule of Reza Shah.

An example of police vigilance is given by the union leader, Shokrollah Mani, who reports that on 2 May 1927 the police raided the printing shops and confiscated leaflets relating to that year's festivities. Consequently, a number of union leaders, including Bagher Nava'i, head of the printers' union; Mohammad Parvaneh, its secretary; and Mehdi Keimaram, head of the shoemakers' union were arrested and held for a period.[83]

Contrary to frequent claims that Iranian workers were apathetic, the Tehran workers continued to participate in May Day festivities in spite of the consequences. Ardeshir Ovanessian describes the semi-secret gathering of six hundred workers in a garden outside Tehran on May Day 1928. Red flags were prominently displayed inside the garden. Later the same day, a number of participants attended an open gathering of socialists sponsored by Soleiman-Mirza and Mirza-Shahab Kermani.[84]

By December 1927 the attitude of the PCP toward Reza Shah was no longer ambivalent. At that time, the Second Congress of the PCP, meeting in Oroumieh in Western Azerbaijan, labeled the shah "the enemy of the political freedom of workers" and called for a joint assault against the monarch and the British, whom they accused of being his supporters. The congress came to the conclusion that the government had eliminated all possibilities of peaceful progress and that henceforth the party must use secret as well as open means to re-establish labor unions. Moreover, the party program called for the elimination of monarchy and the establishment of a revolutionary people's republic. The party pledged itself to maintain Iranian independence against British imperialism and to strengthen bonds of friendship with the Soviet Union.[85]

The 1927 PCP program included many demands on behalf of the workers, among them: recognition of labor unions by the government and employers; freedom to strike; freedom of the press for the workers; establishment of an eight-hour work day; prohibition of night work by women and children; prohibition of work by children under fourteen; establishment for women of four weeks' maternity leave before and after delivery; participation of factory councils in labor-management affairs; institution of collective bargaining agreements; establishment of a minimum wage by the unions; establishment of a forty-two-hour work week; establishment of a two-week annual vacation for all employees with at least six months' service; and prohibition of monetary fines exacted by employers from workers.[86]

By 1928 Reza Shah had drawn almost all political power into his own hands. Having already suppressed the trade unions, silenced the press, and defeated the rebellious tribes, he was ready to subjugate his only other political rival—the Majles. According to a dispatch prepared by the United States legation in Tehran, the government prepared a list of acceptable candidates for the seventh session of the Majles and took steps to prevent the election of any who were not on the list. The U.S. dispatch conceded that previous Majles elections in the provinces had been controlled by "the strongest political power of the moment"; however, the report continued, the elections conducted in Tehran had been conducted relatively freely: candidates had been able to make speeches and to enlist votes openly. In the 1928 elections, however, all public speeches were prohibited by police. Consequently, although political figures such as Dr. Mohammad Mossadegh, Hasan Taghizadeh and Hossein Ala had finally pledged their acceptance of the shah, they were not elected "in spite of the well-known popular demand for their return." The U.S. dispatch concluded its report of the election proceedings by stating that Reza Shah and his influential minister of court, Abdol-Hossein Teimourtash (Sardar Mo'azam-Khorasani), were determined to ensure the election of a docile Majles which would approve all government bills "without the inconvenient expression of criticism of the governmental policies, as is the case at the present time to a very limited extent."[87]

With the conclusion of the 1928 elections, the near-total abolition of the constitutional monarchy was accomplished. Although the unpopularity of the government was reported a few months later to be growing rapidly, no outward sign was apparent because of the "severe attitude assumed by the government toward all demonstrations, or even intimations of independent political activity; its absolute control of the press; and the omnipresence of the military and the police."[88]

In 1929, May Day was celebrated by two thousand workers in an out-of-town garden. The festivities included a number of speeches attacking the government's willful violation of the laws. As soon as the police learned of the gathering, they arrested the union leaders. This time, fifty were arrested,[89] while another fifty went into hiding. Most of those imprisoned, including Nava'i, Parvaneh, and Keimaram, were held without trial until the general amnesty granted on the occasion of a visit by Amanollah Khan, king of Afghanistan.[90]

In the same month, when all potential opponents seemed to be under government control, nine thousand oil workers suddenly struck in Abadan, creating tremors that were felt as far as Tehran. A number of allegations have been made accusing the Soviet Union of having instigated the strike. In his book *Russia and the West in Iran 1918–1948*, for example, George Lenczowski states that prior to the 1929 strike and following the Sixth Congress of the Comintern in 1928, the resident general of the Soviet Intelligence Service (GPU) in Iran had received instructions to intensify his efforts against the APOC in Khouzestan.[91] A month after the strike, the American legation in Tehran informed the State Department that thirty-one "professional" Communists from the Soviet Union had passed through Iran on their way to Ahwaz and that some Communists deported from the United States were headed for Khorramshahr.[92] Two weeks later the same reporting officer stated: "It is known that Soviet 'cells' were established in several towns in Khuzistan. . . . The subversive activities of the Bolshevik agents in Abadan were well known. . . . It is heard [sic] that several arrests were made of Russians, Bulgars [Bulgarians], and other Slavs."[93]

The British did not doubt that the Soviets had a hand in the Abadan strike, and described Soviet intentions in the following terms: "Moscow considers that before attempting to preach Communism in Persia, a state of general unrest in the country must be created. . . . An obvious link in the chain was to promote disturbances in the only industrial undertaking in this country, but that a very big one, the APOC."[94] As a precautionary measure, the APOC had organized a police force of its own, disciplined and trained in military fashion.[95]

The two Western powers were not alone in pointing an accusing finger at the Communists. The veteran Iranian Communist, Kambakhsh, admitted that the PCP had attempted as far back as 1925 to form a union of oil workers, without apparent success. Two years later the party tried a different approach by forming secret cells among the oil workers. Kambakhsh asserts that in 1927 the party succeeded in organizing a labor conference, attended by two hundred APOC workers, at which it was decided to work for greater unity in the face of APOC's efforts to promote dissension; to expand its organization; to establish a cooperative and a club for the workers; to resist fines levied by the company against workers; and to oppose physical punishment and verbal abuse.[96]

The Abadan general strike of 1929 commenced on 4 May with nine thousand of the ten thousand workers participating.[97] According to the leftist newspaper *Setarah-e Sorkh:* "There were police stationed at the scene. The company used its own vehicles for the transportation of the armed forces. As the troops arrived, the workers sang revolutionary songs and shouted, 'Down with A.P.O.C.,' 'Down with British Imperialism.'"[98]

The workers presented a series of demands that included: an increase in wages by 15 percent; recognition of their trade union and of May Day as a legitimate holiday; participation of workers' representatives in hiring and firing decisions; and a maximum limit of seven hours of work for teenagers under the age of eighteen.[99]

Other reports of the strike have claimed that the workers also demanded a revision of the oil concession to the APOC;[100] establishment of a monthly minimum wage of three pounds sterling; provision of housing; the granting of annual leave; representation on the board of management; and equality of pay between Iranian workers and the more highly paid Indian workers.[101]

The company refused to negotiate on any of the workers' demands, economic or political. With the assistance of British Marines from Iraq,[102] Iranian troops attacked with their swords drawn. The workers responded with sticks and stones. As a result, twenty workers and fifteen policemen were injured.[103] The strike continued for three days, and when it was finally broken, according to Elwell-Sutton, "Two hundred men were arrested and imprisoned at Khorramabad, whence they were released after two or three years but forbidden to return to Khuzistan. Five ringleaders were imprisoned at Tehran, and only released after the Shah's abdication in 1941."[104]

Kambakhsh concluded that, although the strike was defeated, it nevertheless indicated the power of a united labor force.[105] Other critics of the regime declared that the Iranian government and the British were seen as cooperating fully and ruthlessly in suppressing the grievances of the working class. As one critic put it, "This company influences and corrupts the leading politicians and officials of present-day Persia."[106] The United States legation in Tehran called the incident "singularly embarrassing to the Shah, to the Anglo-Persian Oil Company and to British commercial interests in South Persia; while the Soviet interests in the North cannot but prosper in direct inverse proportion."[107]

The government's response to the Abadan general strike was predictable—continued suppression and police surveillance. The British obviously supported the repressive policies of the government; they believed that in this "war" with the agents of the Soviet Union any means were justified. The government's repressive posture stiffened a year and a half later when George Agabekoff, a former attache of the Soviet legation in Teheran, exposed a number of Iranian officials as agents of the Soviet intelligence agency.[108]

Soon after the Abadan strike and the Agabekoff revelations, Reza Shah ordered the presentation of a bill to the Majles outlawing communism. The bill, which was approved on 12 June 1931, stated that anyone who organized or joined a group whose objective or program included opposition to Iran's constitutional monarchy or support for communism would be subject to a three- to ten-year term of imprisonment.[109]

Some writers have erroneously concluded that the 1931 anti-communism law put an end to all workers' protests until 1941, but, as Abrahamian points out: "This law failed to have the desired effect, for a year later an unexpected strike broke out among the railway workers in Mazandaran. Mass arrests ended the walkout and destroyed the underground union. However, the organization was quietly rebuilt, and five years later, in 1937, the police discovered the union working not only in the railways, but also in the mines and factories in Mazandaran. Seventeen of the organizers were put in prison, where they remained until 1941."[110]

A number of other sources confirm the view that, in spite of severely repressive measures, the Iranian workers were not totally subdued, but periodically protested their circumstances by participating in strikes. Jowdat, for example, mentions a successful eight-day strike in 1932 by construction workers in Nowshahr, in which they demanded back pay as well as payment of wages for the duration of the strike. In the same year, carpet-makers of Tabriz and Mashhad attempted to reorganize their union, but the arrest of several members frustrated their efforts.[111]

Although Marxism was outlawed, it continued to interest small groups of individuals. One such circle was the Arani group, whose members met and discussed Marxist ideology. They also published a periodical called *Donya*. Leaders of the group were Dr. Taghi Arani, Abdossamad Kambakhsh, Dr. Mohammad Bahrami, Mohammad Shoureshian, and Ali Sadeghpour. On 7 May 1937, a few years after the group's formation, its members were arrested and held in prison until their trial a year and a half later, in November 1938.[112]

Despite a much publicized trial and the forty-five convictions that followed, there appeared to be no reason to suspect that there was any extensive subversive Communist organization at work in Iran. It seemed to an American observer that the Iranian government divided all Iranians into two classes: enthusiastic supporters of the Pahlavi regime and others, "who, for lack of a better and more exact term, are called 'Communists'."[113]

As we have seen, in the late 1910s and early 1920s, Iran experimented with governing itself as a constitutional monarchy. It had begun to develop autonomous political institutions, such as the legislature, the trade unions and the press, when, with the rise of Reza Shah, first as prime minister and then as monarch, this experiment with democracy came to an end. As the state regressed from a constitutional monarchy to an autocracy, the independent institutions that were an integral part of constitutionalism were, one by one, dismantled and replaced by obedient, dependent substitutes. No effort was made during Reza Shah's rule, as there was during the rule of his son, Mohammad-Reza Shah, to replace the Communist-led labor organizations with trade unions controlled by the government. Reza Shah wished to modernize Iran socially and economically without the inconvenience of political development. Thus he enacted a number of laws which were supposed to protect the workers and thereby indirectly reduce the need for trade unions.

According to Fatollah Mo'tamedi, a former official of the Ministry of Labor, the first labor directive in modern Iranian history was issued by Prime Minister Reza-Khan[114] on 19 December 1923 as a result of intervention by the International Labor Office (ILO).[115] It was addressed to the governor of Kerman, instructing him to set limits on hours of work, provide paid holidays, prohibit child labor, and improve working conditions in the carpet-making workshops.[116]

This directive was the first in a series of edicts that can only be regarded as propaganda, for they were never even partially implemented. A senior carpet manufacturer of Kashan recalls an audience with Reza Shah several years after the date of the directive, at which the monarch urged the carpet manufacturers to improve the quality of their work; the manufacturer from Kashan does not recall ever having heard of the 1923 directive and doubts that it was ever implemented in Kerman.[117] Confirming this view, a dispatch from the American legation in Tehran dated 15 October 1934, concerning the implementation of the 1923 directive, stated that "no such reforms have been made and probably were never a matter of serious consideration, except to the official charged with the duty of drafting an appropriate memorandum on the subject."[118]

In the 1930s, as more public and private factories were established, the government decided to draw up a comprehensive bill dealing with industrial plants, and the ILO sent an expert to Iran to assist in drafting the regulations.[119] This bill, which was entitled "Regulations for Factories and Industrial Establishments," was approved by the Council of Ministers on 10 August 1936. It contained a set of regulations pertaining to the construction of factories that stipulated a minimum standard of safety, hygiene, and comfort. There were additional provisions: Expectant mothers were to be granted leave with pay. The alloted time, however, was to be determined by the company physician. Mothers of newborns were to be provided time off with pay to breast-feed their babies. Workers were to be provided with work-clothes and lockers. Employers were required to maintain personnel records and to send a summary of this information to the General Department of Industries and Mines. In the event of illness or injury, the employer, taking the employee's condition into account, was to reduce the length of the employee's work day. Whenever the company physician certified the need of the worker for full rest, the employer was to grant the worker time off until recovery.[120]

Once again, the labor regulations were put on the books without ever being implemented, because the workers had no power to demand their implementation. They could neither dismiss the officials through the power of the ballot, nor could they go on strike. The government, which had implicitly appointed itself as guardian of the workers, had failed even to set up an inspection mechanism. Moreover, the sanctions imposed on employers for infraction of the rules were both insufficient—a fine of 20 to 70 *rials*—and impractical—a prison sentence of three to seven days.[121] On the other hand, the obligations laid on the worker were practical and enforceable, since their implementation was placed in the hands of the employer.

The worker was obliged to carry out properly the duties assigned to him. The employer was granted authority to reduce the worker's wage if he found the latter's performance unsatisfactory. If the worker did not follow instructions from his supervisor, he could be imprisoned from one to five days or fined a sum between 5 and 50 *rials* (equal to half a month's wages or to the fine levied against the employer). Moreover, the workers were obligated to compensate the employer for any losses incurred as a result of inattention or negligence. These regulations were to cover all workshops and factories employing more than five or ten workers, the lower figure applying to those factories that used electrical machinery, and the higher figure to those that did not.[122]

In bringing this review of the 1906–1941 period to a close, it is important to determine what changes—if any—took place in the living standards and working conditions of the laboring class. This is necessary because it was (and still is) often asserted that the price of economic development is the loss of political freedom. It is clearly apparent from this survey that although the price was paid by the Iranian workers, the benefits were rarely received.

To evaluate the socioeconomic accomplishments (as they related to the industrial workers) of the autocracy, which promised to better the life of the oppressed if only they would obey its commands, we may quote from a report written by the United States legation in Tehran about Reza Shah's own modern textile plant in Mazandaran only a year prior to his abdication: "The . . . silk mill at Chalous is doubtless a source of Imperial satisfaction, but the European foremen describe the conditions under which the women and children work as appalling, and the pay they receive as totally inadequate."[123]

Reporting on the living conditions of Iranian workers in general, only a few days prior to the invasion of Iran by the Anglo-Soviet forces in August 1941, the United States Legation stated:

> Wages are certainly insufficient for more than bare existence, amounting for a common laborer to from four to ten *rials* a day with an average of perhaps eight. Disregarding the foreign exchange value of the *rial*, it may be said that it will purchase a loaf of white bread or that a worker must pay from three to seven *rials* a day for his food. Thus, it will be seen that the wage is insufficient even for food for a family, and most workers have a starvation diet consisting of tea, native (not white) bread, cheese

and onions, with occasional greens and grapes and infrequent rice and cheap meat. It is not possible to buy adequate clothing or even to dream of luxuries such as education of the children. Sometimes the workers' one or more wives and the children work to bring in additional income to make possible a slightly higher standard of living.[124]

In summary, a review of the 1906–1941 period leads to the conclusion that the prerequisite for the growth and development of independent trade unions was a functioning constitutional government. It was only during the period in which the spirit of the Iranian constitution was at least partially respected that trade unions came into being and began to develop. As soon as the constitutional monarchy was superseded by an autocratic regime, the trade unions were among the first casualties.

It was in certain ways an accident of history that the development of the trade unions in Iran coincided with the growth of the Communist movement in Russia, Iran's northern neighbor. This accident of history, combined with the massive movement of workers to and from the homeland of the Communist revolution, as well as the hostility of the Iranian elite toward constitutional government, led to the formation in Iran of trade unions whose programs were political and whose leaders were Communists.

Because Iranian trade unions were led by key members of the PCP, it was natural that they would enjoy the general support of the Soviet Union. Conversely, because of their political philosophy and source of support, the trade unions faced the bitter opposition of the British government, which proceeded to counter Communist influence in Iran by supporting an autocratic regime, a regime that employed repressive measures not only against the Communists but, with equal zeal, against all sources of opposition.

The autocratic anti-Communist regime was supported by army officers, landowners, owners of large businesses, and high-ranking civil servants, as well as by the British. In order to cloak its lack of interest in the working class, the monarchy employed a number of public relations maneuvers—one of which was the issuance of labor regulations. Represented as measures designed to protect the workers, these regulations ostensibly removed the need to organize trade unions. The record, however, indicates that these laws did not materially improve the welfare of the workers. Furthermore, little of the social and economic progress that was achieved during the period of autocracy[125] benefited the working class. Thus, without political power—as exercised in independent trade unions—the workers could not influence the content of economic and social reform programs nor could they ensure that they would receive their appropriate share in the fruits of progress.

2

Rebirth of the
Labor Unions

Reestablishment of the Constitutional Monarchy

*T*HE REBIRTH of the labor movement took place in the autumn of 1941 as an indirect result of the invasion of Iran by the British and Soviet forces. Events moved quickly. On 25 August 1941 British and Soviet forces invaded Iran. On 16 September Reza Shah was deposed and left Tehran for exile aboard a British ship. On the afternoon of that same day, the twenty-one-year-old crown prince, Mohammad-Reza Pahlavi, took the oath of allegiance to the constitution before a revitalized Majles. Three days later the new monarch issued a decree granting amnesty to prisoners, and a new era of political freedom had commenced.

The change in the mode of governance was dramatic. The shah became a reigning monarch in the tradition set by Ahmad Shah nearly three decades earlier. The prime minister and his cabinet became responsible for governing the nation. The Majles regained its independence, promulgating laws after considerable debate. The number of newspapers published increased many-fold. Simultaneously, new political parties and trade unions were formed, the most successful of which were the Tudeh Party and the Central Council (Showra-ye Markazi) respectively.

This second opportunity for Iran to attempt constitutional government was granted by a three-year period of cooperation between the Soviet Union and Great Britain, who had united to "fight against fascism for freedom and democracy." Since winning the cooperation of the Iranian public in the war effort required that this slogan be given at least some credibility in Iran, Reza Shah, accused by the Allies of having pro-German sympathies, was deposed and a consitutional monarchy was ushered in. An American legation report offered another reason for Reza Shah's removal: he had become too closely associated in the minds of Iranians with British imperialism.[1]

That the British acceded to constitutionalism reluctantly is shown by their position with repect to the Majles elections in the latter half of 1943.[2] It was not surprising, then, that as soon as the need to cooperate with the Soviets in the war effort had ended, Great Britain reverted to its support of autocratic rule in Iran.

Formation of the Tudeh Party and Its Unions

On 19 September 1941, twenty-seven members of Arani's group[3] were released from prison. Ten days later they met at the home of Soleiman Mohsen-Eskandari (formerly Soleiman-Mirza). A small number of his old colleagues were also present. At this first meeting, the approximately forty people who participated decided to form the Tudeh Party of Iran, to name Mohsen-Eskandari chairman, and to elect a provisional committee of fifteen. Although the founders decided to invite members from all social classes, they planned to make a special effort to recruit workers, peasants, intellectuals, and craftsmen—hence the name "Tudeh," meaning "masses".[4] However, as events unfolded, the party—run by a nucleus of Communists—probably decided on this name rather than the old "Persian Communist Party" in order to appear reformist and to avoid the sanctions of the 1931 anti-Communist law. By October 1942, the party membership totaled four thousand, about 80 percent of whom were workers with the rest mostly drawn from the intelligentsia. In another two years there were more than twenty-five thousand members, 75 percent of whom were workers, 2 percent peasants, and the rest members of the intelligentsia.[5]

The true intent and ideology of the Tudeh Party was a matter of debate from the beginning. The party itself claimed to be a supporter of constitutional monarchy, but the Communist background of many of its leaders and some of their statements convinced its opponents that a Communist ideology and revolutionary program lay behind a facade of reformism. Of the fifteen members of the Tehran Provincial Committee, elected in October 1942 to act as the Central Committee of the party until the convening of the First Party Congress, eight were Arani's disciples and four were Communist activists of the labor movement; only two were former Social Democrats, while one was a newcomer.[6] The influence of Communists in the Central Committee was, in fact, proportionate to their numbers, and this influence increased with time. With the elder statesman Soleiman Mohsen-Eskandari as its chairman, the Tudeh Party achieved some success in projecting a mildly socialist image, resembling that of the German Social Democratic Party, even though the majority of its leaders had been imprisoned as Communist sympathizers by Reza Shah. The early pronouncements of the party were an attempt to reinforce its reformist image by calling for national independence, preservation of Iran's existing geographic boundaries, protection of democracy and constitutional rights, and a campaign against all types of dictatorship and tyranny.[7]

Despite the party's efforts to avoid a revolutionary image, its opponents concluded, as early as June 1943, that "the present aims of the party seem fairly openly Communistic."[8] At the same time, the suspicion grew that the Soviets were behind the Tudeh Party, just as they had supported the Persian Communist Party (PCP) in the 1920s. The United States military attache in Tehran wrote that "although proof has not been established . . . , it is very probable that it [the Tudeh party] is receiving Russian support."[9] Two years later another intelligence dispatch stated: "Although none have admitted it publicly, the evidence of their writings, speeches, and policy clearly demonstrates that a number of the key leaders of the party are Communists."[10]

Direct Soviet support of the Tudeh Party was difficult to substantiate,[11] however. Certainly, in provinces occupied by their forces, the Soviets aided the party indirectly by preventing the civilian and military authorities from suppressing its activities. The Soviet armed forces gave the party a free hand to organize.[12]

Once again, with the reestablishment of constitutional government, a political party was formed, led by a number of dedicated Communists. A related consequence of the reestablishment of constitutional government was the rebirth of Iran's labor movement. The Trade Union of the Workers of Iran (Ettehadieh-e Kargaran-e Iran), commonly known as the Central Council (Showra-ye Markazi), was organized in the autumn of 1941 and reorganized in the winter of 1942. Not surprisingly, all of its founders were members of the Tudeh Party, and the majority of them were Communists.[13] Although little is known about the first attempt at establishing the Central Council in 1941, we do know the reason for its dissolution in the same year: it was thought to be too closely associated with the Tudeh Party. The Council's efforts between 1941 and 1944 to disassociate itself from the party failed to impress its critics.

At the first conference of the Trade Union of the Province of Tehran (a member of the Central Council), in July 1944, the theoretical justification for the separation of the Central Council from the Tudeh Party was presented. According to Anvar Khameh'i, one of the union's founders, the reconstituted Central Council was to be independent of all political parties, because trade unions and parties were governed by different ideological and organizational principles. A trade union, with its class structure, could not be part of or associated with a particular political party. While the membership of the trade union was limited to workers, a party's membership would be open to many classes of people.[15] If the trade union joined a political party, its development would be hindered.[16] Khameh'i concluded that "dependence and association of the trade union with political parties of whatever persuasion is detrimental to the trade union and one must seriously avoid it."[17]

Separation of the two organizations, however, would not preclude the trade union from establishing a "cooperative relationship" with those political parties that were committed to "the struggle against the enemies of the working class and to the betterment of the living standards of the workers, and adjudication of their rights."[18] This relationship would be maintained as long as the trade union could independently formulate its own general policies and make tactical decisions without interference by the party.[19]

To demonstrate the Central Council's independence, a clause in its articles of association stated that members of all political parties could join the trade union. This clause was obviously unobjectionable to the Tudeh Party, corresponding as it did with Lenin's own views on trade unionism: "The wider these organizations are, the wider our influence over them will be."[20]

Despite the Central Council's intention to be politically heterogeneous, there is no indication that members of any party other than the Tudeh joined the trade union.

Whether or not they were effective, the Central Council's articles of association were remarkably liberal. Eligible for union membership was any worker over the age of sixteen, regardless of color, mother-tongue, sex, or religion—as long as the member was willing to fight for his rights under the banner and directives of the Central Council. Not even Iranian citizenship was a requirement for membership.[21]

The membership fee was set at 1 percent of a member's monthly wage for those earning 1,000 *rials* or less, 2 percent for those earning 2,000 *rials* or less, and 3 percent for those earning over 2,000 *rials*.[22] Half of this fee was to be retained by the local union, and the other half was to be passed on to the Central Council.[23] By August 1943, the Central Council claimed a total membership of ten thousand. Another ten thousand were considered to be in sympathy with the trade union, and another thirteen thousand to seventeen thousand workers belonged to Fadakar's trade union in Esfahan.[24]

The Central Council's independence from the Tudeh Party was always difficult to maintain. Although the council had been dissolved in 1941 because it was too visibly a creation of the Tudeh Party, its reorganization did not alter that reality. Once again, the founding fathers, eight in all, were members of the party.[25] Ardeshir Ovanessian, for example, was a member of the Tudeh Central Committee and the party's chief idealogue, and had been an active Communist revolutionary since the 1920s. Other founders included Ebrahim Mahzari, a veteran labor organizer; Zia Alamouti, and Ali Kobari, members of the Tudeh Central Committee; Hossein Jahani,[26] involved in socialist politics since 1925; Mehdi Keimaram, an experienced labor leader who had represented the shoemakers in 1921; and Anvar Khameh'i, a capable journalist who was elected a member of the Tudeh Propaganda Committee in 1944. Always in the background during the formative years of the Central Council (1941–1944) was the veteran Communist and trade union organizer, Reza Rousta.[27]

In August 1944, when the First Conference of the Trade Union of the Province of Tehran was held, it became evident that most of the founders continued to lead the labor organization. Mehdi Keimaram, Ebrahim Mahzari, and Hossein Jahani were among those elected as presiding officers, and Ali Kobari and Anvar Khameh'i were elected conference secretaries. Ardeshir Ovanessian was present, unobtrusively directing the conference proceedings, as he did the following year at the First Party Congress of the Tudeh Party of Iran.[28]

Not only were all the founders of the Central Council members of the Tudeh Party, but three-fourths of them were intellectuals rather than workers. Here again the situation conformed to Lenin's concept of party control over the trade unions. According to T. T. Hammond, Lenin believed that the trade unions could be nominally apolitical but, "wherever possible they were to be secretly dominated and manipulated by the party, by the elite of professional revolutionaries."[29] The members of the trade unions were urged to follow the directives of the Central Council, which, in the words of Khameh'i, aimed to become so strong, widespread, and well-organized that its members throughout the country would follow "a single path according to a single procedure and a single line of thought."[30] Since the highly directive Central Council was, in turn, following the lead of the Tudeh Party, the party ultimately exercised considerable influence over Iran's organized labor movement.

The overwhelming influence of nonworkers in a labor organization did not escape criticism by opponents of the Tudeh Party. To justify its composition, the Central Council's leadership maintained that the party intellectuals were the most natural allies of the workers, since both groups worked to live and were exploited by their employers.[31] Moreover, the intellectuals were performing an essential service by awakening workers to an awareness of their rights. Finally, having motivated workers to form a trade union, the intellectuals helped the union to create an organization capable of dealing with governmental bureaucracy.[32] The non-working-class members of the Tudeh Party were to participate in meetings of the Central Council as "advisers." As soon as the council no longer required their services, the relationship could be terminated.[33]

The founders of the Central Council, when addressing the union at large, openly propounded their Marxist ideology. In his speech to the First Conference of the Trade Union of the Province of Tehran, Ardeshir Ovanessian stated: "The source of all of society's wealth is the labor of the workers. The value of all goods is created by labor and the price of everything is commensurate with the labor that has gone into it."[34]

The preamble of the Central Council's articles of association stressed the interdependence of economics and politics, thereby exhibiting the influence of Marxism on the trade union: "In order to reduce the hours of work, increase wages, and improve their living conditions, the workers of Iran must unite and rise to the struggle. In this struggle the workers have nothing to lose except the heavy chains that have bound the power of their hands and feet."[35]

In their speeches to the First Conference of the Trade Union of the Province of Tehran, Khameh'i and Ovanessian placed different emphasis on the importance of political struggle to trade unionism.

To Khameh'i, the trade union's objectives were essentially economic, yet it was unrealistic to expect the union to remain totally aloof from politics. "Any organization that wants to fight inevitably comes into conflict with the politics of the nation."[36] Ovanessian reminded the workers of the repressive role played by the government on behalf of the owners: "During the past twenty years of dictatorship, while the capitalists were making one-hundred percent profit on their investments, the workers were unable to explain their plight to anyone, or take their complaint to any authority. They were condemned to bear the pressure and remain silent. The dictatorial regime was even afraid of the word 'labor' [kargar] and had officially forbidden its use."[37]

Ovanessian urged the workers to take utmost advantage of the officially declared democracy brought about by international events. The only course for the workers, he declared, was to unite and fight together under the banner of a single national trade union.[38]

The Tudeh leaders themselves counted the establishment of the Central Council as one of their more important accomplishments. At the same time, they feared the repercussions that would follow the admission that the Central Council was their creation. Speaking at the provincial conference of the Tudeh Party in Esfahan in April 1943, one party leader exhibited this ambivalence when he said: "The third success achieved by the Tudeh Party of Iran (this success was, of course, achieved indirectly) has been the formation of trade unions among the workers and the peasants so that [these unions] will defend their economic and class interests against the ruling class."[39]

In the summer of 1943, elections were held for the fourteenth session of the Majles. At that time, the Tudeh Party and the Central Council announced in a joint proclamation that they had formed a coalition in Tehran, and they urged their members to vote for their joint candidates.[40]

Another indication that the Central Council was an auxiliary organization of the Tudeh Party was its use of Rahbar (Leader), the party's official organ. Although the newspaper Giti (World) was used for a time as the medium of communication with its members, in June 1943 the Central Council announced that henceforth Rahbar would serve in its place[41] until the council could publish its own newspaper.[42] Starting with its issue of 21 June 1943, Rahbar devoted a section to issues dealing with "the party and the workers."

A further indication that the Central Council was the creation of the Tudeh Party was the similarity between the structures and articles of association[43] of the two organizations. The basic unit of both institutions was called a "cell" (*howzeh*)—one called "party cell" (*howzeh-e hezbi*) and the other "worker's cell" (*howzeh-e kargari*). Through a series of intermediate units,[44] these cells were represented by a provincial committee, which in turn participated in a national congress. The national congress would elect, in the case of the party, a Central Committee and, in the case of the trade union, a Central Council. As already noted, at the First Conference of the Tudeh Party in Tehran in October 1942, the fifteen-member Tehran Provincial Committee was authorized to carry on the duties of the Central Committee until the First Party Congress was convened.[45] The First Conference of the Trade Union of the Province of Tehran, held on 30 July 1943, adopted exactly the same position: it empowered the thirty-four-member Provincial Committee, which it had just elected, to act in the name of the Central Council of the National Congress.[46] This decision was significant from another point of view. Unlike the Tudeh Party, the Central Council never convened a national congress. A small inner circle of the Tehran Provincial Committee, elected in July 1943 by ninety-five delegates representing, at most, ten thousand workers in Tehran, continued to govern the national trade union until the Council was outlawed in 1949—even though by 1946 the union claimed that its national membership had increased to two-hundred thousand.

One or more workers' cells—whether within a factory, a guild (*senf*), or a geographical area—would form a local trade union, each of which would elect an executive committee of no fewer than three and no more than nine members, to carry out its functions. From among the members of this committee a treasurer was elected. Once a year a provincial conference was held, attended by delegates, each of whom represented ten members of a local union. The provincial conference would then elect a committee that would participate every three years in a national congress. This congress, the highest authority in the national labor organization, would in turn elect a forty-five-member Central Council,[47] which would implement the decisions of the congress and would elect from among its members an executive committee composed of five members, three of whom would be designated respectively as chairman, secretary, and treasurer.[48]

The Central Council's local unions were concentrated in the northern provinces of Iran—Azerbaijan, Gilan, Mazandaran, and Khorasan—bordering on the Soviet Union and occupied from 1941 to 1946 by Soviet forces. Local trade unions were also established in such factory towns as Qazvin, Qom, and Tehran—all located in north-central Iran. Interestingly, no overt attempt was made to organize the sixty thousand workers concentrated in the oil towns of Khouzestan until early 1946. According to the Tudeh leader, Dr. Fereidoun Keshavarz, the Central Council had been unable to gain strength in the south because the British, who were dominant in that area, had allied themselves with reactionaries and the big landowners against trade unions.[49]

A study of the policy of the Central Council and the Tudeh Party toward strikes is essential because it illuminates the relationship of the workers and trade union to the party and the state. The attitude of the two organizations during the formative years of the labor movement (1941–1944) was that strikes were detrimental to the war effort and should be avoided. As a *Rahbar* editorial of November 1943 explained: "International fascism and internal reaction do not allow us to utilize certain methods of struggle at this time. Our government is fighting against fascism. Our factories are operating for war and for the joint victory of our allies. Any action, at this time, that may interrupt production is wrong. . . ."[50]

This policy of "full production" was even extended to May Day festivities. In the 1920s, as we have observed,[51] workers risked imprisonment by gathering clandestinely on May Day to reaffirm their solidarity. On May Day 1943, however, when there was no threat of repression, workers were told to stay on their jobs and to produce goods for the Allies.

The policy against confrontation between employers and the government was adopted for another reason: neither the party nor the trade union was yet strong enough to win. In the words of *Rahbar*: "Internal reaction is waiting for an opportunity provided by any minor and insignificant disturbance, in response to its own well-organized and unending provocations, to give freedom a bad name and to put pressure on liberal political parties—still in their early stages of growth."[52]

Rahbar, however, did not rule out strikes altogether. It conceded that when the workers were placed under great strain and their anger had reached an unbearable level, they could not be expected to remain silent. The employers, *Rahbar* asserted, used the need to produce war goods as an excuse to exploit their workers. When workers reached the limits of their patience and refused to work, employers responded to their protests by calling them "wild, seditious, and saboteurs."[53] According to *Rahbar*, however, the government was ultimately to blame: "The Ministry of Commerce and Industry, using the gendarmes and the police, . . . arrests, . . . workers, forces others back to work, and then claims that peace has been restored. The Iranian worker recognizes through this struggle its real enemies and arrives at its own conclusions."[54]

In the summer of 1944, the official newspaper of the Tudeh unions, *Zafar* (Victory), continued to voice the Tudeh policy on industrial strikes. In its 13 July 1944 issue, the paper advised the workers against damaging the war effort by going on strike. Instead, it declared, the workers should urge the government to improve their living conditions through labor legislation and price control.[55]

Thus, in accordance with the official policy of the Tudeh Party, the union discouraged and, in some cases, interdicted strikes in industries producing war goods. However, once a strike occurred in industries unrelated to the war, the party and its affiliated trade unions were quick to appear on the scene and assume leadership. Thus, *Rahbar* could claim: "Whenever a strike has become unavoidable, [the party] has led the strike to its proper conclusion. Today in any factory whenever the workers are treated unjustly, their only sanctuary is the Party clubs and the Party representatives."[56]

For the second time in Iranian history, the workers could unite and demand that their grievances be heard by their employers. With the monarchy once again controlled by a partially implemented constitution, the workers were at least able to give public expression to their grievances.

The first major strike after the abdication of Reza Shah occurred on 8 February 1942 when fifteen hundred laborers, constructing the new headquarters of the Ministry of Justice in Tehran, stopped work for several days. The workers' demands included a 25 percent raise in pay, establishment of an eight-hour work day, and a paid Sabbath. The strikers tried to convey their demands directly to the Majles, but the police refused to allow them inside the legislature and broke up their demonstration on Baharestan Square. Nevertheless, the workers' demands were partially satisfied when the government agreed to a nine-hour work day, a wage increase of 25 percent for the unskilled and 10 to 16 percent for skilled workers, one day's strike pay, and insurance for all workers, with half the premiums to be paid by the employer.[57]

The strike of construction workers was ultimately provoked by a deterioration in living conditions that were already appalling.[58] The United States minister in Tehran (the post was upgraded to ambassador in 1944,) wrote in March 1943:

Iranians dwell in the same miserable mud huts and exist in the same superstitious and ignorant circumstances. They still wear the same ragged clothing which breed typhus-bearing lice in the winter. In the south of Tehran, people live like animals in cellars, hovels and chicken houses, or sleep in the streets with the dogs. In the villages or in the country they continue to slave for the rich landowners with bent back and careworn face. In the factory, children toil for wages that will not buy even food, for the benefit of capitalists who are able to pay as much as $20,000 for a Buick automobile. These conditions, one may say, have always existed in Iran. That is true, but today there are numerous new elements. First and foremost, the Iranians in Tehran have suffered this winter as seldom before. Bread, their only staple food and the only one their limited funds can buy, has been scarce, and at present is almost not to be had. Due to allied exploitation of the railways for aid to Russia, the vital commodity kerosene is so scarce that women and children wait in block-long queues for hours to get it and then are often disappointed. This in a country which exports petroleum and in a world which talks of Atlantic Charters, a better world and a new order.[59]

As this report suggests, the Allied occupation of Iran aggravated conditions of poverty that had already existed before 1941. A. C. Millspaugh, Iran's administrator-general of finance, stated that the war, more than any other factor, brought about the rising cost of living. Specifically as a result of the war, foreign imports declined, and Allied expenditures in Iran rose—resulting in a decrease in supplies and an increase in the demand for goods.[60]

The strike of construction workers in February 1942 was followed later that year by a food riot, which took place on 8 December in Tehran.[61] Then came demands by workers at the state-owned tobacco factory. They called for equal treatment with civil servants, each of whom had received a grant and an interest-free loan equal to a month's salary. The tobacco workers also called on the factory to provide them with such essentials as rice, cooking oil, and soap at reduced prices.[62] A year later, in February 1943, not having received an adequate response to their demands, the tobacco workers went on strike. This time, however, the government did respond—by discharging sixty workers, allegedly on the orders of Ahmad Qavam, the veteran politician who had followed Ali Soheili as prime minister.[63]

The failure of government to satisfy the workers' grievances was demonstrated in April 1943 when the construction workers once again went on strike. In an open letter to the prime minister and the minister of justice they asked: "How will you provide justice for the oppressed against the oppressor in this building when its foundation has been built on oppression and injustice?"[64]

They then demanded a one-month bonus at *Nowrouz* (New Year); a sufficient increase in wages to cover daily needs; provision of food at cost; insurance; reduction of the work day from nine to eight hours; strike pay; and a promise not to reprimand or discharge the striking workers.[65]

The spontaneous strikes that occurred during the formative years of the labor movement (1941–1944) offered the executive branch, now almost wholly independent of the shah, a chance to show concern for the welfare of the workers. Its failure to do so gave the newly organized Tudeh Party an opportunity to become the exclusive champion of the workers. Recognizing the significance of this political-economic crisis, the American minister, Louis G. Dreyfus Jr., wrote, "Perhaps no country in the world today is more ripe than Iran for socialistic indoctrination. Is it any wonder that the Iranians are being swayed by the promises of the teachers of socialism?"[66]

The Tudeh Party had expressed total support for the workers' general demands as far back as the First Provincial Conference of the party in Tehran, which convened on 9 October 1942. Shortly after the initial strike of the construction workers, the party called for the recognition of trade unions and the right of collective bargaining. It further urged the passage of a labor law that would establish an eight-hour work day and premium pay for overtime work; an old-age pension; annual paid vacation; unemployment insurance; disability insurance; a paid Sabbath, and prohibition of labor by children under fourteen.[67]

Government Response to Labor Unrest

While the Tudeh Party and the Central Council were succeeding in identifying themselves as the defenders of the working class, the government was reacting more often than not by suppressing the workers' protests. For example, in August 1943, shortly after the First

Provincial Conference of the Trade Union of the Province of Tehran, the government-owned copper-smelting factory in Tehran discharged Ebrahim Mahzari, chairman of the Central Council.[68] In an editorial, *Rahbar* claimed that the government, in addition to persecuting trade union leaders, created dissension among workers by exacerbating their religious and ethnic differences.[69]

To be sure, between 1941 and 1944 the Iranian government made a number of pledges to improve the workers' lot, but these statements amounted to no more than unkept promises. As nine cabinets, headed by five prime ministers, succeeded one another within this three-year period, each government would make promises and propose a few legislative measures but implement none of them.

On 7 December 1941, Prime Minister Mohammad-Ali Foroughi had presented his program to the Majles. Among its twelve proposals were "development of national industries as far as possible, entrusting the plants and mills to private organizations" and "efforts to better the lot of workers."[70] Within a few months, Foroughi was replaced as prime minister by Ali Soheili, who, on 12 March 1942, told the Majles that he would attempt "to ameliorate the lot of the workers."[71] The announcement of these intentions was all that was done for the workers until Ahmad Qavam was elected prime minister in August of that year—after being out of politics for nearly twenty years. Following the bread riot of 8 December 1942,[72] Qavam moved to establish a Ministry of Labor and National Economy. He presented a bill to the Majles in January 1943 in which the objectives of the new ministry were given as improvement of the conditions of workers and farmers and a reduction in the cost of living, both to be achieved through a unified plan of economic action.[73]

The proposed ministry did not materialize, however, because Qavam resigned a few weeks later; the issue of establishing a ministry of labor was not reconsidered until he assumed the premiership again in January 1946.[74] During his earlier tenure, Qavam also presented to the Majles a labor insurance bill, which also remained inactive for a period of time.

Ali Soheili, forming his second cabinet, replaced Qavam as prime minister on 17 February 1943 and made an ineffective gesture toward the workers. Three months later, in response to the Central Council's call on May Day for the passage of a comprehensive labor bill and the workmen's insurance bill previously proposed by Qavam,[75] Soheili issued a directive to the Ministry of Commerce and Industry with the following instructions: reduce working hours in factories, especially for women and children; do not employ children under the age of twelve; take effective action regarding workers' health; take serious steps to implement the workers' accident insurance law; provide for washing and recreational facilities; and delegate local committees to implement labor laws and regulations.[76]

Without either legal basis or sanctions this directive, like its predecessors, had little effect. However, in response to the growing demands for labor legislation, on 20 November 1943, the Thirteenth Majles passed a labor insurance law requiring all workers in all commercial, industrial, mining, and transportation enterprises to be insured against physical disability, medical expenses, lost wages, and death due to accident or illness. One-third of the premium was to be paid by the workers and the remaining two-thirds by the employers. Since the necessary infrastructure for its implementation did not exist, the law was to be implemented gradually throughout the country. A fine of 500 to 5,000 *rials* was set as penalty for violations.[77]

It took another five months to establish a Department of Labor Insurance within the Ministry of Commerce and Industry to implement the labor insurance law;[78] and four months passed before the regulations necessary for its execution were prepared.[79] Finally, early in November 1944 the regulations were approved by the Council of Ministers. No evidence exists, however, that the government, after taking a year to enact these regulations, ever put them into practice.

Although the reemergence of constitutional monarchy enabled certain changes to be made in the body politic of Iran, it is clear that the executive branch continued to maintain its unsympathetic, and at times antagonistic, attitude toward organized labor. Nearly all labor laws and regulations purporting to assist the workers were merely expedients to allay the latest outburst of popular discontent. They were rarely carried out.

The unresponsiveness of the government to the workers' legitimate demands reflected its primary allegiance to the wealthy and powerful rather than to the underprivileged. As one analyst stated it, the processes of government were controlled by a group of men who were members of the important land-owning families of the country. Men of this background occupied not only cabinet posts but also most of the important positions in the civil service and in the armed forces. In these circumstances, it was natural that the governments, desiring to maintain the status quo, were unresponsive to the needs of the masses.[80]

In the manifesto of his Hamrahan Party,[81] Mostafa Fateh, an American-trained economist employed by the Anglo-Iranian Oil Company, agreed with the above analysis of post-1941 Iran: "Although the Shah [Reza Shah] had gone," he wrote, "the agents of his dictatorial regime, who were not inferior to him in tyranny, stayed in their position firmly but discreetly, for they now pretended to be democrats."[82]

The group to which Fateh referred comprised less than 1 percent of the population and included not only the major landowners but also the merchants, owners of factories, tribal leaders, and other members of the elite who owned most of the country's wealth. Through their extensive families they also controlled the governing machinery; they or their relatives were deputies of the Majles, senior government officials, and military commanders.[83]

Since this book is concerned primarily with Iranians of the upper class who were employers, it will be useful to review their attitude toward the workers. According to one survey, most employers looked upon their employees as serfs who had no natural rights and upon whom the employers magnanimously bestowed the benefit of jobs. The survey continues:

> The Iranian businessman displays a higher degree of avariciousness than his Western counterpart; the motive of profit maximization is extremely highly developed in him. He is apt to look upon labor costs as an unreasonable restraint on his profits and to cut these costs as ruthlessly as possible. Given these mental attitudes, it is only natural that Iranian employers look upon the labor laws with contempt and as manifestations of governmental weakness. They may therefore be expected to do all in their power to subvert these laws, both by taking advantage of whatever loopholes may present themselves and by bribing government officials to administer them to the advantage of themselves.[84]

The Majles and the Workers

As long as the executive and the legislative branches were dominated by the privileged class, there was little likelihood that the conditions of the workers would improve through constitutional means. Accordingly, their hopes for the future were fixed on the Majles elections to take place in the autumn of 1943. These elections would test the sincerity of those who proclaimed allegiance to the constitution and urged change through constitutional rather than revolutionary means.

With the forced abdication of Reza Shah in 1941, even the Thirteenth Majles, whose members had been hand-picked by him, tried to assert that body's constitutional prerogatives. The Majles did succeed in establishing its control over the ministers and used its right to discuss, criticize, and change proposed legislation. According to a United States government report, the deputies jealously "guarded the rights of the Chamber [Majles] ... against every attempt to infringe them, and, in general, kept the needs of the nation constantly before the public."[85] It is questionable whether most deputies in the Thirteenth Majles exercised their prerogatives out of any regard for "the needs of the nation"; but, however motivated, their independence did prepare the groundwork for the achievements of the session to come.

As the Thirteenth Majles neared its end, a royal decree was issued in June 1943 ordering elections for the fourteenth session. This particular election campaign offers an excellent opportunity to study the attitudes of domestic groups and foreign powers toward constitutional government in Iran. These attitudes would determine whether the trade unions continued to grow or would come to an end.

As far as the Tudeh Party and the Central Council were concerned, the Majles elections were the first real opportunity to participate in the country's governance. As far back as October 1942, during the First Provincial Conference of the Tudeh Party in Tehran, Ardeshir Ovanessian had stated the party's position clearly: "Our party wants to implement its reformist proposals by means of parliamentarianism, and this step requires the presence of our party's representatives in the Majles."[86]

Once the election campaign commenced, the Tudeh Party focused its energies on canvassing the workers. The following editorial from *Rahbar* exemplifies the party's approach: "Constitutionalism and real freedom will only become a reality when the people are able to send their representatives to the Majles, so that they can defend their rights and demand that the responsible officials be accountable."[87]

As a part of the campaign for the elections, *Razm* (Combat), another Tudeh newspaper, published a statement telling the workers that their future well-being depended on the results of the upcoming elections.

Workers: do you know that you must have your own representatives in the Majles so that your wages, food, health, education, and
general welfare will be provided for. . .? Again they want to fool
you with a few *tomans* of money, with a cup of tea, with a dish
of rice; they want to deceive you. Don't be deceived.

Workers: elect representatives of your own class. This is the first
time that you have the opportunity to send the representative of
the workers to the Majles. Success depends only on your serious-
ness of purpose. The Trade Union of the Workers of Iran has
formed a coalition in Tehran with the Tudeh Party of Iran. . . .

Workers: Members of the Tudeh Party will vote for the candidates
of the Central Council of the Trade Union. You must also vote for
the candidates of the Tudeh Party of Iran.[88]

The Central Council selected its chairman, Ebrahim Mahzari,
and secretary, Hossein Jahani, as candidates from Tehran. The Tudeh
Party selected Reza Rousta, Iraj Eskandari, Noureddin Alamouti,
Soleiman Mohsen-Eskandari, Dr. Morteza Yazdi, and Dr. Reza
Radmanesh.[89]

While the Tudeh Party and the Central Council sought increased
political strength—generally, through constitutional means and,
specifically, through participation in the Majles elections—the
British legation in Tehran was reported by the American legation to
"prefer to have the elections postponed indefinitely. They would, as
they have often informed the Department, even prefer to see the
Majles dissolved."[90] A review of internal British documents confirms
this view. Despite their deposition of Reza Shah, the British still
believed that his rule "showed that Persia is more amenable to
complete autocracy than to any other form of government."[91] The
same British report stated that "the so-called 'democratic' parliament,
the Majles, is indulging in an orgy of criticism."

The report is accurate enough; the Thirteenth Majles was, in fact,
only nominally democratic and was much given to petty squabbling,
but, being out of sympathy with the principle of representative
government in Iran, the British preferred deriding the Majles to
helping it improve. The reason the British were against a freely elected
Majles was clear; they feared that it would be filled by deputies
unsympathetic to British interests.

While the British, as before, preferred to deal directly with the
shah and his subordinates, the Soviets took the opposite stance of

supporting the Majles election "since the election of a number of socialist deputies seems likely."[92]

As for the United States, just entering on the scene in Iran, its views toward the Majles were at first mixed. In a dispatch dated 24 August 1942 discussing the prospects of the Qavam cabinet, Minister Dreyfus reported: "Among the more important dangers the cabinet will have to face are the political intrigue of the Majles and the destructive power of the press. Both of these unreliable and unscrupulous elements are likely again to get out of hand and cause another political crisis unless strong repressive measures are taken."[93]

A year later, however, at the time of elections for the Fourteenth Majles, Dreyfus became supportive of the constitutional process: "These . . . will be Iran's first free elections in more than fifteen years. Personally, it would seem to me that the elections should go forward and let the chips fall where they may. This is the democratic way and perhaps, all things considered, the best course from our own point of view."[94] The American minister supported free elections, even though he realized that several Tudeh candidates were likely to be elected. He wrote: "The election of a number of socialist deputies might in the long run be all to the good in bringing about a gradual improvement in the intolerable system of government by the privileged classes. Unless such a change is brought about gradually and in a democratic way, it eventually will have to be achieved suddenly and drastically."[95]

The election results were announced over a period of months. The total number of votes cast for the Tudeh candidates was estimated to be one-eighth of the total votes cast, estimated at 1,500,000.[96] In all, nine of the fifteen Tudeh candidates were elected, although none were elected to the twelve seats for Tehran. Among those elected were Taghi Fadakar, chairman of the Esfahan trade union,[97] and Ardeshir Ovanessian, who represented the Armenians. Of the Central Council and Tudeh Party leaders who stood for election in Tehran, Dr. Morteza Yazdi received 4,719 votes, Ebrahim Mahzari 2, 831, and Hossein Jahani 2,796 out of the 41,000 total votes cast. After the election some observers concluded that the total number of disciplined Tudeh members equaled the number who had voted for Jahani.[98] Even the Tudeh press acknowledged the low number of votes, although construing this outcome as a success.[99]

The Tudeh deputies were in a definite minority, holding only 9 out of 136 seats. The figures, however, are somewhat deceptive. These nine deputies were often reinforced by a dozen or so independents, such as Dr. Mohammad Mossadegh. Moreover, whatever their number, the Tudeh deputies could use the Majles as a forum in which to express sentiments that would be duly reported by the press.

At the beginning of the fourteenth session of the Majles in February 1944, the Tudeh deputies advocated a reformist program. In less than a year, however, their reformist position would become more militant and identifiable with orthodox Communist doctrine.

Unification of the Tudeh Unions

By the spring of 1944, the Tudeh Party was ready to consolidate its power over the labor movement by bringing a number of independent trade unions under the leadership of the Central Council. This move toward consolidation, which began in April and continued through June, has been inaccurately represented as a voluntary and peaceful marriage of four independent trade unions consummated on 1 May 1944.[100] According to the record, however, this unification was not accomplished harmoniously nor on the date that has been reported—though most members of the four unions involved did eventually come under the leadership of the Central Council.

The actual sequence of events was quite different: On 28 April 1944 an extraordinary session of the Executive Board of the Central Council, meeting at the headquarters of the Tudeh Party in Tehran, decided to form a new and enlarged labor organization by merging with its rival, the Central Board (Hei'at-e Markazi),[101] which had been organized by several Socialists at about the same time as the Central Council. Yousef Eftekhari, who had been discharged from the oil company after the 1929 strike, was its chairman; Khalil Enghelab served as publicity manager, and Ezatollah Atighehchi[102] as secretary.

Although little else is known about the origin of the Central Board, the relationship between it and the Central Council was clearly antagonistic. While the Tudeh Party consistently opposed strikes in war industries, the Central Board instigated a number of strikes, placing workers' interests above political considerations. Eftekhari and Enghelab, who held militant socialistic views, were vehemently attacked by the Tudeh Party as provocateurs and agents of capitalists and reactionaries, intent on creating dissension among the workers.[103] Soviet historian M. S. Ivanov echoes these allegations.[104]

The Central Board viewed itself as politically neutral, dedicated solely to the welfare of the workers—a position welcomed by anti-Tudeh newspapers such as *Ra'd-e Emrouz*.[105] Geographically, the Central Board, like the Central Council, concentrated its union activities in the provinces of Mazandaran and Azerbaijan, which were under Soviet occupation. The newspaper *Giti* was, for a time, the official organ of the Central Board.[106]

Subsequent to the Central Council's decision of 28 April 1944, a joint statement was issued on 1 May by the Central Council and the majority faction of the Central Board announcing their consolidation into the Central United Council of the Trade Union of Workers and Toilers of Iran (CUC).[107] Conspicuously absent from among the signers was the Central Board's chairman, Yousef Eftekhari, who chose to follow a separate path.[108] Consequently, the consolidation of the two organizations was marked by recriminations, Eftekhari accusing his former colleagues, Enghelab and Atighehchi, of stealing his union's furniture, documents, and seal.[109] He also denounced them, as well as seventy members of the Central Council, for disrupting his trade union's May Day rally in the village of Asadabad, north of Tehran.[110] In the course of this disruption, Reza Rousta, not yet the official leader of the CUC, suffered a beating and a fractured skull.[111] Eftekhari also claimed that he had previously expelled the Enghelab faction from the Central Board, which he claimed still existed as an independent trade union. With the assistance of these "agents of dissension," Eftekhari asserted, the Tudeh Party was attempting to prevent the meeting of the Central Board's National Congress.

The CUC countered Eftekhari's accusations by contending that it was Eftekhari who had been expelled from the Central Board—not Enghelab and Atighehchi, who were now part of the CUC. Interestingly enough, in less than three months, the propaganda guns of the CUC turned against their recently won colleague, Khalil Enghelab, denouncing him with the same passion formerly directed against Eftekhari. The CUC accused Enghelab of being an agent of reaction and an ultra-leftist at the same time, and urged his arrest.[112]

The official unification of the majority faction of the Central Board with the Tudeh trade union, the Central Council, was followed by the entry of the little-known Trade Union of Toilers of Iran (Ettehadieh-e Zahmatkeshan-e Iran) on 8 May 1944.[113] The much larger Association of Railway Workers (Kanoun-e Kargaran-e Raha-han), formed in August 1943, joined the CUC on 20 June 1944,[114] bringing to four the total number of organizations that had wholly or partially united to form the CUC. Although Fadakar's seventeen-thousand-member union in Esfahan had pledged its allegiance to the Central Council as early as August 1943,[115] it did not formally join the CUC until October 1944.[116] Subsequently, smaller trade unions announced periodically that they too had joined the bandwagon and become a part of the CUC, which became for all practical purposes, Iran's sole labor organization.

As the American labor attache, W. J. Handley, has observed, it is extremely difficult to arrive at an estimate of the membership of the CUC. According to figures provided by its leader, Reza Rousta, in August 1945, the total membership of the CUC was 209,750.[117] Ivanov cites the figure of 150,000 as of June 1944,[118] and 180,000 for the spring of 1945.[119] Handley, having made an on-the-spot survey of the various claims, gives what is probably the more accurate estimate of 100,000.[120] Total estimated employment during the 1940s in 1,239 industrial establishments employing 10 or more workers was approximately 163,790 (see Appendix B).[121] Given this total, Rousta's figure at first glance seems greatly exaggerated, especially since it did not include any of the 62,000 workers in the oil industry. A closer scrutiny of his assessment shows that he claimed only 80,375 of his members to have been employed at industrial establishments. The remaining 129,375 members that he claimed for the CUC were employed outside the industrial category upon which the figure of 163,790 was based. For example, Rousta included 58,000 agricultural workers and 34,000 road and dock workers as CUC members. The records, however, offer no confirmation that such a large number of farmers and road workers, engaged in activities characterized by geographical dispersion rather than concentration, were ever or-ganized. It must be concluded, therefore, that Rousta's membership figure of 209,750 is inflated.

This much can safely be said: By the autumn of 1944, when the period of confrontation began between the CUC and the Tudeh Party on the one hand and the Iranian government on the other, the CUC had organized over 100,000 workers in most industrial centers of Iran. The key factor leading to this development was the reestablishment of the Iranian constitution. Although the executive branch of the government, as well as the army, continued to be controlled by individuals unsympathetic to organized labor, and although the government continued to favor the employers, the workers were able to join and remain members of trade unions because of the protection afforded them by the limited implementation of the constitution.

In summary, the rebirth of the labor movement occurred in 1941, when Iran was given a second opportunity to govern itself according to the constitution. Although the 1941–1944 years brought Iran's economic development to a halt, a significant degree of political development took place during this time. Because the constitution was once again acknowledged, middle- and lower-middle-class Iranians were able to return to the political activities they had been forced to abandon almost two decades earlier. The press began to exercise its proper function in a constitutional society. Political parties were formed. Trade and professional organizations emerged and began to search for their appropriate role. Even deputies who had been hand-picked by Reza Shah to serve as his scribes in the thirteenth session of the Majles were affected by the change of atmosphere, and they too began to demonstrate independence. Thus, with at least partial implementation of the constitution, trade unions were formed and began to represent the workers.

$\mathcal{3}$

Years of Confrontation
1944–1946

Polarization of Politics

$\mathcal{T}$ HE SUMMER of 1944 signaled the resumption of competition
between the Soviet Union and the two Western powers in
Iran.[1] Once again a major shift in the relationship between the major
powers was reflected in Iran's domestic politics. Whereas the years
of cooperation (1941–1944) between the Soviets and the British led
to the reemergence of constitutional government in Iran, the years
of confrontation (1944–1946) precipitated conflict between Iran's
central government and its leftist labor movement. As L. P. Elwell-
Sutton has observed, "1944 saw the gradual widening of the gulf
between Russia and the western powers as the tide of war receded
from Persia and Russia itself; and in sympathy with this the . . . major
groups in Persian politics began to separate along left-wing and
right-wing lines. This process reached its climax in the oil crisis of
the autumn."[2]

The British, suspicious of Soviet intentions, prepared to protect
their interests for the postwar years to come. At the same time, the
wealthy and powerful classes in Iran displayed more aggressively
their traditional pro-British and anti-Soviet sentiments.

In line with the Soviet Union's new attitude toward its Western
allies in Iran, the Tudeh Party shifted from a reformist to a militant
stance. An accident of history hastened this transformation. With the
death of the widely respected socialist, Soleiman Mohsen-Eskandari,

in January 1944, the party leadership passed on formally to younger men who were devoted Marxist-Leninists.

This change in the Tudeh's leadership and attitude was reflected in the newly organized Tudeh labor federation, the Central United Council (CUC), as its leadership, too, passed from reformists to militants who heretofore had been active behind the scenes. On 6 July 1944, it was announced that at a recent meeting Reza Ebrahim-zadeh and Ebrahim Mahzari had been elected co-chairmen of the CUC.[3] This was clearly a demotion for Mahzari, who had been the sole chairman of the Central Council for the preceding 2½ years. His new partner in power, Ebrahimzadeh, was a Communist who had lived for some time in Soviet Azerbaijan and had been imprisoned in Iran during the rule of Reza Shah.[4]

On 18 June 1945, approximately a year later, the title for CUC leaders was changed from "co-chairman" to "secretary" (in conform-ity with the usage of the Tudeh Party), and Reza Rousta was added to the CUC's leadership, making it a triumvirate.[5] In the autumn of 1945, however, Rousta emerged publicly as the sole leader of the CUC.[6] In the intervening months more attention had been given to establishing discipline and centralization within the labor organiza-tion in order to make it more responsive to the policies of the Tudeh Party.

In June 1944, for instance, local chapters had been warned not to take action without written authorization from Tehran.[7] A year later, on 15 June 1945, the CUC's governing body met to review the activities of the first year of the unified labor organization. It was decided to grant more power to the executive board of the CUC and to increase centralization "so that all labor unions throughout Iran [would] operate like an orderly machine and a single body." Hence-forth, all decisions involving strikes, collective agreements, and expulsion of members could only be adopted with the consent of the Central United Council.[8]

In the initial stages of this period of confrontation, the news-paper *Zafar* played an important role in mobilizing the workers. In its first editorial, the CUC organ described Iran's social system as consisting of two parts: on one side were the few "vagrant and pleasure-seeking" rich, and on the other were millions of the oppressed toiling in torn clothes and with empty stomachs. This description of the Iranian masses was commonplace; what was new, and reminiscent of similar writings in *Haghighat* two decades earlier, was *Zafar*'s radical analysis of the social situation: "In a society in which the capitalists, with the support of their capital, have taken power into their own hands and have made the government obedient and submissive to themselves, workers and toilers have no one to support or defend them. In such societies, police, the gendarmerie, and the army are mobilized and equipped to blindly serve the capitalists against the oppressed class and to suffocate their voices."[9] Thus, a battle cry against the government was sounded, and the overthrow of the state seemed to emerge as a CUC objective.

The first instance of confrontation between the CUC and the state occurred not over a labor dispute but over a political issue of major importance—the oil concession demanded by the Soviet Union. This confrontation clearly revealed a close collaboration between the CUC, the Tudeh Party, and the Soviet Union. When, in October 1944, the government of Prime Minister Mohammad Sa'ed turned a deaf ear to Soviet demands for an oil concession in the northern provinces of Iran, the Tudeh Party and the CUC jointly organized a march of 12,000 people. The demonstrators demanded the dismissal of the prime minister and the settlement of the oil problem "in Iran's national interests and not in the interest of English and American oil monopolies."[10] Moreover, according to the political scientist Sepehr Zabih, the CUC instigated walkouts and sit-down strikes in important industrial cities such as Shahi in the north and Esfahan in central Iran, as well as in the capital, where armed workers actually assumed control of some major factories.[11] Soviet historian M. S. Ivanov states that about half a million people participated in the demonstrations that were held in Tehran, Tabriz, Esfahan, Mashhad, Ahwaz, Rasht, and other cities.[12]

Soviet troops provided the demonstrators with protection. The U.S. Office of Strategic Services (OSS), predecessor to the Central Intelligence Agency, reported that during the Tudeh-CUC demonstration on 27 October, "several truckloads of Russian soldiers appeared on the scene, apparently to discourage the Iran military from restraining the marchers."[13] In provinces under their occupation, the Soviets intervened even more forcefully. In Tabriz, for instance, they disarmed the local police in order to keep them from preventing a pro-Soviet demonstration.[14]

The oil question was temporarily shelved on 2 November 1944 as the result of a motion proposed by Dr. Mohammad Mossadegh, the nationalist leader of the Majles, prohibiting any discussion of an oil concession as long as foreign troops occupied Iran.[15] The Tudeh Party and CUC, finding another occasion to rally their followers, planned a mass commemoration of the October Revolution. The government, however, banned further demonstrations,[16] and the conflict deepened. On 17 November the military governor of Tehran ordered the occupation of the local Tudeh Party club, and posted the police to keep everyone out.[17] According to the leftist newspaper *Ajir*, the police removed CUC's billboard and paraded it through the streets of Tehran in order to demonstrate the power of the military authorities.[18] At the same time, Gholam-Hossein Ebtehaj, the mayor of Tehran, discharged all Tudeh employees of the municipality. When the Tudeh deputy, Iraj Eskandari, protested, it was reported that Ebtehaj ordered all the garbage from the district in which Eskandari lived dumped in front of his house.[19]

Represented by deputies in the Majles, whose public protests could not be silenced, and enjoying Soviet, as well as considerable popular support, the Tudeh Party was not easily intimidated. On the contrary, *Rahbar* challenged the prime minister and the executive branch in the most explicit terms:

> On Friday 27th October 1944 . . . [we] demonstrated our strength, action, courage, and perseverance. Today we have in our ranks thousands of devoted individuals, ready for self-sacrifice, who as a result of organizational training, have become familiar with the techniques of governing the nation. We state explicitly that Sa'ed is a usurper of the rights of the Iranian people; and by remaining in the office of premiership, he is a liability to the nation. The Majles . . . must remove this thorn and rubbish from the path of the people.[20]

Zabih, in *The Communist Movement in Iran*, summarized the situation well:

> As the Right and Left moved further and further apart, the Communist movement in Iran returned to a policy of open offensive, reminiscent of 1920–21 and aimed, at the least, at an ending of oil concessions [to the West], and, at the most, at the establishment of a pro-Soviet government in Iran. So far as the tactics in the country as a whole were concerned, the hardening of the line meant dumping the still basically non-revolutionary Tudeh party in favor of a revolutionary organization.[21]

The events of October and November 1944 led to the fall of the Sa'ed government through a vote of no confidence in the Majles initiated by Tudeh representatives. In a speech on the floor of the Majles, Dr. Fereidoun Keshavarz condemned the government for closing the Tudeh club in Tehran and removing its billboard, and for preventing workers from holding meetings even in their own homes. As for Tudeh support of the Soviet oil concession, Keshavarz said that by supporting the Soviets, the party was neutralizing British influence in Iran.[22]

Prime Minister Sa'ed was replaced by Morteza-Gholi Bayat on 26 November 1944 with the backing of the Tudeh Party and the independent deputies in the Majles. As his first act, Bayat removed the restrictions placed on the leftists. However, this period of relative conciliation between the executive branch and the opponents of the status quo was brief, as the Majles withdrew its support from Bayat and on 2 May 1945 replaced him as prime minister with Ebrahim Hakimi, the much respected but old and ineffective veteran of the constitutional revolution. Hakimi himself remained in office for just a month, during which the war in Europe came to an end.

Hard Line against the Left

The mild-mannered Hakimi was succeeded as prime minster by hard-liner Mohsen Sadr (Sadr-ol-Ashraf) a few days after a strike by workers of the Anglo-Iranian Oil Company (AIOC)[23] in Kermanshah. This first major strike at an AIOC installation since 1929 occurred on 30 May 1945.[24] Four days later the shah appointed Sadr prime minister. A controversial politician, Sadr had opposed the constitutionalists in 1908. His appointment and his decision to assume office before his cabinet could be presented to the Majles[25] provoked accusations from the Tudeh Party and its supporters that the "Anglo-American imperialists" were the real sponsors of Sadr.[26] Two days later the AIOC, assuming an uncompromising posture, dismissed nearly 400 of the 650 striking workers who did not return to work before the deadline set by the company.

The appointment of a hard-liner to deal with the militancy of the Tudeh Party and the CUC was adding fuel to the fire. Dr. Mossadegh opposed Sadr for a number of reasons. He argued that the new premier must be considered neutral by Iran's "neighbors" (the Soviet Union and Great Britain) and by participants in the upcoming elections for the Fifteenth Majles.

With the end of the war in Europe, war-related employment in Iran declined drastically, and unemployment took on critical proportions. Not surprisingly, *Zafar*, on behalf of the Tudeh Party, was the first and only publication to address the problem. The editor noted that while in the Soviet Union millions of soldiers were being employed in productive work, the number of unemployed Iranians was increasing because of the corrupt and selfish members of the ruling class. The only solution, concluded *Zafar*, was to overthrow them and their incompetent government.[27]

Prime Minister Sadr's response to these threats was to answer in kind. General Moghaddam, military governor of Tehran, placed the city under martial law. At midnight on 24 August 1945, the headquarters of the CUC and the Tudeh Party were searched and occupied. Over a dozen Tudeh and CUC leaders were detained,[28] and about fourteen newspapers, including *Zafar*, were shut down. Ivanov goes as far as to claim that there was a virtual state of war in the city.[29]

In reaction to these assaults on the Tudeh Party and the CUC in the capital, militant worker groups in the northern province of Mazandaran occupied major towns, factories, and railroad junctions.[30] Zabih further reported: "The so-called self-defense service assumed control of roads and communication networks. Attempts by the government to enlarge their security forces in these areas were blocked when Soviets refused to allow troop movements."[31]

The confrontation between the CUC and the executive branch was not confined within Iran's borders. The World Federation of Trade Unions (WFTU) and the International Labor Office (ILO) invited Iran's trade unions to attend their conferences to be held in Paris in the autumn of 1945. These conferences were to be a source of conflict in both Tehran and Paris.

The selection of a workers' delegate to the ILO conference took place at a time when repressive measures were being employed against the CUC, and the Iranian government found itself in a difficult predicament. American Labor Attache William J. Handley described its position:

> Such a delegation would have to include two government representatives and one each from management and labor with their respective advisors. But how could the government send a genuine

representative of labor when organized labor does not have legal status in the country? Furthermore, if the delegation, in accordance with the provisions of the ILO, were a member of the most representative union in the country, he would have to be a member of the Central United Council of Trade Unions, which is affiliated with the Tudeh party. This would then be anathema to the government and to the employer representatives, and it would immeasurably strengthen the Tudeh.[32]

Since the CUC was obviously the most representative trade union in Iran, a CUC member should have been selected as the workers' delegate. Instead, the government chose Shams Sadri, chairman of an employer-sponsored, anti-Tudeh labor organization in Esfahan.[33] As substitute delegate, the government chose Yousef Eftekhari, who by mid-1945 represented no more than a few hundred unionized workers. Unwilling to accept the government's decision as a *fait accompli*, the CUC decided to send a rival delegation to Paris. When W. J. Handley, the American labor attache, suggested to Habib Naficy, director of the Ministry of Commerce and Industry's labor office, that the government would be embarrassed at the conference by this situation, which was of the government's own making, Naficy remarked with a smile that "perhaps the Tudeh representatives would not be able to find transportation when the time came for them to leave Iran."[34]

Naficy's prediction came true.[35] On the eve of their departure to attend the WFTU conference, Reza Rousta, Ali Shamideh, and a number of CUC leaders were arrested and imprisoned. They protested to various authorities, including attendants at the Foreign Minister's Conference then meeting in London,[36] Dr. Mossadegh, and other deputies in the Majles. But in spite of this, they remained in detention. In their letter to the Majles, Rousta and his colleagues declared, "Our illegal detention is the best proof of the existence of despotism and terror in the country."[37] Although Rousta was released from prison on 2 October, after an alleged visit by a Soviet officer named Rasuloff,[38] he was denied permission to leave the country and therefore was unable to attend the Paris conference.

As a result, it was Iraj Eskandari, a secretary of the Tudeh Party and a Majles deputy, who was assigned the task of representing the CUC in Paris. When Eskandari applied for a diplomatic passport, normally granted to any Majles deputy, his request was ignored. After much delay, however he was finally issued an ordinary passport.[39]

Eskandari, together with a few other CUC delegates, arrived in Paris via Moscow on 3 October, four days before the end of the WFTU conference.[40]

Although Shams Sadri was seated as the Iranian workers' delegate, the Credentials Committee saw fit to criticize the Iranian government for its lack of attention to the ILO's regulations. The committee also established that two of the workers' advisers were employers, two others were officials or state employees, and that the traveling expenses of two workers' advisers (Eftekhari and Amir-keivan)[41] had been paid by their employers.[42]

The government of Mohsen Sadr faced harsher criticism at home, from both its opponents and disaffected supporters. Clearly, his repressive domestic policies had failed to achieve results. The membership in both the Tudeh Party and the CUC had grown even while their headquarters and clubs were occupied and their news-papers suspended. The province of Azerbaijan was being lost to Ja'far Pishevari, a founder of the Persian Communist Party of the 1920s, whose credentials as a newly-elected deputy from Tabriz had been rejected by the Fourteenth Majles.[43] In foreign affairs, the prime minister had fared no better. He had incurred the wrath of the Soviet Union by refusing to meet its renewed demands for an oil concession.

Conciliatory Moves toward the Left

The Sadr cabinet fell, predictably, in late October; and once again, Ebrahim Hakimi, who held office from 4 November 1945 to mid-January 1946, served as a bridge between two opposing policies. For the next six months, Hakimi's successor, Prime Minister Ahmad Qavam, followed a policy of conciliation with the Soviet Union and its proteges in Iran.

It should be stressed at the outset that Qavam did not pursue his policy of conciliation out of any genuine sympathy with the labor movement or with Communist ideology. His tortuous policy, so far as it can be reduced to any guiding principles, seems to have been based on political expediency. He tried to accommodate competing factions while building up a political party of his own.

At the time of Qavam's selection by the Majles, the status quo was seriously threatened by revolutionary activity, supported by the presence of Soviet troops. Qavam reassured backers of the status quo and relieved the fears of most other Iranians by engineering the departure of Soviet troops from Iran and by obtaining assurances from the Soviet Union that it would abstain from interfering in Iran's domestic affairs. This he accomplished by promising the oil concession in return. Simultaneously, he pacified the Tudeh Party and the CUC by a number of conciliatory gestures, such as introducing a comprehensive labor law and inducing employers to negotiate with workers.

Inspired as they were by political expediency, Qavam's concessions were not necessarily in the best interests of those who approved them. In fact, they proved to be double-edged. While pacifying the Communist and labor organizations, Qavam had also to assure the British and the shah that he was not playing into Communist hands. Thus, measures such as his labor law offered advantages to both sides. While the law sanctioned the establishment of trade unions, it also allowed employers to negotiate with labor representatives of the employers'—not the union's—choice. An example of Qavam's equivocation is found in the events of May Day 1946. Acceding to the CUC's demands, he allowed Reza Rousta to broadcast a May Day address, but the frequency carrying the address was one that could not be received by radio sets in Tehran.[44]

Ahmad Qavam was no neophyte in politics.[45] He had first become prime minister in June 1921 when Reza-Khan served as his minister of war and Dr. Mossadegh as minister of finance.[46] He had been returned to office in August 1942 and served for a brief period of six months. During both terms Qavam had aroused the anger of the trade unions, the press, and other opponents of the status quo by his assertion of governmental authority and his adoption of repressive measures. In January 1946, however, Qavam was supported by both proponents and opponents of the current regime.

The United States, Great Britain, the shah, and other members of the ruling elite favored Qavam's return to office because, in the words of George Allen, the newly arrived United States ambassador to Iran, Qavam was "the most energetic and forceful man on the scene in Iran" at the time, and the most likely person "to prevent one more country from falling completely into the Moscow orbit."[47] Moreover, as a politician with a record of friendship toward the West, and as a man of wealth,[48] Qavam was unlikely to stray into Soviet arms.

The opponents of the status quo, led by the Tudeh Party and the CUC and supported by the Soviet Union, were pleased by Qavam's recently adopted policy of conciliation toward them. They concluded that the "new" Qavam was their best available option—short of their own takeover. Consequently, they made the tactical decision to disregard his record and give him the opportunity to carry out his promises.

As soon as Qavam had been selected by the Majles in the final days of January 1946, the CUC made a number of demands: that freedom of action be guaranteed to the CUC; that their clubs, which had been closed during the preceding five months, be reopened; that freedom of the press be restored; and that the labor bill pending before the Majles be approved.[49]

In response to these and similar demands made by other critics of the regime, on 11 February 1946 Qavam revoked the martial law edict of August 1945 against political activity, thereby returning their clubs to the Tudeh and CUC. Curbs on the press were removed two weeks later.[50]

Because the fourteenth session of the Majles was to end on 12 March 1946, Qavam was able to proceed with his plans without having to coordinate them with the legislative branch. He moved quickly to reopen discussions with the Soviet Union over the question of an oil concession in the northern provinces. This was done in total disregard of the November 1944 law forbidding such talks. Assurances by Qavam that the Fifteenth Majles would grant such a concession, combined with intense international pressure, led to a comprehensive agreement between the Soviet Union and Iran on 5 April 1946,[51] including an understanding that Soviet troops would leave Iran by the 6th of May 1946.[52]

Having alleviated Soviet pressure on his government, Qavam moved to reduce internal tensions. One such initiative was his introduction of direct labor-management discussions and negotiations. During the normally inactive Nowrouz holidays,[53] he ordered his deputy, Mozaffar Firouz, to meet with representatives of the CUC and employers to establish temporary machinery for resolving their disputes. At a historical meeting attended by Reza Rousta, the secretary of the CUC, and Abdol-Hossein Nikpour, president of the Tehran Chamber of Commerce and a confidant of Qavam, it was agreed that Nikpour would arrange for the employers to elect representatives to negotiate with representatives of labor. Issues not settled by mutual agreement would be decided by Firouz or referred by him to the Arbitration Commission of the Ministry of Commerce and Industry.[54]

Cognizant of Qavam's desire for prompt action, on 4 April 1946 Nikpour convened a meeting of the employers from Qom, Semnan, Qazvin, and Tehran and founded an employers' association called the Industrial Council of Iran.[55] Representatives from the Industrial Council and the CUC met two weeks later. It was indicative of Qavam's authority that no high government official was present to coerce the two sides into negotiating. The major achievement of this meeting was the resolution of a dispute at a factory in Tehran which manufactured glass goods. Moreover, it was agreed that the joint commission would continue to meet once a week to discuss other labor disputes as they arose.[56] These meetings, however, were no longer held after the second and final meeting of 23 April 1946, because the labor law enacted on 18 May provided for other arrangements.

Qavam initiated cooperative action between labor and management in the public sector as well. In April 1946, a series of joint labor-management meetings commenced at the State Railway Organization. Dr. Hossein Jowdat, the veteran Communist and Tudeh leader, led the CUC representatives at these meetings.[57]

At the same time that Qavam's government was prevailing upon employers to meet with CUC representatives, it acted directly to redress some of labor's grievances. One of these was against factory owners who were closing down their plants now that peacetime had brought an end to wartime profits and ushered in a troublesome period of labor disputes.[58] On 3 April 1946, the minister of commerce and industry, Ahmad-Ali Sepehr, warned employers not to close their factories on the pretext that they were incurring losses. Repeating the accusation often made by the CUC, Sepehr reminded the employers that in previous years they had reaped profits of "several hundred" percent on sales when the commercial law had permitted a return of only 12 percent. If they did not heed his warning, the minister said, the government would authorize senior staff and labor to operate those factories on behalf of the owners.[59]

On 7 April, the prime minister took the unprecedented step of inviting the CUC leaders to meet with him in his office. After listening to their grievances and demands, Qavam agreed that (a) the Council of Ministers would recognize the CUC by decree; (b) the hours of work per week would, by decree, be reduced to forty-eight, and Fridays would be declared a paid holiday; (c) the minister of war would release all CUC members still in prison; and (d) representatives of the CUC would be allowed to participate in those meetings of the

Supreme Economic Council at which labor matters were to be considered.[60] After more than two decades of struggle, the Iranian trade unionists had finally reached many of their social and economic goals—a direct result of their recently gained political power and influence.

The Qavam Labor Law

Qavam's most significant conciliatory gesture prior to the Soviets' departure was to order a labor bill to be prepared for consideration by the Council of Ministers. This bill would be the first comprehensive labor legislation enacted in the history of Iran. Also for the first time, those Iranians who would be affected by enactment of a law were invited to participate in its preparation. The bill, later to become law, was prepared by a commission that included Reza Rousta, Engineer Zavosh, and Engineer Tabrizi—all members of the CUC.[61]

On 18 May 1946 the long-awaited labor bill was approved by the Council of Ministers, which pronounced it in effect pending its final approval by the Fifteenth Majles. The Qavam labor law recognized, at least nominally, the right of workers to pursue their economic interests through unionization. Previously, the only labor law on the books was an act passed on 10 August 1936 known as the Regulations for Factories and Industrial Organizations. While the 1936 act provided for minimum hygienic conditions in factories, it prohibited employees from "faction formation, connivance, and other activities leading to disturbance of the smooth running of factory affairs and progress in production."[62]

Since trade unions were not legally recognized prior to the Qavam labor law, the usual procedure for settling industrial disputes was for representatives of the Ministry of Commerce and Industry to act as mediators or arbitrators. Since employers had considerably more influence over government officials than the workers, it was not surprising that most mediators sided with the employers. W. J. Handley reports that on one occasion, when one of the more successful government mediators was unable to settle a dispute, "he agreed to the demands of the workers' spokesmen and thereby succeeded in having the workers return to their jobs. He then proceeded to have the spokesmen, or 'troublemakers,' as he called

them, arrested one by one. Another tactic which he used on several
occasions was to threaten to bring in Indian workers to take the place
of those who were striking."[63]

Even when verbal agreements acceptable to both sides were
concluded, they were rarely implemented. According to Handley, this
failure to abide by their provisons resulted in many strikes.[64] Between
1944 and the approval of the Qavam labor law in May 1946, two labor
bills were presented to the Majles by as many cabinets in response
to an increasing incidence of strikes and other agitation.[65] Both of
these bills, however, severely restricted the unions from participating
in the settlement of labor disputes.

In the summer of 1945, Habib Naficy, of the General Department
of Labor, had told Handley that the government was reluctant to give
legal status to the Tudeh-led trade unions while Soviet troops still
remained in Iran.[66] In the middle of May 1946, a week after the Soviet
troops had departed, Iran passed its first labor law ever to recognize,
in principle, the bargaining power of trade unions. The Qavam law,
however, like most of labor's gains during his premiership, was
equivocal; for the specific provisions of the law, and especially their
elaboration in the form of regulations, provided the government with
the legal means to enter the industrial relations arena, reducing the
influence of organized labor, and preventing it from representing the
workers before the employers and the state. Once the Ministry of
Labor was established, the workers were expected to look on the
government as their true protector, thereby eliminating the need for
a militant trade union.

Article 21 of the law recognized the right of workers engaged
in the same factory or trade to form a union. The board of directors
of the union was simply required to register the articles of association
of the union "with a view to securing legal status." While this
requirement seemed innocuous enough, the note following the article
was a clue to its ominous nature: "The rules concerning unions shall
be laid down in a regulation to be approved by the Council of
Ministers."

Writing laws that enunciate general principles, to be made
specific by regulations at a later time, and the entrusting of these
regulations to the Council of Ministers, has been a familiar political
ruse in contemporary Iran. The same Majles deputy who voted to
pass the law—unobjectionable in its general nature and lack of
specificity—might object to subsequent regulations. These con-

troversial regulations, however, were passed by the executive branch, not the Majles, without publicity or public debate.

It was in line with this tradition that the Qavam labor law of 1946, prepared in cooperation with CUC representatives, recognized the right of workers to organize trade unions and required them only to "register the articles of association." The subsequent regulations,[67] eagerly awaited by the AIOC and the British Foreign Office, [68] were prepared by Kenneth Hird of the British embassy and A. C. V. Lindon of the AIOC. They were approved by the Council of Ministers on 3 March 1947, when the CUC was no longer a political force.

Article 2 of the regulations required founders of trade unions, before proceeding to form a union, to notify the Minstry of Labor in writing of their intentions, at the same time enclosing copies of their identity certificates and certificate of clear record from the police and a questionnaire duly completed. Having received these documents, the Ministry of Labor was to state, within a month, its approval or disapproval of the workers' intention to form a union. If the ministry withheld consent, the workers' only recourse was to appeal the decision to the ministry's High Labor Council, the majority of whose members were representatives of the government and the employers.[69]

The provisions of the Qavam law, as they related to the settlement of disputes, were even more blatantly biased against the unions, prohibiting, for all intent and purposes, the use of strikes. According to article 32 of the regulations, a strike would be permitted only after the dispute had been considered by the factory council, the arbitration board, the umpire, and the Board for Settlement of Disputes, which was composed of three representatives from the government, two from labor, and two from employers. The procedure for selecting the representatives sitting on both boards, as well as the manner in which the boards performed their duties, was to be determined by regulations issued by the Council of Ministers. Only after the arbitration board had failed to settle a dispute within twenty days and the Board for Settlement of Disputes within another twenty days, did the workers have the right to go on strike.[70] These provisions placed so many obstacles in the way of a strike as to make it an unlikely eventuality. No less prejudicial to the unions was the law's failure to specify how labor representatives on the factory council and the boards were to be selected. Even if a union had succeeded in becoming legally established, there was no assurance that one of its members would sit on the council or board.

Conceivably, a union could exist and yet be given no part in the settlement of labor disputes.[71]

This is in fact what took place once the regulations were approved by the High Labor Council in December 1946. One of the principal points in dispute was the method by which the labor representatives on the factory council should be elected. Throughout the discussions, the CUC representatives on the High Labor Council insisted that labor leaders from outside the factories should be permitted to represent employees on the factory councils. While the CUC insisted on this point as a means of gaining a foothold inside the factories, the AIOC representatives, for obvious reasons, were just as adamant in opposing the idea. As finally drafted, the AIOC position prevailed. The regulation provided that the labor representative must be an employee. Not only did the CUC lose out on introducing experienced labor organizers into the factories, but—even more important—the employers retained the right to discharge any employee, thereby leaving the door open to the possibility of discharging "undesirable" labor representatives.[72]

It is not clear why the CUC embraced a labor law that was, in fact, detrimental to its interests. The repressive character of the law was obvious enough to others. A member of the British House of Commons stated that the law "curtailed the right to strike and would not be tolerated in this country in peacetime."[73] Perhaps the CUC detected pitfalls in the law, but had become so intoxicated by its own rise in power that it participated blindly in the preparation of a labor law that was eventually used to eliminate it. Rousta even took pride in and credit for having played a major role in the final draft of the bill.[74] The newspaper *Zafar* called the labor bill "progressive."[75]

Qavam's Move to the Right

By ridding Iran of Soviet troops and by lulling the Tudeh Party and CUC into a false sense of security, Qavam had surely helped to protect the status quo against revolution and Soviet incursion. Nevertheless, Great Britain and the United States were soon to yield to the shah's pleas and retract their support for Qavam. Once he had lost his authority, the government would reject his policy of "conciliation" for one of repression. The failing fortunes of Qavam, therefore, held serious consequences for the Iranian labor movement.

It was mainly events in the oil fields of Khouzestan that turned the British against Qavam. A series of unexpected strikes in Abadan and Agha Jari, a May Day procession of tens of thousands in Abadan, and the appearance of Tudeh leaders to negotiate on behalf of the AIOC workers had greatly disturbed the British.[76] Although the provincial authorities were more than willing to follow British directives and forcibly suppress the strikes, Qavam—fearing political repercussions—did not agree. Hence the British blamed his leniency for their problems in Khouzestan, which persisted through the summer of 1946.

After a lengthy debate as to whether the Tudeh Party was an independent reformist movement or "an instrument of a foreign power,"[77] the British Foreign Office came to the latter conclusion and subsequently instructed their ambassador in Tehran, Sir John Le Rougetel, to inform Qavam that unless he took steps to eliminate Tudeh influence, Iran risked being partitioned "as in the 1907 period." "You presume," Le Rougetel was advised, "that Qavam as a patriotic Persian would wish to do what he can to avoid such a development. Surely, therefore, he can take energetic action to keep Tudeh in order and to prevent further interference with British interests."[78]

Responding to messages of alarm originating in the AIOC and being transmitted by the British consuls in Khouzestan,[79] the Foreign Office sent yet another message to Le Rougetel on 22 June 1946. "You should leave the P.M. in no doubt of the paramount importance which H.M.G. attaches to uninterrupted working of the Company oil fields and of the very serious view of the situation which we should take if this was threatened by illegal actions or violence which the Persian Govt. should themselves be unwilling or unable to restrain."[80]

As Great Britain was expressing its dissatisfaction over Qavam's leniency toward the Tudeh Party, the shah began to voice his deep resentment against Qavam to American Ambassador George V. Allen. According to the ambassador, the Shah, feeling threatened by Qavam's initiatives as early as May 1946, wondered whether he himself should rule rather than reign. Reportedly, the shah told Allen: "The Iranian people had not reached the stage where the king could be only a symbol. If he continued to exercise no substantive authority in Iranian affairs, the people would become unaware, after a time, of the value of a monarchy and unappreciative of the needs thereafter."[81]

Although Qavam was fully aware of the increasing opposition to him and took note of British insistence that he should stamp out

Tudeh influence, he did not oblige the British. He believed that a campaign of repression against the Tudeh and CUC would defeat its own purpose by inflaming their militancy.[82] Responding to Qavam's progressive policies, the Tudeh Party came to his aid. An editorial in *Rahbar* declared, "As long as the prime minister remains firm in his decision and puts into practice these fundamental democratic reforms, we assure him of our full support."[83]

Besides considerations of public safety, Qavam had his own reasons for rejecting a policy of repression. With the British and the shah withdrawing their support from him, Qavam determined to build his own base of support in the form of a popular political party. On 29 June 1946, in a broadcast from Tehran radio, Qavam announced the formation of the Democratic Party of Iran. The party's ideology was to be nationalist and reformist, as distinct from the Tudeh's pro-Soviet, revolutionary line. At the same time, the Democratic Party would join the Tudeh Party in opposing those individuals and groups allied with the court and the army, whose sole concern was for maintaining the status quo.

Most of Qavam's statements and actions after February 1946 had been consistent with the proposed ideology of his new party. It is especially worth recalling a statement that he had made in May 1946 which announced his determination to see his program through and attacked the "reactionary elements" in the Majles who damaged Irano-Soviet relations, rejected the credentials of veteran Communist Ja'far Pishevari,[84] did nothing for the welfare of the people, and maintained relations with foreign embassies for their own enrichment.[85]

Qavam's strategy, characteristic of his political style, was to incorporate the Tudeh Party into his own Democratic Party rather than exterminate his rivals. Accordingly, instead of forcibly suppressing the CUC, as he was urged to do by the British and factory owners, on 23 June 1946, he warned all labor organizations and "those calling themselves labor organizations" to "refrain from interfering in the affairs of the government under the pretense of safe-guarding the rights of the workers or some similar excuses." He concluded his statement by warning all such dissident elements, "who may be reactionaries in the clothes of labor," that he would deal with them severely.[86]

The Tudeh-CUC tide, however, had gained too much momentum to be held back by verbal warnings alone. The Abadan general strike of 14–17 July 1946,[87] for example, was probably the greatest challenge to government policy as expressed in the labor law and Qavam's statement of 23 June.[88] Even though Qavam had severely criticized organized labor in that statement, he nevertheless continued his efforts to win the workers over to his Democratic Party. He therefore dispatched his deputy, Mozaffar Firouz, along with a number of Tudeh leaders, to conduct negotiations to end the strike at Abadan.

Qavam's most daring move to enhance his own position and to contain Tudeh influence came when he reshuffled his cabinet and brought in three of the most prominent Tudeh leaders. Qavam's motives for taking this unprecedented step are not entirely clear. It is possible that he intended to limit their party's ability to oppose him. Another interpretation put forward by the American ambassador was contained in his report to Washington: "I feel confident changes of ministers resulted from Qavam's belief he can handle Tudeh better inside government than out and from his effort to absorb Tudeh organization into his political party."[89]

As early as 8 June 1946, Qavam had told the British ambassador that he was considering a different approach—that of bringing a few Tudeh leaders into the cabinet "in the hope of sobering them with responsibility."[90] After a temporary rapprochement with the shah in late July, when the monarch conferred upon him the title of "Highness" (Jenab-e Ashraf),[91] Qavam decided to go ahead with his experiment of assigning the Tudeh leaders to the various ministries. At the same time, he created a Ministry of Labor and Propaganda, and placed his deputy, Mozaffar Firouz, in charge. By this move, he prevented Iraj Eskandari, the new minister of commerce and industry, from exercising any control over labor affairs, which, up to the time of the reshuffling of the cabinet, had come under the Ministry of Commerce and Industry.[92]

Although the establishment of the Ministry of Labor was represented as signifying the government's concern over the plight of the workers, in actual fact the date of the formation of this ministry can be considered to mark the beginning of organized and systematic suppression of the labor movement by the government. The CUC either did not realize, or did not want to admit, that a ministry of labor in the hands of a government which was totally unaccountable to the working class could become an instrument of control and repression.

An American observer was more clear-sighted: "There can certainly be hardly anything more anomalous or undesirable than a Ministry of Labor openly and officially connected with the propaganda machine of the Government. Such a union only confirms the suspicions of the skeptical that the Government's pronouncements on labor and social reforms are mere propaganda."[93]

As soon as the Tudeh leaders had joined his cabinet, thereby endorsing his ministry, Qavam could afford to deal with the CUC and the Tudeh Party more harshly. On 6 August a procession of Democratic Party followers walking past the Tudeh and CUC headquarters after a Constitution Day rally led to a disturbance and several injuries. At about the same time, the CUC protested Democratic Party efforts to recruit members. Qavam responded by pointing out that under the new labor law all workers were entirely free to join whatever party or union they wished and that any attempt by such an organization to force workers to join its ranks was illegal.[94]

In the meantime, leaders of the Abadan general strike, composed of CUC and local labor leaders with whom the government and the AIOC had negotiated, were being arrested. It was becoming gradually clear that by joining Qavam's cabinet the Tudeh Party was quickly moving toward its own destruction. In a dispatch of 8 October, British Ambassador Le Rougetel confirmed this view. During the first six months of 1946, Le Rougetel reported, the strength and influence of the Tudeh Party had developed rapidly, "but during the last three months it has encountered set-backs in spite of the inclusion of three Tudeh leaders in the cabinet at the beginning of August."[95]

Despite his repressive measures against the Tudeh and CUC, Qavam continued to lose the support of foreign and domestic proponents of the status quo. His political ambitions were obvious and alarming to the shah and his supporters. In theory, his plan had been a sound one: to occupy the considerable space between the extreme left and the extreme right. The sincerity of his party leaders and their determination to carry out the party platform, however, were another matter. While the party's slogans were reformist, the majority of the leading members were anti-reformists who had gathered around Qavam as a means of protecting themselves against the Tudeh. Qavam's followers soon realized that the shah and the army—with British and American support—were a much better rallying point against the Communist threat than was Qavam. While the shah demanded only loyalty, Qavam's strategy required them to surrender certain privileges and live in the uncertain climate of a pluralistic society. The shah, therefore, had little to fear from the

Democratic Party, and on 16 October 1946 he was able to force Qavam's resignation. This event marked what George Allen referred to as "the turning point in . . . Iranian history."[96]

Allen was right. Although Qavam did not by any means become a totally weak opponent of the Shah after his resignation, the balance changed steadily in the Shah's favor from that time on. The change that took place on 16 October 1946 marked the beginning of the end of an era during which, for the first time since the early 1920s, a number of independent political institutions had developed in Iran.

4

Suppression of the Tudeh Labor Unions
1946–1949

Reemergence of Autocracy

*I*RANIAN TRADE UNIONS were reborn in 1941 and developed during subsequent years with the reestablishment of constitutional government. In spite of all its imperfections, the government of Iran from 1941 to 1946 was more constitutional than at any time since the early 1920s. The executive powers of Reza Shah were transferred to the prime minister and the cabinet. The Majles, particularly the fourteenth session (1944–1946), reasserted its constitutional prerogatives. True, the supporters of the status quo, who made up a very small minority of the national population, continued to control the majority of the seats in the Majles; but there were important departures from the autocratic past. The Majles majority, not having been hand-picked by the monarchy, no longer blindly followed the shah's will; rather, it considered the interests of its own constituents. Moreover, a small number of popularly elected deputies did enter the Majles, which then became an effective forum for the expression of public opinion. A free press, though acting irresponsibly on occasion, provided another means of exposing governmental abuses, informing the public, and mobilizing its support. In short, as Ervand Abrahamian, the Iranian historian, has observed, Iran's political system during this period became pluralistic, although not democratic.[1]

Iran's constitutional government, however, was greatly weakened in October 1946 when the United States ambassador, George

Allen, encouraged Mohammad-Reza Shah to discharge an independent prime minister and so take a major step toward becoming a ruling rather than a reigning monarch.

It is now clear from reading the released diplomatic dispatches of the United States and Great Britain that the youthful shah, who had come to the throne in 1941, had been dissatisfied from the first with the inactive role he had been assigned by the constitution. In his view, Iran required a strong ruling monarch like his father, Reza Shah. Slightly over a year after swearing allegiance to the constitution, the Shah ordered Prime Minister Qavam to resign so that the military could rule. This attempt was made immediately after the disturbance—sometimes referred to as the bread riot—that occurred in Tehran on 8 December 1942. There have been a number of allegations since that time blaming the shah and members of his court for instigating the riot in order to topple Qavam. It has also been suggested that the British had a hand in the event in order to bring their troops into Tehran. Qavam, however, ignoring the shah's proposal, reestablished order and, encouraged by the British minister Sir Reader Bullard,[2] repelled the shah's first attempt "to dominate the government through his own trusted supporters [acting] as ministers."[3]

On 5 July 1943 the U. S. Office of Strategic Services (OSS) reported that Mohammad-Reza Shah had been energetically, though cautiously, strengthening ties with the army officers.[4] Two weeks later, the United States minister (the post was upgraded to ambassador in 1944), Louis Dreyfus Jr., reported that the shah had succeeded in taking control of the army, a critical first step toward the return of autocratic rule.

Although a high-level commission appointed by the Majles had decided that under Iran's constitution the general staff was to be subordinated to the minister of war (and thus remain under the control of the prime minister), the shah had refused to sign regulations implementing this decision. Instead, the minister of war was ordered to tell the press and the Majles that the minister of war was fully responsible for the army and the general staff.[5] By August 1943 the shah was issuing orders directly to the general staff.[6]

The shah's justification for this significant move was that a strict interpretation of the constitution was inappropriate for Iran. In December 1944, the shah, now only twenty-five years old, told a visiting American diplomat, Averell Harriman, that the country could not be truly democratic, as he desired, "until the people had acquired sufficient education to understand the principles of democratic

government and be able to form intelligent individual opinion."[7] This
rationalization in support of autocracy was to be repeated frequently
by the shah and echoed by his foreign and domestic supporters for
the next thirty-five years.[8]

Possibly the shah did initially wish to see Iran become a
democracy, and so had assumed his autocratic power with mixed
feelings. Abbas Eskandari, who had served in Reza Shah's government and was a founder of the Tudeh Party, said of the young shah:
"He is one half the son of Reza Shah and one half a sincere democrat."
Because of bad advisers, he continued, "the son of Reza Shah is in
the ascendancy . . . and the democratic, social justice-minded young
king is less and less evident."[9]

In May 1946, as soon as Prime Minister Qavam had succeeded
(with the aid of the United States and the United Nations) in
persuading the Soviets to withdraw their troops from Iran, the shah
began his campaign to enlist the support of the American and British
governments in removing Qavam from power and replacing him with
a more amenable substitute.[10] Although initially the two Western
powers received the shah's suggestion unenthusiastically, within the
year they agreed to his proposal, and on 14 October 1946 Ambassador
George Allen urged the shah to dismiss Qavam.

Power was sufficiently dispersed among existing independent
political institutions in 1946 that the shah could not have returned
autocratic government to Iran without foreign support. It can be said,
therefore, that Great Britain and later the United States indirectly
hindered the development of the labor movement in Iran by their
decision to support a strong anti-Communist government headed by
a ruling rather than a reigning monarch. Great Britain and the United
States, being themselves democracies, could have pressed for a
constitutional government in Iran. They did not do so, however,
because their overriding considerations were geopolitical and commercial. In deliberating on the best means of protecting these
interests, the two governments saw themselves faced with a choice:
to support an "unstable constitutional monarchy" that might fall prey
to the Soviet Union and would in all probability be unsympathetic
to their national interests, or to encourage the reestablishment of a
"stable autocratic monarchy" that would fight Communist influence
vigorously and would be sympathetic to their interests. Seeing their
choice limited to these two options, they decided to ignore Iran's
constitution, thereby restoring a political system intrinsically hostile
to independent trade unions.

There was an element of truth in the Anglo-American perception
of the political situation in Iran. The road from an autocratic to a

democratic system of government in a developing country such as Iran was inherently precarious, providing many opportunities for well-organized and disciplined Communists to influence events and even take control of the government. However, instead of encouraging an interplay of competing political factions and using their own considerable influence to promote the development of democratic institutions, Great Britain and the United States chose to encourage the elimination of all political contestants but one—the monarch. Although this course was the safer of the two, and certainly the more profitable in the short run, it was also an indication that the two Western powers had little faith in the applicability of democratic government to a developing country.

This is not to deprecate or ignore the strong element of reformist idealism present in United States policy in Iran during the 1940s. This idealism, however, was focused on social and economic issues and was rarely concerned with the political structure of the state. The supposition was that education, health, agriculture, industry, and even income distribution, could be improved if only a strong leader was able to establish domestic order and improve the efficiency of the bureaucracy. He would then, with or without prodding by the United States, proceed to direct and preside over the implementation of socioeconomic reforms. The most optimistic assessment of such a paragon was that he would not only seek but also heed advice, both domestic and foreign, in determining the country's welfare, its goals, priorities, programs, and projects. Moreover, the model of development supported by the United States assumed that the discipline imposed by the accountability of the executive to the legislature, the judiciary, the press, and other independent political agencies representing the public—the ultimate beneficiary of the reforms— was a luxury not affordable by an underdeveloped country like Iran. In short, socioeconomic reform could be divorced from political reform.

After United States troops entered Iran in 1941 to expedite the shipment of war goods to the Soviet Union, both military and civilian planners took notice of Iran's postwar strategic importance to the West—especially in the light of Britain's decline as a world power. In 1945 a United States military planner commented on Iran's role in the future:

> Unfortunately, Iran's position geographically, bordering Russia on the north, with British oil interests in the south, and its important strategic location in any war, will continue to make this country

an object of basic interest to the major powers. It must be borne in mind that in any future war, control of any part of Iran will allow the bombing either of the Russian oil fields in the north or of the British oil fields in the south. In the post-war period Iran's location is of importance in connection with . . . transit landing facilities for various world airway projects. It is these inescapable factors that give Iran an international importance and one beyond what its size and population would otherwise warrant.

It is, therefore, not for any sentimental reasons nor even for any idealistic democratic principles, worthy as these may be, that the United States is forced to take a continuing interest in Iran.[11]

As early as September 1942, plans for controlling and manipulating Iran's government were being considered by the American legation in Tehran. One American memorandum discussed the "urgent advisability of placing Americans in strategic positions in the Iranian Government, and, in particular, . . . the necessity of sending a military mission to observe and, if possible, check any internal plots in the Iranian Army which might lead to the coup d'etat which Dreyfus [the American minister in Tehran] fears."[12]

Subsequently American missions were assigned to the Ministries of Finance, Interior, and War. An indication of the conflicting loyalties of at least some members of these missions was revealed in a dispatch from Colonel H. Norman Schwarzkopf, commander of the Iranian gendarmerie until June 1948, to the American ambassador in Tehran. Referring to a recent incident involving workers at the Shahi factory and Soviet soldiers, Schwarzkopf wrote: "It is my definite and expressed intention to conform with American policy, and information is respectfully requested as to what action on my part American policy dictates in this situation."[13]

United States interest in Iran was further increased by the Tehran Conference of December 1943, attended by President Roosevelt, Prime Minister Churchill, and Marshal Stalin. In a memorandum to the State Department after the conference, the president wrote: "I was rather thrilled with the idea of using Iran as an example of what we could do by unselfish American policy."[14]

As the United States' major objective in Iran narrowed down to "stability and order," the diplomatic corps cast about for some means of achieving that goal. Reporting in September 1944 on his first impressions of the shah, the new American ambassador, Leland Morris, stated: "On the whole I received a good impression of the shah, and it might be possible that the strengthening of his hand would be one of the roads out of the internal political dilemma in which this country finds itself. One thing is certain, that the weakness at the top which is apparent here must be eliminated either through the hands of the shah or by the rise of a strong individual."[15]

While Ambassador Morris was praising the shah and advocating the "rise of a strong individual," he was at the same time showing impatience with constitutional government in its infancy. In disussing the future of the Majles, the cornerstone of that government, the ambassador observed that the legislature by its past actions had not shown itself "an intelligent, patriotic, and sincere body."[16]

In April 1946, George Allen became the American ambassador to Iran, a position he held for the next two years. During Allen's tenure the United States became more deeply involved in the domestic affairs of the country. Witnessing the decline of British imperial power, Iran's governing elite sought a new ally to counter Soviet influence. It was not surprising, then, that the ambassador was besieged by "Iranians" urging a more active role by the United States in the country's internal affairs.[17] Initially, Allen rejected these requests, contending that the United States was endeavoring to prevent interference in Iran's domestic concerns.[18]

Reportedly the shah was among those who favored direct involvement by the United States. He was described at the time as "extremely pro-American, even to the extent of urging . . . the United States to accept a valuable oil concession."[19] In return, the United States was to support the shah's quest for absolute power. Ambassador Allen resisted the shah's proposal because in May 1946 he considered Qavam more capable of achieving his country's main objective in Iran: "to prevent one more country from falling completely into the Moscow orbit."[20] In the American ambassador's view Qavam was "the most energetic and forceful man on the scene in Iran at the present time."[21]

By October of that year, however, Allen no longer considered Qavam "the most likely instrument" to contain Soviet influence. Already aware that members of the ruling elite were ready to abandon Qavam in favor of the shah,[22] Allen told the shah on 14 October that he "should force Qavam out and should make him leave the country or put him in jail if he causes trouble."[23] In explaining this momentous change of mind, George Allen declared: "Things had been going from bad to worse for several weeks, with the Tudeh members of the cabinet tearing the government to pieces, installing Tudeh Party members in all the ministries they could control, and Qavam seemed helpless before their organized attack, engineered by the Soviet Embassy here."[24]

Unable to enlist the help of the Majles, since it was not in session, Qavam chose to submit to all of the shah's conditions for remaining in office. He dismissed six members of the his cabinet, including three leaders of the Tudeh Party, and agreed to "fight the Tudeh to the last ditch in the elections."[25]

Although Qavam's purge of his cabinet was correctly labeled by Ambassador Allen "the turning point in . . . Iranian history," this one act did not put an end to constitutional monarchy. Iran's return to autocracy was accomplished in stages. Within a period of 2½ years, beginning on 16 October 1946, there were three specific occasions (cited by three ambassadors as "historical") on which the shah increased his political power.

Destruction of the CUC

Prior to October 1946, Qavam's strategy of defeating the Tudeh Party had been to follow the dual course of conciliation toward party leaders and assimilation of Tudeh and CUC members into his own Democratic Party of Iran and its affiliated trade union. The shah strongly objected to Qavam's tactics. Like his father, the shah preferred a policy of elimination by the use of armed force. Qavam never had the opportunity of implementing his strategy.

After purging his cabinet and submitting to the shah's demand to "fight the Tudeh to the last ditch," Qavam, wishing to remain prime minister, agreed to use force to eliminate the Tudeh Party and the CUC. The CUC had become too prominent, both domestically among the workers and internationally among such labor organizations as the World Federation of Trade Unions (WFTU), to be suppressed by the security forces alone. The CUC was to be eliminated legalistically, with due regard for internationally accepted methods of dealing with "subversive" organizations. It was therefore the Ministry of Labor rather than the police or army that initially directed the campaign of repression against the CUC.

Soon after the cabinet purge of October 1946, Qavam replaced a number of managers of state-owned enterprises who were sympathetic to labor with anti-Tudeh managers as one means of stamping out Tudeh influence. One of those replaced was the popular head of the State Railway Organization, Engineer Ahmad Mossadegh, son of Dr. Mohammad Mossadegh, prime minister from 1951 to 1953. His successor was Khosrow Hedayat, a leader of the Democratic Party and reportedly supported by the Shah's twin sister. The change was significant because the railway organization, with thirty-five thousand workers, was the second largest employer in Iran—the largest being the AIOC.

As soon as Hedayat had assumed his new position, he prohibited outsiders from entering the railway offices and installations unless they first applied to the chiefs of section for permission to speak with an employee. This order obviously hampered the ability of professional CUC organizers to visit the work place. The Tudeh papers thereupon attacked Hedayat for establishing a "fascist dictatorship,"[26] and the CUC notified the High Labor Council of its intention to call a strike unless the appointment of Khosrow Hedayat was canceled. The council rejected the CUC demand as improper.[27]

While these events were taking place in early November 1946 an inspector of the railway warehouse beat a railway porter. In response to the assault, the warehouse porters, all CUC members, decided to take revenge and on 10 November a large number of them attacked the inspector, delivering a severe beating. At this point the railway police and, according to Ambassador Le Rougetel, "Democratic Party toughs"[28] intervened, and in the ensuing fray eight porters were injured and one porter was killed.[29] Tudeh papers, always ready to publicize antilabor events, headlined the incident the next day, calling it a "massacre of oppressed workers."[30]

On 11 November, the CUC issued a manifesto that called for a general strike in Tehran on the following day, and demanded the punishment of those responsible for the "massacre," including Khosrow Hedayat, "the imposed director of the railway." The manifesto also threatened to "tell the whole world of the dictatorial tendencies of the present Iranian government."[31]

On the day of the strike, the Ministry of Labor issued an announcement criticizing the CUC for not allowing the High Labor Council to investigate the beatings and refer the issue to the Labor Appeals Commission. The council had no choice but to regard the strike as unlawful.[32] Following the legalistic mode of repression mentioned earlier, the Tehran police and the military governor of Tehran, in conjunction with the Ministry of Labor, proceeded to break the strike, arresting about 130 workers.[33]

Since the government was not yet ready to totally disregard the CUC, Reza Rousta, leader of the Tudeh trade union federation, was invited to help resolve the issues raised by the strike. The agreement

worked out by the two parties included release and reinstatement
of all the arrested workers; reinstatement of 400 railway warehouse
workers who had been discharged; and permission for newsboys to
sell Tudeh newspapers in factories and industrial establishments.[34]

As we shall see in Chapter 5, in November 1946 the army was
preparing to move against the Soviet-backed autonomous regime in
Azerbaijan led by Ja'far Pishevari. Although the Tudeh Party and the
CUC had not been directly implicated in the Azerbaijan affair,
nevertheless the assault against Pishevari was combined with a
campaign against the Tudeh Party and the CUC—initially in the
provinces and then in Tehran. On 16 November 1946, as the army
occupied the city of Zanjan and prepared to move toward Tabriz,
provincial capital of Azerbaijan,[35] twenty-five CUC leaders in
factories located in the northern province of Mazandaran were
arrested and a military governor was appointed by the central
government over those factories. On 25 November, martial law was
declared by the government and additional military forces dispatched
to the industrial cities of Mazandaran.[36] A few days later, a regiment
of soldiers occupied the Chalous silk factory on the grounds that its
300 workers were "threatening" insurrection. The workers were
thereupon arrested and put in prison to await trial.[37] Early in
December there was a riot at the Zirab coal mine in the province
of Mazandaran, in which the striking workers allegedly fired at the
military forces and attempted to sabotage the mine. On orders of a
military commission 140 workers were arrested, and on 8 December
three of the strike leaders were executed on the spot. More than 100 of
those arrested were brought to Tehran, where four were later sentenced to five years in solitary confinement, and 70 were banished to
other parts of the country. At the same time, those workers who had
taken part in the riot were discharged from their jobs.[38] On the same
day, publication of *Rahbar* and *Zafar* was suspended in response to
their attacks against United States policy in Iran. The ban was lifted,
however, by the end of the month.

On 13 December, two days after the capture of Azerbaijan,
pro-government demonstrators in Tehran denounced members of
the Tudeh Party as Soviet "stooges." The next day, the Tehran
headquarters of both the Tudeh Party and the CUC were closed down
"as detrimental to the interests of the state" and were occupied by
security forces.[39]

With ever-increasing suppression of its activities and without
powerful domestic allies, the CUC urged the World Federation of

Trade Unions (WFTU) to send a delegation to Iran to investigate the government's actions against one of the federation's members. Realizing that an investigation by the Communist-dominated WFTU would be a major source of embarrassment to the government, most of the members of Qavam's cabinet advised against admitting the delegation, arguing that Iran, as a sovereign nation, was not accountable to the WFTU. Ahmad Aramesh, formerly vice minister of commerce, who had recently become minister of labor, countered by arguing that this was a unique opportunity for the government to tell its story to the world. The Ministry of Labor had documentary evidence, he said, to prove that the CUC was conspiring with the Soviet officials and that some of the CUC leaders were guilty of acts of treason. He would be personally responsible for the results of the investigation, he told the Council of Ministers, if the WFTU were allowed to undertake one. Aramesh's argument was seconded by his deputy, Habib Naficy. Prime Minister Qavam accepted Aramesh's recommendation and rescinded his provisional instructions[40] that no visas be issued to the WFTU delegates.[41]

In order to accomplish what he had promised the cabinet, Aramesh, with Naficy and Mehdi Sharif-Emami (an official in the Ministry of Labor and president of the new government-organized labor union federation known as ESKI)[42] began to plan the reception for the WFTU delegation. As a first step, Aramesh decided to undermine the position of Reza Rousta, head of the CUC, by "democratic methods."[43] He directed Sharif Emami to plan a coup in the Executive Committee of the CUC which would repudiate Rousta before the arrival of the WFTU delegation.[44]

On 13 February 1947 a number of workers claiming to be CUC members invited several press correspondents to CUC headquarters. These workers were, in fact, sponsored by ESKI, and the Ministry of Labor. After forcefully expressing their dissatisfaction with Rousta and other leaders of the CUC, they proceeded to "elect" a new Executive Committee that included "moderate" CUC leaders such as Dr. Hossein Jowdat, Taghi Fadakar,[45] and Engineer Tabrizi, none of whom were present.[46]

The plot by the Ministry of Labor was doomed from the start. Jowdat and Fadakar issued statements the next day expressing disgust at this government-inspired tactic to cause dissension among CUC members; most of the other CUC leaders followed suit. Rousta also protested and proceeded to move his office into another building, to which he affixed a sign announcing that it was the new headquarters of the CUC. Since *Zafar*, the official organ of the CUC, was still under suspension by the government, *Mardom*, an organ of the Tudeh Party, opened its columns to Rousta.[47]

When acceptable "democratic" methods failed to remove Reza Rousta from office, the Ministry of Labor decided to use more "traditional"—but still peaceful—methods to reduce the influence of the CUC upon the WFTU delegates. On 25 February, while Rousta and a large CUC welcoming party awaited the arrival of the delegates at Tehran's Mehrabad Airport, Habib Naficy, acting for the government, diverted their aircraft to the city's military airfield, where he and other government officials were waiting.[48] The delegation was then driven to the Darband Hotel, located in the northernmost corner of Tehran, a good twenty miles from the city's center and without access to public transport. Police agents had replaced the regular hotel staff. Moreover, Mohsen Khajehnouri (a ministry official) and his wife stayed at the hotel to keep an eye on the delegates, and especially on their visitors.[49]

An important goal of the Ministry of Labor was to show the WFTU delegates that the workers had defected en masse from the CUC and were now solidly lined up behind the government-sponsored union, ESKI. Naficy and Sharif-Emami therefore arranged a number of "spontaneous" anti-Rousta demonstrations. As E. P. Harries and Maleffetes, the British and French delegates, reached the Darband Hotel, they were greeted by a chorus of "workers" shouting anti-Rousta and anti-CUC slogans.[50] A second demonstration took place at the Tehran tobacco factory entrance, where crowds of workers shouted "Death to Rousta!" and "Rousta stole our money!" This second display so disgusted Harries and the delegates accompanying him, one of whom was Borrisov, the Soviet representative, that they left the factory before completing their tour.[51]

After the delegation had visited Tehran, the province of Khouzestan, and the northern provinces of Mazandaran and Gilan, the Lebanese chairman of the WFTU delegation, Mostafa Al-Aris, sat down to prepare a report. Harries disagreed so strongly with Al-Aris' draft that he decided to write a minority report. The main point of difference between Harries and his colleagues was that the British delegate found some justification for the government's action against the CUC in view of the union's identity with the Tudeh Party, which he considered to be a militant revolutionary organization intent on overthrowing the Iranian government. In his view, CUC members in Mazandaran and elsewhere had been imprisoned not because they

were workers exercising their legitimate trade union rights, but
because they were members of the Tudeh Party.[52] In his report,
Harries wrote: "Unfortunately, the Central Council of Trade Unions
became indistinguishable from the Tudeh party. I therefore regard
the prisoners mentioned in the report as being political prisoners who
took part in a civil armed revolt which failed, and not as persons
imprisoned or penalized because of trade union activities."[53]

The documents available to this writer do not offer evidence
supporting Harries' contention that the jailed workers in Mazandaran
had "taken part in a civil armed revolt."[54] Much more credible are
the often-repeated allegations that the CUC was an auxiliary organization of the Tudeh Party whose "intention" was to overthrow the Iranian
government, although it was not for association with the party but
for a criminal action that the prisoners were punished. What Harries
failed to consider was that the government—especially after the
purge of Prime Minister Qavam's cabinet—had been installed not
by free and democratic methods but by the will of a small circle of
powerful men who wanted to maintain the status quo. Therefore, the
workers and the rest of the public had no constitutional means of
changing the government that held power over them.

The association between the Tudeh Party and the CUC, regarded
as unfortunate by Harries, was actually a necessary consequence of
conditions existing in Iran during the postwar period. As Harries was
by no means the only Western observer to overlook these conditions
and their bearing on the labor movement, they warrant further
comment.

Given the new political realities after October 1946, it seems
obvious that constitutional and nonrevolutionary means of expressing protest and demanding change were becoming less and less
available to the workers. While the privileged had exclusive access
to military and financial instruments of power, there were only two
peaceful avenues that were theoretically available to the workers: that
of exercising their constitutional right to elect representatives to the
Majles, and that of forcing consideration of their grievances upon
the employers and the state through strikes and demonstrations.

Preceding chapters have already explored the fact that the
power to exercise the constitutional right of electing representatives
to the Majles was never fully available either to the masses or to the
industrial workers. The only time after 1941 that a small number of
representatives sympathetic to the needs of the general public and
the cause of labor were allowed to be elected was for the Fourteenth

Majles (1944–1946). The elections to the Fifteenth Majles were conducted in the undemocratic tradition of the past;[55] nearly all of the deputies elected represented the wealthy and powerful, all of whom had joined Qavam's Democratic Party. As the elections were conducted under martial law, they were boycotted by liberals such as Dr. Mossadegh, and on 16 December 1946 the Tudeh Party announced its intention to join the boycott. Mossadegh and thirty-six other nationalists sought "royal refuge" at the shah's palace on 12 January 1947 to protest the government's method of conducting elections. The next day government troops were ordered to guard the palace to prevent any increase in the number of protestors.

Because the workers were unable to elect legislators mindful of their grievances, the only other nonviolent means by which they could demand redress was, as noted earlier, through strikes and public demonstrations. Even the most ardent opponents of the CUC were forced to admit that almost all such demonstrations were orderly and peaceful and that they therefore had to be tolerated under civil law.

The labor law of 1946, for all intents and purposes, made strikes illegal; and the government, by imposing martial law in all the major industrial centers of the country, prevented mass demonstrations. Thus, the only alternative remaining to the workers, other than apathetic submission, was the revolutionary activity to which Harries, the British delegate, took exception.

Because Al-Aris did not want the delegation to appear divided, and because Harries believed "that there was already enough friction between Britain and the Soviet Union without adding yet another item to the account,"[56] they agreed on a new draft. The recommendations finally approved were that the WFTU should continue to recognize the CUC; that the WFTU should urge the Iranian government to release innocent workers from prison; that clubs belonging to the CUC should be vacated by the occupants and returned to the CUC; that in the future, CUC elections should be supervised by the WFTU; and that before these elections took place, a congress of the CUC should be held, also under the supervision of the WFTU.[57] As the work of the delegation came to an end, Minister of Labor Ahmad Aramesh realized that his efforts were lost on the delegates, whom he viewed (with the exception of Harries) as "straight-line Communists receiving instructions from the Soviet Embassy."[58] He had learned secretly—through an attractive Armenian secretary whom he and Sharif-Emami had planted in Rousta's office[59] —that the delegation's report was thoroughly critical of the Iranian government.[60] At the same time, he was reassured by Harries' minority report and the continuing support of the British Embassy. He and Naficy, therefore, came around to the view that they need not make any apologies for the government's actions against the CUC. According to the American labor official, W. J. Handley: "Their defense, if it could be called that, would rest not so much in denying that repressive and harsh measures had been taken, but on showing that no government could have done otherwise."[61]

Having given up all efforts to win the goodwill of the WFTU and its delegates,[62] Aramesh and Naficy embarked on yet another offensive against the CUC. This initiative began as part of a general offensive against opponents of the regime. On 31 March 1947 Kurdish rebel leaders Ghazi Mohammad and his brother Sadr Ghazi were executed by the army for sedition. A short time later, Major Sadegh Ansari, Davar Taghizadeh, and Fereidoun Ebrahimi, members of Pishevari's government, were executed in Tabriz. It was in this tense atmosphere that on 14 April Reza Rousta was himself arrested. Together with two former cabinet ministers, Dr. Fereidoun Keshavarz and Dr. Morteza Yazdi, Rousta at the time of his arrest was calling on the military governor of Tehran to plead for the release of a number of imprisoned workers. Initially, Naficy explained that Rousta was not being arrested for political reasons but for civil offenses, including alleged misappropriation of nearly 1 million *rials* of union funds,[63] and that a civil warrant for his arrest, issued after complaints by private individuals, was now being put into effect by "normal common law process."[64]

British Ambassador Le Rougetel commented wryly: "They [the government] apparently feel unable to continue to hold the process of common law in suspense any longer."[65] Undoubtedly, the officials of the Ministry of Labor reasoned that since Rousta would eventually be taken into custody in any case, it was just as well that the arrest was made while the WFTU delegation was still in Iran; otherwise, Rousta's supporters would be able to claim that the government did not have the courage to carry out the arrest while the WFTU delegation was on hand.[66]

Within a few days the charges against Rousta became much more grave; they now included treason as well as embezzlement. About a week after his arrest, Minister of Labor Aramesh declared: "Reza Rousta has been arrested and will be charged for having undermined the security of the country, having cooperated with the [Azerbaijan] rebels and secessionists with prejudice to the independence of the country; incited the citizens to insurrection and murder and encouraged armed forces to mutiny and divulgence of military secrets."[67]

Aramesh's accusations against Rousta were amplified by General Ahmad Amir-Ahmadi, minister of war, who claimed that a search of Rousta's house at the time of his arrest revealed documents showing that the July 1946 riots in Abadan,[68] which caused several deaths, had been directed by Rousta from Tehran.[69] Naficy claimed that evidence had been found among Rousta's effects proving his complicity in attempts to subvert the army. He also indicated that, because of this, the shah had himself taken personal interest in the case and considered the matter to be very serious. Naficy told Handley that it was not unlikely that Rousta would be executed.[70]

Naficy's version of events was contradicted by Aramesh just two months later, after he had been relieved of his duties as minister of labor in June 1947. According to Aramesh, "Twenty-four hours before [Rousta] was arrested, he packed his documents and belongings and entered the precincts of the Russian Embassy. When his house was searched, little of real value was found."[71]

The arrest of Reza Rousta and his detention for the next six months, combined with the general repression of the CUC, was judged by the American embassy to be a "crippling blow" to the labor union.[72] For example, no May Day rallies were organized in 1947 by the CUC, which the year before had massed some eighty thousand marchers in downtown Tehran.[73] Now led by the veteran Communist Ghazar Simonian,[74] the CUC was forced to continue its work in semi-secrecy, awaiting more favorable political conditions to come back into the open.[75]

On 17 June 1947 Qavam took an important step in normalizing conditions in Tehran by lifting martial law, which had been in effect intermittently since the invasion of Iran by Great Britain and the Soviet Union in 1941. This gesture had little meaning, however; martial law was reimposed on 17 July, a few days before the inauguration of the fifteenth session of the Majles which had been in recess for almost sixteen months.

Rousta, like most other labor leaders, was detained in prison for many months without a trial. During this period, Naficy was working closely with the public prosecutor in preparing the case against the labor leader, even though officials of the Ministry of Labor more than once maintained that Rousta's trial was no concern of theirs, but a matter for the Ministry of Justice. Shortly after the rejection of the Soviet oil concession by the Majles on 23 October 1947, it was reported that because of lack of evidence and fear of Soviet reaction,[76] the government preferred to postpone Rousta's trial as long as possible. As Naficy expressed it, "Time more than anything will finish Reza Rousta. Three or more years in jail, and the workers will forget about him." Rousta's supporters, however, both in and outside of Iran, continued to press for a speedy public trial.[77]

In November 1947 Rousta was released on bond for 1 million *rials*, given by Dr. Keshavarz, following a three-to-two vote by the Tribunal of the Criminal Court. According to a source in the American embassy, Prime Minister Qavam was responsible for the decision of the tribunal that Rousta was eligible for release on bail. Qavam was said to have ordered Rousta released as a result of pressure from the Soviets "and also as a devious appeal for Tudeh political support."[78]

Rousta remained quiet after regaining his liberty. The Tudeh newspaper *Bashar* (Human) carried the story that Rousta was ill and, to his regret, was unable to see friends. Actually, according to the American embassy, Rousta was observed walking about the streets of Tehran, "usually in the company of three or four huskies." Although not delivering speeches at the Tudeh or CUC clubs in town, he was reported to be holding private conversations with leading Tudeh Party members.[79]

No date was set for Rousta's trial. This, on top of his release from prison, turned even the normally loyal Ministry of Labor officials against Qavam. They feared that Rousta's release on bail was, in the embassy's words, "the edge of the wedge and that this [would] be followed by further concessions to Tudeh by Qavam,"[80] who by this time had lost the allegiance of all those supporters of the status quo who had brought him to power. Understandably, the officials of the Ministry of Labor were disturbed by Rousta's release. At considerable personal risk, they had destroyed the CUC organization, of which Rousta had been the leader, employing both legal and illegal means. Now their clever arch-enemy was walking freely on the streets of Tehran.

Rousta's release from prison presented the shah with another opportunity to convince the British and American ambassadors that Qavam must go. In a dispatch dated 18 November 1947, Ambassador George Allen questioned whether the release of Rousta was a conciliatory move by Qavam toward the Soviets. The shah certainly thought so, reported Allen. He had told the ambassador that Rousta's release was further evidence of Qavam's flirting with the Soviets.[81] After all, the shah's own military forces had arrested Rousta, and it was the minister of war who had elevated the charges against him from embezzlement to treason.

The second "historical" advance toward autocracy occurred in December 1947. By that time Soviet troops had left Iran, Azerbaijan was once again under the authority of Iran's central government,[82] the Tudeh Party and its trade union federation the CUC were in disarray,[83] the Fifteenth Majles was packed with supporters of the status quo, and the Soviet oil concession had been rejected by the Majles.[84] The shah and his allies now concluded that Qavam was expendable.[85] Using as his pretext an alleged veiled criticism of himself by the prime minister, the shah let it be known that the continuation in office of Qavam's cabinet was no longer tolerable. Accordingly, on 4 December 1947, all members of the cabinet, except two who were absent from Tehran, resigned, leaving Qavam totally isolated. Suddenly there were demands for Qavam's arrest and trial on charges of corruption and unconstitutional rule. Appearing before the Majles, Qavam reminded members of his own Democratic Party that more than seventy of them had signed an oath pledging to support their party leader until the end of the fifteenth session of the Majles. He then warned them and the nation of the gravity of what was taking place: "If we intend to maintain a constitutional government in Iran, then we must make the various powers in the country cognizant of their constitutional limitations and prevent them from opposing and interfering with each other. If we permit this [interference] to take place, we will lose our democratic system, and the government by other methods will impose itself on the people of Iran."[86]

After receiving a vote of no confidence Qavam was relieved of his duties and allowed to leave for France on an ordinary passport; his requests for a diplomatic passport, normally granted to former officials, had been rejected.[87]

This was not a routine change of cabinets. Clearly, the shah removed Qavam only after securing the blessing of the British and American ambassadors. British dispatches mention that the removal of Qavam had been discussed by the shah with the British ambassador on 12 November 1947,[88] and the tone of the American ambassador's report indicates that he, too, was in sympathy with the ouster of Qavam: "The Shah kept Qavam in power to make him assume responsibility for refusing the Soviet oil concession, since the Shah did not want Qavam ever to be able to return to power with Soviet support. Finally, when Qavam had served his usefulness, the Shah gave the nod and the Majles kicked him out."[89]

Removal of Prime Minister Qavam from office eliminated one of the shah's most formidable political rivals. In the words of British Ambassador Le Rougetel: "The fall of Qavam seems likely to mark the end of a phase in the development of Persian politics."[90] The decision to encourage the shah to take a more active part in governing Iran was preceded by considerable debate within the British Foreign Office and the U.S. State Department. In the United States, the decision to support the shah followed a vigorous debate within the State Department on the advisability of increasing the Shah's power. Some State Department officials argued that such an increase in power "might not be a bad thing since strong governments in countries bordering the Soviet Union have generally been better able to resist Soviet domination."[91] John D. Jernegan, acting chief of the Division of Greek-Turkish-Iranian Affairs, although subscribing to the principle of containing Soviet power by supporting strong neighboring governments, doubted the applicability of this principle to Iran and the person of Mohammad-Reza Shah. The shah, he said, had deplored the lack of progress in Iran and attributed it to his personal lack of constitutional power, but where he did have control, as over the army, his record was "less than inspiring."[92]

Oddly enough, George Allen, who played a key role in the transfer of greater power to the monarch, agreed with Jernegan's analysis of the Iranian situation:

> One is tempted by the thought that, although a dictatorship of the Reza Shah variety would be undesirable, perhaps a middle ground of a somewhat stronger government would be preferable to the chaotic and corrupt conditions we now have. However, I have steadfastly resisted the temptation, and my own policy continues to be based firmly on support of democratic principles no matter how badly they may be carried out in practice. The Shah sometimes uses cogent arguments with one on the subject, but I continue to argue for the ways of democracy. The best way for Iran to become a decent democracy, it seems to me, is to work at it, through trial and error. I am not convinced by the genuinely held view of many people that democracy should be handed down gradually from above.[93]

Unfortunately, neither Ambassador Allen nor his successors followed this advice. Time and again, when a critical step was taken toward autocratic rule, they either applauded and justified the action or maintained an approving silence, explaining their behavior as "non-interference."

When Ahmad Qavam's premiership ended, former Prime Minister Ebrahim Hakimi once again was given the post by the Majles. One of Hakimi's first moves was to relax political restraints as he had done before (only to tighten the screws a little later), ending martial law in Tehran and in most of the other major cities.[94]

Hakimi's example of political moderation was followed by Habib Naficy, still in his post as vice minister of the Ministry of Labor, who declared that a "reformed" Tudeh Party could register its unions according to the provisions of the labor law and receive official recognition. He said further that he would welcome a left-wing labor union provided it was not foreign-directed, because he believed such an organization could do much to further the labor movement in Iran.[95]

Prime Minister Hakimi's honeymoon with the opponents of the status quo lasted for less than four months. In April 1948, under pressure from the shah and the army, the government once again suppressed a number of newspapers which had allegedly attacked the Shah's court, and these moves against the press were followed by actions against dissident workers. A number of employees in government factories who belonged to the CUC were transferred from the northern provinces of Mazandaran and Gilan to Tehran, and on 10 April martial law was declared in the cities of Chalous, Shahi, and Shahsavar. At the same time, three hundred people reported to be Tudeh members were arrested, and the Iranian State Railway, at the request of the army,[96] dismissed several hundred "undesirable" employees. Police closed the Tudeh club at Esfahan and jailed several of the union members.[97] In the meantime, sixty-five newspaper editors and journalists adopted a resolution requesting the Majles to defend civil liberties. Once again, however, lacking support from both the Majles and a free press, CUC activities were confined largely to semi-secret meetings.[98]

Abdol-Hossein Hajir, minister in several cabinets, who enjoyed the full confidence of the British and the shah, became prime minister on 13 June 1948 and was immediately greeted with an angry demonstration by his opponents. Police fired on the demonstrators, injuring several of them. Hajir responded by following the tradition of offering an olive branch to the opposition before suppressing it. Taking advantage of this opportunity, a deputation of the Tudeh Party met with the new prime minister and presented him with a list of political measures which the party considered essential for the restoration of internal and external stability.[99] These recommendations included the abolition of martial law; release of political prisoners; restoration of freedom of the press and of assembly; creation of work for the unemployed; a return to work for those who had been dismissed from their jobs because of their political views; protection of Iran's industry against the influx of foreign imports; reduction in the cost of living; and improvement of living conditions for the workers.[100] As reasonable as these demands seemed, they were promptly dismissed by Prime Minister Hajir and the British ambassador because, in his words, "these demands were much as would have been expected had they been dictated, as [Prime Minister] Hajir believes they were, by the Soviet Embassy."[101]

Although Hajir was even more indifferent to the tenets of democratic rule than his recent predecessor, for tactical reasons he permitted a number of Tudeh and CUC clubs to reopen in Tehran and other cities. As usual, the Tudeh-CUC leaders lost no time in resuming their activities.[102] Interpreting these developments for American embassy officials, former Labor Minister Ahmad Aramesh expressed the belief that the Tudeh Party was planning an offensive along the lines of the Czechoslovakian coup of 1948. The Tudeh Party did not expect to seize power in Iran by revolution, Aramesh stated; it viewed itself not as a Communist army but as a voting bloc. Accordingly, the Tudeh Party was concentrating on gaining seats in the Sixteenth Majles, elections for which were scheduled to take place in early 1949. The party also planned to disrupt production, encourage demonstrations, and generally create an unsettled situation in which the Tudeh deputies could easily seize power. Finally, Aramesh criticized the policy of allowing the Tudeh Party freedom of action.[103]

The presentation of the Tudeh program to Hajir and the reopening of the Tudeh-CUC clubs were followed by the reappearance in public of the CUC leader, Reza Rousta. Having avoided the public eye since his release from prison in November 1947, and with the charges against him apparently forgotten,[104] Rousta suddenly emerged with an open appeal to the workers of Iran to donate one day's wages to the CUC. This appeal was not accepted by his opponents at its face value. As the American embassy viewed it:

"Rumor had it that Tudeh has received a large sum of money from some unrevealed source and that the appeal for workers' contributions was a cover-up by which Tudeh will explain how it got its funds."[105]

The last quarter of 1948 witnessed a renewed growth in the influence and membership of the Tudeh Party and its affiliate, the CUC. On 8 November 1948, the shah, having returned from his first official visit to the United Kingdom, replaced Prime Minister Hajir with his trusted elder statesman, Mohammad Sa'ed, and appointed Hajir minister of the court. A month later the British embassy had become clearly alarmed about the revitalized Tudeh organization. In a 7 December dispatch, the British ambassador stated: "Further preparations for subversive action are reported to have been made in Tehran. The town has been divided up into operational areas, and Tudeh agents have been instructing their followers about their duties in an emergency."[106]

There were ominous signs, in the British view, that the Soviets could be involved in this conspiracy. The British report referred to a number of immigrants and "Caucasians" from Soviet Azerbaijan who had appeared in Tehran. Tudeh activity had also increased in the schools and at Tehran University. An official ban on political activities, imposed by the Hajir government, had led to a strike by university students. Even more alarming for the British were reports received that a number of Tudeh leaders previously expelled from the AIOC concession area after the Abadan general strike of 1946[107] had recently returned.[108]

Seven years of open and semipublic activity by the CUC came to an end in February 1949, following an unsuccessful attempt on the life of the Shah. On 4 February, Nasser Fakhr-Ara'i, a photographer for *Parcham-e Eslam*, a newspaper with a religious orientation, fired a number of shots at the shah as he arrived for his annual visit to Tehran University.

Initial reports correctly identified the would-be assassin as a member of a radical Islamic group[109], but then the government—mainly Chief-of-Staff General Ali Razmara—determined to place total blame for the event on the Tudeh Party. Prime Minister Sa'ed claimed that the government had "unearthed indisputable evidence of a plot on the part of the Tudeh party" and that there was no question but that the would-be assassin was a Tudeh member. Chief evidence for this accusation was that the walls of Fakhr-Ara'i's apartment were allegedly "covered with pictures of Stalin, Lenin, and other Soviet leaders." A notebook had also allegedly been found in which the man "had expressed a number of pro-Communist and highly subversive opinions."[110]

The government's campaign to discredit and remove the Tudeh Party from the political scene achieved its desired end. Riding on the wave of a national sense of shock following on the attempt on the Shah's life, the government issued a decree outlawing the party without a hearing or a judicial inquiry.

It is unlikely that the assassination attempt was planned and executed by leaders of the Tudeh Party. No hard evidence was ever put forward to substantiate the government's claim of Tudeh involvement, and this study of the record points to the conclusion that in 1949 the Tudeh Party had little to gain and much to lose by a premature grab for power. Only a few hours before the assassination attempt, the United States embassy had reported to Washington that on the two days preceding the attempt on the shah's life, the Tudeh Party appeared to have emerged from a long hibernation and resumed overt activities. Citing information from a local Associated Press correspondent with reliable Tudeh contacts, the report also stated that the party had decided to participate actively in the forthcoming elections for the sixteenth session of the Majles.[111]

A dispatch by a reporter on labor affairs at the U.S. embassy (there was no official labor attache at the time) confirmed this view: "The reporting officer does not accept the government's assertion that the Tudeh party leaders approved or knew of Fakhr-Ara'i's plan to kill the Shah. The signs point to the shooting's having been the individual expression of a fanatic rather than an organized plot. The organizational ability of the Tudeh leaders, as demonstrated in the past, is wholly lacking in Fakhr-Ara'i's attempt on the Shah's life."[112]

The United States' charge d'affaires himself reported the day after the assassination attempt that Fakhr-Ara'i was probably not a member of the Tudeh Party, but, on the contrary, had been known for some time as a reporter for the *Moslem Paper*.[113] Later, however, he encouraged Prime Minister Sa'ed to accuse the Tudeh Party of having organized the plot. In this first meeting with the prime minister after the assassination attempt, the charge d'affaires told Sa'ed that "it was unfortunate from a publicity standpoint that the first reports regarding the assassination attempt had identified the man as a member of a Moslem group."[114]

As it turned out, a clandestine radio station based in the Soviet Union was a more accurate reporter of the news, claiming, correctly, that the government was using the episode as an excuse to oppress the Tudeh Party and the CUC.[115]

In the view of the chief-of-staff, General Razmara, "the incident was providential"[116] except for the slight discomfort to the shah.[117] The general now believed that the military could take steps to eliminate "subversive activities"[118] throughout Iran. Subsequent to the government declaration on 5 February that the Tudeh Party was illegal and therefore must be dissolved, the army and police moved quickly. The Tudeh and CUC clubs were seized for the last time; they were not reopened until after the Islamic Revolution of 1979. Of the Tudeh-CUC leaders who could be found, five hundred were arrested.[119] Among the first group were such familiar figures as Dr. Hossein Jowdat, Ebrahim Mahzari, Dr. Morteza Yazdi, Noureddin Kianouri (later to become the leader of the Tudeh Party), Amanollah Ghoreishi, and Zia Alamouti.[120]

Unable to receive assistance from any source within Iran, the arrested Tudeh-CUC leaders turned to the outside world once again and addressed an appeal to the secretary-general of the United Nations, protesting their unfair trial by a military court.[121] These appeals proved to be futile; the shah and his foreign and domestic supporters were determined to eliminate their enemies. In the first series of trials, which came to an end on 16 May 1949, eighteen Tudeh leaders (most of whom had escaped from prison and had subsequently left the country) were charged with "creation and direction of an organization hostile to the constitutional monarchy, crimes affecting national independence, assistance to separatists, and the attempt of February 4 against the shah's life."[122] Eight of the accused were sentenced to death, and the remaining eight were given five- to ten-year sentences. Leaders of the CUC found guilty by the military court were Reza Rousta and Ardeshir Ovanessian (death penalty); Gholam-Ali Babazadeh,[123] and Amanollah Ghoreishi[124] (ten years), and Yousef Jamarani[125] and Petros Shamoun[126] (eight years).[127]

The third major step toward reestablishment of autocratic government was taken in April 1949, when a constitutional assembly was hastily and undemocratically summoned to amend the constitution so as to grant greater powers to the court. Consultation with the British and American ambassadors regarding changes in the constitution had been in process for more than a year. According to Foreign Office documents, on 1 November 1947, the shah had solicited the

British ambassador's advice.[128] After consulting with London, Le Rougetel, on 6 January 1948, concurred with the shah's contention that the current composition of the Majles made it virtually impossible for his government to reform the administration or to enact a constructive economic policy.[129] Although the shah's foreign supporters had given their assent, he could not proceed with his plan of amending the constitution because of considerable domestic opposition.[130] Subsequent to the assassination attempt in February 1949 and a surge in the shah's popularity, the constitutional assembly was convened in April.[131] As for the degree to which this assembly's action reflected the consent of the people, suffice it to say that the one participating labor leader not associated with a government union was Shams Sadri of Esfahan,[132] who was in the employ of the textile mill owners.

Referring to the shah's most recent seizure of authority as "a turning point in the current history of Iran," John C. Wiley, who had replaced George Allen as American ambassador in April 1948, declared:

> Iran is now on a new orientation. It must be watched with greatest care. The Shah must be prevented from leaping on his horse and charging simultaneously in all directions. There is so much good he wants to do and so much harm he might do—if he does not proceed wisely. It is important that we and the British—the British ambassador has considerable influence on the Shah—leave nothing undone to follow closely the immediate course of events.[133]

Confirming the statement by Ambassador Wiley that henceforth "the Shah will rule and not merely reign,"[134] the monarch reduced the powers of the prime minister further by personally presiding over cabinet meetings. Later, reporting on a conversation he had had with a former prime minister, Ali Mansour (1940–1941), Ambassador Wiley wrote:

> [The Shah was] dedicating himself to the minutes of administration. On even the smallest details he was communicating directives, even to section heads. He was . . . wasting his energy and time and undermining governmental coordination. The worst phase of the situation, according to Ali Mansour, was the fact that the Shah was . . . surrounded by sycophantic advisors who were constantly

urging [on] him the necessity of increasing his royal prerogatives, exercising authority, and ruling in the pattern of his late father.[135]

Having revised the constitution in favor of the court and taken over direct command of the executive branch, the shah next proceeded to extend his control over the legislative branch. In September 1949, Ambassador Wiley reported that the shah had cast aside his plan for free elections for the Sixteenth Majles because, in the shah's words:

> "corrupt and venal political influences were effectively working to take improper advantage of free elections." The Shah was now convinced that with the great illiteracy among and backwardness of the great mass of Iranian people, any application of electoral principles of Western democracies would be premature and bad. His Imperial Majesty[136] was determined to have a Majles with which he could work in harmony. He intended moreover to make considerable reform of governmental structure but he wanted me to be completely assured that he had no idea whatsoever of setting up a dictatorship.[137]

Following the practice of his father, Reza Shah, who had maintained the façade of a functioning constitutional monarchy, the shah preserved the legislative branch as a matter of form, but increasingly selected the deputies to the Majles himself.

Despite his assurances to Ambassador Wiley, the shah did proceed to concentrate executive power in his own hands. As a first step, the Tudeh Party and its trade unions were eradicated. Later, non-Communist trade unions were dissolved,[138] freedom of the press curbed, independent non-Communist political parties suppressed, and even the Tehran Chamber of Commerce was brought under the control of the court. Independent political institutions had no place in an autocratic system of government. Trade unions, for example, would unify an important segment of the urban population, could demand that employers and the state redress their grievances, and could call strikes to back up their demands. Although later events demonstrated that it was independent political power that the governing elite feared, the initial attack upon the Tudeh-backed trade unions was based on considerations of national security. In Chapter 8 we shall consider the status and fate of the non-Communist trade unions that were in fact organized by the government itself.

Soviet Influence on the Labor Movement
The Case of Tabriz

Introduction to Tabriz

𝒯HE SOVIET UNION is held responsible for organizing labor unions in Iran during World War II when its troops occupied the northern provinces of that country. One of the aims of this study is to evaluate this claim and to determine to what extent it is valid. It has already been noted that the Soviet Union aided the Communist labor movement in Iran by opposing the reemergence of autocratic monarchy and by providing the Communist-led trade unions with strategy, training, and funds. Although this support was usually covert, the Soviets openly applauded in their press and other media those workers in Iran who—in revolutionary parlance—united to cast off their chains.

To determine the role of the Soviets in the formation of Iranian labor unions, we have chosen as an example the northwestern city of Tabriz, the provincial capital of Eastern Azerbaijan, which was under Soviet occupation from August 1941 to May 1946. The second largest city in Iran, Tabriz in 1943 had a population of about two hundred thousand, nearly all of whom were Shiite Moslems and spoke Azari (an ancient dialect of Persian spoken in Azerbaijan).

Azerbaijan had been one of the most neglected areas of Iran during the preceding two decades, and it was this neglect that

undoubtedly helped provoke the extraordinary militancy of Azerbaijan nationalism that culminated in its short-lived autonomy of
1945–1946. In other respects, conditions in Tabriz did not differ
greatly from those in other Iranian cities. The American counsul,
Samuel G. Ebling, who served in Tabriz in 1944, divided the
population of Tabriz into two categories—the "notables" and the
"rabble." Included among the former, and numbering fewer than four
hundred, were the landed proprietors and factory owners, who were,
for the most part, supporters of the West and intensely anti-
Communist.[1]

In the opinion of the privileged class of Tabriz—an opinion
shared by the privileged in other areas of Iran—if it were not for
the interference of the Soviets and the Tudeh Party, the workers
would be satisfied with their lot in life.[2] The existing order was
perfectly acceptable to the notables; any dissatisfaction with it was
irrational and could only be accounted for by the meddling of outside
agitators. Thus Ebling expresses the notables' social views: "God has
created different classes of people; servants to be servants, merchants
to be merchants, peasants to be peasants, and the higher classes to
direct and manage."[3]

According to Ebling, the landed proprietors were determined to
resist any reform of the existing agricultural system. It was alleged
that in one district, the owner of a village had encouraged the use
of opium by his tenants in order to dissipate their interest in reform.[4]

In his account of May Day festivities in 1944, Ebling vividly
describes his second category of people in Tabriz, the "rabble":
"These under-privileged people in their rags and tatters, many
without shoes, accompanied by their infants and children showing
evidence of malnutrition and disease, presented a depressing sight.
It is doubtful if a more unprepossessing crowd of humanity could
be assembled in any other part of the world."[5]

The underprivileged "rabble," as he called them, were estimated
by Ebling to comprise about 44 percent of the residents of Tabriz.
They included factory workers, unskilled day laborers (such as
porters, or *hammal*), chauffeurs, transport drivers, itinerant peddlers,
rug weavers in household industries, the indigent, and the unemployed.[6]

Among the "rabble," the factory worker is of special interest.
The total "industrial" population of Tabriz in 1943 was estimated at
20,000, of which about 4,300 were employed in large, mechanized
factories, 3,000 in several small textile mills, about 7,000 in small

rug-weaving workshops and 5,000 in the production of handmade fabrics at home. In addition to these "industrial" workers, there were several thousand, less easy to classify, who were engaged in various small jobs as shop attendants, clerks, porters, truck drivers, garage mechanics, and even camel drivers.[7]

Eight large factories accounted for the employment of almost all of the 4,300 industrial workers mentioned above. These works, established between 1910 and 1936, included the Azerbaijan, Pashmineh, and Boustan textile mills owned by the Calcatehchi and Jourabchi families; the Iran and Tavakoli match factories, owned by the Kho'i and Tavakoli families; the Khosravi and Iran tanneries; and the Zafar sock-making factory. The number of workers in these factories ranged between 253 for Zafar and 650 for Tavakoli Match.

The average factory worker earned 25–40 *rials* (about one dollar) per day in the autumn of 1944.[8] He was living in one or two rooms with mud walls and mud floors. Water had to be carried from an underground channel in the vicinity; light was furnished by candles or kerosene lamps. The staple diet was bread, tea, sugar, and a few vegetables, supplemented on rare occasions by liver or mutton.[9]

Children in the family of an average worker were fortunate to receive four or five years of education. Many never attended school, but at the age of five or six began to earn small wages by weaving rugs. Those youths who did attend school usually left after four or five years to be apprenticed to a shoemaker, tailor, or some other artisan. Teachers of long residence in Tabriz asserted that in all their years of teaching, they could not recall one worker's child who had been able to continue in school beyond the elementary grades.[10]

The Years of Soviet Nonintervention

Between August 1941 and the summer of 1944, Soviet influence on local politics and on trade unionism was very limited. Even though the Soviets occupied Tabriz, they did not interfere in local politics, even allowing the governor-general the privilege of curtailing political meetings organized by Communists.[11] One explanation for this restraint was that the Soviets were totally absorbed in the defense of their country against the invading Germans. Tabriz was a supply route and a source of manufactured products. Maintenance of order and tranquility in the city, therefore, was of prime importance to them.

The Soviets' posture of noninterference held another advantage for them: it helped to dispel the low esteem in which they were held by various segments of the Tabriz population, especially the middle class. A 1942 report by R. W. Urquart, the newly arrived British consul, indicates both the unpopularity of the Soviets and their success in dispelling it: "I had heard so much before leaving London . . . of Russian intransigence, of their machinations and unscrupulous methods, that I approached my consular district warily, ready for trouble at the first post. I met with none. If anyone wishes to learn from my two months' experience in Russian-occupied Azerbaijan let him register that the Russians, certainly no angels, are equally certainly no ogres."[12]

According to Ebling, the Tabriz population shared Urquart's favorable impression of the Soviets: "The local Iranian population appear to place more emphasis on the exemplary conduct of the occupying Soviet forces, rather than to question the motive of the occupation. The self restraint of Soviet officers and enlisted personnel, lack of drunkenness and disorderly conduct, and a minimum of interference with civilians have deeply impressed the Iranian population."[13]

During the years 1941–1944, when the Soviets in Tabriz were refraining from interference in local affairs, the provincial officials appointed by the central government in Tehran exercised a surprising degree of authority over the Soviet-occupied zone. In particular, they exerted considerable effort toward weakening the local Tudeh Party and the labor movement. In this undertaking the governor-general enjoyed the blessing and advice of the British consular officials[14] and the total support of the local business community.

One would have expected the Tudeh Party to proceed without delay to establish a trade union in Tabriz once the city came under Soviet occupation in August 1941. The party did not do so, however. Consequently, Tabriz later became one of the few cities in Iran where a non-Tudeh union competed effectively with the Tudeh-led union for the loyalty of the working class.

As noted in Chapter 2, the Central Committee of the Tudeh Party opposed any action by the workers or the trade unions that would interfere with the production of goods for the Red Army.[15] This policy was faithfully implemented in Tabriz. Not only did the Tudeh Party oppose strikes in the city of Tabriz, but it made no zealous attempt to organize the workers in that city since most of the large factories were producing goods for the Soviet war effort. Understandably, the Soviets, too, were reluctant to excite the workers. Reported the British consul: "Even anti-Russian employers admit that the Russians are not attempting to woo the workers of Azarbaijan."[16] Thus, in spite of the fact that Tabriz was occupied by an army friendly to the Tudeh Party, the first trade union in the city of Tabriz was organized on 1 September 1942, not by the Central Council (Showra-ye Markazi, a trade union formed in Tehran by leaders of the Tudeh Party in 1942) but by Khalil Enghelab (later known as Azar), a leader of its main rival, the Central Board (Hei'at-e Markazi, a labor union formed in Tehran by a group of independent Socialists in 1942).[17]

Enghelab (Revolution) was born in Azerbaijan around 1907. During the rule of Reza Shah he was employed by the Tabriz Department of Justice until he was imprisoned for three years for allegedly preaching revolution. Released in 1941, he remained in Tehran until the summer of 1942, when Khalil Fahimi (Fahim-ol-Molk), governor-general of Azerbaijan, appointed him advocate-general in the High Court of Tabriz. Late in September 1942, a notice was posted throughout Tabriz announcing that Khalil Enghelab had been authorized to form a labor union affiliated with the Central Board. Attached to the notice was a copy of a letter from the governor-general approving the formation of the union, provided that it would not "interfere with political affairs."[18]

The support of a governor-general for the establishment of a trade union, even though it was to refrain from interfering "with political affairs," was a unique event, strikingly at odds with the antagonism of successive Iranian governments toward trade unions. The British consul was puzzled at the time by the governor-general's action, and explained it as a piece of calculated expedience.

Ali-Asghar Sartibzadeh, a veteran of the constitutional revolution, became the first leader of the Tudeh Party in Tabriz in 1941.[19] According to the British counsul, Governor-General Fahimi attempted to seize the initiative from the Tudeh Party by supporting Enghelab, and the scheme backfired. Enghelab fomented industrial disputes that Fahimi, the employers, the Tudeh Party, and the Soviets neither anticipated nor appreciated.[20] Despite the prohibition against strikes by the Tudeh Party and the Central Council, rising prices and Enghelab's agitation did produce a number of labor conflicts.

The high inflation rate experienced in Tabriz during the war years, one source of those conflicts, was even greater than the national average.[21]

Indifferent to political considerations, Enghelab expressed concern over the consequences of inflation for the worker. Despite his official position as advocate-general, he spent much of his time in the autumn of 1942 visiting local factories, notably the textile mills where overcoats were manufactured, and the leather factory making boots for the Soviets. A Soviet inspector attached to the leather factory had said that "the 1917 speeches of the Russian revolutionaries were mild compared with Enghelab's."[22]

One of the first labor disputes in Tabriz occurred in November 1942. In response to demands for a wage increase, and threats of a strike if those demands were not met, Abolghasem Javan, an important rug manufacturer, arranged to have Enghelab severely beaten and then detained in the police station for twenty-four hours. Upon his release on 20 November 1942, the advocate general of the High Court organized a series of strikes that resulted in wage increases of 25 to 35 percent in the larger Tabriz factories. These increases brought the daily wages of a common laborer to about 11 *rials* and those of a skilled worker and a trained technician to 20 and 33 *rials* respectively.[23]

Having had second thoughts about allowing Enghelab to organize the workers, Governor-General Fahimi, along with the employers, petitioned Tehran to have him removed from Tabriz. When on 27 November 1942 Prime Minister Qavam ordered the recall of Enghelab, the labor leader proceeded to appoint agents at each factory to carry on union activities in his absence. Finally, after numerous delays official patience was exhausted; Enghelab was arrested and forcibly taken out of town.[24]

Now that trade unionism had been introduced into Tabriz factories, the Tudeh Party had no choice but to attempt to take control of the movement. To accomplish this task and to unify the Tudeh Party of Tabriz, which had been in disarray from the start, a three-man commission that included Ali Amir-Khizi[25] and Ardeshir Ovanessian, members of the party's Central Committee, set out for Tabriz. Amir-Khizi, who had been born in Tabriz, took up residence there as the party's local chairman.[26]

The Tabriz Tudeh Party assigned to Mohammad-Ali Helal-Naseri, a local Tudeh leader described by the United States consul as a "trained Bolshevik,"[27] the task of drawing away the workers from Enghelab's union into the Tudeh fold. On 2 December 1942, a Tudeh labor organization calling itself the "Provincial Council of the Union of Workers of Azerbaijan" (*Showra-ye Ayalati-e Ettehadieh-e Kargaran Azerbaijan*) published a proclamation disclaiming any connection with the "fraudulent" labor organization of Enghelab (the Central Board) and associating itself instead with the Tudeh Party's Central Council.[28] The proclamation clearly revealed that the Central Council's major motive for taking over Enghelab's movement was to prevent strikes: "The Union of Azerbaijan Workers from the date of this proclamation calls upon all workers in local factories to remain at their jobs producing goods for the Red Army. If workers have any demands, they should present them to the local union, in order that they may be considered here or be forwarded to the Central Union in Tehran to be taken up there with the appropriate authorities."[29]

After issuing its proclamation, the new Tudeh union, or Provincial Council, achieved little during the next two months, partly because the Central Board's offices and funds were in the custody of the police. In early February 1943, however, the new governor-general, General Hasan Moghaddam, formerly the military governor of Tehran, agreed to release the funds to Helal-Naseri, leader of the Provincial Council.[30] This act, once again, did not signify a change to a pro-union policy on the part of the government. Rather Moghaddam considered Helal-Naseri to be relatively docile, saying if he "had not accepted him as labor leader here, there was a risk that one Ali Amir-Khizi . . . would secure the leadership and be a good deal more dangerous."[31]

In spite of the brakes placed on strikes by the Tudeh leaders because of the war and the expulsion of Enghelab from the city, the deteriorating economic conditions of the workers led to a number of spontaneous strikes.[32] In February 1943, for example, 450 workers of the Khosravi leather factory went on strike, demanding, among other things, provision of bread and other essential foods by the factory at prices that they could afford.[33] Other than the publication of their demands in *Rahbar*, organ of the Tudeh Party, the Khosravi workers received no support from any source.

Given the Central Committee's policy of strict opposition to strikes, the local party and union leaders had no choice but to limit their activities to speeches denouncing fascism. "All this talk about fascism," reported the British consul, "meant little or nothing to workmen whose wages are 10 *rials* [30 cents] a day, whereas a kilo of gritty bread costs 12. Indeed, a bitter jest was circulating among the crowd that anti-fascism was some new kind of bread."[34]

May Day 1943 was the first opportunity for the Provincial Council of the Union of Workers of Azerbaijan to organize a mass rally. The foreign consuls were invited, but all declined to attend, including the Soviet representative, who continued to keep his distance from organized labor. The outstanding events of the rally were speeches about labor everywhere toiling for the defeat of fascism.[35]

The conflict between the concerns of the masses and those of the Tudeh leadership was bound to lead to frustration and anger. On 19 February 1943, for example, after Amir-Khizi, representing the Central Committee in Tabriz, had finished speaking and was leaving the podium, he was followed by a jostling, hostile crowd. The police intervened before any harm came to the frightened Tudeh leader.[36]

While the Soviet forces of occupation and the Tudeh Party acted to inhibit strikes in Tabriz, the employers applied their own ingenuity to prolonging industrial peace. According to the manager of the Iran leather factory, the new labor leaders appointed by the Tudeh Party in various factories had all "accepted" an increase in salary as the price of not making trouble. While the new union leader, Helal-Naseri, was referred to as a "very reasonable fellow," the Soviets were commended for remaining "scrupulously neutral as between employer and men."[37] In this way all the parties cooperated and benefited at the expense of the workers.

It was not surprising that the return of Khalil Enghelab to Tabriz in August 1943 was greeted with enthusiasm by the workers and with extreme alarm by the governor-general, the employers, and the Tudeh Party.[38] Returning to Tabriz, Enghelab attempted to revive his old union, and delivered a number of speeches which, as usual, embarrassed his opponents. In a speech delivered on the first anniversary of his now dissolved union, Enghelab pointed out the absurdity of plentiful crops in the villages and starving people in the towns of Azerbaijan. He asked why the sugar ration should be 700 grams in Tehran and only 300 in Tabriz. No sooner had Enghelab delivered his speech than he was once again arrested and sent out of the city,[39] without a word of protest from the Soviets or the Tudeh Party.

Heartened perhaps by the absence of protest against Enghelab's expulsion, the factory owners became more intransigent. In response to a strike at the Pashmineh textile mill, the owner advised his workers that he could not afford to increase their wages and told them to present their demands to his customers, the Soviets. The Soviet consul-general, however, refused to see the workers, suggesting that they take up the issue with Iranian authorities.[40]

While the strikes at the Iran match and Pashmineh textile factoʋ. were in progress, Yousef Eftekhari, chairman of the Tehran-based Central Board,[41] arrived in Tabriz to continue Enghelab's work.[42] The police, anxious to prevent any intensification of labor unrest, wasted no time in giving Eftekhari the same treatment accorded Enghelab.[43]

On the following day, 30 September 1943, about two thousand factory workers congregated in front of police headquarters to demand the release of Eftekhari. In an attempt to disperse the protestors by firing over their heads, the police wounded two workers. In spite of the Soviets' protestation of neutrality in local affairs, the workers took their wounded to the Soviet consul. There, according to his British counterpart, "the shocked Consul-General, much after the fashion of an outraged gentleman denying the paternity of an unexpected foundling," turned them away after heatedly disclaiming any responsibility in the matter.

After Eftekhari's removal the workers were once again without a leader willing to support their demands. They were obliged to submit, and industrial peace was imposed until the summer of 1944,[44] when an unprecedented wave of labor militancy was instigated and led by the Tudeh organizers.

As noted in Chapter 2, on 1 May 1944, the Central Council, led by the Tudeh Party, and a faction of the Central Board, led by Enghelab and Atighehchi, agreed to form a single labor organization to be called the Central United Council (CUC).[45] Within a week of the May Day unification in Tehran, Khalil Enghelab arrived in Tabriz[46] and on 7 May chaired a joint meeting of about 120 members of the Tudeh Party and his own unions. At that meeting it was agreed to combine the two organizations into the Provincial Board of Trade Unions of the Workers of Azerbaijan and thus "end the unnecessary disagreement between the labor groups."[47]

A few days after the 7 May meeting called by Enghelab, the CUC sent a telegram from Tehran to the Tabriz Department of Commerce and Industry announcing that Enghelab had been expelled from the CUC and had no authority to act on its behalf. At the same time, the new governor-general, Mehdi Dadvar (Vossough-os-Saltaneh), received an authorization from Tehran to deport Enghe-lab from Tabriz "should he cause any trouble."[48]

Enghelab having been disowned by the CUC and, in effect, outlawed by the central government, the governor-general promptly issued orders for his arrest. Unexpectedly, the Soviet consul-general, Marchenko, intervened to prevent the arrest. This change of Soviet strategy was apparently related to the imminent expulsion from the national legislature of the veteran Communist Majles deputy from Tabriz, Ja'far Pishevari.[49] According to the British consul-general, the Soviets intervened with the intention of using Enghelab to inflame popular opinion in favor of Pishevari.[50]

Enghelab did deliver a number of speeches in support of Pishevari, as well as on labor issues, creating a good deal of agitation. As a result, on 13 July, Enghelab was expelled from Tabriz for the last time. Having convinced the new Soviet consul-general, Matveev, that Enghelab was a danger to public order, the governor-general had reissued orders for his arrest.[51] Armed with the arrest order, police and soldiers surrounded the office of the union, where several thousand workers were assembled. Upon the arrival of the police, Ahmad Barazandeh, Enghelab's assistant, appeared on the balcony of the union office to address the crowd. While speaking, Barazandeh was shot dead.[52] In the confusion that followed, a number of workers were killed and more than a dozen others were wounded.[53]

During the fray, Enghelab was arrested, and was deported immediately to Tehran. In Tabriz, the incident led to bitter controversy, the Soviets maintaining that Enghelab should have been arrested quietly and without bloodshed. Local government officials contended that the workers fired first on the soldiers and the police, stressing the allegation that Enghelab's supporters were armed.[54] This incident, whether it was accidental or planned by the provincial government, ended the career of Khalil Enghelab as a labor leader in Tabriz, and with it the chances of a non-Tudeh labor movement taking root in that city. Also noteworthy were the forces that had combined to defeat the non-Tudeh labor movement: the employers, the provincial, civilian, and military officials, the Tudeh Party, and the Soviet consulate-general. Henceforth, a new Soviet strategy gradually emerged, that of keeping the local government at bay while the workers, led by Communist labor leaders, intimidated their employers.

Soviet Intervention

The summer of 1944 signaled the resumption of competition between the Soviet Union and the West in Iran. Once again a major shift in the relationship between the major powers was reflected in Iran's domestic politics. The Soviets, beginning to take the offensive against Germany, tended to their interests in Iran, which included the acquisition of an oil concession in the north.[55] Subsequent to the defeat of their protege, Ja'far Pishevari,[56] by the pro-Western majority of the Fourteenth Majles, the Soviets began to act more directly and forcefully against their opponents. In pursuing their interests, they naturally collaborated with Azerbaijan's Tudeh Party and Tudeh-led labor union, the Provincial Council. They also enjoyed the unintended cooperation of an incompetent central government that showed no interest in the deteriorating life of the people of that province.

The domination of the labor movement by pro-Soviet Communists was accomplished in July 1944. After Enghelab's abortive attempt to unify the Tabriz unions and within a few days after his final expulsion from Tabriz, the CUC sent Ebrahim Alizadeh-Nami, a former leader of the Central Board who had become a CUC loyalist, to Tabriz to bring the Tudeh-backed Provincial Council and the rebellious pro-Eftekhari faction of the Central Board under the banner of the Tudeh Party. Although temporarily restrained by the local police chief, the CUC representative, Alizadeh, did succeed on 30 July 1944 in gathering 129 representatives of the two competing unions and forming the Provincial United Council of the Trade Union of Workers and Toilers of Azerbaijan (AUC).[57]

Subsequently Mohammad Beriya, a poet and militant Communist,[58] was elected chairman of AUC. A fellow Communist, Hossein Akhoundzadeh-Ganji, who had immigrated from Soviet Azerbaijan, and Mashhadi Mottalab, a local factory worker, were elected vice-chairmen. The Tabriz union was following the same path traveled by the CUC in Tehran. There, only three weeks earlier, Ebrahimzadeh, another Communist from Soviet Azerbaijan, had become co-chairman with Mahzari, a worker from a local factory.[59]

The British consul-general informed the Foreign Office that Beriya's appointment had been prompted by the Soviet consul-general.[60] He also predicted, correctly, that henceforth the newly formed labor organization would be under direct Soviet control.[61]

Beriya was routinely accompanied by two Red Army soldiers as he went about the city,[62] and on the twenty-fifth anniversary of the independence of the Soviet Republic of Azerbaijan, a Soviet officer was added to the men assigned to protect him.[63]

Led by Beriya and backed by Soviet force, the AUC embarked on a course of unprecedented militancy. On 27 July 1944 the workers of the Iran match factory occupied the premises and threatened to kill the manager if they were not paid their extra production bonus, which, because of slow-downs and stoppages related to the furor over Enghelab's arrest, had not been earned. Moreover, the workers demanded that wages be paid to one hundred workers who had absented themselves from their jobs to attend demonstrations. Kho'i, owner of the factory, was forced to meet these demands, having been told by the governor-general not to expect any protection from the police. Other factories were experiencing similar behavior on the part of their workers. Ahmad Esfahani, a Tudeh member and a contender for the leadership of the AUC, was urging the workers to kill the factory owners "as suckers of workers' blood."[64]

During the first two weeks of August 1944, the treasurer of the Azarbaijan spinning factory was assaulted, and the younger brother of the owner of the Iran match factory was imprisoned by the workers.[65] The British consul-general had no doubt that the militants were in touch with the Soviet consulate and had "received encouragement and protection" from the Soviets. Realizing that he could do nothing in the face of Soviet intervention, the governor-general advised patience on the part of employers and appealed to the Soviet consul-general to restrain the workers.[66] While the president of the Chamber of Industry was making similar appeals to the Soviets, the employers telegraphed Prime Minister Sa'ed asking for assistance and threatening to close their factories. The owners complained that they could not even state their case during negotiations with the workers for fear of physical violence.[67]

Extortion and violence came to an end when an agreement was worked out in October giving AUC workers a 45 percent increase in wages over those received in May of the same year. A more important feature of the agreement allowed Beriya to collect 10 *rials* per month from each worker without having to reveal how the funds were applied. The employers, howevers, resisted other AUC demands, including a closed shop, a check-off system, and the exclusion of the Chamber of Industry from any part in the settlement of disputes.[68] The employers had been intimidated but not yet totally subdued.

No sooner had agitation for higher wages ended than a series of mass meetings was organized to support the granting of an oil concession to the Soviet Union. The motivation behind these demonstrations was more economic than political. The province of Azerbaijan, endowed with rich natural resources and hard-working people, was nevertheless one of the more backward and depressed areas of Iran. As World War II drew to an end, local factories were gradually closing down with the termination of Soviet orders. Truck drivers had already lost their jobs transporting war supplies to the Soviet Union. Thus, the local populace believed that the granting of the oil concession would save the province from a disastrous economic depression.[70]

Demonstrations in favor of granting the oil concession commenced late in October 1944 and were held daily. On 30 October, as Beriya addressed a meeting of Tudeh and AUC members held outside police headquarters, the crowd became unruly. An Iranian army officer who happened to be crossing the street was seized and beaten. Beriya himself was seen joining the assault. When the mob then tried to force its way into police headquarters, the police fired, injuring a number of people.[71] The Soviet authorities, taking advantage of the incident, disarmed the local Iranian police and military.[72] In effect, the government of Azerbaijan was transferred to the AUC and Tudeh Party by the Soviets. The Britain consul-general reported two months later: "It is beginning to be felt that the leaders of the Workers' Union can do very much as they like without interference from the local government, least of all from the governor-general."[73]

This state of affairs led to an exodus of "notables" from Tabriz; employers feared for their physical safety. Moreover, the factory owners, including Jourabchi of the Pashmineh and Calcatehchi of the Azerbaijan textile mills, had been declaring themselves for some time to be near bankruptcy. Only by severely reducing the workers' wages, they declared, could they avoid complete financial ruin. The AUC took the position that the wages it had demanded could be paid out of the enormous profits made during the war. The owners' reply—that the shareholders had pocketed the profits and that they themselves had nothing—did not impress the AUC.[74]

Employers such as Jourabchi were unwilling to continue operating at reduced profits and unable to improve the efficiency of their operations. They therefore prepared to leave Tabriz for Tehran.[75] The exodus was not limited to a few factory owners; many of the well-to-do, having sold their homes, were "sitting in hired rooms waiting for the moment to flee."[76] Contributing to this atmosphere of insecurity were recent evictions from Tabriz by Soviet authorities of Iranian army officers and members of the American Economic Mission.[77]

Meanwhile, the AUC steadily extended its influence and membership. Laborers never before organized, such as porters, were drawn into the fold; wages were fixed at higher levels;[78] and a closed shop was imposed on that bastion of city conservatism, the bazaar. As of February 1945, all porters were to be union members, and all merchants employing them were obliged to contract for their services through a central office. The same plan was being implemented for all factory workers. The employer was given the right to fire anyone once. A replacement, however, was provided by the union's central office, and this replacement could not be dismissed without the office's consent.[79] In short, the AUC was dictating its own terms to the employers. However, not all of the AUC's methods of preventing further unemployment were coercive and negative. By May 1945, the union claimed it had managed to register more than six thousand unemployed.[80]

Hard-liner Mohsen Sadr, who came to power in 1945, was the worst possible choice for prime minister as far as the province of Azarbaijan was concerned. His government expressed no interest in reform; in fact, it so ignored the province that the month of June 1945 saw Tabriz without a governor and East Azerbaijan without a governor-general.[81]

Consequently, unemployed workers formerly employed by the Pashmineh factory took to the streets demanding "bread and work" and complaining that "minerals remain under the ground while we are unemployed."[82] Unable to do much else, the Tudeh Party and the AUC organized meetings of five to six thousand unemployed on 6 June and 5 July. At the latter meeting a speaker demanded the removal of Prime Minister Sadr because, "through the fault of a supine government, thousands of Azerbaijanis are out of work and starving."[83] Unemployment had reached such proportions that even owners of small local businesses were sending cables to the Majles describing the tragic plight of the unemployed on the city streets.[84]

With no new stimulus to the economy forthcoming, the AUC relied increasingly on force to prevent further unemployment. On 18 July 1945, the AUC posted pickets on the main roads leading out of Tabriz. All trucks leaving the city were stopped, and none were allowed to proceed until the driver had obtained a permit from Beriya.

This permit was granted only after the truck owner had given security for the truck's return to Tabriz, and had agreed to hire a second driver from the pool of unemployed drivers in the town.[85]

The AUC policy of preventing the dismissal of the idle workers was extended. Although two of the most important factories had produced nothing for months past, they continued to pay a full complement of workers. This anomaly was the result of union power. To the employer's economic arguments the AUC responded that the factory owners had made staggering profits when times were good; they must now keep the workers on when times were bad. Whenever a factory owner resisted this argument, he faced either intimidation or violence. There were occasions, however, when the AUC, faced with the threat of large-scale unemployment, accepted some compromise and sanctioned the dismissal of superfluous workers.[86]

Clearly the AUC benefited the workers of Tabriz. Even the staunchly anti-Communist consul-general of Britain acknowledged that the union had been "largely successful in its legitimate struggle for better rates of pay and working conditions."[87] He also credited the AUC with successfully combating the exploitation of workers.[88]

Soviet Support of Azerbaijan Autonomy

The combination of callous neglect by the central government in Tehran with militant local leadership (enjoying Soviet support) led to a call for autonomy in Azerbaijan. In this episode Ja'far Pishevari played the key role. Pishevari, as noted earlier, had become an ardent Communist at the time of the Russian revolution while he lived in that country. Upon his return to Iran around 1920, he became a leader of the Persian Communist Party and an editor of the newspaper *Haghighat*. He was later imprisoned during the rule of Reza Shah.

After his release from prison in 1941, Pishevari became one of Azerbaijan's most ardent and vocal champions, displaying a deep concern for the plight of the people in his province. In a series of articles in the newspaper *Ajir* (Alarm) in April 1944, Pishevari described the dismal state of affairs in Azerbaijan. The Pashmineh factory was about to close and leave eight hundred workers unemployed. When the rug factory of Abolghasem Javan had closed, four hundred people were put out of work. Twelve-year-old children were being paid two *rials* a day when they should have been going to school. Since Azerbaijan had too few schools and teachers, however, Pishevari believed it would be the lesser of two evils to assist in the opening of factories employing child labor so that the children could work and at least earn a few *rials* to keep from starving.[89] Regarding the employers, Pishevari wrote:

> One cannot expect the factory owners to act against their self-interest. They consider people the same as commercial commodities. One of them even said: "I am the owner of the house. If I see that I cannot afford the expenses, I will reduce the expenses of my house and will discharge my servants." This is the class mentality of the employers. Even now these gentlemen are unwilling to listen to the logic of others. The worker says, "I am not your servant. I will sell you my labor for a certain number of hours. As a result of my labor during the last four years, you have made millions. At least for a short period you must take care of me on account of the days that I made those immense profits for you."[90]

Although Pishevari had never formally joined the Tudeh Party, he was one of the party's candidates for the Fourteenth Majles from Tabriz and was elected upon receiving the largest number of votes cast for any candidate from that city. During his two-month tenure in the Majles, Pishevari took advantage of the opportunity to bring the plight of the people of Azerbaijan to the attention of the nation. One such occasion was the meeting of the Majles on 11 June 1944 when he said: "At present Tabriz has been transformed into a ruined village. The city hospitals have been closed for the past six months. . . . In Tabriz there are only twenty-seven primary and high schools, of which only six are state-run, the rest being private schools. I have seen most of them closely myself. You would not be willing to lodge even your horse in those quarters."[91]

Of the many factors precipitating the autonomy movement in Azerbaijan, one of the most important was the expulsion of Pishevari from the Fourteenth Majles. His credentials were rejected by a bare majority of his fellow deputies in July 1944.[92] Clearly, Pishevari had regarded his election to the Majles as a mandate to obtain assistance for his province from the central government. His expulsion therefore confirmed his constituents' conviction that no redress was to be gained from Tehran, whether the government was representative or autocratic.

The unseating of Pishevari accelerated the trend toward militancy in his province. The demonstration organized in October of the same year in favor of granting an oil concession to the Soviets was followed by local demands for a program of administrative and social reform. In November 1944, speakers at rallies in Tabriz made a number of demands, among them the establishment of freely elected town and provincial councils to govern, in accordance with the provisions of Iran's constitution, in place of officials traditionally appointed by the central government in Tehran. The transfer of government land to the peasants was also advocated.[93]

By August 1945, the central government realized that it had serious problems in Azerbaijan, but instead of sending economic experts armed with funds, General Amanollah Jahanbani, a veteran of the Persian Cossack Division married to a Soviet woman, arrived on 18 August as the head of a military commission dispatched by the shah to investigate a variety of local complaints. While the visit raised great hopes among merchants and landlords, who presented the commission with a petition, a counter-petition was presented by Beriya and other Tudeh leaders, demanding, among other things, the immediate establishment of town and provincial councils, recognition of Azari as the language of instruction in Azerbaijan schools, and employment for all those out of work.[94]

In the same month Pishevari, after returning to Tabriz, organized the Democratic Party of Azerbaijan (DPA), which was to be the driving force behind the autonomy movement. On 3 September the DPA issued a manifesto which revealed a policy nearly indistinguishable from that of the Tudeh Party.[95]

Mohammad Beriya became the most loyal and effective partner in Pishevari's party program. As the Azerbaijan autonomy movement began to gather momentum, the Executive Committee of the Azerbaijan United Council (AUC), the Tudeh-affiliated labor union, implemented one of the DPA's objectives by announcing that henceforth correspondence addressed to the committee in the Persian language would be ignored. All communications would have to be written in Azari.[96]

In November 1945, as Pishevari's party began to organize an autonomous government, armed clashes took place between the DPA and national armed forces. In the events that followed, the Soviet Union used its own occupation army to support the rebels. On 16 November, armed members of the DPA attacked and disarmed the gendarmes in several villages outside Tabriz. On the following day, they took control of the road to Tehran, searching all travelers and detaining all Iranian army officers. In response to a request from the Iranian army commander in Tabriz to be allowed to send his own troops to the other parts of Azerbaijan, the Soviet commanding officer in Tabriz replied that he would allow troops to go but he "strongly advised him [the Iranian army commander] not to send them."[97]

A meeting called for 18 November by the DPA was attended mostly by factory workers. Pishevari, leader of the party, chaired the meeting. Beriya, chairman of the AUC, also spoke: "We are not plunderers; there is no need for anyone to fear for his life or property. The military and police are our brothers: we intend them no harm; but if they try to repress us by force they will be drowned in the blood of the people of Azerbaijan. We have now taken matters into our own hands. We are stronger than Tehran thinks, and under the flag of Iranian independence we demand local autonomy."[98]

An Azerbaijan "National" Congress was held at Tabriz from 19 to 21 November, attended by about 650 delegates from all parts of Azarbaijan. The congress, then acting as a constituent assembly, composed a declaration of principle and set up a temporary "National Committee."[99] In the meantime, Iranian armed forces dispatched from Tehran to Tabriz had been turned back by the Soviets at Qazvin. Election notices for a new Azerbaijan Majles (which was to make the province semi-independent from Tehran) were posted by the National Committee throughout the province the next day. Polling began on 28 November and was completed by 1 December. In Tabriz, 23,950 people voted (out of a total population of about 200,000), but there is little indication of the relative freedom of the elections. Ten days after the elections, the Azerbaijan Majles was opened in a cinema in Tabriz. Although all foreign consulates were invited to attend, only the Soviet consul-general was present. At the opening session, Pishevari was elected prime minister (indicating that he was not merely a locally elected provincial governor), and in the second session, the cabinet was announced. Mohammad Beriya, leader of the AUC, was named minister of education. A Ministry of Labor was established (six months ahead of Prime Minister Qavam's), headed by Pishevari himself.[100]

Among the domestic policies of the new government were the rehabilitation of industry and the establishment of employment for all.[101] Within a month the Pashmineh factory was reopened, after the new government had made a prepayment for an order of the factory's cloth of 1 million *rials*. Iran Leather was actually managed by the government.[102] In April a law was passed prohibiting the importation into Azerbaijan of industrial products similar to those produced within the province, except for essential imports listed by the Azerbaijan Ministry of Commerce and Economics. All government employees were obliged to wear clothing manufactured locally.[103]

The Azerbaijan labor law, another initiative of the Azerbaijan Democrats, was approved on 12 May 1946—six months before the approval of the national labor bill by Prime Minister Qavam's cabinet. Although the national bill recognized trade unions and their right to strike, "every dispute occurring between a worker and an employer had to be settled by a ruling of the Ministry of Labor."[104]

The Azerbaijan labor law also provided for full pay on all official holidays and for those days when work was suspended by order of the factory owner. When a factory was closed by circumstances beyond the owner's control, workers were to receive half-pay. Annual paid vacations, from fifteen days to a month depending on the type of work performed, were also instituted. The principle of a minimum wage was recognized, although the figure was to be determined by future legislation.[105] An eight-hour work day and a forty-eight-hour work week were set by law. An overtime premium was set at 50 percent. Illiterate workers were to be allowed to leave work half an hour early in order to attend daily, one-hour literacy classes. All previous labor contracts were annulled.[106] These were the main features of the Azerbaijan labor law, but it is not clear now much of the law was actually implemented.

The government of the Azerbaijan Democrats came to an end on 11 December 1946, exactly one year after it had been formed. As the Democrats had been installed through the support of Soviet armed forces, so the government's collapse followed the evacuation of Soviet troops from the province on 6 May 1946.

The Soviets departed, it will be recalled, on the condition agreed to by Prime Minister Qavam, that they be granted an oil concession. At the same time, Qavam, following his conciliatory policy, entered into negotiations with DPA leaders. An agreement signed on 16 June 1946 raised hopes for a peaceful political resolution of the conflict between Azerbaijan Democrats and the central government. These hopes gradually dimmed, however, as Qavam was increasingly urged by the shah and the two Western powers to adopt a hard line against his opponents. Consequently, in late October 1946, after the publication of notices announcing the forthcoming elections for the Fifteenth

Majles (not to be confused with the elections of the previous year
for the Azerbaijan assembly),[107] Qavam insisted that prior to the
casting of ballots in Azerbaijan, inspectors from Tehran would have
to be admitted freely to all parts of the province. After sending
gendarmes to Zanjan (the entry point to Azerbaijan province) on 10
November, Qavam announced that on the twenty-second he would
send forces to all parts of Iran to preserve order during the elections.
He proposed to send a token force to Azerbaijan of one thousand
soldiers.[108]

After the Soviet ambassador protested Qavam's decision to
dispatch troops to Azerbaijan, George Allen, the United States
ambassador, announced publicly that "the Government's decision to
send security forces to all parts of the country to maintain order
during elections seemed . . . entirely normal and proper."[109]
Encouraged by this show of support, Qavam protested the Soviet
attitude to the Security Council of the United Nations; and on 11
December 1946, Iranian troops entered Azerbaijan. The conflict was
over within forty-eight hours. According to Allen, military casualties
on both sides amounted to about twenty killed and one hundred
wounded, and perhaps five hundred Azarbaijan Democrats and
Caucasian immigrants were killed by "local people"—an indication,
if the report was accurate, that their popularity had reached a low
ebb. However, Dr. Fereidoun Keshavarz, a Tudeh member of
Qavam's coalition cabinet, gives a totally different account from that
of the American ambassador, claiming that sixteen thousand natives
of the province were killed by the army.[110] Pishevari, along with a
number of his close associates, fled to the Soviet Union. He was later
killed there under suspicious circumstances in an automobile accident.[111] The fate of Beriya, who also fled to the Soviet Union, is
unknown.

In a report written after the fall of the autonomous government,
the United States consul in Tabriz praised the Democrats for having
gained tangible results: "They built roads and paved streets—things
that people could see and things that the Tehran government had
not bothered to do for years and years. They emphasized education,
revamping the schools entirely, and thereby showed a true instinct
for perpetuating their control."[112]

The rule of martial law imposed by the central government
throughout Iran was especially severe in the conquered province of
Azerbaijan. With the fall of the Democrats in December 1946, the
life of the AUC came to an end. No trade union was permitted to

be organized; no new leadership was allowed to emerge. As a matter of fact, no reference to trade unionism was to be heard in Azerbaijan for the following three decades. The official rationale was that the government was replacing the traitorous labor leaders with government officials who would look after the needs of the workers. A 1948 report by the British consul in Tabriz gives an impression of the kind and quality of official attention received by the workers: "Improvements in working conditions and educational facilities have been suggested and requests made that loudspeakers should be installed in factory canteens so that employees may listen to the special workers' programme."[113]

There was little question that prohibition of trade unions, combined with mass arrests and deportations, had succeeded in temporarily intimidating the workers—once among the most militant in Iran. The employees of the Administration of Posts, Telegraph and Telephone in Tabriz, for instance, declined to follow the example of their colleagues in Tehran by going on strike for higher pay, saying that the strike would be "disloyal."[114] Instead of holding demonstrations to protest that they had not been paid for two months, about one hundred employees of Iran Leather were seen waiting meekly on the acting governor-general to complain.[115] Before the reemergence of autocracy in 1946, the workers had presented their appeals to their union leaders, the party, their Majles representatives, and the press. In February 1949, however, it was the United States consul to whom they appealed. The municipal street employees told him that they had not received the raise in salary the government had approved for them. They were appealing to the United States consulate because they had already petitioned the mayor and the governor general to no avail.[116]

Once again, ineffective and corrupt officials sent from Tehran were ruling over the local residents. The American consul reported, "Nothing of the sort has been seen since the days just before the fall of the Kajar [Qajar] dynasty."[117] His British counterpart agreed: "The populations continue to feel more and more that too little is being done for them by the Government. Many Persian officials in Azerbaijan are inefficient, if not corrupt; most of them fail to take kindly to service here and look upon it as banishment."[118]

It must be noted in conclusion that Soviet policy with respect to trade unions in Tabriz was dictated wholly by self-interest. During the war years the Soviets gave a free hand to local government officials to administer city affairs in such a manner as to ensure order and full production for the Red Army. Once the end of the war was in sight, they supported agitation through the Communist-led labor union. As long as the oil concession they sought was withheld, they lent support to an autonomous movement led by Pishevari. As soon as Prime Minister Qavam had assured them of an oil concession, they withdrew their support from Pishevari, consigning his government and its program to certain destruction.[119] In the words of Fereidoun Keshavarz, the former leader of the Tudeh Party, the lesson of Azerbaijan is that no liberation movement would "count on foreign support even if that foreign regime has a socialist name, because the cost of such assistance can mean surrender of independence and freedom of action."[120]

6

British Influence on the Labor Movement
The Case of Abadan

Introduction to Abadan

*A*S EARLY AS 1921, the British had looked on the Communist movement and the labor unions under its influence as another manifestation of Soviet designs upon Iran inimical to British interests in the region. Britain therefore supported the reestablishment of an anti-Communist autocracy in the person of Reza-Khan (later Reza Shah), in order to "do with Persian hands that which the British had wished to do with British hands"[1]—that is, to block the spread of communism into the Middle East. After the fall of Reza Shah from British favor and the return of constitutional government to Iran in 1941, Britain decided to intervene more openly to protect her geopolitical and commercial interests.[2]

It is obvious that Great Britain worked deliberately against the trade unions for two reasons. First, as the largest industrial employer in Iran, the British government-owned Anglo-Iranian Oil Company (AIOC) did not relish the idea of negotiating with its employees—whether Iranian, Indian, or British. Second, because the Iranian labor unions were Communist-sponsored, the British government, fearing a Communist takeover in Iran, resolved to eliminate what it considered to be an instrument of Soviet policy. In this second resolve, Great Britain enjoyed the total support of the United States govern-

117

ment. The policy of eliminating the Communist-led trade unions was implemented through the Iranian civilian and military authorities, as well as through the personnel of the AIOC. In pursuit of this policy, extra-legal as well as legal means were pursued. The two Western powers, fully cognizant of and witness to the illegal acts, not only withheld dissent but often condoned and justified them.

This chapter will examine the dynamics of British intervention by focusing on the city of Abadan in the province of Khouzestan.[3] In this city was located Britain's major oil refinery. Long before 1941, the province of Khouzestan, and its oil installation in particular, had been a virtual enclave controlled by the AIOC. From the invasion of Iran by Great Britain and the Soviet Union in 1941 to early 1946, British troops occupied the province, serving as the company's security force and giving Britain greater control over it.

Khouzestan is located in southwestern Iran, bordering on Iraq and the Persian Gulf. The whole of this area was once the center of the Persian empire. Abadan itself is an island at the head of the Persian Gulf. Like the adjacent districts, it is a desert, broken only by a fringe of date palms near the river. The earliest oil refinery was completed there in 1912.[4] Since that time, Abadan has grown from a small village to a city containing one of the largest oil refineries in the world. In 1946, its annual capacity was 20 million tons of oil.[5]

The operations of the AIOC in Khouzestan were carried on partly in Abadan and partly in the foothills of the Zagros Mountains, more than a hundred miles away. Between the refinery at Abadan and the oil fields in the foothills lies the desert.[6] The oil fields in descending order of production were located at Haft Kel (9.8 million tons per annum), Masjed-e Soleiman (2.7 million tons), Agha Jari (2.4 million tons), and Gach Saran (1.9 million tons).[7]

Nearly all of the industrial employment of the province of Khouzestan was provided by the AIOC. Containing about 52,000 AIOC employees in 1946, Khouzestan could easily be considered a "company province." Abadan itself had a population of about 115,000 in 1943. A February 1943 census indicated that of the 39,000 adult males residing in Abadan, more than 30,000 were company employees. Another 60,000 residents were dependents of employees. Another 10,000 persons were believed to be earning their living indirectly from the company, for example, as shop-keepers.[8]

The working hours at AIOC installations were superior to those of other industries in Iran. The employees worked on the average 8 hours per day, 44½ hours per week in the winter, and 45 in the summer—well within the limits set by the May 1946 labor law.[9] The basic wage rate for ordinary unskilled laborers in Khouzestan was 40 to 50 *rials* (approximately $1.30) per day in 1944. While the AIOC paid a lower daily wage of 14 *rials*, it provided its workers with a full ration of flour, sugar, and tea each month.[10]

The relationship between the British government and the Anglo-Iranian Oil Company was extremely close. In 1901 Mozaffar-ed-Din Shah granted an oil concession to W. K. D'Arcy, a British subject. In 1933 Reza Shah replaced this agreement with a sixty-year concession to the AIOC under which the government of Iran received an annual royalty on petroleum products sold and a share in the total profits of the company. It was estimated that such payments constituted 10 percent of the total revenue of the Iranian government. The Iranian government, however, took no part in operating the AIOC, the headquarters of which were in London.[11]

Since 1914 the British government had owned over 50 percent of the stock of AIOC; representatives of both the Admiralty and the Treasury held seats on its Board of Directors and could exercise a veto on any matter affecting imperial interests. Since the British fleet, which converted to oil in 1913, was largely dependent upon Iranian oil, the company's importance in the protection of British interests can hardly be overemphasized. Moreover, the fact that the oil fields lay in the strategically important Persian Gulf was another factor of some importance to British imperial interests.[12]

There was a close, though unofficial, working relationship between the Foreign Office and the AIOC. Communication between the two was conducted through the intermediary agency of the Ministry of Fuel and Power in London, the British embassy in Tehran, the British consul-general (in the mid-1940s, Alan C. Trott) in Ahwaz (provincial capital of Khouzestan), and the consul in the province's port city of Khorramshahr. A primary topic of discussion between AIOC representatives and the British government was Tudeh-led union activity in Khouzestan. After an unsuccessful Tudeh-led strike at the AIOC's Kermanshah refinery, which began on 30 May 1945,[13] the British ambassador in Tehran wrote to his consul-general in Ahwaz:

> If the Anglo-Iranian Oil Company want our advice on the way to handle the Tudeh they are at liberty to ask for it, and I do not wish to press it on them unasked. They know, presumably, that we cannot do anything much to protect them from Tudeh slanders,

and that it is up to them to seek legal redress if they consider it
worthwhile to attempt this in a country where the law is something
worse than an ass. . . . We cannot be over-nice about legality and
fair play where it is a question of our vital oil interests.[14]

The British policy of eliminating Tudeh influence in Khouzestan
was accomplished through the civilian and military officials of the
Iranian government in the province. Since the high officials of the
Iranian government were generally unsympathetic to the working
class and shared the Foreign Office's anxiety over a possible
Communist takeover, cooperation between provincial and British
officials was easily achieved. It was also effective. In Khouzestan,
armed forces could be employed to "preserve the peace" with greater
impunity than in other areas of Iran, as the province enjoyed the
unofficial status of a British enclave. What happened there was the
business of the British. Thus, no labor union activity was permitted
there before April 1946 or after September of the same year.

Once their occupying forces were evacuated from Iran in the
winter of 1946, the British relied wholly on local officials to employ
"exceptional measures" against the Tudeh Party. They carefully
scrutized the appointment of Iranian officials to civilian and
military posts in Khouzestan, and even exercised some power of
selection, as indicated by a letter from British Ambassador Reader
Bullard to the Ahwaz consul-general, in which he wrote: "I do not
know what possessed Prime Minister Sadr to make appointments in
the South without consulting us. . . . It is a bad moment to appoint
in the South officials who may be useless or harmful, since it now
seems certain that in six months our troops will have gone for good
. . . I will try to ensure co-operation in other cases."[15]

Once a new Iranian official arrived in Khouzestan, he was
constantly evaluated by the officials of the British consulates and the
oil company. The AIOC, on its part, secured the cooperation of local
officials by granting favors that put them in debt to the company.
In addition to food and shelter given to Iranian authorities, for
example, company transport, including aircraft, was at times placed
at their disposal.[16]

After the appointment of local officials sympathetic to British
interests, and the encouragement of such sympathy through company
favors, there remained the task of persuading these pliant officials
to serve the interests of the AIOC. In the mid-1940s, this responsibility
was delegated to the British consul in Khorramshahr,[17] Lieutenant-

Colonel V. W. D. Willoughby, and to the AIOC's "political adviser," Colonel H. John Underwood.[18] The British consul-general in Ahwaz, A. C. Trott, and the British ambassador in Tehran completed this network.

This arrangement among the Foreign Office, the AIOC, and the Iranian government produced the intended results—so much so that even the British consuls would describe one local police chief as "notoriously friendly to the Anglo-Iranian Oil Company and British interests in general."[19] It was not surprising that certain provincial officials of the Iranian government displayed greater loyalty toward British officials than toward their own Iranian colleagues and superiors.

The Formation of Labor Unions in Abadan

The labor movement in Abadan, in contrast to that in Tehran, Tabriz, and Esfahan, was extremely short-lived. It first became active late in April 1946 and was suppressed in mid-August of the same year. The brevity of the movement was due largely to the efficiency with which the British manipulated the local authorities. This efficiency is best illustrated by the outcome of national elections for the Fourteenth Majles held in the autumn of 1943. These elections, relatively free in other parts of the country, enabled the workers of Tabriz and Esfahan to send their representatives to the legisature. Because the British controlled the political life of the oil-producing area, however, the workers of Abadan, who constituted the majority of the city's population, were denied representation. Zia-ed-Din Neghabat, a man of wealth and a supporter of the status quo, was "elected"[20] to the Majles from the Abadan district.

The brief period of trade union activity in Khouzestan came in 1946 when Ahmad Qavam returned to power as prime minister. Qavam, who had demonstrated his lack of patience with Communists and trade unionists as far back as 1922,[21] was reluctant, on assuming office, to use extreme measures against the Tudeh Party and its labor unions. Until he had persuaded the Soviet troops to evacuate Iran in May 1946 and had successfully involved Tudeh leaders in his cabinet, Qavam held in check such anti-Tudeh zealots as Governor-General Ali-Naghi Mesbah-Fatemi.

In July 1945, the Labour Party had triumphed in Great Britain, and its alignment with organized labor placed certain constraints on British representatives in Iran. The AIOC had to recognize, at least outwardly, the principle of collective bargaining. It was no longer feasible to dismiss workers' grievances out of hand and then to employ force, if necessary, to deal with the consequences. Instead, the British protected their political and economic interests in Iran through the labor law enacted by the central government in May 1946 and through the Ministry of Labor and Propaganda, created in August of the same year. Thus, in response to any accusation in Britain or Iran that the company was exploiting its workers, the AIOC could reply that it was simply complying with the laws and governmental procedures of Iran. To the extent, however, that the company dealt with its labor problems through the bureaucracy in Tehran, it gave up the capacity for dealing quickly and decisively with situations as they arose. This partial loss of effectiveness presented the labor movement with a brief opportunity for action.

Before 1946, attempts to organize the oil workers were notably unsuccessful. The Provincial United Council of the Trade Union of Workers and Toilers of Khouzestan (KUC), a branch of the Tudeh trade union federation (CUC), was briefly established in Abadan in March 1944 by Farhad Falahati, a discharged employee of AIOC.[22] After less than a month of limited activity, the union was closed by order of the military governor on 16 April. Falahati, secretary of the union, was "advised" by the city governor to stop his activities. Two days later, he attempted to reopen the union office and was arrested. He was tried by the military court of Abadan and sentenced to deportation from Abadan.[23] On 10 May 1944, at which time the Central United Council (CUC) was being organized in Tehran[24] and two competing labor unions united in Tabriz,[25] Falahati secretly returned to Abadan to attempt once again to organize the workers. However, the police, the oil company, and the local government again demonstrated their total control over the city: Falahati was rearrested the next day and sent off to Ahwaz once again. This was not the end of the KUC, however.[26]

As Falahati was attempting to plant the seeds of trade unionism in Abadan, Hossein Tarbiyat, an employee of the British-owned Imperial Bank of Iran, was trying to recruit members for the Tudeh Party.[27] His activity, however, was limited to distribution of a dozen or so copies of the Tudeh newspaper, *Rahbar*, in the port city of Khorramshahr.[28] A major reason for this small distribution was the energetic enforcement of a ban by the AIOC and the local authorities on the purchase and reading of *Rahbar* and *Zafar*,[29] the penalty for which was often dismissal from the company.[30] Soon, Hossein Tarbiyat was arrested and his activities terminated by the local police.[31]

The severe limitations placed on the Tudeh Party and the KUC did not dampen the interest of the two organizations in Khouzestan. Such a large concentration of workers was unique in Iran. Moreover, the AIOC was an outstanding target for protest, being both an "oppressor" and an "imperialist"—a distinction enjoyed by no other employer in the country. Finally, oil, the product of the company's operations, was a national issue in itself.

As the Allied victory came within sight, the Tudeh Party unshackled its press and began a campaign of denunciation against the British and the AIOC. Ashouri, later a labor organizer in Abadan, sounded the type of ominous warning that made the British more anxious than ever to deny the Tudeh Party a foothold in Khouzestan: "Oh, brothers, you may know that the laborers of Khouzestan have no more patience to carry on their shoulders the heavy burden of the spongers. . . . They have no more patience to bear the vexation and calamities of a few low and mean individuals. They rather choose to be killed and torn to pieces than to obey the authorities and to see this company continue its activities."[32]

Judging by later events, articles like this made a significant impression on the workers. They established the Tudeh Party and the CUC as the only organized forces willing to support the aspirations of Iran's workers. At the same time these articles further convinced the British that the Tudeh-sponsored labor union movement was not solely, or even mainly, interested in the workers' welfare. Taking at face value the Tudeh statements published in the press and spoken at rallies, the British in Khouzestan labeled the KUC a totally political organization.

In the autumn of 1945, when confrontation between the CUC and the central government reached a violent pitch[33] and an autonomous regime was being established in Azerbaijan,[34] the British authorities became aware of the activities of the Tudeh Party in Abadan. At the time, party membership in Abadan was estimated to be about one thousand, composed of unemployed and employed AIOC workers. Initially, the party did not hold open meetings; the principal leaders, about twenty in all, frequently met in private, their main objective to forward information about AIOC and Abadan officials to Tudeh newspapers in Tehran as grist for union propaganda.[35] These leaders were drivers, fitters, and plant attendants employed by the AIOC. On 11 March 1946, at the height of the dispute between the Soviet Union and Iran over the evacuation of Soviet troops,[36] and after the departure of British troops from southern Iran, the Tudeh opened a branch of the party in Khorramshahr.[37] The first contact between the AIOC and the KUC, however, did not occur until 29 April 1946. On that day, Mehdi Hashemi-Najafi (commonly referred to as Najafi), correspondent of *Zafar* and *Rahbar*, accompanied by two prominent members of the local Tudeh Party, called on the management of the AIOC. He wished, he said, to make a tour of the works, discuss labor troubles with the workers, and negotiate with management on behalf of the fifty-eight workers in the locomotive shop, who had a complaint.[38] He was informed that the company would receive him as a correspondent of *Zafar* but was definitely not prepared to recognize him as a trade union leader.[39] The company then arranged a tour of the works and residential areas. The next day, the locomotive shop went on strike.[40]

The complaint Najafi had referred to involved the British superintendent of the locomotive shop, who allegedly had not only verbally abused Iranian workers but on a number of occasions had actually struck some of them. When the complaint was lodged by the representative of the aggrieved worker, the company had discharged the representative. As a result, the local KUC, led by Najafi, urged the workers to demand not only reinstatement for the discharged representative but also an apology from the superintendent. Following the company's refusal to negotiate with Najafi, the KUC decided to hold a demonstration on May Day in order to exhibit its numerical strength.[41]

As 6 May 1946, the date for the withdrawal of Soviet troops from Iran, grew near, Prime Minister Qavam became engaged in a very sensitive balancing act. To appease the Soviets, he was prepared to allow celebration of May Day. To reassure the British and Mohammad-Reza Shah, he issued orders that demonstrations must be contained within club premises. These conflicting messages left the pro-British local authorities in a difficult predicament.[42] Unable to call on reinforcements, if the need arose, from the army divisional command post at Ahwaz, the Abadan police chief suggested that "Indian soldiers in civilian dress should be kept at Abadan, or else that the European employees should be embodied and issued with arms."[43]

Meanwhile, following Qavam's orders, the local police chief informed the Tudeh Party representatives that the government wished all workers who were members of any party to meet in their respective club premises to celebrate May Day. The initial order was diluted by a second telegram allowing overflow crowds to gather outside the clubs and ordering the police chief "to plead this too in a friendly manner with party leaders."[44]

The KUC, taking advantage of the confusion and disunity among the central and provincial authorities, organized an elaborate parade through the streets of Abadan. The procession, reported the AIOC security officer, was well organized. Contrary to later claims—and typical of Tudeh demonstrations—order was maintained by special marshals wearing white arm bands. Each section of the procession, made up mostly of workers, had its own cheerleaders, or slogan shouters. The most common slogans were "Long Live Qavam," "Long Live our Young Shah," "Long Live the Freedom Lovers," "Down with Laborers' Enemies," and "Down with the Enemies of the Tudeh."

In spite of KUC's show of strength, the AIOC continued to ignore the demands of the locomotive workers, and on 5 May, 350 employees in the distillation and bitumen plants of the Abadan refinery commenced a sympathy strike.[45] While British crews manned these units, a KUC deputation demanded reinstatement of the locomotive shop strikers, full pay for strike days, removal of the unpopular superintendent, and the formation of an arbitration committee to investigate labor conditions and complaints. This committee was to consist of two members each from management and the KUC.[46]

Because of Qavam's policy of conciliation with the Soviets, the Azerbaijan Democrats, and the Tudeh Party, local government officials were unable to quell the strike by force. As reported by a high AIOC official: "The local government officials were disinclined to take preventive action because of personal consequences, . . . for fear of violent personal attacks in the press."[47]

The local authorities were even more explicit, advising the company of their probable inability to prevent intimidation should the Tudeh Party call out workers in other departments as they threatened to do.[48] The minister of finance also conceded that "the company's policy must be one of appeasement."[49]

Without the backing of the army and the police, the AIOC officials were powerless. They therefore decided to negotiate and yield to part of the workers' demands. The strike ended on 6 May, after the company sent a deputation to the KUC and agreed to reinstatement of the locomotive strikers and full pay for strike days. The KUC in turn, agreed to a reprimand rather than dismissal, for the superintendent. With respect to the arbitration committee proposed by the KUC, the AIOC promised to give the matter consideration, as it would in any case be obliged to accept such a committee once the newly drafted labor law was passed by the Council of Ministers.[50] Once the strike was settled, company representatives did, in fact, meet regularly with representatives of the KUC to discuss workers' grievances.

Only a few days after the resumption of work at Abadan, news came that the workers of Agha Jari, which was producing 44 percent of the total crude, had walked off their jobs. The strike began on the afternoon of 10 May and extended even to the domestic servants of British personnel.[51] The company estimated that three thousand field workers had joined the strike; the KUC claimed ten thousand.[52]

The motive for the Agha Jari strike was clearly economic. British Ambassador John Le Rougetel cabled the Foreign Office that housing and general amenities in Agha Jari were substandard, offering a fruitful field for Tudeh propaganda. The company was willing to improve conditions, Le Rougetel continued, but had to wait until the yield of a new field could be estimated with sufficient certainty to justify the erection of permanent housing.[53] After his visit to Agha Jari a few weeks later, Jack Jones, a Labour member of Parliament on a fact-finding mission to Iran, confirmed Le Rougetel's report: "Here were to be seen Persian labour living in squalid conditions under tents, etc., and without doubt this was the worst place we visited from the point of view of social amenities."[54]

Although the Agha Jari strikers were not yet members of a union, the strike may well have been promoted by KUC organizers. An American diplomat claimed that union organizers had been active in the area prior to the walkout.[55] An article in *Zafar* declared that although the KUC had not ordered the walkout, once the strike began, the Tudeh press in Tehran certainly supported the workers' demands.[56] These demands included those made at Kermanshah the previous year, as well as a better distribution of ice and drinking water, the provision of one or two midwives and other medical services, and special hardship pay.[57]

The company at first refused to consider these demands, dismissing them as "ridiculous."[58] Instead, following their usual practice, the local AIOC representatives at Agha Jari asked that military forces be sent in to maintain order. An officer and twenty-seven men were at once dispatched, and an additional hundred men were sent from Ahwaz on 8 May.[59] In the meantime, the AIOC managers in Abadan were advised by London to negotiate only with their own employees' representatives and not with Tudeh Party officials. Moreover, the company was not to make any new commitments until it knew what would be required of it by the forthcoming labor legislation.[60] These instructions had little effect, however, since the representatives of the company's workers were invariably members of the Tudeh Party.[61]

Meanwhile, the Tudeh press unleashed a barrage of criticism against the company, charging that the conditions of employment were intolerable and that the AIOC, hoping to starve the workers into submission, had stationed troops around the strikers in such a way as to cut off their water and food supply.[62] The AIOC itself confirmed this allegation, in reporting on 14 May that there were "absolutely no supplies of food or drink in the Agha Jari area, and [that] the workmen will, therefore, starve if they do not go back to work."[63]

As the Agha Jari strike continued through 16 May, conflicting pressures were brought to bear on Prime Minister Qavam. First, the KUC leaders of Ahwaz again complained that the strikers were surrounded by troops and cut off from food and water.[64] Qavam's response was equivocal. He cabled Governor-General Mesbah-Fatemi that order must be maintained, but he also directed that the workers' grievances be investigated and, where justified, redressed.[65]

The pressure applied on the same day by Northcroft, the AIOC's representative in Tehran, was more effective. In a response to the company's representation, Qavam promised to send another telegram to the governor-general in Ahwaz, emphasizing the imperative need to maintain public order and instructing him to tell the Tudeh leaders that they should cease from further activity in Khouzestan.[66] On 18 May, the day that the Qavam labor law was approved by the Council of Ministers, Ambassador Le Rougetel called on Qavam to pressure him into futher action. Qavam told him that under the new labor law a commission would be appointed to investigate the Agha Jari dispute. Le Rougetel was not satisfied: he wanted assurance "that effective measures would be taken without delay to prevent activities of political agitators in the Abadan area." Qavam assured him that the necessary instructions had already been issued. He added that he "was well aware that the company treated their employees well, and the main function of the proposed commission would therefore be to dispose of all allegations to the contrary."[67]

Governor-General Mesbah-Fatemi, who was more eager than the cautious prime minister to take action against the KUC, assured the company that "given necessary authority, trouble could be quickly checked at present by arrest of some half a dozen leaders. . . . Utmost pressure should be applied by British Embassy as only means left of achieving results."[68]

The Agha Jari strike had been peaceful and the workers' demands were legitimate. Even so, British Consul-General Alan Trott wanted the labor leaders arrested and urged the British ambassador to ask the prime minister to allow the arrests.[69] Le Rougetel was not enthusiastic, however. He told Trott, "I am reluctant to ask the Prime Minister to take specific action until I have seen the situation for myself. If you consider it essential, I will, however, consider doing so."[70]

Changing their approach, Governor-General Mesbah-Fatemi and Consul-General Trott, in cooperation with AIOC officials, prepared a list of "principal ringleaders" whose removal "would have an immense and salutary effect" and sent it to Qavam.[71] But the moment was not yet ripe, and the prime minister refused to grant permission for the arrests.

In the meantime, in direct response to British pressure and to increasing labor unrest in Khouzestan, the Council of Ministers who had approved the labor law, on 18 May,[72] dispatched a four-man commission to Agha Jari to negotiate settlement of the strike.[73]

The Agha Jari strike came to an end on 25 May 1946, after the company had made a number of concessions for the second time in less than a month. As part of the settlement the AIOC agreed to grant pay for the period of the strike. This extraordinary concession was disguised as an *ex-gratia* payment, "an indication of the company's benevolence toward its employees."[74] In fact, the company had yielded because of the Tudeh threat of a general strike that would have spread the work stoppage to other oil fields. The company realized that for the moment it was not in a position of strength, since Tudeh power was at its height, and government resolve to combat the Tudeh Party was at its lowest point because of Iran's sensitive relations with the Soviet Union.

The agreement also provided for: (1) a minimum wage of 35 *rials* per day beginning the first of June, coupled with the elimination of all rations of tea, sugar, and bread, which probably reduced the gain in minimum pay by about 50 percent;[75] and (2) company observance of the new labor bill. The company refused, however, to grant the demand for Friday pay (a paid day of rest), or for thirty days' annual leave with pay.[76] As for a thirty-day paid annual vacation, the AIOC maintained that it was already giving more time off with pay than the labor law required. Commenting on the Agha Jari labor agreement, the U.S. military attache in Tehran observed: "It seems that the British are being grudging when they should be generous."[77]

The Abadan General Strike

On 14 July 1946 the workers of the Abadan oil refinery commenced a general strike that lasted for three days and led to 50 deaths and 165 casualties.[78] At the time, the strike seemed a triumph for the KUC; it demonstrated the workers' solidarity and drew some concessions from the AIOC management. Ultimately, however, the strike was disastrous for the KUC: it was followed by the mass arrest of the strike leaders and the total destruction of the KUC and the Tudeh Party in Khouzestan. The Tudeh press claimed that the disburbances and casualties that followed the strike were instigated by the British to provide them with a pretext for vigorously suppressing the labor union. It does seem more than coincidental that the general strike was so immediately and effectively followed by the complete annihilation of the KUC and the Tudeh Party in the province. A more balanced conclusion, however, based on careful scrutiny of documentary evidence, is that a combination of factors led to the general strike, which the British then seized upon to their own advantage.

According to the available evidence, the strike was initiated by dissatisfied rank-and-file workers in Abadan against the advice of the CUC in Tehran, and most probably against the better judgment of the KUC leadership in Abadan. The workers' dissatisfaction with the terms of their employment was certainly aggravated by the AIOC's unwillingness to deal directly with the workers' representatives. By negotiating with CUC leaders in Tehran at the Department of Labor (the Ministry of Labor and Propaganda was formed in August 1946), the company delayed resolution of the strike issues, feeding the impatience of the workers, who were not easily mollified even by their own leaders.

There is ample evidence to suggest that, once the strike commenced, the KUC had no intention of introducing violence into the conflict. On the contrary, as a part of its tactical planning, the union adopted a number of measures to prevent the outbreak of violence from either side. The violence that caused the large number of deaths and casualties resulted from provocative actions on the part of the two British colonels, Underwood and Willoughby. The provincial officials also helped create an explosive situation by declaring martial law even before disorder had threatened to break out.

After decades of silence and obedience, the workers were suddenly presented with articulate leadership and the relaxation of repressive measures. This development was evident in the May Day procession of 1946 in Abadan, the Abadan strike of 5 May, and the Agha Jari strike five days later. These events generated a spirit of revolt among the excitable workers that soon surpassed the zeal of their leaders. This climate of revolt was reported by Colonel Underwood six weeks before the general strike: "Reliable sources state the younger hot-headed Tudeh leaders wish to stage a general strike but the more sober elements are advocating postponement until a really good reason for a general strike can be discovered."[79]

A month later this deterioration of union discipline was confirmed by K. B. Ross, the Abadan works manager, who reported that the KUC leaders appeared to be losing their hold over the workers. In one incident, it took Najafi, the KUC leader, an hour to persuade a number of shift workers to end a sit-down strike; previously, his orders had been obeyed at once. A few days earlier, local leaders at Agha Jari had declared that they recognized neither the KUC nor the central government.[80] In the first week of July, a British intelligence officer told a visiting American diplomat of "overhearing" a telephone conversation in which self-appointed strike leaders refused, in spite of all threats, to carry out an order from headquarters to return to work.[81] Moreover, in reference to a number of work stoppages prior to 14 July, the British consul in Khorramshahr noted "a marked lack of cohesion between the Tudeh leaders around the various fields."[82] The consul's observation can be taken as a tacit admission that the general strike was spontaneous. In short, the workers had had enough of their low wages, poor housing, inadequate diet, and lack of medical facilities and wanted immediate solutions to their problems. The Tudeh leadership, on the other hand, had a more objective outlook and wished to manage the workers' dissatisfaction in such a way as ultimately to alter the political system.

The AIOC management in Abadan declined to negotiate in good faith with a KUC leadership that appeared suprisingly well-intentioned and accommodating. The list of demands for which the Abadan workers struck was first presented to the company on 3 July. The major items on the list were (a) payment of wages for Friday, the day of Sabbath; (b) appointment of worker representatives in workshops for the settlement of disputes between the workers and the company; (c) an annual increase in wages, and (d) transport facilities for workers who had to walk several miles from their homes to work.[83] At the same time, the company was given notice that if no satisfactory reply were received by 5:00 P.M. on 5 July, the workers would use "drastic means" to obtain their rights.[84]

Even though the KUC, according to company sources, "seemed bent on showing quick results to labor," its leaders did demonstrate a good deal of understanding and patience with the company's position. After meeting with company representatives on 4 July, KUC leaders agreed that the issues had to be referred to London and that the deadline had therefore to be extended.[85]

On 7 July, KUC leaders and AIOC representatives met again. At this meeting the union leaders frankly admitted that the main issue was pay for Fridays. They said that other points could be settled by discussion, but that the main issue had to be decided at once. The AIOC explained that this demand, if agreed to, would cost them about £ 1 million per annum and that they would have to refer the matter once again to their London office. While KUC representatives agreed that more time was necessary for consideration of their main demand, they, in the words of the British consul, "naively hinted that they must have something definite to show to workers in the immediate future and asked the company to suggest a date. AIOC suggested 13 July and the leaders agreed."[86]

Instead of welcoming the union's readiness to negotiate and their honesty in admitting that they were under pressure from the rank-and-file, AIOC officials, intent on the destruction of the labor movement, interpreted the union leaders' behavior as a sign of weakness and decided to hold their ground. By 8 July, they had received authorization from London "to accede to main demand in an emergency.[87] The company, however, deluded the union leaders into thinking that it was still awaiting instructions from London.

In the time gained by this deception, the company, through the services of Britain's visiting labor attache, Audsley, arranged a meeting at the Labor Department in Tehran between CUC leaders and its own representatives. The agendum of the meeting was to arrive at a minimum wage which would also settle the question of Friday pay. The first meeting of the wage committee took place in Tehran on 8 July, the day after the company had told the KUC that it would take six more days to receive instructions from London. According to Audsley, who attended the initial meetings of the wage committee, it was agreed at the first meeting that further discussions over wages and Friday pay should not take place at Abadan while negotiations were proceeding in Tehran.[88] Whether the KUC leaders were ever aware of these discussions is not clear. It is fairly certain, however, that the agreement was reached without the participation or consent of the KUC leaders in Abadan.

While the committee formulating the minimum wage continued its work, the company and the central government were clearly anticipating a strike and braced themselves accordingly. The Council of Ministers in Tehran authorized the governor-general of Khouze-stan to declare martial law at his own discretion in any part of the province, and on 10 July Mesbah-Fatemi returned to Ahwaz[89] ready to lend support to the company.

The central government's attitude toward the Tudeh Party and its auxiliary trade unions had obviously hardened since the early spring of 1946. Since that time, Soviet forces had vacated Iran and a provisional agreement with the Azerbaijan Democrats had been reached. Once relieved of pressure from the north, Qavam had come under heavy pressure from Great Britain.[90] So, while still maintaining cordial relations with the CUC and the Tudeh Party in Tehran, the prime minister agreed on a hard line against them in Khouzestan.

Not fully reassured by Qavam's resolve to crush future strikes, the British government itself prepared military plans for various contingencies, including the occupation of Abadan and the oil fields. At the same time, AIOC officials maintained a direct channel of communication with the British military authorities in neighboring Iraq—often without the knowledge of either the British embassy in Tehran or its consulates in Khouzestan.[91]

In the meantime, Colonel Underwood and his assistant, Jaecock, had succeeded in persuading the Arab sheiks in and around Abadan to form an "Arab Union"[92] consisting of five thousand armed men, to deal with Tudeh agitation. According to a report by a secretary in the American embassy in Tehran, Colonel Underwood, in conjunction with Colonel Willoughby, the British consul in Korramshahr, planned to bring the armed men of the Arab Union into Abadan on 15 July—two days after the expiration of the latest negotiation deadline—on the pretext of celebrating the opening of Arab Union headquarters, but actually for the purpose of eliminating Tudeh influence in the city.[93]

Only a few days before the bloody confrontation of 14 July, the American ambassador in Tehran reported: "Indications are that the British are gathering forces to strike a hard and, if possible, a fatal blow to the Tudeh at the appropriate moment. The local people, Tudeh as well as Arabs and British, seem to be spoiling for a fight, almost as if they had hoped something would happen."[94]

When the deadline of 13 July 1946 arrived, the company claimed that the issue of Friday pay was still under discussion in Tehran and that the KUC would have to wait longer for a decision. At the same time, KUC leader Najafi received a cable from the CUC in Tehran urging him to prevent the strike.[95] However, the KUC Executive Committee, under pressure from the rank-and-file, met on the evening of 13 July and authorized a strike for the next day.[96]

The Abadan general strike began at 6:00 A.M. on Sunday 14 July 1946. A. C. Trott, the British consul-general, admitted that the strike was "surprisingly" well-organized and orderly.[97] When the workers left their jobs, approximately one thousand began distributing pamphlets outlining strike issues.[98] As a precaution against possible mischief initiated by the company, other workers were posted as guards at strategic positions throughout the island of Abadan. These guards were ordered to prevent damage to company property and looting by provocateurs, for which the KUC could be later blamed, and to forbid the shipment of food from the island by the company as a means of breaking the strike.[99]

As soon as news of the strike reached Ahwaz, Governor-General Mesbah-Fatemi, instead of dispatching a mediator to the scene, delcared martial law in Abadan—even though there were no signs of violence. He advised the British consul-general against any appeasement by the AIOC, and asked for British moral support for whatever he might to do restore order.[100] The British complied. Consul-General Trott cabled Ambassador Le Rougetel: "I feel we must leave the details to him [the governor-general] and that his first task is to re-establish governmental authority here."[101]

What had started as a peaceful and orderly strike turned into a violent nightmare on the evening of 14 July. According to the U.S. military attache in Tehran, the riot began at the Arab Union in Abadan, where a large group of Arabs were engaged in a native dance known as the *jazli*, which was used by Arabs to rouse "the passions of the participants."[102] The spark that ignited the blaze took the form of a shot fired from an undetermined source at about 8:30 P.M. Subsequently, fighting broke out in and around the Arab Union between several hundred Arabs armed with pistols and rifles and several thousand KUC members armed with clubs and knives.[103] Fighting soon spread to other parts of Abadan. During the riots, Colonel Underwood moved his office next door to that of Military Governor Ahmad Fateh, in order to coordinate their efforts.[104] Government troops, assisted by two hundred Iraqi Arabs brought from across the border, began firing on the crowd. Order was restored at about 10:30 P.M. after two hours of rioting.[105]

When the heavy fighting had ended, KUC leaders including Najafi, Mottaghi, Vafa'izadeh, Tarbiyat, and Kabiri, as a conciliatory gesture, gathered some firearms seized from the Arabs during the fray and took them to the office of the military governor. They delivered the arms, obtained a receipt, and were then jailed. On the same day, the Council of Ministers authorized the dispatch of an additional battalion of soldiers to Ahwaz from Tehran and the arrest on sight of the "so-called Tudeh police." The governor-general was instructed to telegraph to Tehran the names of the agitators so that the government could order their arrest or expulsion from Khouzestan. In extreme circumstances, the governor-general was authorized to arrest them himself.[106]

Once again, the central government was demonstrating its total lack of sympathy for the workers. If people were to be arrested for their part in the riot, the names of Colonel Underwood and Major Fateh should have topped the list. The American military attache had no doubts about Underwood's role: "He [Underwood] also knows that he has been playing with dynamite in organizing the Arabs. Proper organizing might be acceptable, but organization of a fighting rival to Tudeh, which has shown its willingness to bear arms, if necessary, to put down the enemy, might not be looked on with favor in high political circles."[107]

Although Prime Minister Qavam had responded to the strike by the use of force, he could not ignore the outcry of protest led by the Tudeh press. He therefore dispatched his right-hand man, Mozaffar Firouz, at the head of a delegation which included Dr. Reza Radmanesh and Dr. Hossein Jowdat, leaders of the Tudeh Party, to investigate the strike. As his first act, Firouz demanded the immediate release of the five KUC leaders,[108] ordered a cease-fire, and began a series of conferences with union officials, Arab leaders, and company representatives. He also attempted to replace Military Governor Fateh and Police Chief La'li, but in this he was overruled by Qavam.[109]

On the evening of 15 July, G. N. S. Gobey of the AIOC and C. P. Skrine, the British embassy counselor, were summoned to a meeting with Firouz at the Abadan governor's office. Ahmad Aramesh, of the Ministry of Commerce and Industry (he soon became minister of labor), and Governor-General Mesbah-Fatemi were also present. While Firouz maintained that the AIOC's refusal to grant Friday pay had caused the strike, Gobey responded that Friday pay and minimum rates could not be divorced and that the company had awaited the result of Tehran's deliberations. Firouz replied that the wage committee in Tehran had already agreed on a procedure for fixing the minimum wage, which was to list the items necessary for the subsistence of an average-sized family. The items on the list and their quantity had been agreed upon, said Firouz, the resulting sum amounted to a minimum wage of 45 *rials* per day, and he was prepared to instruct the company to pay this wage retroactively to 18 May. Aramesh disagreed with Firouz, however, and proposed instead a lower minimum wage of 35 *rials* per day plus one day's payment for Fridays. Gobey agreed with the latter proposal, pointing out, however, that the company would not give in on the strike pay issue.[110]

As soon as Firouz had the Tudeh leaders released from prison, British diplomatic channels were clogged with protests against him and his actions. British Consul-General Alan Trott, for instance, cabled Tehran: "Unless Firouz and his four companions are recalled at once and the law breakers re-arrested I fear it will be vain to expect any further help from the Governor-General, who hitherto has in my opinion done extremely well. Releases have undermined his authority and made his position impossible."[111]

Firouz was extremely close to Qavam, but British pressure was overwhelming, and the prime minister recalled his assistant to Tehran the next day,[112] leaving the governor-general in Khouzestan to carry out the British policy of eradicating Tudeh influence from the province. As his first act, Mesbah-Fatemi canceled Firouz's cease-fire, authorizing the division commander of the army to open fire when necesary.[113]

After the departure of the Firouz delegation, Najafi publicly announced that the entire affair had been referred to the central government by the CUC for arbitation, and that the KUC expected the government to meet union demands. He stressed that no further strikes would be called in the foreseeable future. The issue of minimum wages and Friday pay had been settled; the sharpest issue still outstanding was the refusal of the company to grant strike pay. The KUC demanded pay for the three-day strike period and double pay for those who had remained in vital jobs.[114] Also not yet agreed upon were improvement of transportation facilities, increased medical facilities, housing, and especially the removal of Colonel Underwood, his assistant Jaecock, Governor-General Mesbah-Fatemi, Military Governor Fateh, and Police Chief La'li, all of whom Najafi described as British stooges.[115]

Najafi, as leader of the KUC, was obviously confident of the future of the labor movement, which he considered to be under the protection of the central government. In the words of the U.S. military attache in Tehran: "There is about Najafi a glow of certainty that he has won."[116]

The union leader seemed unaware that the central government's earlier restraint of Military Governor Fateh and other local officials hostile to the KUC had been motivated by considerations of political expedience that no longer prevailed.

The British Analysis of the KUC Initiative

As a consequence of the locomotive shop and Agha Jari strikes in May and the union's show of force on May Day, the British Foreign Office entered upon a comprehensive assessment of the Tudeh Party's position in Iran, with particular reference to Khouzestan. Contributing their views were AIOC officials, British embassy personnel, and a parliamentary mission. When one compares these various opinions, expressed in correspondence and reports, two opposing viewpoints emerge. On one side, a minority opinion held that the

Khouzestan labor movement had begun spontaneously, was born out of the dissatisfaction of the workers with their difficult living conditions, and was not controlled by the Soviet Union. It is significant that the two individuals most closely involved with daily operations at the Abadan oil refinery—K. B. Ross, the works' manager, and McQueen, the labor manager—believed that there was "no outside pressure" and that the trade union movement had sprung up because of the lack of improvement in working conditions resulting from six years of war.[117] Also siding with the minority view was Jack Jones, a Labour Party M.P. and member of the parliamentary mission. Although in his report and subsequent statements, Jones took a surprisingly unsympathetic attitude toward Iranian labor, some portions of his report did demonstrate an understanding of the Iranian situation: "It is, of course, humanly impossible to expect even a Persian to advance his knowledge technically in the interest of British oil production and at the same time expect any individual Persian or Persians not to acquire knowledge which creates within them a desire for a much better existence than has obtained theretofore."[118]

In Jones' opinion, the Soviets were not creators of trade unionism in Iran, but once it had come about, they had been ready to take advantage of the movement to further their own interests. In Jones's view, a major cause of the 1946 labor disputes was the anachronistic and anti-trade union attitude of the AIOC management.[119] The Foreign Office itself was already aware that the company was remiss for not having established an orderly procedure for airing labor's grievances. The sharpest statement on the subject was made by none other than Ernest Bevin, the Secretary of State for Foreign Affairs. In referring to a Foreign Office paper that emphasized the political aspects of the Iranian labor movement, Bevin responded:

> Your paper leaves out of account the history of this business and the action of the Anglo-Iranian Oil Company in their dealings with labor in the past. The first point I would like to make is that there was a law in Persia which prohibited work people from joining a trade union, and that law, I understand, was carried at the request of the oil companies,[120] for, be it remembered, it was only at the outbreak of this last war that the oil companies in England were willing to recognize a union for their transport people. . . . This

background of anti-trade union organization by the companies has inevitably brought the present situation to a head.[121]

Those who considered the workers' demands to be just, their movement spontaneous, their leadership genuine, and the degree of Soviet involvement minimal were in the minority. The majority subscribed to the view advanced by the AIOC, that the KUC was an instrument of Soviet design on the oil fields. This misrepresentation by the company of what was basically an indigenous movement was a calculated tactic on the part of AIOC officials, who were aware that they could elicit little support from a Labour government for their repression of the KUC if they admitted that the union's demands were non-political.

It must be remembered that the Foreign Office based its analysis of the Khouzestan situation principally on reports and opinions prepared by the British embassy in Tehran and the consulates in Ahwaz and Khorramshahr. It is significant that a major portion of these consular reports and dispatches were based on communications received from the security officer of the AIOC, Colonel Underwood, and could hardly be considered unbiased. Moreover, during the critical months of 1946, there was close collaboration and even collusion between Colonel Underwood and the British consul in Khorramshahr, Lieutenant Colonel Willoughby.

Much of the information contained in the monthly consular diaries prepared by the British consul in Khorramshahr was based on secret reports prepared by Colonel Underwood's informers.[122] The British ambassador in Tehran and the Foreign Office in London were bombarded with situation reports full of alarm, often asserting without any supporting evidence that the KUC was a creature of the Soviets and that the union's grievances were largely unjustified, being essentially a pretext for political agitation instigated by the Soviet Union through Tudeh organizers.

While Colonel Underwood was disseminating misinformation, the AIOC management in Abadan, Tehran, and London pressed its view of the Abadan situation directly on the British government. Time and again AIOC officials exaggerated the extent of the KUC threat. In one communication they claimed that "the Tudeh party, at the instigation of the Russians, are doing their best to put the company out of business by making their oil production unremunerative in world markets."[123]

Since the majority opinion, that of the British diplomatic corps heavily influenced by the AIOC, was that labor demands were politically motivated, the solutions considered appropriate by the majority tended to be political. The measures adopted in response to the Tudeh initiative were to exert pressure on the Iranian government to suppress the Tudeh Party and its unions; to discredit the Tudeh Party and publicize the progressiveness of the AIOC through a public relations campaign; to endeavor to improve wages, housing, and labor-management relations in the AIOC; and to sponsor political parties and groups that would oppose the Tudeh Party and its unions.

The prevailing view of the labor movement as being politically inspired had an influence on Britain's policy in Iran that extended beyond its response to the KUC initiative. "The Persians are not strong enough nor morally sound enough ever to form a really democratic government and rule their own country,"[124] wrote W. N. Cuthbert, the Conservative member of the parliamentary delegation to Iran. An official of the Ministry of Fuel and Power concurred: "The Persians are a weak and shiftless people, ill prepared for democracy, and their present drift towards the Tudeh Party can, in the opinion of the Ambassador, be arrested."[125] Given this diagnosis of the country as a "hopeless case," an interventionist prescription was inevitable. As early as 5 June 1946, the British embassy had settled on an interventionist approach to the problem of the Tudeh Party.[126]

The growing sentiment in favor of intervention was hardened into resolve by the Abadan general strike. Henceforth, under such overt pressure by the British as military maneuvers off the Abadan coast, the central government would eradicate the KUC without reservation or delay.

Suppression of the KUC

The active life of the KUC lasted only four months—from May to August 1946. Within a month after the general strike, the leaders of the union were arrested and exiled from Khouzestan, their headquarters and clubs were closed, and their public meetings banned. This sudden termination of the KUC occurred as the result of British insistence that Tudeh influence must be eradicated from the province. In retrospect, it seems clear that the Abadan general strike, with its violence, provided the British with the necessary pretext to destroy the trade union by force.

It seems likely that if the general strike had not occurred spontaneously the British would have had to bring it about, for it enabled them to argue that the KUC was not an ordinary trade union to be dealt with by constitutional methods, but was, on the contrary, a violent, subversive organization whose elimination justified the use of equally violent means. The fact of the matter is that, with the exception of the violence that was instigated by the two British colonels on the evening of 14 July, all other KUC strikes and demonstrations were notably peaceful.

Once the bloody events of the evening of 14 July had taken place, the British embassy in Tehran led the chorus in blaming the Tudeh Party for everything that had happened in Abadan. Not a word was said about the organization by Colonels Underwood and Willoughby of the Arab Union, which had engaged the striking workers in combat. The British embassy was well aware that on at least two occasions, on 3 and 7 July, KUC representatives had formally presented their demands to AIOC officials and had accepted postponements of the company's decision until 13 July. It is against this background that the British ambassador's cable of 16 July 1946 to the Foreign Office must be read: "Although friendly discussions were in progress regarding conditions of labor, no demands were presented to the company by the workers before the strike began and it therefore seems clear that it has been organized for purely political reasons.[127]

Britain decided to flex its naval muscles even though no British personnel had been lost or injured. Ernest Bevin himself admitted this in response to a question in the House of Commons. "I have had no reports of casualties among the British and Indian staff of the company."[128] On 16 July, the British sloop *Wild Goose* anchored off Abadan in Iraqi waters. Two days later she was joined by the British light cruiser *Norfolk*, which was anchored four miles further down the river Shatt-ol-Arab.[129] On 3 August, after the British warships had disappeared from the scene, Britain dispatched fifteen thousand troops to Iraq from India. When Iran, a week later, protested this action, the Foreign Office rejected the Iranian note, claiming these troops were "replacements"—a statement that a large number of Foreign Office documents prove to have been untrue. To add insult to injury, a Foreign Office spokesman stated that, if necessary, Britain would act unilaterally to quell any violent or sudden threat "to her oil interests in Iran."[130]

With warships off Iranian shores and Indian troops on their way to a base in Iraq a few miles from the Iranian border, Ambassador Le Rougetel's recommendations to Prime Minister Qavam obviously carried new weight. On 17 July, the Foreign Office instructed Le Rougetel to try to "stiffen the Persian Prime Minister"[131] and Qavam gave a free hand to Governor-General Mesbah-Fatemi to carry out a mass arrest and deportation from Khouzestan of KUC and Tudeh leaders.

The first labor leader of any stature to be arrested and deported was Hafezollah Kiyani from Agha Jari. He was taken into custody on 23 July and deported to Tehran the same evening.[132] As Iraj Eskandari, Dr. Morteza Yazdi, and Dr. Fereidoun Keshavarz, the three Tudeh leaders, were assuming their ministerial posts in Qavam's coalition cabinet,[133] a new wave of arrests commenced in Abadan on 13 August. Among those seized were Najafi and another KUC leader, Gholam-Reza Moradi. Najafi was handcuffed and taken out of Abadan in an oil company truck. After being held for a time in the Ahwaz prison, he was taken to Tehran.[134]

The removal of Najafi and Moradi from Abadan ended the active life of the KUC. Further arrests were carried out during September, October, and November, including those of less prominent leaders, among them Ezattolah Dashtipour, organizer of the Abadan stevedores,[135] Makki-Rabi'i, acting president of the Khorramshahr Tudeh Party,[136] and Mohammad Kaveh, party treasurer in Abadan.[137] Because both the Tudeh Party and the KUC drew on a small pool of educated, capable leaders, and were highly centralized organizations, the removal of a comparatively few such men had the devastating effect forecast by Mesbah-Fatemi before the general strike.[138] In October 1946 Le Rougetel was able to report: "In the province of Khuzistan most of the party's agitators have for the time being been banished or shut up, and martial law has imposed severe restrictions on party activities of all kinds."[139] Moreover, according to the British labor attache, the AIOC cooperated with local police to "discourage" new leaders from replacing those who had been banished.

Since the summer of 1946, the AIOC had devised several methods of demoralizing the union's leaders and members. Not surprisingly, Colonel Underwood was entrusted with carrying out this portion of the anti-Tudeh program. He was well placed to do so: it was reliably reported that his agents had successfully infiltrated the Tudeh cells in Abadan.[140] He could therefore receive detailed reports of the inner workings of the KUC and the party and issue instructions to be carried out within these organizations.

As a part of the oil company's anti-union activities, Underwood suggested ways of planting suspicion in the minds of workers as to what was happening with the funds collected for the union. He also devised other methods of creating dissension. These he listed as current or future projects for his department: issuing propaganda leaflets charging certain party officials with embezzlement of party funds and posting false notices that a meeting of the party was to be held, for example, at 4:00 P.M. on a certain afternoon instead of at 5:00 P.M., its originally scheduled time.[141]

Reports of these and other activities were given directly to the general manager of the AIOC, with copies to the British embassy in Tehran, consular officials in Ahwaz and Khorramshahr, and the Foreign Office in London. There is, therefore, no doubt but that those outside of the company were aware of these actions.

After the general strike, as we have seen, devious ploys were supplanted by direct action. The expulsion of the Tudeh ministers from Qavam's cabinet in mid-October 1946 and the collapse of the Azarbaijan Democrats signaled the final and most repressive phase of the government's campaign against the party in the province of Khouzestan. Following an order issued by the authorities on 30 November 1946, the headquarters and all branch offices and clubs of the Tudeh Party in Khorramshahr and Abadan were closed and their signboards removed by the police. Members found in the clubs were arrested, and the landlords of the various buildings used by the party were ordered to find new tenants.[142] Henceforth the Tudeh Party and the KUC were forced to carry out their activities clandestinely.

The KUC secretly reorganized in Abadan. Selected workers were each instructed to recruit several trustworthy followers, each of whom had in turn to enroll other members, with all members working on the "cell" principle.[143] According to Iranian military intelligence, there were 179 different cells in Abadan alone.[144]

As the KUC was being driven underground, the attention of the British embassy turned to the CUC and the Tudeh Party in Tehran. In Ambassador Le Rougetel's words, the only thing that kept the KUC alive was "the sustained vigour of the party headquarters in Tehran, the vitality of its chief organs of publicity, the Tehran newspapers *Rahbar* and *Zafar* and its eight provincial journals."[145] Something had to be done, therefore, to eliminate the problem at the source. Since the British could do nothing to put an end to radio broadcasts emanating from the Soviet Union, they concentrated their efforts on suppressing the anti-British publications. On 3 November 1946, Secretary Bevin cabled Le Rougetel, instructing him to "take a suitable opportunity of pressing Qavam either for the suppression or effective control" of *Zafar* and *Rahbar*, the two newspapers that were most violently anti-British.[146] By the end of the following month, the two papers were silenced.

The suppression of the KUC in the autumn of 1946 coincided significantly with elections for the Fifteenth Majles, the outcome of which was a matter of considerable apprehension to the British. On 5 June 1946 the counselor of the embassy declared: "The Tudeh party, encouraged and inspired by Moscow, is making such headway that a Communist landslide in the forthcoming elections is an absolute certainty unless something drastic can be done about it."[147]

By 18 October, when the order to hold elections was displayed in Abadan, the KUC had been destroyed. Destroyed too was the KUC's hope of sending representatives from Khouzestan to the Fifteenth Majles. On 6 November, Reza Rousta, head of the CUC, cabled to the British Trade Union Congress (TUC): "At Khuzistan these circles [the government and the AIOC], encouraged by the presence of British troops at Basra and Sibe [in Iraq], took away the last remaining liberties of workers in order to be victorious at the forthcoming legislative elections. At Khouzestan, where 98 per cent of the working population are organized in their trade unions, the worker's candidates have been deported and placed under guard."[148]

The Foreign Office, misleading the members of its own Trade Union Congress (TUC), denied Rousta's accusations, declaring: "The allegation that the Anglo-Iranian Oil Company [is] conducting a general campaign against trade unionism [is] contrary to the information in the possession of this department, and the report now received from His Majesty's ambassador at Tehran confirms that it is without foundation."[149]

The election for the Fifteenth Majles, which took place in Abadan from 14 to 18 February 1947, was "won" by Dr. Abdol-Hossein Raji, formerly an executive of the AIOC and now a member of Qavam's Democratic Party. Colonel Underwood provides a detailed description of the balloting, which was so blatantly rigged as to evoke even his astonishment.

The ballot box, wrapped in white canvass and covered with official
seals, was placed in the Seyed Ali Reqi Mosque [sic] close to two
tables at which were seated in turn members of the local electoral
committee of 9. These individuals kept a register of voters under
the supervision of a young clerk inspector of the Ministry of
Interior. Voters coming to the Mosque were handed [already]
prepared voting papers (mostly in the same handwriting) for the
popular candidate, Dr. Raji. They were then taken into the Mosque
where their identity papers were scrutinized and stamped as having
voted. The voting paper was then taken from them and placed in
the box! Individuals arriving at the polling booth with a number
of . . . identity papers had all of these scrutinized and stamped,
and an equivalent number of voting papers all prepared were
placed in the ballot box. Anyone arriving with a voting paper made
out for any other candidate usually had this substituted unless the
electoral committee were prepared to allow a certain number of
voting papers to be placed in the box in another candidate's name
so as to make things appear normal.[150]

Through the combined efforts of the British and Iranian governments and the AIOC, the KUC and its leadership were decisively
defeated. The spirit of defiance persisted, however. It was voiced by
Kal-Faraj, an AIOC worker, at a secret meeting: "Comrades, we are
only asking our valid rights so that we may live under better conditions. In every country of the world workers are crying for increases in
pay. They are not crying with intent to create mischief or hooliganism
but honesty. . . . The company, instead of healing our wounds, is
spraying salt over them. They should, however, remember that we
also await a favourable opportunity and then we will take our revenge
item by item.[151]

The Creation of "Nonpolitical" Unions

As we have seen, the AIOC and the newly established Ministry
of Labor and Propaganda cooperated in removing the last public
vestiges of the KUC, justifying their actions as a response to the threat
of communism. Both the company and the ministry claimed that they
were not against genuine, nonpolitical trade unions; indeed, they
welcomed them. In Chapter 8 we shall discuss the Ministry of Labor's
actual position on the issue of nonpolitical trade unions. It will be
noted that the anti-Tudeh labor unions, sponsored by the Ministry

of Labor, never developed an enthusiastic or loyal following. The AIOC's efforts to sponsor a nonpolitical union met with similar results.

The AIOC had not always proclaimed itself in favor of nonpolitical unions. Prior to 1945, it was so vehemently opposed to trade unions of any kind that it denied representation even to its British employees. As the Labour Party came to power in Britain in July 1945 and strife increased in AIOC installations in the spring of 1946, the British government urged the company to change from a policy of total opposition to trade unionism to one of supporting "nonpolitical" unions.

To implement the Foreign Office's new directive, the AIOC augmented its staff with a succession of industrial relations advisers, among them, A. C. V. Lindon. The company was receptive to a proposal from Mostafa Fateh,[152] the AIOC distribution manager, who was given a top administrative job in Abadan as a means of reducing Colonel Underwood's influence and strengthening the company's community relations. Fateh proposed to the general management the need to form "a new union opposed to the Tudeh, and for this purpose suggested Yousef Eftekhari as the organizer."[153] The general manager agreed to Fateh's plan because, as he said, "it is infinitely better for the workers to belong to a genuine labor union rather than have no union at all.[154]

On 20 January 1947, eleven individuals (including Yousef Eftekhari, founder of the labor union known as the Central Board), all of them either current or former employees of the AIOC, "after obtaining official permission," issued a manifesto to their fellow workers[155] in which the signatories announced the formation of the Oil Worker's Union (OWU) and invited everyone to join. Although the AIOC was obviously eager to ensure the success of its own creation, it realized at the same time that it must not display any outward interest in the OWU; that the workers would not join the union if they suspected that it was sponsored by either the company or the government.[156] For the same reason, AIOC officials planned to provide OWU with opportunities to claim victories in its negotiations with the company. One item in Eftekhari's program was the reinstatement of workers who were discharged in 1929.[157] The British consul in Khorramshahr reported to London: "The company may be able to make limited 'concessions' in this direction—they certainly are prepared to go a long way to assist the new movement."

Although the company attempted to hide its sponsorship, leaders of the union did not disguise their pro-company and pro-government attitudes. On a number of occasions OWU leaders went out of their way to praise the AIOC and the local government and to urge their members to adopt a conciliatory attitude toward them. For instance, in a meeting held in February 1947 the workers were told: "This new union of ours has nothing to do with politics. It is simply for the welfare of the workers. Do not abuse the government and the company which are always working for your welfare. It is useless to do so as the government has the right to imprison anyone abusing peaceful citizens or government officials."[158]

OWU's collusion with the company was revealed in other ways. Eftekhari, the union leader, had been abused by the Tudeh press as a tool of the British ever since his disagreement with the party in May 1944.[159] By subsequently joining the Ministry of Commerce and Industry in order to "study and organize trade unions in Iran,"[160] he had lent plausibility to these accusations.

On several occasions the OWU received special treatment from local authorities. For example, at a time when no formal procedure for the registration of unions had been adopted, the Ministry of Labor issued special instructions to the Abadan Department of Registry that "any application for registration by the Trade Union of Oil Workers [OWU] should be accepted immediately."[161] Moreover, the military governor of Abadan, having confiscated the KUC premises and furniture, turned them over to the OWU.[162]

With government and company support of the OWU so flagrant, it was not surprising that most workers refused to join the new union. In March the Khorramshahr consul reported, "Though a fair number of workmen have already enrolled,[163] the general enthusiasm expected by the union leaders has not so far been forthcoming."[164] In June 1947 it was reported that Eftekhari was becoming discouraged[165] and two months later he left for Tehran, having informed the military governor of Abadan that he would not return.[166]

As the company's initiative in establishing an anti-Tudeh union in Abadan was clearly failing, the government took the lead in achieving that end. In June 1947, Dr. Shapour Bakhtiar, the director of the Khouzestan Department of Labor, undertook formation of a labor union,[167] and on 2 September he issued a proclamation urging the workers to form unions, independent from political parties: "A legal union should certainly not be attached to any political party or policy and should have no idea and purpose except the improvement of their social situation and raising the standard of education and living."[168]

The Central Council of Khouzestan Worker's Unions (CCK) was formed by AIOC employees in February 1948 and was composed of four separate branches: Abadan, Masjed-e Soleiman, Haft Kel, and Lali. The leaders of the new unions were workers' representatives on the factory councils. In line with Dr. Bakhtiar's directive and AIOC policy, the unions had announced that they were strictly professional trade unions and had no interest in politics. The CCK was therefore quickly recognized by Dr. Bakhtiar as a bona fide trade union.[169]

The public reception given to the CCK was not much different from that accorded its predecessor, the OWU. AIOC workers called it "a tool of the company and Dr. Bakhtiar."[170] Even officials of the AIOC referred to the CCK as "Dr. Bakhtiar's Union." The chief industrial relations adviser asked company officials to refrain from this practice, which, he said, played into Tudeh hands.[171]

By September 1948, approximately three thousand workers had joined the CCK.[172] Lacking a large or enthusiastic membership, the union led an uneventful existence in Abadan, similar to that of ESKI in Tehran. Having destroyed the KUC and failed to replace it with a sizable union of its own, the AIOC concentrated instead on expanding the network of factory councils within the company as a means of responding to the workers' nonpolitical grievances.

Employers' Influence on the Labor Movement
The Case of Esfahan

Introduction to Esfahan

*T*HERE CAN BE little doubt but that Great Britain and the United States, in their effort to establish an anti-Communist regime in Iran that was sympathetic to their national interests, were allied with the shah, the landowners, the owners of large businesses, and the officer corps of the army, as well as with high-level civil servants. It can also be said that these domestic groups firmly opposed constitutional government. Since, in their view, any gain by the masses would mean a loss of their own privileges, they were eager to reestablish an autocratic monarchy.

So far we have been concerned with the influence of foreign powers on the labor movement in Iran. The present chapter, which focuses on the city of Esfahan, capital of Esfahan Province, will examine the interaction between labor unions and domestic—rather than foreign—supporters of the status quo. Located in central Iran, unoccupied by foreign troops during World War II, Esfahan provides the opportunity for such a study. Moreover, the province's textile industry, concentrated in its capital city, did not contribute significantly to the Allied war effort. Hence, labor activity in Esfahan—unlike that in Tabriz and Abadan—was not seen by the Soviet Union or Great Britain to have a direct effect upon their national interests.

Accordingly, the two powers intervened less strenuously in Esfahan than elsewhere; there, the antagonists of the labor movement were chiefly domestic forces, of which the employers were, of course, the most zealous.

Esfahan, after Tehran, was the most important trading center in Iran. Of more immediate importance, however, is the fact that in Esfahan were located nine of Iran's twenty-one textile mills—the largest concentration of textile mills in the country. These nine mills employed about 10,000 workers, Risbaf employing the largest number (1,870) and Nakhtab the smallest (500).[1] Of the 10,000 textile workers, 74 percent were men, 20 percent women, and 6 percent children. The rate of literacy among them was about 18 percent.[2]

The population of the city of Esfahan, estimated at 194,000 in 1945, was described by one observer as thrifty and hardworking. The Esfahanis, like residents of other provinces, considered themselves to be Esfahanis first and Iranians second. Made up of a homogeneous population of Persian stock, speaking the Persian language, and adhering to the Shiah branch of Islam (there was a small but economically significant minority of Armenians, Jews and Baha'is), the Esfahanis were among the more religious people of Iran.[3]

Working conditions in Esfahan textile mills were similar to those in factories of similar size in other parts of Iran.[4] The mill's work force included many children, who worked twelve-hour shifts. In 1944 the average textile worker was paid 40 *rials* ($1.10) for a twelve-hour workday. A skilled worker received about 100 *rials* ($2.70) a day.[5]

According to Charles Gault, the British consul in Esfahan during World War II, the Esfahan area was not particularly receptive to Communist doctrine. A large proportion of Esfahani peasants, numbering about 500,000 in the entire province, worked their own land, in contrast to the peasants of Azarbaijan, who were largely tenant farmers and eager for land reform. The tradesman was independent of both large landowners (who numbered a few thousand) and major businessmen. The local trade guilds were also strong and able to exercise considerable influence on their members, especially at election time.[6]

The mill owners were extremely close-knit, bound by financial as well as familial ties. British Consul Gault described them as "some dozen men, all rascals, . . . at the same time the richest merchants in the bazaar, the biggest factory owners and the biggest landowners."[7] The mill owners of Esfahan construed the relationship between employer and worker as analogous to that between autocratic monarch and subject: It was the employer's absolute and exclusive right to determine the workers' compensation. If the workers asked for more, the employer either ignored the demand or promised an increase that was never granted. If the workers then went on strike or otherwise inconvenienced the employer, the local authorities were called in to restrain them by force.

After the deposition of Reza Shah in 1941 until the reemergence of autocracy in 1946, the mill owners could no longer rely on local officials to exercise force against their ungrateful employees. Although the mill owners enjoyed the support of the young shah, Mohammad-Reza Pahlavi, and the successive provincial commanders of the army who were appointed by the shah, they were not fully supported by the incumbent governors-general, who were appointed by the prime minister. Thus, prior to 1947, before the shah had extended his authority over the prime minister and the cabinet, there were many conflicts between the governors-general of the province and the divisional army commanders. While the former's attitudes toward trade unions varied in accordance with the fluctuating policies of the incumbent prime minister in Tehran, the army commanders' inclination was more consistently to use force on the side of the mill owners against all forms of dissent—whether Communist or otherwise. The army's support for the mill owners derived from the court, with which the mill owners had had direct links ever since the 1930s, when all nine mills were established under the patronage of Reza Shah.

When disagreements arose between the provincial commander and the governor-general over the handling of labor disputes, the latter found an influential ally in the person of the British consul in Esfahan. In its formative years, the Esfahani labor movement enjoyed the sympathy of the British consul because it was, as we shall see, the most notably independent labor movement in Iran and as such posed no immediate danger to British interests. It was unique by virtue of its independence from the Tudeh Party, as well as from the employers and the central government's Department of Labor. (Until August 1946, when the Ministry of Labor and Propaganda was created, the Labor Department of the Ministry of Commerce and Industry was responsible for labor affairs.) Where British commercial interests were not directly involved, the Foreign Office looked favorably on a non-Communist union and regarded the indiscriminate, forceful repression of trade unions as creating conditions of discontent that could be exploited by revolutionary agitators. The

British consul, therefore, befriended the various leaders of the Esfahani labor movement during the years from 1942 to 1944, when it functioned separately from the Tudeh Party and the Tudeh national labor organization, the Central Council (Showra-ye Markazi).

The Formation of Iran's First Independent Union

The deposition of Reza Shah and the reestablishment of a constitutional government created a situation in which trade unions, for the first time in nearly twenty years, were able to organize. The emergence of trade unions in Esfahan first became apparent in the summer of 1942, when the workers in nine textile mills joined in a concerted strike.

Unable to stir the provincial government into suppressing the strike by force, the mill owners signed a comprehensive agreement in the presence of a neutral, Governor-General Nasr.[8] The agreement, signed on 7 September 1942, provided for: reduction of daily hours of work from ten to eight; payment of extra wages for overtime work; provision of 20 percent premium pay for night work; a minimum wage of 10 *rials* for men; a minimum wage for women and male children (under the age of fifteen) of 4.5 *rials;* a minimum wage for female children of 4 *rials;* referral of disputes to the Provincial Department of Commerce and Industries for settlement; provision of two suits per year to every worker—one free and the other at the expense of the worker; improvement of hygienic conditions and washing facilities in the mills; and arrangement for the education of illiterate boys working in the factories.[9]

To celebrate their victory, the workers held a mass meeting on 19 August 1942 at Bagh-e Beh (the quince orchard) on the banks of the Zayandeh River.[10] At this gathering a number of speeches were delivered, including one by Taghi Fadakar,[11] a local lawyer, in support of the strike. At the end of the meeting, it was announced that a city-wide industrial union encompassing all nine textile mills would soon be formed.[12] It was primarily Fadakar who implemented this decision, and who, more than anyone else, determined the union's independent character.

In 1942, Taghi Fadakar was 39 years old and in the prime of life. He was born into a clerical family and was accordingly influenced by religion. His father had studied in the holy city of Najaf in Iraq and subsequently became a religious leader in Esfahan. Like a surprisingly large number of other Iranian labor leaders, he became an orphan at an early age[13] and was forced to become independent and partially self-supporting while still a child.[14]

As a young man, Fadakar was drawn to the ideologies of Marx and Lenin. About the year 1920, while in Tehran attending the College of Political Science, he became acquainted with Soleiman-Mirza Eskandari (later called Soleiman Mohsen-Eskandari), the veteran Socialist. He also fought briefly in the Jangali Movement, in which his older brother lost his life.[15]

During the reign of Reza Shah (1925–1941), Fadakar lived in his native city of Esfahan. His first position was with the Soviet commercial firm of Sherkat-e Panbeh-e Sharqh (Eastern Cotton Company), where he learned Russian.[116] Subsequently, he practiced law and represented a number of Bakhtiari tribal leaders, a profession he continued until after the abdication of Reza Shah.[17]

An advocate of social reform, Fadakar was intensely national-istic, and therefore did not qualify as a Communist. He was widely respected, even by his opponents, who remembered him as the genuine leader of a spontaneous labor movement. Workers followed him because he remained true to his origins; he continued to wear the local cotton shoes (*giveh*) and to ride a bicycle, while his Tudeh colleagues in the Majles wore smart European clothes and rode in the latest automobiles. Born in Esfahan and having grown up there, Fadakar was considered by the workers one of their own, a leader who understood them. Moreover, speaking of social issues in the humorous style of the Esfahani dialect, Fadakar presented a distinct contrast to the typical Tudeh leader, who lapsed into the jargon of scientific socialism when addressing the "working class."[18]

Fadakar assumed leadership of the Esfahani labor movement from its beginning. After the mill owners had capitulated—tempo-rarily—to their workers' demands in September 1942, Fadakar met with the representatives of the workers of the nine mills. Out of this meeting came the statement of purpose published on 6 December 1942:

> Because the occurrence of disputes between workers and em-
> ployers in the absence of labor laws or regulations leads to
> strikes and, as a result, to misinterpretation by seditious ele-
> ments of the workers' legitimate demands, therefore, on 5 De-
> cember 1942, to support workers' rights and to prevent any kind

of disorder, the representatives of the workers' unions [from each mill] held a joint meeting and established a union by the name of [Ettehadieh-e Kargaran-e Esfahan] Union of the Workers of Esfahan [UWE].[19]

Clearly, in this declaration the new union disowned any revolutionary intent—without, however, assuming a posture of subservience. By its emphasis on maintaining social order and conforming to the laws of the land, the UWE placed itself squarely in the reformist camp.[20] In its organization, too, the union distinguished itself from those dominated by the Central Council—even though a number of UWE leaders were members of the radical wing of the Tudeh Party. In Tabriz and Abadan, the union leaders at the factory level were generally appointed by the leader of the city-wide union, who was himself an appointee of the Tudeh Party. By contrast, the UWE grew from the bottom up. Each mill elected a representative and an assistant representative.[21] The UWE was governed by a seven-man council composed of the representatives of seven of the nine largest mills. The internal affairs of each mill were handled by the mill's own Board of Directors, half of whom were production workers, the rest representative of the clerical staff.[22]

The Tudeh Party had taken part in the UWE from the start. According to Shams Sadri, who initially worked with Fadakar but later led an employer-backed union, the strikes of 1942 had been instigated by Ali Shamideh, a founder of the Tudeh Party in Esfahan. Shamideh, an immigrant from Soviet Azerbaijan, had been arrested in 1931 in Bandar Anzali and exiled to Esfahan.[23] While Shamideh strongly favored the use of strikes as a weapon to force employers into submission, Fadakar was not so aggressive,[24] and although he was a native of Esfahan and an excellent orator, his leadership of the union was challenged by Shamideh. To resolve the dispute, the two men met with the Central Committee of the Tudeh Party in Tehran, where the influence of another reformist, Soleiman Mohsen-Eskandari, moved the Central Committee to confirm Fadakar's status as leader of UWE, even though the majority of the committee preferred Shamideh.[25]

The mill owners' response to the UWE was far from cordial. In January 1943, a month after its formation, workers of various mills went on a second major strike; their principal demand was the implementation of the agreement reached between their representatives and the employers on 7 September 1942, before the formation of the UWE. The mill owners had been using delay tactics in dealing with the union. Charles Gault, the British consul, more perceptive than the mill owners, warned them and the new governor-general, Mostafa-Gholi Kamal-Hedayat, that "the workers cannot remain downtrodden indefinitely."[26] Aware of the social upheaval taking place in northern Iran and the part played in it by Tudeh agitators, Gault wished to immunize Esfahan from similar disturbance by the recognition by employers of workers' legitimate grievances.

While the UWE was trying to force the mill owners to honor the agreement they had signed the previous September, the people of Esfahan were experiencing unprecedented suffering. According to Gault, the food shortage and high inflation rate[27] had resulted in widespread malnutrition among the masses. This malnutrition had in turn caused more sickness and death than the people of Esfahan could remember. Typhus had also reached epidemic proportions.[28]

As a result of Gault's prompting and his own assessment of the situation, Governor-General Kamal-Hedayat instructed the director of the Provincial Department of Commerce and Industries to convene a meeting of the mill owners and urge them to take some action to alleviate the workers' plight. On 14 February 1943, the textile mill owners agreed to grant a general wage increase of 10 percent,[29] a very small concession in the light of triple-digit inflation and reported profits by the mills of "several hundred" percent.[30]

The agreement reached on 14 February met the same fate as the one signed the previous September. Assured privately of support from the Esfahan chief of police and the director of the Provincial Department of Commerce and Industries, the mill owners continued to ignore the two agreements. Instead, they talked of the dangers of communism and the need for martial law to prevent it.[31] Clearly worried by the mill owners' procrastination, Gault reported to his government: "This may be dangerous in the end, for the workers are now more or less organized in unions and have the power to make serious strikes if they should be too badly treated. The owners still believe that force is the only weapon and that they must block any attempt at organized representation among their workers."[32]

Gault also suspected the mill owners of deliberately provoking strikes, which they could then present to Governor-General Kamal-Hedayat as arguments for the forceful suppression of trade unionism.[33] Unable to prevail upon the governor-general, the owners took their cause to the newly arrived army commander, General Shahbakhti, urging him to stamp out the union's influence. Upon learning of this, Gault advised Kamal-Hedayat "not to tolerate interference in civil matters."[34] In this he was following his government's temporary policy of supporting the Iranian prime minister and containing the influence of the shah and the army.

Unable to sway the governor-general, the army commander, or the British consul, the employers pinned their hopes on Tehran. They urged the transfer of the governor-general, whom they characterized as being "in the pocket of the Tudeh Party and therefore a dangerous man." They also severely attacked Fadakar and the UWE for making unreasonable demands and creating disturbances.[35]

To the government's queries about UWE's demands, Fadakar responded that his union's expectations were reasonable. Justifying the workers' demand for higher wages, he pointed out that the owners, who had increased their prices by a factor of five to six during the past year, were unwilling to pay their workers a living. Instead they used their financial power to scheme against the labor union and to create disorder. Fadakar further accused the employers of providing funds to the owner of Nour (Bargh) mill, so that by bribing Tehran officials, martial law would be brought to Esfahan.[36]

In response to Fadakar's arguments, the central government granted concessions to both sides. In the first week of April 1943 Governor-General Kamal-Hedayat was recalled to Tehran.[37] At the same time, the Ministry of Commerce and Industry dispatched to Esfahan its vice minister and chief labor expert, Dr. Abolghasem Sheikh. On 27 April, Dr. Sheikh, together with the acting governor-general, Shahrokh, succeeded in concluding a new agreement between the mill owners and the UWE. In this agreement, the employers promised to:

Provide the men with a daily ration of 3.5 lb. of bread; and for women, 3/4 lb., for workers under the age of 18 half the ration for men.

Complete the building of a hospital as soon as possible where workers could be treated free of charge.

Provide workers with two suits each year as well as two shirts and underclothing.

Set minimum wages for men at 15 *rials,* for women at 10 *rials,* and for children (under 14 years of age) at 8 *rials.*

Establish a premium pay of 20 percent for certain hardship posts in the mills.

Provide workers with a cafeteria.

Refrain from employing children under the age of twelve.

Provide for medical examination of workers once a month and free treatment for those found to be ill.[38]

Workers were committed to obey the rules and regulations in force in the factories and to refrain from interfering in any administrative matters. The workers also agreed to obey the "Regulations for Factories and Industrial Establishments" of 10 August 1933, under which workers could be fined for dereliction of duty.[39] An arbitration committee, composed of the city governor, a representative of the Provincial Department of Justice, and the director of the Provincial Department of Commerce and Industries, was established and charged with investigating and settling disputes. The committee's decisions were final, thus precluding strikes.[40] It can fairly be said that in agreeing to these stipulations the union conceded as much as it gained.

The agreement of 23 April 1943 marked a high point in Fadakar's popularity among the workers; union membership had grown from 1,600 in 1942 to 14,500 in April 1943.[41] Limiting himself to economic issues and rejecting any form of violence, he had succeeded in forcing the mill owners to agree to the workers' demands.

The employers, however, refused to accept the new relationship, which they viewed as an infringement on their prerogatives.

They were encouraged in this unyielding attitude by the arrival of Mostafa Fateh, a native of Esfahan and the distribution manager of the Anglo-Iranian Oil Company, to form a branch of the Hamrahan Party.[42] This effort was unsuccessful; the local branch of the Hamrahan Party, headed by another employee of the AIOC, failed to attract members, a testimony to the political judgment of the workers.[43] Unable to convince the local authorities to use force against the UWE, one mill owner, after consultation with the other mill owners, decided to raise his own army. In late June 1943, Fazlollah Dahesh, the senior owner of the Nour mill and an important landowner, recruited a large number of men from one of his villages to intimidate the UWE. The villagers were implausibly represented as members of the National Movement Party (Nehzat-e Melli) who were outraged by the Tudeh Party. In the ensuing fight between peasants and workers, several people were injured, and a scuffle took place between Fadakar and Abbas-Gholi Dahesh, son of Fazlollah.[44]

Now it was Fadakar's turn to complain to Tehran. He cabled Prime Minister Ali Soheili protesting that employers–in collusion with reactionaries—were harassing workers in the name of a fictitious political party, the National Movement.[45] Not only were gangs, under the party's banner, attacking workers physically, but inside the factories workers were being harassed into becoming party members. Fadakar warned that if the government failed to protect members of his union from violence and harassment, the UWE would take whatever measures were necessary to protect itself.[46]

Charles Gault expressed his sympathy for the UWE in a report to his superiors, accusing the mill owners once again of attempting to frighten the citizens of Esfahan by warning that communism was on their doorsteps. In Gault's view, this fear was "far from being the case." The consul's report also accused the Shah and wealthy Esfahanis of masterminding the National Movement Party as a means of combating Tudeh influence. Displaying once again his influence over local politics, Gault admonished the senior Dahesh, Farajollah Bahrami (Dabir-A'zam), the newly arrived governor-general, and Fadakar to prevent repetition of such incidents in the future.[47] The governor-general agreed, and in early July expelled from Esfahan Dahesh, his son, and Dr. Ahmadi, the local leader of the National Movement Party.[48]

Governor-General Bahrami, like all his predecessors since 1941, refused to identify himself with the mill owners. He went even further and tried to make them implement the agreements of 7 September 1942, and 14 February and 27 April 1943. According to Amir Amirkeyvan, then a young leader of the workers of the Nour mill,[49] Governor-General Bahrami called a meeting of the mill owners in early July at the home of Sarem-ed-Dowleh (Akbar Mas'oud), the Qajar prince and a senior notable in Esfahan.[50] To set the stage for his offensive against the employers, Bahrami had only two chairs placed in the meeting room—one for himself and one for the host. As the first order of business, the governor-general announced the immediate banishment of six of the mill owners present to the southern port city of Bandar Abbas.[51] He next instructed the remaining employers to make immediate payment of all unpaid wages to the workers, add 30 percent to their wages, and provide them with a free ration of bread. Anyone failing to follow this order, he warned, would be immediately exiled.[52]

This meeting was followed by the signing of an agreement on 10 July 1943 that marked the zenith of the UWE's power and of Fadakar's influence. This oddly worded document gave Fadakar unusual responsibility for the maintenance of order:

Aghai [mister] Fadakar [undertakes] to do his best to prevent
differences arising at all. He promised to take good care to avoid
any losses in the production of the factories. If any of the workers
are seen to be involved in any plot or organization for the purpose
of creating disorder in the factories or the town, Aghai Fadakar
can ask the factory (giving the reasons and evidence) to dismiss
that worker, and if the worker has anything more to say, he can
refer [the matter] to the governor-general and his decision will be
final.[53]

It was not surprising that Bahrami became unpopular with the
mill owners as a result of his efforts to balance the power of the mill
owners with the growing strength of the UWE. Once again the mill
owners attempted to expel an uncooperative governor-general while
at the same time seeking military assistance. The newly arrived army
commander, Brigadier General Ghadar, told Bahrami that the Shah
had instructed him "to establish a military governorship [in Esfahan]
but that he preferred to cooperate with the governor-general if
possible." Gault had no doubt that the mill owners were attempting
to replace Bahrami with a military governor.[54] When in late July the
employers succeeded in engineering the recall of Bahrami, Gault
pulled a few strings of his own. Through the intervention of the British
legation in Tehran, the instructions for Bahrami's recall were
canceled, and he retained his post for the next twelve months.[55]

It was the intransigence of the mill owners more than any other
factor that led to the eventual domination of the UWE by Tudeh Party
members and to the subsequent suppression of trade unions in
Esfahan. The Tudeh Party took steps to expand its foothold in
Esfahan in late March 1943, when the First Provincial Conference
of the Tudeh Party in Esfahan met in the province's capital city.
Although Fadakar was given a seat on the Provincial Committee of
the party,[56] the superior post of committee chairman was entrusted
to Mahmoud Boghrati,[57] formerly a member of Taghi Arani's
Marxist group and a founding member of the Tudeh Party, who was
elected a member of the party's Central Committee in 1944.[58] Boghrati
was one of the party's most experienced and trusted members. Once
in charge of party affairs in Esfahan, he tried to extend Tudeh
influence over the UWE through workers who were also party
members. One such worker was Ne'mattollah Bahrampour, who
became highly instrumental in the Tudeh Party's annexation of the
UWE.

From the time of Boghrati's appointment as committee chairman in Esfahan until October 1944, the UWE was associated, but not integrated, with the Tudeh labor organization, the Central Council. At the party conference in Esfahan, Fadakar described his union as an "iron ring around the Tudeh Party"[59] but not as a wheel within it.

Although the Tudeh Party was inclined to rebuff Fadakar because of his reformist stance, it took pride in its association with the UWE. On one occasion, Anvar Khameh'i, a Tudeh leader, described the Esfahan union as the most successful example of the labor movement.[60]

During the campaign for elections to the Fourteenth Majles, Shams Sadri claims, the Tudeh Party preferred the more radical Boghrati to Fadakar as their candidate.[61] British Consul Gault, however, by supporting the more moderate Fadakar, dissuaded the party from opposing him. In July 1943, Gault urged Iraj Eskandari, the visiting Tudeh leader, not to oppose Fadakar with a Tudeh candidate; otherwise, he argued, neither the Tudeh Party nor Fadakar would succeed. Fadakar was not personally disliked by the rich Esfahanis, Gault contended, whereas a Tudeh candidate from outside would be.[62] Recognizing the validity of Gault's argument, the Tudeh Party lent its support to Fadakar, who already enjoyed the strong support of UWE members.

The collaboration of Gault, Bahrami, and Sarem-ed-Dowleh helped elect UWE's leader to the Fourteenth Majles. The three men agreed that the election of Fadakar would hearten the working class of Esfahan and so prevent the Tudeh Party from making inroads in that city.

The prospect of Fadakar's election had been assured when Governor-General Bahrami returned from Tehran to inform Gault that, "after discussion with the Legation and with the government, an 'official' list of candidates . . . [had] been agreed upon. These are Fadakar (workers), Dowlatabadi-Emami (mills and bazaar merchants) for Isfahan town."[63]

Aware of the party's ambivalence toward him, Fadakar joined Heidar-Ali Emami and Hesameddin Dowlatabadi in a coalition.[64] The "official" slate was, in fact, elected: Taghi Fadakar finished first with 30,499 votes (twice the number of votes cast for Dr. Mohammad Mossadegh, the top candidate in the Tehran elections),[65] Hesameddin Dowlatabadi was second with 29,740 votes and Heidar-Ali Emami third with 28,730.[66]

On the day Fadakar departed for the Majles, 26 February 1944, elaborate ceremonies were held in honor of the event. The factories closed for a time and at 9:00 A.M. blew their whistles. Workers lined up on both sides of the road leading to the city's "Tehran Gate." Many workers and three of the owners (Mohammad Ali, Mohammad Ja'far Kazerouni, and Ali Hamedanian) accompanied him to the villages of Mourcheh Khord and Delijan, and one workman even offered to decapitate one of his children as a token of his admiration for Fadakar's work for the union.[67]

While the workers were overjoyed that their popular leader was about to represent them in the nation's legislature, the employers also celebrated the event; with Fadakar out of the way, they hoped to reestablish absolute authority over the workers.

The Disintegration of the UWE

The departure of Fadakar for Tehran proved, ironically, to be the most important factor contributing to the destruction of the UWE. Deprived of his immediate, unifying presence, the union fell into internal strife. The outcome of this dissension was the takeover of the UWE by the radical Tudeh faction of the union, and the formation of a separate employer-sponsored union for those workers who could be persuaded or coerced to leave the UWE.

This schism in the UWE occurred during the period of confrontation discussed in Chapter 3. As soon as the end of World War II was in sight, groups that had tolerated each others' differences for the sake of a united front against fascism set about eliminating each other. Political ideologies polarized into militant communism and repressive conservatism.

Taking advantage of Fadakar's absence, the mill owners commenced their offensive against the union, aided by other notables who had established branches of anti-Communist political organizations in Esfahan—the Hamrahan, Vatan, and National Movement Parties.[68] These parties assisted the mill owners by organizing "demonstrations of anti-Communists"—in reality, mobs of toughs and malcontents recruited from the bazaar and nearby villages. By means of these demonstrations, the mill owners attempted to intimidate striking workers and to create civil disturbance that would justify the imposition of martial law.

The mill owners began their offensive against the UWE by declaring that as of 27 March 1944 they would impose a lockout unless the union severed its ties to the Tudeh Party.[69] If the UWE did in fact take such a step, it would lose a powerful ally; if the union stood firm, the ensuing lockout could lead to an outbreak of violence for which the UWE could be blamed. Although the governor-general dissuaded most of the owners from carrying out their threat, the owner of Shahreza textile mill declared a lockout in early April.[70] On 18 April a riot broke out at Shahreza and Risbaf mills between UWE members protesting the lockout and strike breakers recruited by the mill owners. The ensuing fight, in which two men died and about thirty were wounded, was ended by the police and the army, led by General Ghadar.[71] Cooperating with the mill owners were leaders of the Vatan Party and the Da'i-Javad organization, an anti-Tudeh group established in Esfahan by an influential bazaar merchant and aided financially by the city elders and mill owners.[72]

Reacting to the 18 April incident, the UWE called a strike to demand an inquiry into the riot and immediate action against the instigators. Otherwise, the UWE declared, under the terms of the 10 July 1943 agreement,[73] it would expel from the factories all workers belonging to the reactionary parties implicated in the riot. At the same time, the mill owners traveled to Tehran[74] where they succeeded in arranging the dismissal of yet another governor-general: less than two weeks later Bahrami was replaced by Reza Afshar.[75]

With the arrival of Reza Afshar, the mill owners gained another ally; for the first time since 1941 the governor-general and the army commander were of one mind concerning organized labor. The day after his arrival, Afshar called the leaders of the UWE to his office and threatened them with exile if they continued to cause trouble.[76]

On 1 June 1944 another fight broke out between the UWE and its opponents at the Pashmbaf mill.[77] This was followed by a similar disturbance at the Rahimzadeh mill a month later. The employers were accused by the UWE of locking out the workers and bringing in hired thugs to attack them.[78] A report by the U.S. Office of Strategic Services (OSS) confirmed the legitimacy of the workers' grievances, dismissing the mill owners' claims that the organizers of the strikes were "men trained in Soviet schools training labor agitators."[79]

At this point, Fadakar's presence in the Majles proved of some benefit to the Esfahani workers. Speaking to the chamber, Fadakar charged that the new governor-general, Reza Afshar, had been sent to Esfahan at the request of the textile mill owners with instructions to eliminate the UWE.[80]

As a result of further protests by Fadakar, who was a member of the Tudeh Party bloc, and other Tudeh deputies in the Majles, Prime Minister Sa'ed was forced to recall Afshar as governor-general and replace him with the more moderate Mohammad-Ali Varasteh.[81] A man of some political skill, Varasteh arrived in Esfahan on 13 July[82] after which the level of violence dropped dramatically.

The UWE's next crisis originated not from any action of the employers but from within its own ranks. When leaving Esfahan to take his seat in the Fourteenth Majles, Fadakar had entrusted the union's affairs to its seven-member board composed of Ahmad Kaf'ami, Ne'mattollah Bahrampour, Hasan Omrani, Ali Ayazi, Karim Teimouri, Hasan Sarrafian, and Shams Sadri.[83]

As originally established, the board's membership was divided fairly evenly between adherents of the Tudeh Party and those opposed to the party's domination. In line with Communist doctrine, and contrary to the wishes of the more moderate leaders, the radical Tudeh members on the board—Ne'mattollah Bahrampour, Hasan Omrani, and Karim Teimouri—would have subordinated the union to the party and placed part of its funds at the party's disposal. The two factions also differed over the ideological issue of private property.[84] Within a few months, Shams Sadri, an employee of the Risbaf mill, set about with employers' support tipping the balance of power established by Fadakar. Sadri and two other board members, Ahmad Kaf'ami and Ali Ayazi,[85] succeeded in expelling a Tudeh partisan, Hasan Omrani, and replacing him with one of their own men, Amir Amirkeyvan, giving them a majority on the UWE governing board.[86]

Sadri had risen to prominence during the brief term of Governor-General Afshar. When Afshar expressed his intention of dissolving the UWE,[87] Sadri, according to his own memoirs, appealed for continuation of the union: "Do not disappoint the workers. Do not throw them deliberately into the arms of foreigners. Do not turn them into traitors. These workers love their monarch. These workers love their country. Aside from bread, education, and health-care, they do not demand anything else."[88]

Sadri's plea achieved its intended purpose. Because of its obsequious tone, Sadri became a favorite of the mill owners. Later he was seen as the obvious choice to lead the anti-Tudeh union sponsored by the mill owners.

Sadri's intention was to sever the bond between the UWE and the Tudeh Party. To this end he attempted to exploit the dissension between Fadakar and the increasingly radical members of the Tudeh Party that was beginning to be noticed as early as August 1944.[89] Upon his return to Esfahan from the First National Party Congress, Bahrampour, a Tudeh leader on the union's board, delivered a report to a group of UWE members criticizing Fadakar and his past activities.[90] Prompted by Bahrampour's attacks against the popular Fadakar, Sadri traveled to Tehran to persuade the union's leader to make an open break with the party. Refusing to do so, Fadakar told Sadri that any open break between the Tudeh Party and the UWE would be to the disadvantage of the union. Without powerful allies, Fadakar believed the UWE would become prey to labor's opponents, foremost among whom he listed the "Anglo-Saxons." Once they succeed in separating the union from the party, Fadakar argued, they could then destroy the union with one blow.[91]

Having failed in his mission, Sadri attempted the ouster of his main Tudeh rival in the union, Ne'mattollah Bahrampour. Bahrampour was not easily defeated; on 26 September 1944 he issued a statement in the name of the Pashmbaf mill workers criticizing the "selfish acts" of the other UWE leaders and calling for new elections in all the mills. At the same time, the Pashmbaf workers declared their independence from the board of directors of the UWE, defended Bahrampour, and expressed their support for the Tudeh Party.[92] Further, they accused non-Tudeh leaders of the UWE of being in collusion with the mill owners and other "reactionaries."[93] The dissension among members of the governing board was gradually spreading to the general union membership.

By this time Fadakar had lost some of his former influence over the workers of Esfahan. Sadri's group rejected him as a friend of the Tudeh Party; Bahrampour and radical Tudeh supporters viewed him as a weak-willed moderate. This loss of support became apparent in late September 1944, when Fadakar returned to Esfahan to reconcile Sadri and Bahrampour and was prevented from speaking by the workers at Pashmbaf mill. In his place, the Tudeh Party sent the veteran Communist leader and Majles deputy, Abdossamad Kambakhsh. After he too was shouted down by workers loyal to Sadri, both he and Fadakar returned to Tehran. The Tudeh Central Committee then assigned Dr. Morteza Yazdi, another Tudeh deputy in the Majles, the task of resolving the Esfahan dispute. After consultation with the opposing factions, a joint meeting was convened on 7 October at which an agreement was signed by all parties.[94]

The agreement marked the complete takeover of the UWE by the Tudeh Party and the beginning of the end of Fadakar's influence on the Esfahan labor movement. The agreement stated that henceforth the UWE, being a part of the Central United Council (in May the Central Council had merged with a number of other pro-Tudeh unions to form the Central United Council), would be known as the Provincial United Council of the Unions of Workers and Toilers of Esfahan. Furthermore, as a CUC union, the Esfahan United Council (EUC), like all other affiliates, would scrupulously follow the political policies of the Tudeh Party.[95]

Although Sadri and his allies reluctantly signed the 7 October agreement, they continued their efforts to undermine the Tudeh-led trade union. Thus, on 25 December 1944, a Tudeh delegation composed of Taghi Fadakar, Dr. Fereidoun Keshavarz, and Abdossamad Kambakhsh, all Majles deputies, arrived in Esfahan to put an end to Sadri's opposition and to supervise the election of new representatives for each mill.[96] After anti-Tudeh representatives were elected in most of the mills, the board of directors of the EUC, on 8 January 1945, resigned in order to make way for new elections.[97]

After resigning from the board of the EUC, Sadri and his allies formed a union that was sponsored by the mill owners themselves.[98] The union's militant anti-communism disrupted the labor movement as effectively as gangs of hired toughs had done in the past. Formed in January 1945, the new organization called itself Ettehadieh-e Kargaran, va Pishevaran va Dehghanan-e Esfahan or the Union of Workers, Artisans, and Peasants of Esfahan (UWAPE) and claimed to represent workers in all the mills.

On 27 March 1945, the new union made its first public appearance. A procession of approximately a thousand workers set out from the mills and proceeded toward the union's headquarters, where the articles of association were to be read and approved.[99] As soon as the procession reached Chahar Bagh Avenue, pro- and anti-Tudeh shouts—and later rocks—were exchanged between Tudeh members on the roof of the party's headquarters and UWAPE members on the street. The marchers then attacked Tudeh headquarters, inflicting considerable damage on the building, destroying the furniture and injuring two of the Tudeh leaders. In order to preserve their "nonpolitical" image, and to disprove the accusation, made by

Radio Moscow, of pro-British sympathies, the UWAPE marchers moved on to the unoccupied offices of the three conservative parties, Vatan, Hamrahan, and Mardom, and totally destroyed them. Having taken care of the first order of business, the new union held its mass meeting at which fifty-two articles of association were read and approved by acclamation.[100] Late in March, the OSS reported that the Tudeh Party and the EUC had been eclipsed by Sadri's union.[101] The companies, as one of the mill owners remarked to W. J. Handley, the American labor attache, "were against all unions, but company unions could at least be tolerated as the lesser of two evils."[102]

The disturbance on 27 March was the first of several such incidents during the next few months. On 23 April 1945 Mahmoud Boghrati, leader of the Tudeh Party in Esfahan and a leading figure in the EUC, was physically attacked by the party's enemies.[103] On 22 May Ne'mattollah Bahrampour, the foremost Tudeh partisan among the Esfahan labor leaders, was attacked and injured by Tudeh opponents. The next day Bahrampour and his friends took revenge on Amir Amirkeyvan, Sadri's lieutenant, who had allegedly directed the attack against Bahrampour on the previous day.[104]

On the morning of 25 May, Hasan Sarrafian, formerly a UWE leader and more recently a leader of the UWAPE, was assassinated as he and six colleagues were standing in front of their union headquarters. British Consul Gault accused Bahrampour of plotting this murder, as well as having planned to assassinate two Majles deputies who were sponsors of the anti-Tudeh union.[105]

The deterioration in relations between Britain and the Soviet Union, and the takeover of the UWE by the Tudeh Party, totally changed Gault's attitude toward the union. Hence he took a leading role in the offensive against the Tudeh organizations in Esfahan. In June 1945 he reported, "If the anti-Tudeh can keep its ranks closed up and allow its leaders to direct its activities, I think it will succeed, for its position is strong." In a more direct reference to his own participation in the anti-Tudeh movement, Gault stated: "It happens that the Workers' Union [UWAPE] and the vested interests are now both in opposition to the Tudeh, not because of any community of ideological interest, but because both fear revolution, both have been offended by the Tudeh's contempt for religion, and neither wishes to see Persia fall under Russian, or for that matter, British influence. A nameless directorate can keep the two running together."[106]

Although Gault had joined forces with the mill owners to defeat the Tudeh-controlled EUC, he believed that the factory owners had "no sense of responsibility or social consciousness and are not sufficiently astute to realize the disservice they do themselves in trying to maintain the status quo."[107] He told the Foreign Office that the employers were the root of most trouble in Esfahan. They measured everything in terms of immediate financial profit or loss and had become accustomed to calling in the police whenever they had difficulties with their workers.[108]

Shams Sadri's violent antipathy to the Tudeh Party was appreciated not only by men of wealth and power in Esfahan, and by the British consul, but was also taken note of in Tehran. In the late summer of 1945, when the government was selecting a workers' delegation for the ILO conference to be held in Paris in November, Sadri and Amirkeyvan were among the four selected.[109] At the meeting, Sadri claimed that his union now had 153,000 members throughout Iran,[110] an exaggeration by a factor of about thirty.

In the remaining months of 1945, during which Prime Minister Mohsen Sadr imposed martial law and other repressive measures on most of the country, Sadri and his union became the dominant force in Esfahan. After Ahmad Qavam became prime minister the following February, and during a six-month period of conciliatory gestures toward the Soviet Union and the Tudeh Party, the EUC revived and attempted to regain its former control of the Esfahan unions.

On 26 March 1946, it was reported that street fighting had broken out between pro- and anti-Tudeh groups of factory workers, due in part to a recent decision by the mill owners to discharge nearly 1,000 workers because of low demand for their goods. On 6 April more than 900 discharged workers took sanctuary (bast) in the telegraph office and voiced their complaints to a representative of the prime minister's office, demanding that the mill owners be instructed to provide work for them.[111]

On 10 April, a month after the termination of the fourteenth session of the Majles, Fadakar returned to Esfahan to mediate the dispute over unemployment. According to Zafar, a Tudeh journal, every time a group of workers came to welcome his return, they were attacked by mobs sent by the employers.[112] The army commander, on the other hand, charged that Fadakar had entered Esfahan accompanied by a large number of "Caucasian thugs."[113] Gault reported that on the day of Fadakar's arrival, 2,000 partisans of the EUC took over all the mills in Esfahan,[114] and retained their control for the next six months.[115]

In response to objections by the mill owners to Fadakar's presence, the prime minister ordered his immediate return to Tehran.[116] Fadakar replied that the workers were physically restraining him from leaving town, insisting that the prime minister prevail upon the mill owners[117] to rehire those workers who had been discharged. The dispute was finally settled a few days later by the prime minister's emissary, Boroumand, Governor-General Varasteh, and Fadakar,[118] who then returned to Tehran, where he remained for several weeks.

All workers gained by the return of Tudeh power to Esfahan. The prime minister, for example, was persuaded to issue an ultimatum to the mill owners; if they did not pay the workers their overdue wages by 23 May, he would order their arrest.[119] A month later the prime minister warned all labor organizations and "those calling themselves labor organizations" to refrain from interfering in the affairs of the government under the pretext of safeguarding the rights of laborers. He concluded by declaring that all such disruptive elements, "who [might] be reactionaries in the clothing of labor," would be severely dealt with. The principal reason for this announcement, reported the American embassy, was "the anarchic state of affairs in Isfahan, where the Tudeh unions had seized control of the factories, discharged workers who refused allegiance to Tudeh and replaced them with Tudeh supporters, and had refused the factory owners access to the factories. The factory owners were physically threatened, and nearly all of them withdrew to Tehran for safety."[120]

The brief period of EUC supremacy ended on 7 September 1946, when Mozaffar Firouz, the new minister of labor and propaganda in Qavam's coalition cabinet, arrived in Esfahan, declared martial law, and issued orders for the arrest of Fadakar, who had returned to Esfahan sometime after May 1946. Having received word of Firouz's plans, Fadakar escaped to Tehran, where the Tudeh Party still held three cabinet posts. In a letter to the party, Fadakar acknowledged sixteen mistakes made by the leadership, including their attacks upon religion and their agreement to join Qavam's cabinet. Fadakar cabled his "condolences" to his party colleagues, warning them that "the old fox [Ahmad Qavam] has tricked you." Subsequently, he withdrew his active support from the party and practiced law in Tehran, where he frequently met with other dissident Tudeh members.[121]

Led by Shams Sadri, the UWAPE became inactive in April 1946, when the ban on political activities was lifted by Prime Minister

Qavam and the EUC made a comeback.[122] Once martial law was imposed in Esfahan in September and hundreds of EUC members were arrested, the UWAPE once again became active. By December all employees were considered members of the employer-sponsored UWAPE.[123]

The Disintegration of the Employer-Sponsored Unions

At the time of its formation, Sadri's union, the UWAPE, served to draw workers away from the EUC. But after the EUC was forcibly repressed, the local authorities and mill owners regarded the UWAPE as an annoyance. In fact, Sadri's union, having become an affiliate of the government-organized Union of the Syndicates of Iranian Workers (Ettehadieh-e Sandika-ha-ye Kargaran-e Iran, known as ESKI)[124] in early 1947, was in the words of the British consul "a very docile watch-dog indeed." Even so, the mill owners rendered it even more harmless by creating dissension between Shams Sadri and his ambitious lieutenant, Amir Amirkeyvan, which resulted in the formation of a separate union by Amirkeyvan and his followers. The new union became the nucleus of the Central Union of Workers and Peasants of Iran (Ettehadieh-e Markazi-e Kargaran va Keshavarzan-e Iran), known as EMKA, during the first half of 1947.

The British consulate in Esfahan was extremely annoyed with the turn of events:

> The owners are a thoroughly bad lot and are, really, the cause of all this trouble because they will always intrigue against each other among themselves and among their workers. For instance, the owners were instrumental in creating the anti-Tudeh Workers' Union [UWAPE] eighteen months ago as a counterbalance to the Tudeh [EUC], which was then strong. When they later saw that the Tudeh were defeated and that the union they built up was becoming too strong for their liking they began to undermine it.[125]

The rivalry between Sadri and Amirkeyvan spilled over into the Labor Congress held in Tehran in October 1947. By this time the fifteenth session of the Majles, packed with members of Prime Minister Qavam's Democratic Party, had convened. The workers of

Esfahan no longer had a representative in the legislature; the Tudeh Party was being suppressed, Fadakar had withdrawn from political life, and Esfahan was represented exclusively by members of the privileged class: Haj-Seyyed-Habibollah Amin (Amin-ot-Tojjar), Azizollah Ezaz-Nikpay and Safa Emami.

In order to weaken Amirkeyvan's position in Esfahan, the mill owners, through their Majles representative Azizollah Ezaz-Nikpay, succeeded in preventing Amirkeyvan's attendance at the Labor Conference, despite Vice Minister Naficy's best efforts to seat Amirkeyvan's delegation.[126] Naficy considered Sadri "an undesirable element in the labor movement and a traitor to the workers' cause."[127]

With the weight of governmental authority behind it, the ESKI dominated the labor scene in Esfahan from 1946 to the early 1950s. The elections of worker representatives in the factories, which were held in September and October 1947, resulted in an almost complete victory for the ESKI candidates. In the one factory where an EUC leader was expected to be elected, the mill owner selected the representative himself.[128]

The civilian and military authorities in Esfahan insisted that the local EMKA union, under the leadership of Amir Amirkeyvan, must merge with ESKI, led by Shams Sadri,[129] whom the British consul described as the "puppet of the government and the employers [who] displays little real interest in the workers' conditions."[130] Although Amirkeyvan reluctantly agreed to cooperate with ESKI for the limited objective of fighting the Tudeh Party and the EUC, the authorities were not satisfied, and continually threatened Amirkeyvan and his associates with exile from Esfahan. Moreover, Amirkeyvan's followers underwent all manner of persecution, including arrest. Amirkeyvan lacked funds,[131] and his main protector, Vice Minister Naficy, was prevented from defending him too energetically by the uncertain position of the Ministry of Labor itself.[132] Naficy had, however, expressed a desire to see Amirkeyvan's EMKA become the stock from which a "genuine trade union might develop."[133]

In Esfahan, as in other Iranian cities, independent trade unions were short-lived. The UWE was taken over by the Tudeh Party, a move that led to its repression. Taghi Fadakar, the only labor leader who could be considered "independent," was attacked by both the right and the left, and was expelled by the Tudeh Party in April 1948.[134] The central government did not allow him to return to Esfahan until 1951, when Dr. Mohammad Mossadegh was elected prime minister. When a second-best substitute, Amir Amirkeyvan, turned up to take Fadakar's place, the combined power of the mill owners, the army, and the Shah immobilized him. Instead of a true trade union, the workers were given an ineffectually paternalistic Ministry of Labor. As Fatollah Mo'tamedi, the director of the Esfahan Department of Labor, asserted in 1947, the workers no longer had any sincere interest in trade unions; they knew that the government was very strong in Iran and would "protect" them.[135]

One way in which the government was supposed to protect them was to set a minimum wage. Although at Abadan a minimum wage of 35 rials was established after the general strike of July 1946 (see Chapter 6), no such determination was made for Esfahan's workers until June 1948. At that time, the High Labor Council established a daily minimum wage, based on an eight-hour day, of 43 *rials* for unskilled adult workers in Esfahan. The cash wage, however, was set at 29.5 *rials*. The balance was made up by a bonus of a month's wage at Nowrouz (21 March, the Iranian New Year), by the distribution of 67 kilograms of bread a month, and by the issue of two suits of clothes a year.[136] This minimum wage was not implemented as of 1949, or, to the knowledge of this writer, at any time thereafter. Consequently, as the British consul reported, the wage rate applicable to the vast majority of workers was "so low that overtime beyond the legal eight hours . . . [had] to be worked systematically to enable the operators to earn a living wage."[137]

Inadequate wages were not the workers' only problem; sometimes wages were not paid at all. In June 1948, the British embassy reported that the wages of the 1,300 employees of Pashmbaf mill "were two months in arrears, and the directors, who were assumed to have misappropriated the funds, have fled to Tehran."[138] Even the director of Esfahan's Department of Labor, who, in lieu of a union, was supposed to be looking after the interests of the workers, was charged with embezzlement of workers' aid funds and with connivance with employers. He was relieved of his duties pending an investigation of charges.[139] Such was the sordid conclusion of the labor movement organized by Taghi Fadakar.

In summary, the years between 1941 and 1944 offered a unique opportunity for the workers of Esfahan, unhindered either by foreign interference or repression by the central government, to establish their own independent trade union. An important feature of the UWE was its willingness to negotiate patiently and to compromise with the employers and the government to further the economic aims of its members. As the nation entered the years of confrontation and the lines were drawn between pro- and anti-Soviet forces, Esfahan, too, became an arena of conflict. A first casualty of this conflict was the independent and moderate UWE, which split into two extreme factions: the Communist-led EUC and the company-sponsored union affiliated with ESKI. Once the years of repression arrived, Esfahan was one of the first cities to come under martial law, during which the labor movement was easily eradicated. Only Shams Sadri's union remained to maintain the façade of trade unionism in Esfahan.

Rise and Fall of
Government-Controlled Unions
1946–1953

Formation of Anti-Tudeh Unions

*T*HE MINISTRY OF LABOR and Propaganda was formed in the summer of 1946 at the urging of Great Britain to combat the growing influence of the Communist-led labor unions.[1] Once this mission had been accomplished, the emerging autocracy used the ministry in conjunction with the security forces to subjugate and eliminate the remaining labor unions, even though they were led by anti-Communists.

Suppression of the anti-Tudeh labor unions was not sponsored by Great Britain or the United States. As labor strikes increased at the Anglo-Iranian Oil Company (AIOC) installations in 1946 and the Labour Party came into power in Britain, British policy in Iran changed from one of total opposition to trade unionism to one of supporting "nonpolitical" unions. This was also in line with the U.S. government's view of the proper role of labor unions. But this policy of supporting "nonpolitical" trade unions within an increasingly autocratic political system was untenable for a number of reasons. First of all, the expectation that an autocracy would tolerate any kind of independent association, whether union or not, was unrealistic. In the second place, it was at best naive to think that workers, once unified, would refrain from exercising their potential power to challenge a government which so blatantly ignored even the most basic tenets of the country's constitution.

Thus, the primary Anglo-American policy of supporting an autocratic monarchy was in conflict with the subordinate policy of promoting "nonpolitical" labor unions. Since the former policy superseded the latter, it was natural that the two Western powers would witness the elimination of the anti-Communist independent labor unions without using their influence on the unions' behalf.

The principal anti-Communist trade union was created by the Ministry of Labor and Propaganda. Discussions in the spring of 1946 between the British embassy in Tehran and the Foreign Office had led to a two-pronged attack against Communist influence among Iranian workers: the destruction of the Tudeh trade union federation, CUC, by whatever means possible, and the creation of "nonpolitical" labor unions to take its place. This approach had already been attempted on an ad hoc basis in Tabriz[2] and Esfahan[3] by provincial government officials. In September 1946 the Ministry of Labor and Propaganda in Tehran sponsored the most ambitious project of this kind: the creation of Ettehadieh-e Sandika-ha-ye Kargaran-e Iran (Union of the Syndicates of Iranian Workers) that became known by its acronym, ESKI.

The chief motive for the establishment of ESKI was never in doubt. According to one of its founders, Ahmad Aramesh, then the vice minister of the Ministry of Commerce and Industry and from January to June 1947 the minister of labor: "The government could not destroy the Tudeh union by force, since suppression of unions leads to a reaction in their favor among the workers."[4]

The best strategy, Aramesh explained, was to organize another labor union to rival the CUC, and this the Ministry of Labor and Propaganda, in conjunction with the ruling Democratic Party of Iran, proceeded to do. Habib Naficy, the first vice minister of labor, while professing that he had wished for a *spontaneous* nonpolitical union, justified the ministry's sponsorship of ESKI by asserting that "the danger of Tudeh was too great . . . to have waited for a non-Communist union to develop from grass roots." Naficy expressed the hope that the ministry's support of ESKI would eventually be endorsed by the emergence of leaders from the union's ranks and the evolution of ESKI into "a genuine union led by and for the workers."[5] The ministry had justified its sponsorship by declaring that the workers were "ignorant of their rights and of the procedures of organizing, and [were] in need of direction." Except for Tudeh

organizers, who were accused of receiving their instructions from the
Soviets, the ministry alleged that no leader had been available from
the ranks of the workers.[6]

Naficy's desire for a "genuine union" was sincere, though perhaps shortsighted. What he had not considered was the inherent
antipathy of the emerging autocracy toward the development of an
independent union. It should be remembered that the CUC had
flourished only at a time (1941–1946) when political power was not
yet concentrated in the court. We have already noted that on every
occasion when the monarch had the opportunity of bringing other
centers of power—the legislative branch, political parties, the press,
and labor unions—under his own control, he moved with vigor to
do so. Although acquainted with the political views of the government
and its supporters, Naficy seemed to believe that they would
voluntarily permit the growth of a new power center that would
gradually diminish their own prerogatives.

In the autumn of 1946, the executive branch was acting without
the restraints of a Majles in session. Earlier that year, Soviet troops
had withdrawn from Iran, leaving a relatively clear field to conservative groups allied with the shah. The young monarch, Mohammad-
Reza Pahlavi, with the encouragement of American Ambassador
George Allen, was becoming more openly assertive, and the most
powerful independent politician—Ahmad Qavam—was losing adherents. This was surely an inauspicious time for establishing a "genuine
union."

Ahmad Aramesh delegated the formation of ESKI to Mehdi
Sharif-Emami, his brother-in-law and director of the Dispute
Settlement Department of the Ministry of Labor and Propaganda.[7]
Sharif-Emami reported that in mid-September 1946, "a number
of workers and engineers who were members of the Council [CUC]
met . . . and formed a new union."[8] The American labor attache,
William J. Handley, later wrote that ESKI was run "nearly entirely
by government functionaries, many of whom [were] entirely socially
illiterate."[9] The social gulf between ESKI's leaders and the workers
partially explains the union's lack of success.

Established by the ruling Democratic Party of Iran and directed
by the officials of the Ministry of Labor and Propaganda and
government-appointed factory managers, ESKI had little difficulty
in adding names to its membership lists. According to Handley,
workers employed in government-owned factories were obliged to
join the union as a condition for holding their jobs.[10] Another

observer stated that familiar methods of bribery and coercion were used to recruit ESKI members.[11]

Although ESKI succeeded in enrolling a relatively large number of members, and even in drawing crowds to its rallies, it clearly lacked a loyal, enthusiastic following.[12] As one reporter remarked two years after ESKI's formation, "Its achievements other than in obtaining names on its membership rolls have not been remarkable."[13] This was confirmed by another American Embassy dispatch: "ESKI has at least become Iran's dominant union in terms of membership, but there are no signs yet that the workers themselves are gaining control of ESKI or that ESKI had made deep inroads on workers' loyalty."[14]

As a result of the arrest in April 1947 of Reza Rousta, leader of the CUC, and the suppression of activities by the union and the Tudeh Party, the two organizations were unable to hold mass demonstrations on May Day 1947. ESKI attempted to fill the vacuum, but, as the U.S. military attache reported: "Where Tudeh used to put thousands and thousands of screaming workers on the streets for a demonstration, Qavam's labor boss, Sharif-Emami, . . . found it necessary to hold no demonstration because of the apathy which surrounded his group."[15]

Entry of the Court into Labor Affairs

Following the purge of Qavam's cabinet in October 1946, the shah, assisted by his twin sister, Princess Ashraf Pahlavi, moved at a faster pace to rebuild the power of the court and to extend its control throughout the body politic. They realized that an independent ESKI, or a union in the hands of Qavam or some other political opponent, could present a stumbling block in their efforts to strengthen the monarchy. To avoid this possibility, they decided to bring ESKI under their own control with the assistance of the army chief-of-staff, General Ali Razmara. In the spring of 1947, several important moves were made within a few weeks: Reza Rousta was arrested,[16] and Sharif-Emami, a labor expert, was removed as head of ESKI and replaced by Khosrow Hedayat, a court loyalist.[17] Considering his aristocratic background, his managerial position as director-general of the State Railway Organization, and his unpopularity with the workers, Hedayat could hardly be presented as a credible representative of labor.

In June of that year, following the changing of the guard at ESKI, Aramesh was replaced as minister of labor by Salman Assadi, another Democratic Party leader. According to Aramesh, who was not happy with the turn of events, Hedayat, soon after his appointment as president of ESKI, lost "every semblance of kinship with the workers." He "developed into a great dandy, with pomaded hair, perfumed handkerchiefs and flashy cravats." He would come to ESKI meetings, stay ten minutes, and then leave. "He actually thinks he has the workers behind him," said Aramesh, "and does not realize that the workers cannot feel loyalty to a person so out of touch with the working class."[18]

In line with the court's desire to do away with all independent centers of power, the replacement of Sharif-Emami by Hedayat was a significant step toward the assimilation of non-Tudeh trade unions. The independence of Prime Minister Qavam was already severely circumscribed after October 1946. The Fifteenth Majles was much more responsive than its predecessors to the wishes of the court,[19] and the press was coming under greater control. The activities of the Tudeh Party and the CUC had already been curtailed, and steps were now being taken to ensure that ESKI, which was created to destroy one power center, would not itself become one.

The term "nonpolitical" was never properly applicable to ESKI; its creation and its actions were as politically motivated as those of the CUC. As a key member of Qavam's newly organized Democratic Party of Iran, Aramesh formed ESKI as an auxiliary of the party—a mirror image of the CUC and the Tudeh Party.[20] Moreover, as of April 1947, ESKI was headed by a "political" appointee of the court who was commissioned to take control of the labor union away from Qavam and the Ministry of Labor.

A brief review of the stated policies of the union shows that ESKI *had* adopted positions on major political issues. The chief difference between the CUC and ESKI was that the CUC followed the Tudeh line, which was sympathetic to (and perhaps dictated by) the Soviet Union, while ESKI followed the political line of the court, which was sympathetic to the United States. The specifics of ESKI policy were described by the American embassy:

> The basis of ESKI's existence is political opposition to Tudeh. ESKI is opposed to international and domestic Communism, and,

on the positive side, is pro-Court, and, to a lesser degree pro-army. It has no wish to see imprisoned Tudeh members released; it favors the formation of the Senate [in addition to the Majles], as does the Shah; it is on record as supporting . . . a request for a large loan from the World Bank; it approves of the utilization of foreign specialists, including the American Military Mission.[21]

While the court intended to make ESKI serve its own purposes, Habib Naficy, in his role as vice minister of labor, continued to pursue his original plans for the development of independent labor unions. In April 1947, when Sharif-Emami was forced to resign from ESKI and Reza Rousta was arrested, Naficy candidly admitted to William Handley that ESKI was created for the purpose of "smashing" the CUC. "This it succeeded in doing," he said, "and now it must go. Last year we destroyed and this year we shall build."[22]

Naficy, with the enthusiastic support of the anti-Communist coalition composed of Great Britain, the United States, the court, the army, the Democratic Party of Iran, and the factory owners, had been able to destroy the CUC. He was now attempting to build a "nonpolitical and independent" trade union movement without considering which of his allies in the "destructive" phase of his plan would now support him in the building phase. The truth was that in his effort to build "independent" labor unions, Naficy could only count on the support of the British and American labor officials, a small number of colleagues in the Ministry of Labor,[23] and a handful of pro-government labor leaders.

The factory owners were violently opposed to the Ministry of Labor and all its works. Whereas the shah wished to use the ministry for his own ends, the industrialists, led by the Esfahan textile mill owners, wanted to abolish it.[24]

Commenting on the antagonistic view of the factory owners toward the Ministry of Labor in June 1947, K. J. Hird, the British labor attache, reported: "If present legislation is not applied to private Iranian industry, it will not be because the aim is primarily to attack the Oil Company, but because the ministry's proposals with regard to private Iranian industry clash with the private interests of individuals high in government office and power."[25]

E. P. Harries, the British member of the World Federation of Trade Unions (WFTU) delegation that visited Iran in the winter of 1947,[26] came to the same conclusion. In his report, Harries stated that there were a few enlightened people, such as Naficy in the

Ministry of Labor, who could improve the situation, "but this group [does] not hold real political power, and their efforts could and probably would be undone at any moment by the wealthy factory owners who [have] influence in the cabinet."[27] As Harries remarked, Qavam had surrounded himself with men who opposed any kind of trade unionism.

Naficy wished to make the Ministry of Labor the protector of the workers, and in August 1947, when he was promoted to the post of acting minister of labor, he made an effort to convince the workers that henceforth they could rely on the ministry for support. As proof of his good intentions he followed the unprecedented policy of permitting strikes. One such strike, involving 4,500 brick kiln laborers in the Tehran area, began on 26 August of that year. The major issue involved in the dispute was the employer's attempt to take advantage of anti-CUC sentiment to reduce wages. During the previous year the CUC had succeeded in increasing the wage rates of the brick kiln workers from 40 *rials* to 65 *rials* per thousand bricks delivered. Now that the CUC had been suppressed and ESKI was attempting to champion the workers' rights, the employers reduced the rate to 60 *rials* per thousand bricks. In response to ESKI's appeal of the case to the High Labor Council, the Council proposed a compromise rate of 64.5 *rials*. The workers rejected these terms and called a strike, which Naficy's Ministry of Labor unexpectedly recognized as legal. The dispute was finally settled by the intervention of Prime Minister Qavam, who, at Naficy's urging, presided over a meeting on the matter at his residence.[28]

In spite of opposition to the Ministry of Labor by a powerful domestic political bloc led by Esfahan industrialists, Qavam continued to support it for two reasons. First, Naficy had made a passionate appeal to Qavam, declaring that the prime minister and the Democratic Party needed the ministry to demonstrate their support of the workers' cause. Otherwise, he said, "the workers would say Qavam was not their friend, that he had formed a Ministry of Labor only as counter-propaganda against the Tudeh Party, and was abolishing the ministry now that the Tudeh Party was no longer strong."[29] To add force to his argument, Naficy told Qavam that he would no longer carry out his duties if the role of the ministry was diminished. Anglo-American pressure was the second and perhaps more compelling reason why Qavam decided to maintain the ministry as it was. On 24 September, Ambassador George Allen urged the prime minister to continue the ministry, and his appeal was followed a few days later by a similar recommendation by his British counterpart, prompted by instructions from the British government.[30]

By far the strongest advocates of the Ministry of Labor were the British. To the AIOC, the ministry was a shield against the pressures of the CUC. When Ebrahim Hakimi replaced Qavam as prime minister in December 1947, Le Rougetel, the British ambassador, during his first call on the new prime minister, discussed only one point of substance: the future of the Ministry of Labor. He urged Hakimi not to yield to "some influential persons in this country. . . [who] desire this ministry to be suspended or reduced to vanishing-point." Prime Minister Hakimi reportedly assured Ambassador Le Rougetel that he had no such intention and as a matter of fact was assigning the task of supervising the Ministry of Labor to Dr. Mohammad Sajjadi, the minister of national economy.[31]

As far back as January of that year, the British embassy had begun urging the Ministry of Labor to proceed with the amalgamation of all trade unions into a single federation corresponding to their own Trade Union Congress (TUC). The proposed Iranian Trade Union Congress (ITUC) could claim to represent all the Iranian workers. "As non-Tudeh unions expand in number and membership the Minister [of Labor] may more actively support the policy of federation," reported Ambassador Le Rougetel.[32] By May 1947, when the CUC had been further weakened and its leader, Reza Rousta, imprisoned, Naficy was ready to hold a congress of all registered unions in Iran and to bring them together into some sort of federation. If this was not successful, he would leave the various unions unfederated until such time as a "natural and spontaneous movement toward federation" manifested itself.[33]

As a public relations gesture, Naficy, on 25 May 1947, invited the few remaining leaders of the CUC to attend a congress for all labor unions. With its leader in prison, the CUC refused to respond to the call, and the congress did not convene until October.[34]

Naficy was not a man easily discouraged. While ESKI, with the backing of the court and the army, had become the dominant union among those recognized by the Ministry of Labor, a number of smaller non-Tudeh unions were also developing. These included the Central Union of Workers and Peasants of Iran (Ettehadieh-e Markazi-e Kargaran va Keshavarzan-e Iran), known by its acronym, EMKA—which was led by Ali-Asghar Noureddin Ashtiani. The CUC having refused to cooperate, Naficy's next goal was to bring together

ESKI, EMKA, and other small non-Tudeh unions to form a national federation.

As a gesture of goodwill toward the smaller unions, Naficy offered them status equal to that of the larger ESKI within a national labor organization. Moreover, the ministry suggested dividing the country into zones and assigning to ESKI and the smaller unions specific areas in which each would have sole right to organize. The smaller unions would be free to initiate their own policies, and would be bound in no way by ESKI. Naficy argued that their presence in a larger body with ESKI would enable them to form a labor front on points of common agreement and to present their case more effectively to the Ministry of Labor.[35]

Naficy's efforts seemed to bear fruit, when, on 30 August 1947, the leaders of ESKI, EMKA, and a smaller organization reached an agreement to coordinate their labor union activities.[36] Two weeks later, however, the two larger unions decided to dispense with the third, and signed an instrument of affiliation without giving up their independence.[37]

The ESKI–EMKA agreement led to the call for a labor congress, which was eventually held on 28 October 1947 in Tehran.[38] Of the 130 delegates, 46 represented EMKA; the rest were from ESKI unions. Most parts of the country, except the AIOC area of Khouzestan, were represented;[39] the largest number of delegates were from Tehran (50), followed by Esfahan (19), Mazandaran (16), and the railway areas (17).[40]

Disintegration of Government-Controlled Unions

The Labor Congress of 28 October 1947 put to an initial test the Ministry of Labor's stated policy of supporting independent labor unions. ESKI, as already noted, was led by Khosrow Hedayat, a court appointee. Although the union was nominally affiliated with Qavam's Democratic Party, it had in fact become an instrument of the court and the army. In Esfahan, ESKI was affiliated with the employer-sponsored union (UWAPE) led by Shams Sadri.[41]

EMKA,[42] on the other hand, proclaimed itself the only real organization of workers and peasants of Iran. An EMKA publication announced that the union enjoyed "full independence and happily is not supported by any party or political body."[43] Agreeing with this contention, the American embassy stated, "At the moment EMKA is indeed the labor union which comes closest to being independent of party and politics."[44]

EMKA was led by Ali-Asghar Ashtiani, who maintained his personal loyalty to Qavam in spite of the prime minister's imminent fall from power. Also associated with EMKA was Sadri's adversary, Amir Amirkeyvan,[45] who had refused to enter into collusion with the Esfahan employers, thereby inviting their opposition.

In order to undermine Amirkeyvan's position in Esfahan, the mill owners had asked their Majles deputy in Tehran, Azizollah E'zaz-Nikpay, to prevent Amirkeyvan's attendance at the October congress. Naficy, however, in accordance with his policy of assisting "independent" trade unions, supported Amirkeyvan and opposed Shams Sadri, who was supported by the factory owners.[46]

To prevent the collapse of the congress,[47] which was supposed to create a united front against the CUC,[48] Naficy reached a compromise with E'zaz-Nikpay, whereby both Sadri, leader of the employer-sponsored union UWAPE, and Amirkeyvan, leader of EMKA, were to be permitted to attend the congress.[49] This was not to be, however: ESKI, under the leadership of Hedayat, was covertly collaborating with the mill owners and failed to keep the agreement. Amirkeyvan did not receive his invitation until the day the congress opened.[50]

The second phase of the scheme to prevent Amirkeyvan's attendance at the congress occurred on 5 November when Sadri challenged the credentials of Amirkeyvan and his group. "What trade union do the gentlemen in question belong to?" Sadri demanded. "If they have a union, where is it situated? What number of workers do they have? How are these [union] representatives elected?"[51]

Amirkeyvan, Ashtiani, and the forty-five EMKA delegates were forced to leave the congress and to convene a congress of their own.[52] The main congress, now limited to unions controlled by the court, elected an Executive Committee of twenty-one members and reorganized the union's administration before adjourning on 7 November.[53] Khosrow Hedayat was elected general secretary of the ESKI federation, and a newcomer to the labor leadership, Aziz Ghezel-bash (a railway worker), was chosen as assistant to Hedayat.[54]

Clearly, Hedayat was swimming with the current while Naficy was not. Naficy had been badly humiliated by Hedayat, Sadri, and the influential Esfahan employers in a single move. While Hedayat was supported by those attempting to preserve the prerogatives of the privileged, Naficy, the reformer, was without powerful domestic allies. His only visible source of support was Prime Minister Qavam, who himself was discharged the following month, and the labor officials of Britain and the United States.

After the split between ESKI and EMKA and the dismissal of Prime Minister Qavam, Hedayat led the drive to push EMKA out of the labor field altogether. He justified his position by arguing that the primary purpose of ESKI was to fight the Tudeh Party and that betterment of the workers' lot was a secondary issue. By competing with ESKI, he said, EMKA was playing into the Tudeh Party's hands.[55]

The fight against communism was becoming sufficient justification for the most undemocratic tactics. When Prime Minister Qavam, himself an aristocrat, could be removed from office and his political party taken over by force[56] on the pretext that he was flirting with the Soviets, the elimination of a small labor union like EMKA was easily justified. With the once powerful Qavam out of office, the powerless Naficy could no longer stand in the way of the Hedayats, who were so agile in joining the winning side.

From 1941 to 1947, the major division of political loyalties was between the pro- and anti-Tudeh forces. Henceforth, however, political figures were compelled to be either pro-court or anti-state. Politicians who supported the status quo easily changed their labels from anti-Tudeh to pro-court; for them it was one and the same thing. Those who were not willing to switch sides overnight, however, invited the same fate suffered by Ahmad Qavam. One such person was Ali-Asghar Ashtiani, leader of EMKA, who continued to express publicly his loyalty to Qavam even though the former prime minister's fortunes had collapsed.

On the afternoon of 14 December 1947, ESKI toughs descended on the EMKA club and took possession.[57] This unlawful act was engineered by Khosrow Hedayat, who was, at the same time, head of the ESKI, secretary of the High Labor Council, a deputy of the Majles, and a member of the new (anti-Qavam) Executive Committee of the Democratic Party of Iran. The raid on the EMKA club had obviously been cleared with the court and coordinated with, if not directed by, the army, since soldiers were on hand to give assistance to ESKI "on the pretense of keeping order."[58]

With the Soviet army out of Iran, international labor organizations rebuffed, CUC leaders in prison, an independent prime minister turned out of office, and Western embassies silent, the emerging autocracy no longer needed the cooperation of the Ministry of Labor to achieve total control of the labor unions. The army could carry out the assignment much more efficiently. It is well to remember that on exactly the same day in the previous year, 14 December 1946, the army, in cooperation with the Ministry of Labor, had closed down and occupied the headquarters of the CUC "as detrimental to the interests of the state."[59] Now, ESKI was used as a weapon against a more independent labor union. In 1946 the justification was that the CUC was an agent of a foreign power. A year later the justification was that "EMKA was using its clubhouse for political rallies and supporting an ousted prime minister who had fallen out of favor with the Shah." It would not be long before ESKI and Hedayat himself outlived their usefulness.[60] Two years later it was reported that the former leader of ESKI was totally discouraged and was living in voluntary exile in Switzerland.

In point of fact, EMKA's only "crime" was that Ashtiani, its leader, had remained loyal to Prime Minister Qavam at a time when everyone was being required to show their allegiance to the court. According to the American embassy, "Ashtiani had been a supporter of Qavam, since the beginning of Qavam's term, ostensibly because Qavam had promised in return for Ashtiani's support to pass a basic labor law and to increase the farmer's share of the crop."[61]

In spite of Ashtiani's anti-Communist credentials, he was treated not very differently from the Tudeh leaders. The usually courageous Naficy was uncharacteristically timid in the face of court-inspired aggression against EMKA. He asserted that the Ministry of Labor had played no part in ESKI's raid on the EMKA club, "but remained strictly neutral."[62] An American embassy report suggested a reason for Naficy's inaction following the attack by ESKI: "The personal relations between Naficy and the court are close. Naficy's father was tutor to the shah, and Naficy's wife (Nee-Ozma Adle) by his second marriage is a confidante of Princess Ashraf. Naficy is also close to Princess Ashraf . . . . Naficy has easy access to the shah's ear, and counts upon him as one of the best sources of political support."[63]

The American embassy's response to the attack, however, could not be excused by a plea of impotence. Embassy officials now adopted a defensive attitude toward a political situation they had helped to create. They pretended to believe that the expulsion of Qavam, encouraged by their own ambassador, George Allen, and the subsequent actions of the pro-American victors were unconnected.

After giving support to the court and the army to oust independent leaders, they were now taking a condescending view of the "natives." "The disposition of the clubhouse is of small concern. The fracas, however, throws a revealing spotlight on the kind of leadership and the type of activities which constitute trade unionism in Iran."[64]

The British embassy's attitude was the same—feigning ignorance. While the British ambassador, "to preserve Iran from Communism," was actively aiding the country's emerging autocracy, the British labor attache was deriding his own proteges by reporting to his government that "there is little real understanding here of what unionism and democratic government mean or how they work."[65] While the army was occupying the premises of anti-Communist unions, as well as those of CUC affiliates, the same labor attache was suggesting that Iranian trade unionists be invited to visit Great Britain "for intensive study of first essentials, such as the administrative procedures and the activities of union branches, the work and responsibilities of shop stewards, and the practical procedures of joint negotiations."[66]

The attack on EMKA headquarters by ESKI thugs was followed several months later by another assault—this time from within. On 10 July 1948, EMKA's founder, Ali-Asghar Noureddin Ashtiani, and his aide, Dr. Afrashteh, were expelled from the union on the charge that they were "toadies" of Mozaffar Firouz, now exiled, and were steering the union on a "political" course.[67] The leaders of the new Executive Committee of EMKA were Engineer Majid Mohiman and Amir Amirkeyvan,[68] who was now beginning to demonstrate his political agility. The American embassy offered its own explanation for the attack against Ashtiani: "The Ashtiani faction is pro-Qavam and therefore not a partisan of court or army."[69]

Once again the reaction of the two Western embassies was revealing. The British labor attache, K. J. Hird, was clearly delighted to learn of Ashtiani's ouster. Apparently, the union leader had not been sufficiently pro-British or sufficiently receptive to his advice. Keeping in mind that the new EMKA leader, Majid Mohiman, was not a worker, but the manager of the government-owned Tehran Silos, it is interesting to read Hird's comments on Ashtiani's expulsion: "I believe I forecast the Trade Union split . . . It is, I think, a wise move, for Ashtiani is not a bona fide Trade Unionist. Mohiman is far more intelligent and reliable, and has a very high regard for British achievements; both he and Amir Amirkeyvan, who under the new organization is in charge of international affairs, continuously seek our guidance and honestly try to follow it."[70]

In the EMKA dispute, not only the British but also the Ministry of Labor were siding with Mohiman against Ashtiani. While the ministry was advising Mohiman on how to respond to Ashtiani's counteroffensive, Amirkeyvan was conferring with Vice Minister of Labor Naficy, as well as with Mohiman, about future EMKA strategy. Naficy, always ready to put the best face on things, was frank about his support for the Mohiman-Amirkeyvan faction of EMKA. In his opinion EMKA, purged of Ashtiani, was the closest thing Iran had to a "nonpolitical" union.[71]

And yet in another year Naficy would concede privately that freedom of association did not exist in Iran. He would also admit that the Ministry of Labor was unable to protect unions from army interference or to force an unsympathetic governor-general to allow union organization in his province. The Ministry of Labor, for that matter, had not even been able, in the face of management opposition, to seat a labor representative, properly elected by the workers, on the factory council of the government-owned silo in Tehran. Nevertheless, Naficy would continue to assert that "for public dissemination the Ministry of Labor would insist that Iranian workers enjoy freedom of association."[72]

Khosrow Hedayat had demonstrated more than once his adaptability to a changing political environment and his skill in games of intrigue. It will be recalled that in the autumn of 1947, when Qavam's fortunes were declining and the power of the court was increasing, Hedayat had been able to shift his loyalties to the winning side very quickly. Consequently, he was a co-conspirator with the faction in the Democratic Party of Iran that included Reza Hekmat (Sardar-Fakher), president of the Majles, and that took over the party headquarters and organization from the Qavam faction. At about this time, ESKI, now under the control of the court and the army, disassociated itself completely from the Democratic Party, even though the party was then under the control of Hedayat's friends. Thus, the ESKI newspaper, *Kargaran-e Iran*, carried the message at the top of its front page: "We are not connected with any party. Our aim is to obtain the rights of the workers and farmers."[73]

With the CUC's public activities at a standstill and the small, semi-independent EMKA recently split into two factions, ESKI was the only labor union that operated both openly and as a single unit. The November 1948 Congress of ESKI, however, brought this state of affairs to an end. For some time there had been indications that trouble was brewing between Hedayat and his deputy, Aziz Ghezelbash, who seemed convinced that he could seize control of ESKI from Hedayat.

While Hedayat came from a prominent family and was educated in Europe, Ghezelbash was a worker of the "horny-handed" type that other workers could understand. Naficy conceded that Hedayat was resented and considered an outsider by the workers, but felt that Ghezelbash was not capable of meeting employers, government officials, and politicians on equal terms. In his view, therefore, Hedayat was needed until ESKI was strong enough to stand unaided.[74]

Nevertheless, Ghezelbash, who enjoyed the support of about 70 percent of the ESKI members, made his bid to unseat Hedayat. The struggle came to a head in November 1948 at the Tehran provincial conference, which met to appoint delegates to the Second Annual General Congress of ESKI. Under Hedayat's orders the conference was held in the ESKI club room at the tobacco factory where Hedayat's faction had absolute control. Soon after the meeting opened, the Hedayat group began a verbal attack on Ghezelbash that eventually led to blows. Ghezelbash proposed to Hedayat that the conference meet in a neutral club room.[75] Hedayat ignored Ghezelbash's proposal, and instead called a separate conference of pro-Hedayat representatives, who faithfully appointed a Hedayat slate of delegates to the General Congress.[76]

ESKI's Second Annual General Congress was held in Tehran from 22 to 29 November 1948. It was attended by 105 delegates from Tehran and the provinces and claimed to represent 71 separate trade unions and a total membership of 70,000.[77] When a representative from the provinces asked publicly why the deputy-director, Ghezelbash, was not present, he was told that the workers had failed to appoint Ghezelbash as a delegate.[78] Hedayat, in his report to the members, admitted that very little had been achieved during the preceding year.[79] The congress then passed a resolution expelling Ghezelbash and his friend Abbas Pour-Hashemi, voiced due "recognition of the services rendered and sacrifices made by Engineer Khosrow Hedayat," reappointed Hedayat as secretary-general of ESKI, and elected 31 persons to the Central Board of Directors, among them the controversial Esfahan labor leader, Shams Sadri.[80]

Once again it was made clear that popular labor leaders could not compete with leaders appointed by the court. According to the

American embassy, Hedayat won over Ghezelbash not because the former had the support of the working class, but because he "had influence in the Majles, in government circles, in the army, and in the Court."[81] Without political power the workers could not even begin to achieve their goals.

More specifically, Chief of Staff General Ali Razmara, who, with the shah's backing, was taking an increasing role in labor affairs,[82] called in Ghezelbash and his followers and "advised [them] not to attempt to form their own union or to break up ESKI." To make sure that the message was understood, Ghezelbash and his associates were given the same stern warning by the local police.[83]

In many ways Ghezelbash was the Ministry of Labor's last prospect as leader of a "genuine, nonpolitical and independent" trade union. If the government had been sincere in its profession of support for trade unionism, the Ministry of Labor would have demonstrated the same vigor in denouncing Hedayat's dictatorial methods as it had done in criticizing the CUC. However, recognizing the new political realities, the ministry officials uttered not a word of public protest.

As vice minister of labor, Naficy was undoubtedly concerned with army and police interference with labor unions' affairs. Powerless to put an end to such interference, he nevertheless attempted to have a voice in security measures that might affect workers. At his urging, a board was formed which was to have the responsibility of coordinating internal security measures.[84] The board first met immediately after the ESKI Congress of November 1948. It consisted of the mayor of Tehran, representatives from the army, gendarmerie, national police, Ministry of the Interior, and Ministry of Labor. This meeting was the first formal step toward involving the Ministry of Labor in internal security matters.

At the end of June 1950, General Ali Razmara was elected prime minister, the first prime minister since Qavam to take a personal interest in labor affairs. He had been dealing with the question for a number of years in his previous capacity as army chief-of-staff. Wanting to give support to the Ministry of Labor's unification drive, Razmara spoke at a workers' rally in October, the first Iranian prime minister to attend a trade union function. Following the rally and during Asadollah Alam's tenure as minister of labor, a workers' congress was held in Tehran in February 1951. It was organized by Amir Amirkeyvan, Ezattollah Hedayat (Khosrow Hedayat's cousin who had replaced him as head of the Railway Organization and then of ESKI), Baba'i (leader of the Association of Employees of Government Offices), Mahmoud Moshar, and Aziz Ghezelbash acting as organizers. As a result of this congress a new national labor federation called the Iranian Trade Union Congress (ITUC) was formed which included ESKI and EMKA.

The assassination of Prime Minister Razmara by Khalil Tahmasbi on 7 March 1951, as Razmara was attending a memorial service for a deceased religious leader, discouraged any immediate hope of unifying government unions. As an American embassy report suggested: "It is likely that if Prime Minister Razmara had lived the [unified] trade union would have proved, however short the duration, the rallying point of most non-Communist labor leaders."[85]

The Strike of the Oil Workers

The veteran Hossein Ala, member of the Fifth Majles and ambassador to the United States at the time of the Azerbaijan crisis of 1946,[86] was given the task of forming a caretaker government after Razmara's death. The assassination of the prime minister at the height of the country-wide debate over the nationalization of the oil industry was followed by a strike of the employees of the AIOC—the first since the Abadan strike of July 1946.[87]

The strike began on 22 March 1951, at Bandar Shapour on the Persian Gulf, but the first large-scale walkout occurred three days later at the Agha Jari oil field northeast of Abadan. The next day, Prime Minister Hossein Ala proclaimed martial law after "Communists" called for a general strike in the oil region. On 27 March all communications between Tehran and the strike-bound oil fields were cut by the government, and the government sent troops to the region. The cause of the strike was the AIOC's sudden withdrawal of housing allowances and certain other amenities. A report prepared by the American embassy in Tehran described the situation:

> It is very unlikely that the company would have been able to persuade workers, especially those of technical and skilled labor categories, to go to the isolated fields areas if such extra allowances had not been offered. The company contended, however, that in Agha Jari and certain other parts of the fields areas the housing and amenities program previously initiated by the company, was largely completed. The workers resented the proposed withdrawal

because they had by this time come to consider the allowances as a part of their anticipated income. No one questioned the company's legal right to withdraw these allowances, but few doubted that the timing of the withdrawal, and the manner of the announcements, were badly timed and executed from a public relations point of view. Many Iranians resented what they contended was an arbitrary withdrawal, although the company claimed to have consulted the workers.[88]

The strike, which moved swiftly from Agha Jari to the Naft-e Sefid, Lali, and Masjed-e Soleiman oil fields in Khouzestan, was followed by student agitation in Abadan. Having carefully screened the apprentices earlier to exclude those who might be "Communists or Communist sympathizers," the company did not consider the agitation to be serious at first, but soon realized that it faced a major crisis.

The crucial day of the general strike was 12 April, when an estimated four thousand workers and sympathizers, resisting police efforts to break up an outdoor meeting of apprentices, were fired on by military forces attempting to disperse the crowd. Three British nationals and six Iranians were killed and six British and eleven Iranians wounded. "This tragic affair" the American embassy reported, "served to make the leaders of both the British and the Persians more cautious. The strike tapered off as it began. There had been no real crystalization of strike intentions at the beginning and no concrete, final and friendly solution at the end." On 20 April, the strike ended when the AIOC announced a bonus of 35 percent to those workers who "resisted all efforts of intimidation." At the high point of the strike, virtually all thirty thousand Abadan refinery workers were idle, as well as a fourth of the workers in the fields areas.[89]

The Mossadegh Government and Labor

About two weeks after the Khouzestan strike, the Majles elected Dr. Mohammad Mossadegh as prime minister with a mandate to implement the oil nationalization law. Thus Mossadegh's top priority was to resolve the oil problem through negotiation with the still powerful British government. Consequently, a number of domestic issues, such as policy toward labor organizations, were given secondary importance. Morever, Prime Minister Mossadegh paid no particular attention to workers as a group; nor did he have any especial interest in the formation of labor organizations or political parties. To him labor was just another segment of the Iranian population which supported him. He demonstrated neither support for nor opposition to trade unions. According to the American embassy, the prime minister had told a visiting delegation of the International Confederation of Free Trade Unions (ICFTU) in November 1952 "in plain language" that he had "no use for organized labor, nor did he intend (nor think it useful) to enlist its support for his government."[90]

Mossadegh, like his predecessors, chose his ministers of labor on the basis of their compatibility as members of his cabinet rather than on the basis of their qualifications for the job. This was illustrated by the selection of Mohammad-Ebrahim Amirteimour (Kalali), a veteran Majles deputy and an independent-minded tribal leader from Khorasan Province, as his first minister of labor. It seemed that the appointment of aristocratic landowners to that post was becoming a tradition: in 1946 Iran's first minister of labor, Mozaffar Firouz, a Qajar prince, was replaced by his uncle, Moham-mad-Vali Farmanfarmaian, a major landowner in Azerbaijan. And General Razmara appointed Asadollah Alam, heir to the lands of Birjand, as his minister of labor in 1951.

In November, however, Amirteimour was transferred to the Ministry of the Interior, and on 19 July 1952 Dr. Ebrahim Alemi, a professor at Tehran University, was appointed to replace him. Subsequently Naficy resigned as vice minister of labor, and was replaced by Dr. Afshar, another professor from Tehran University. In July, Dr. Shapour Bakhtiar replaced Afshar.

The reaction of the American embassy officials to these changes is noteworthy. They derided the Ministry for being "chaotic and confusing," and criticized Amirteimour for his attitude toward the Ministry. Vice Minister Afshar was described as a man "without previous knowledge of labor who entered the post of undersecretary without ambition to learn and left the post with the reputation of being vain, lazy and incompetent." By contrast, Dr. Bakhtiar, who replaced Afshar, was described as "hard-working, ambitious, and aggressive."[91] Nevertheless embassy officials were displeased with his appointment because, as noted by the reporting officer: "There has periodically been some doubt about the political reliability and Western leanings of Dr. Bakhtiar, who consistently talks a moderate socialist philosophy, but who occasionally makes appointments far to the left of Fabian socialism. It is thought that he is so far left of center that his politics, coupled with his ambition and 'drive,' makes him, from the American point of view, one of the weak pegs in the coterie of Ministers and undersecretaries."[92]

The Iranian Trade Union Congress, led by Amir Amirkeyvan and Aziz Ghezelbash, was publicly critical of Prime Minister Mossadegh and his policies. Its criticism, however, placed the ITUC and its leaders in an unenviable position, because the union, in the words of the American embassy, had "rather ineptly named itself 'Iranian Trade Union Congress,' a name too closely modeled on the British organization, which allegedly contributed to its support."[93]

Dr. Mossadegh, however, unlike his predecessors, tolerated criticism and did not attempt to suppress the union. Instead, he utilized a much more effective means of dealing with his critics: the two labor leaders were publicly chastised for their failure to support a government that was engaged in a life-and-death battle against Great Britain. The effectiveness of this approach was confirmed by the American embassy: "Because of the popularity of the Mosadeq [sic] Government with the poorest members of the Iranian social community, there is no doubt but that these leaders lost prestige with their own followers."[94]

In July 1952, Dr. Mossadegh resigned following a dispute with the shah over control of the military. When the shah appointed Ahmad Qavam as prime minister to replace him, there was a national uprising referred to by the Persian date on which it occurred—Siyom-e Tir (26 July)—and Dr. Mossadegh was returned to power.

The Mossadegh government was under attack from both the right and the left—from the right by the pro-Western conservatives led by the court; from the left by the pro-Soviet radicals led by the revitalized but still illegal Tudeh Party. As a means of limiting the growth of communism, the Ministry of Labor ceased to register labor unions after May 1952. This action was taken, according to the American embassy, "because the Ministry [of Labor] feared that it would be inviting government endorsement of Communist-front organizations masked as nonpolitical trade unions."[95]

This policy was extended to the newly nationalized oil industry. In its annual Labor Report for 1952, the American embassy reported, "There is lack of government support of any trade union organization in the nationalized oil industry and great pressure on the oil workers not to organize against their own government." At the same time, it was reported that the membership of the only government-recognized union in the oil industry, the Central Union of Oil Workers of Khouzestan, had declined to as few as five hundred members.[96]

In August 1953 the shah issued a decree dismissing Dr. Mossadegh as prime minister. The prime minister refused to obey the order, declaring it to be illegal. Within three days the Mossadegh government was overthrown by the armed forces and by paid street mobs in an operation coordinated by the United States Central Intelligence Agency.

Although it would appear that the policy of Dr. Mossadegh toward labor unions was not very different from that of his predecessors, unlike previous governments, Mossadegh seemed to enjoy the support of the workers: "One of the testimonies to the strength of the Mosadeq [sic] Government with the working people of Iran has been their willingness to follow his request not to strike and to conduct their affairs in such a way as not to embarrass the government."[97]

9

Workers Without Unions
1953–1963

Government Attitude toward Labor

*A*FTER THE COUP D'ETAT of August 1953, in which
the government of Dr. Mohammad Mossadegh was overthrown, the relationship between the government, the employers, and
labor reverted to what it had been during the autocratic rule of Reza
Shah. From 1941 to 1946, the arbitrary power of the government had
been tempered by the reinstatement of a constitutional monarchy.
No longer enjoying the total support of the government in their
dealings with the workers, the employers had become less formidable.
The workers, on the other hand, had been strengthened by their new
allies: the Tudeh Party, a handful of deputies in the Majles, and a
number of sympathetic newspapers. In short, the political power of
the workers vis-à-vis their employers and the government had
increased during this period.

As noted above, the ascendancy of the court over the cabinet
and the Majles, which began in October 1946 and continued until
1951, when Dr. Mohammad Mossadegh became prime minister,
eroded most of the political gains made by labor. The coup d'etat
of August 1953 completed this process. Henceforth, all pretensions
of government support for organized labor ended, even though the
shah and his ministers periodically spoke favorably on the subject.

Prior to 1953 the government publicly claimed to favor independent trade unions; it objected only to labor organizations it branded

193

as "political." After the overthrow of the Mossadegh government, the autocracy entered a new phase in its development; it relied more heavily on a modernized military and, as of 1957, on the newly established State Organization for Information and Security or Sazman-e Ettela'at va Amniyat-e Keshvar (SAVAK) to stamp out any kind of opposition or dissent.

R. E. Cunningham, an officer of the American embassy, accurately described the relationship among the Iranian government, the ruling elite, and the workers. In the "Basic Survey of Labor Conditions in Iran," dated 26 September 1955, Cunningham stated:

> The Government of Iran traditionally has been controlled by the "thousand families." In practice this means that, except for the Mosadeq regime, the processes of government have been controlled by the Shah and a group of men who are members of the important landowning families of the country. In these circumstances, it is natural that Iranian governments have been extremely conservative in internal affairs, desiring to maintain the *status quo*, which in Iran is the nearest modern manifestation of feudalism, and making only the minimum concessions to the demands and pretensions of the working classes.[1]

As long as it was restrained by the constitution, the government was obliged to take account of the workers' demands. As soon as political power once again became concentrated in the court, the position of the workers deteriorated while that of the employers improved, as noted by Cunningham: "The various Governments of Iran have never been interested in improving the lot of workers as a humanitarian or social end in itself, but have concerned themselves only with preventing the rise in the ranks of labor of elements which might prove a threat to the wealthy landowners."[2]

The government of General Fazlollah Zahedi, the leader of the anti-Mossadegh collaborators and prime minister from 1953 to 1955, looked upon labor affairs primarily from the point of view of internal security. According to Cunningham, the government of Hossein Ala (1955–1957) retained to a large extent the same orientation.

As for the officials who were charged with implementing the laws, R. C. Johnson, an officer of the American embassy asserted: "Government officials generally may believe in progress and modernization . . . But they too spring from the entrenched ruling classes, share the same anachronistic if not feudalistic attitudes, and have not broken with their past associations as did Mosadeq."[3]

Ministry of Labor

The reemergence of autocracy transformed the Ministry of Labor, which under Habib Naficy (its vice minister from 1946 to 1951) *intended* to promote "nonpolitical" labor unions into a department for internal security. According to the "Basic Survey of Labor," the ministry was looked upon by the rest of the government as "a security agency and it is expected to insure that potential threats to national security within the ranks of labor are suppressed before they have a chance to do any harm."[4]

As the youngest and least important government department, the Ministry of Labor was never seriously expected to engage in extensive improvement of the lot of the workers. It was commonly agreed by most observers that the generally poor condition of the workers was not due to a lack of legislation. The problem continued to be that of enforcement. This was confirmed by R. C. Johnson in 1957, as he reported to Washington:

> It is virtually impossible in Iran today to visit any business establishment in which the labor law is not being violated in a number of important ways. The most common violation, to be seen in nearly every plant of any size, is the employment of child labor. Even in the most progressive establishment in Iran, children under the legal minimum of 12 can be found doing production work (sometimes under the guise of training) on a full-time basis at a rate of 10 *rials* (13 cents) a day.[5]

One indication of the low priority assigned to the Ministry of Labor and a reason for its ineffectiveness in law enforcement was its small budget. For the fiscal year 1954–1955 (Iranian year 1333) the Ministry's budget was less than one-third of 1 percent of the total budget; the following year it had declined to one-fourth of 1 percent. As the Labor Survey observed, "If this amount of money were used only for paying the Ministry's 537 employees it would yield an annual salary of only 60,279 *rials* ($803.72) per year to each from the Minister down. It is therefore obvious that there is no money left to perform even the most elementary tasks usually alloted to [the Ministry] of Labor."[6]

Inadequate pay to civil servants was the major cause of corruption. Few cabinets, however, were willing to tackle the problem at its roots. According to the Labor Survey, "Every Iranian government [had] begun its term of office with a pledge to root out corruption in the Civil Service. The Shah periodically [made] pious statements on his resolution to end this menace."[7] However, little ever came of these resolutions, since, as noted earlier, in the lower echelons of government the problem was due to "employment of too many people at wages which [were] too low to provide a decent living."[8] In the upper echelons the problem was of a different nature; it was a question of "follow the leader." As corruption in high places was tolerated and, according to some, even encouraged (as a means of cementing political loyalties), it continued.

Employers

Since the Ministry of Labor and the labor law did not give adequate protection to the employees, working conditions depended almost entirely on "the goodwill or benevolence of the individual plant owner."[9] Since government did not give high priority to the plight of the workers, the undisciplined employers continued "to follow a feudal pattern in which the workers [appeared] to acquiesce."[10] Under such circumstances no employer voluntarily allowed the formation of labor unions in his plant. In his book, *Mission for My Country*, published in 1961, the shah alluded to this when he said:

> Employers often adopted a most reactionary view of democratic as well as other trade unions. Unconsciously or not, they copied some of the worst anti-union practices of employers in Britain or America in the days before the legitimate role of unions was recognized in those countries. Instead of giving sympathetic consideration to the workers' requests for better wages and

improved conditions, employers would place on their payrolls gangs of toughs hired just to intimidate the workers.[11] These men received much higher wages than the regular employees and employers chose to pay good money to such characters instead of using it to meet the workers' rightful demands.[12]

The employers' attitude toward labor relations also characterized the way they managed their production. Low wages served as a disincentive to improve efficiency. In the words of the U.S. Labor Report:

> There are many modern mills and much machinery, but the same master-servant atmosphere prevails as has prevailed for centuries in the bazaar shops. In spite of modern automatic German or Japanese looms that are designed to permit one worker to operate 16 to 22 at a time, Iranian mill owners are content to have one worker operate 4 looms at a time. The proof that Iranian workers can learn and can produce in terms of modern production is demonstrated by the American-managed Chitsazi mill where workers run 20 looms per man.[13]

Although the older generation of employers was unlikely to change its attitude toward labor relations and production management, the appointment as factory managers of a younger generation of managers, many of whom had been educated in the West, was seen as a hopeful sign by some observers. Most members of this new breed, however, while technically competent, had little or no socio-political awareness nor much understanding of the lot of the working class. Many of them viewed workers as a factor of production and from an "industrial engineering" point of view. Workers were to be utilized in ways contributing to improved efficiency and reduced unit cost.

Private employers were not alone in their unsympathetic view toward workers' rights. A large proportion of the industrial labor force was employed in enterprises owned or controlled by the government. In these firms the prospect for trade unions was even more bleak, as government officials looked upon "concerted action by [their] workers as a form of subversion and [employed] national security forces quickly to suppress such action."[14]

Workers

The labor force of Iran had shown itself to be highly trainable. Workers had been able to acquire new skills when offered a reasonable opportunity to do so. "There have been problems in connection with skill levels and productivity of workers," reported an American labor specialist, "but since the solution of these problems lies largely with management, such deficiencies should not be charged to labor."[15]

As can be seen from Table 2, by 1955 the size of the nonagricultural labor force had increased to a little over a million.[16]

TABLE 2
Nonagricultural Labor Force in 1955

Type of Work	Number of Workers	% of Total
Crafts and Miscellaneous Jobs	268,000	25.2
Professional and White Collar Jobs	229,000	21.4
Armed Forces, Gendarmerie and Police	185,000	17.4
Private Manufacturing Industries	150,000	14.0
Civil Service	125,000	11.7
Petroleum Industry	62,000	6.0
Government Controlled Industries	46,000	4.3
Total	1,065,000	100.0

After the coup of August 1953, the security measures employed by the government to eliminate what it regarded as Communist influence had succeeded, at least temporarily, in destroying all remnants of the labor movement and subjugating the workers, or—as it is said in Persian—"putting them in their place." This outcome was interpreted differently by different observers. The description of the Iranian workers by an American embassy official only six months after the overthrow of the Mossadegh government typifies the view of many foreign and most upper-class Iranian observers: "The lethargy of the Iranian workers is such, their labor unions so feeble, and their Moslem fatalism in accepting their lot so complete, that without outside agents fanning the latent grievances into strike action, there would be little overt strike activity by the workers."[17]

R. E. Cunningham, the American diplomat, made the same erroneous judgment as he mistook what was on the surface for what was underneath: "The workers have become accustomed to receiving a small share of the country's income, and it is difficult to convince them that they might be entitled to a larger share. Workers often accept the most flagrant violations of their rights with hardly a murmur of protest."[18]

To substantiate the above claim, he wrote: "The largest textile factory in Isfahan had not paid its workers for almost three months. Work finally stopped, and there was considerable manipulation and negotiation to get the factory in production again. A temporary board of directors was appointed. They agreed to pay one month of the wages in arrears, with a vague promise of the remainder sometime in the future. Under these conditions the workers returned to work and their morale was reported high."[19]

These statements seemed to be making certain assumptions regarding the character of Iranian workers—that they were inherently submissive and that their behavior was unrelated to the political-security measures employed against them. Moreover, the statements raised a number of questions. Was the behavior of Iranian workers inherently different from that to be found in other lands? Was not their behavior a testimony to the effectiveness of government repression? Cunningham seemed unaware of recent Iranian labor history and the government's relentless opposition to the labor movement. It is not surprising, then, to find many adherents of this view even today, puzzled and in a state of disbelief as they view the behavior of these same "lethargic" and fatalistic Moslems in the unfolding drama of the Islamic Revolution.

Apparently not considered by Cunningham was the dire poverty that brought about the workers' revolt. No mention is made of the role of the security forces in Esfahan and their treatment of the leaders who would have led a continuation of the strike referred to by Cunningham.

R. C. Johnson of the U.S. embassy, the first of a series of more open-minded labor officials, was able to delve into the root causes of the current predicament of the Iranian workers. In his report to the embassy, he called their working conditions "abominable in most industries and individual factories throughout Iran," and, he continued, "little is being done to improve them."[20] As for the workers themselves, Johnson wrote in January 1957: "The labor force in this country is probably the most docile in the world. Its demands are few and its expectations are small. The average worker asks only for fair treatment, for the opportunity to earn the minimum amount of money to feed, clothe, and shelter himself and his family and to be paid the money he earns. He will work long hours in extremely poor conditions if those two simple demands are satisfied."[21]

With unusual impartiality Johnson declared, "part of this docility and general tractability is attributable to labor's lack of organization."[22] "It is necessary to state here that the lack of conflict between labor and management is partially attributable to labor's lack of spokesmen and organizational outlets for protest, and its acceptance without much question of its general lot."[23]

Tudeh Unions

After 1947, the workers no longer enjoyed the protection of trade unions independent of the state. From 1941 to 1946 the Tudeh Party, whatever criticism it may have earned, must be given credit for effectively advocating and advancing the cause of the working class and labor unions. Even the American embassy could not ignore this fact:

> The first serious threat to the *status quo* in modern times was [made by] the Tudeh Party, which, through its labor arm . . . made the first successful effort to organize labor and to inspire united effort in favor of change.[24]

> The only true labor leaders this country ever produced, the only workers' representatives who were willing to go out on a limb on behalf of labor, were for the most part unfortunately Tudeh Party members, some perhaps driven to that extreme by economic and social adversity of a kind that can only be compared with conditions in England almost a century ago.[25]

This support by the Tudeh Party for labor continued at a much reduced rate from 1947 to 1949, since the party was itself under attack from the government. In February 1949 the abolition of the Tudeh Party and the Central United Council (CUC), its trade union federation, effectively ended the public status of the two organizations. Although they temporarily surfaced during the Mossadegh era (1951–1953), they were severely dealt with in the following years.

In September 1953, a month after the overthrow of the Mossadegh government, the Office of the Military Governor of Tehran (predecessor to SAVAK) announced that a Tudeh Party network and a cache of weapons had been found. The following year a secret military organization of the Tudeh Party was discovered. In October 1954 the first of a series of executions of Tudeh army officers began; nine were shot in that month and five the following month. In November a secret printing house and an alleged[26] storage area for ammunition belonging to the party were seized, and in January 1955 the party's youth organization was discovered and 68 of its members held in custody. In March, thirty-five leaders of the Tehran Provincial Council of the CUC were arrested.

Although the CUC could no longer represent the workers, no other labor union had been able or permitted to take its place. It was not surprising, therefore, that the CUC continued to be popular with a large number of workers. Although the suppression of the CUC had deprived it of the bulk of its active members, nevertheless it was estimated in 1955 that a hard core of leaders numbering around five hundred continued to maintain a cadre organization "which could be activated with very little difficulty when the occasion arose."[27]

As long as the workers were unable to have their grievances redressed, or at least heard through legal channels, the Tudeh Party and its trade union federation remained their sole champions. This view was confirmed in the 1957 report by R. C. Johnson: "Iranian conditions cannot but favor the long-term growth of Communism in the Iranian working class, and the fact that there was no visible increase in Communist activity during 1957 is a result of official vigilance."[28]

Government Unions

While destroying those trade unions organized by the Tudeh Party, the government professed a desire to see genuine, nonpolitical unions take their place. These promises were not fulfilled, however; there were no genuine autonomous labor unions in Iran after 1947. In his report, Johnson wrote: "True, there are labor unions in Iran, but [they] bear only a slight resemblance to the organizations in Western countries. They must operate under government and management restrictions and suspicions that make almost any functioning at all practically impossible."[29]

As already noted, various Iranian administrations since the early 1940s had reacted to the Tudeh challenge in different ways. Prime Ministers Mohammad Sa'ed, Mohsen Sadr, and Ali Razmara tried suppression, which did as much to inhibit the development of independent labor unions as to damage the CUC. Prime Minister Qavam, after his conciliatory gestures toward Tudeh unions in the first half of 1946, created his own captive labor union federation, ESKI, with which to counter the Tudeh threat. These unsuccessful strategies were characterized by the U.S. embassy as having "done much to discredit in the eyes of the workers the potential non-Communist labor organizations which might otherwise have attained positions of strength among the workers."[30]

The "labor unions" that were formed after 1953 were described by an American observer as "weak and ineffective, often dominated by management, and with leaders who [were] more interested in personal political power than bettering the lot of the workers."[31] Many of these "labor leaders," he declared, were in fact "individuals in the pay of the security authorities for the purpose of reporting on the activities of workers and attempting to impose government policy upon them."[32]

As noted in Chapter 8, the remnant of ESKI and its rival EMKA were consolidated by the Ministry of Labor, and with the advice of British labor attache, K. J. Hird, were assimilated into the Iranian Trade Union Congress (ITUC) (Kongereh-e Ettehadieh-ha-ye Kargaran-e Iran). Thus the ITUC inherited membership in the International Confederation of Free Trade Unions (ICFTU), of which ESKI had been a founding member.[33]

Although the ITUC had been defunct since 1951, the government of Prime Minister Zahedi decided to resurrect it because the stance taken by Aziz Ghezelbash and Amir Amirkeyvan against the Mossadegh government[34] had returned them to favor. Ghezelbash was given the post of ITUC president, which he retained until at least 1963, Amirkeyvan was appointed secretary-general, and Majid Mohiman was put in charge of its international affairs.[35]

Although little pretense of support for organized labor was made within Iran, the government was eager to present a progressive image abroad. Accordingly, the Ministry of Labor each year sent a delegation that included the ITUC leaders to the International Labor Office (ILO) conference in Geneva.[36] Iranian workers, however, gained very little from these gatherings. As the 1955 report by R. E. Cunningham stated: "Every year the delegation returns with the recommended conventions approved at the Conference. Every year these conventions are solemnly submitted to the Parliament. To date, not a single one of these conventions has been ratified by Iran, and in no case has the Government ever made a serious effort to urge ratification."[37]

In summary, officially approved labor unions were reduced to a handful, and were led by individuals who often had no previous connection with labor; rather, they were "politicians who [had] chosen this field as their particular sphere of influence."[38] The ITUC leaders, for example, had little contact with the workers and made no significant efforts to obtain better conditions for them. As a testimony to their political maturity, the workers of Iran, who had so enthusiastically supported the nongovernment trade unions during the 1940s, refused to be associated with any of these governmental creations.

Syndicates and Factory Councils

The labor laws of 1946 and 1949 had recognized the workers' right to form unions, or "syndicates," as the government preferred to call them. Use of the term "syndicate" as a synonym for labor union was misleading in the Iranian context—perhaps intentionally so. A syndicate (*sandika*) was defined as an association, or guild, of workers or employers in one craft. Thus an association of self-employed tradesmen, such as bakers, was represented as a labor union.

The section of the labor law dealing with the formation of syndicates was so designed as to make such association extremely difficult. Under the 1949 labor law, for example, no union was legal until it had applied for registration with the Ministry of Labor and had its constitution and officers approved. The law went into minute detail as to what the constitution had to contain.[39] Also, the founding members had to pass a security clearance.[40]

Although the 1949 labor law severely restricted the abililty of workers to form syndicates and to strike, it nevertheless gave them the right of electing their representatives within their place of work on the factory councils. In practice, however, even this basic right

was denied. The employer, either by virtue of his established influence
in high places or because he could and did bribe poorly paid local
officials, controlled the factory council. The law provided for a factory council made up of three representatives—one each for the
employer, the worker and the Labor Department: "The laborers
nominate candidates for this position. The names must then be
submitted to the provincial Labor Officer, who sends it to the police
and Army . . . [Army Intelligence][41] either of which agency may
disqualify a candidate for political reasons."[42]

Officials of both the army and the police were known to be
subject to bribery, and it was possible for a desirable candidate to
be eliminated by the employer even before voting. Another hurdle
was the election itself, in which management could bring pressure
to bear and the labor officer who supervised procedure could
influence the election almost at will.[43]

Given an increasingly autocratic system of government, un-
enlightened employers, and workers without unions, labor's situation
was truly unenviable. With their organizations suppressed and their
leaders banished, the workers, nevertheless, were not permanently
subdued. Whenever their conditions became intolerable, they struck
back. Little is known of the frequency of these work stoppages because no records were kept in a central location by the government.[44]
It is known, however, that these strikes were rarely the result of
premeditated action on the part of a union or group of workers.[45]

The principle of government control over labor affairs was
firmly established in the labor law of 1949. Disputes had to be settled
through a series of three successive boards, each of which had a
minimum period for arriving at a decision. No strike was legal until
this procedure was exhausted. Employers could force postponement
of strike actions for six months or longer by making full use of board
action.[46]

On those rare occasions when the representative of the Ministry
of Labor was not subservient to the employer, the decision regarding
a labor dispute was already two (employer and workers' "representative") to one (government) before the case was heard. If for some
reason the company's factory council could not settle the matter, it
was placed before the Settlement of Disputes Committee (Hei'at-e
Hal-e Ekhtelaf) in the area. According to an American observer,
"Here too, the employer has usually rigged the selection of the
committee so that he loses only when he wants to."[47] In Tehran this

general condition was tempered a little by the fact that there the government, ever sensitive about collective action, was quicker to end the strikes by concession or repression.[48]

Wages and Working Conditions

Since political issues could no longer be raised after 1953, the workers' demands were limited to economics—particularly wages. Iran's minimum wage, set for the first time in 1947 following the Abadan general strike,[49] had remained unchanged notwithstanding the tremendous rise in rents, food, clothing, and other costs of living.[50] In 1947, the cost-of-living index stood at 780, based on the 1937 index of 100. By 1961 it had increased by an average of 67 index points per year.[51]

In 1961 the Ministry of Labor conducted a survey of prices in Tehran for workers' market basket commodities.[52] The result was not published, for it revealed that a worker with a wife and two children had to take home a minimum of 178 *rials* ($2.37) a day in order to feed and clothe his family at a minimum standard of decency and health. This compared to a minimum wage of 50 *rials* a day in Tehran. The minimum wage for the rest of the country remained the same as in 1947—35 *rials* a day.[53]

As low as the minimum wage was, an American labor official reported that in many segments of Iran's industry, this rate was "avoided by the hire of underaged minors and women."[54] Thus, many unskilled workers—children and women particularly—were "lucky if they [could] get the minimum wage."[55] A comprehensive survey of wages and living conditions conducted in Qazvin, a city about eighty miles west of Tehran, revealed that 22 percent of the work force were earning between 10 and 29 *rials* per day. In Yazd, a city in central Iran, many workers were receiving as little as 6 *rials* a day.[56]

On the other hand, the twenty-one thousand seasonal employees who worked only seven months a year had struck for higher wages a number of times in recent years,[57] winning an average wage of 80 *rials* a day. However, thirty-five thousand of their co-workers were unemployed from 1960 to 1962 as a result of the economic crisis. Employees of the National Iranian Oil Company (NIOC), were among the highest paid, receiving a minimum wage of 99 *rials* a day.[58]

Low wages were not the workers' only concern. Sometimes they had gone as long as six months without receiving any pay. Even government payrolls had been as much as two months in arrears.[59]

Although the labor law of 1949 provided for an eight-hour day and six-day week, the traditional practice of "sunup to sundown" continued, except in the few modern plants where working hours were planned along with all other aspects of their operations.[60]

Two-Party System

As a result of the imposition of martial law and the arrest and execution of Tudeh leaders and officers, few labor disturbances occurred during the administrations of General Fazlollah Zahedi (1953–1955) and Hossein Ala (1955–1957). The year 1957, however, brought to an end this four-year period of silence. With the elimination of Tudeh labor unions, the political demands of workers had come to an end. Neither could labor make any economic demands since "nonpolitical" unions had also been suppressed. With the press under severe censorship and the Majles under increasing control by the court, the workers could no longer write individual letters of appeal, as they had done in the 1940s, and even in the early 1920s.[61] Nevertheless, conditions could and did become desperate enough for spontaneous strikes to occur in 1957. As a result, according to R. C. Johnson, the shah felt obliged to do something about this new unrest.

> The absence of union organization and a heavy-handed anti-labor policy on the part of the government for the most part deny Iranian workmen an avenue of protest, and much of the dissatisfaction is hidden below the surface as a result. It often takes the form of sabotage—deliberate fouling of machines and breakage of replacement parts are widespread practices among factory workers. But after a long period of surface calm in labor-management relations . . . labor erupted in at least eight important strikes during the last six months of the year, and several other walkouts were only narrowly averted.[62]

Four of these strikes were in the oil industry. Others occurred in the brick kilns of south Tehran, in a government textile mill at

Shahi, at Pashmbaf textile mill in Esfahan, and at a lead mine in the Khorasan province. In most of these strikes low wages were the key factor in dispute. During the Shahi strike in November, a thousand unemployed workers demonstrated in the streets of the town.[63]

The walkouts appeared to be spontaneous; the strikers had apparently taken all they were going to take without protest. R. C. Johnson reported the situation accurately and sounded one of a series of alarms: "Conditions are so unfavorable to workers that strikes of this kind can occur without strong organization or firm leadership, among workers [who are] accustomed to almost indescribably poor working conditions and low wages—and [are] characteristically phlegmatic about it. There is a real danger for the regime that opposition groups will see in this situation a golden opportunity and will attempt to utilize it for political ends."[64]

While the workers were suffering from inadequate wages and intolerable working conditions and were beginning to protest in spite of the consequences they would face, the shah decided to experiment with a two-party system within the general framework of his autocracy—an unlikely task. In April 1957 he instructed his newly appointed prime minister, Dr. Manouchehr Eghbal, to form the Melliyoun (Nationalists) Party and another of his close aides, Asadollah Alam, to form the Mardom (People's) Party. This sponsorship by the shah of a two-party system was to give assurance to his Western allies that Iran was led by a progressive monarch and was enjoying a democratic system of government.

While the Melliyoun Party was to rule, the Mardom Party was slated as the loyal opposition. Headed by Asadollah Alam, minister of the interior in the Ala cabinet, the Mardom Party adopted a "liberal" platform and organized a faction of some forty members in the Nineteenth Majles. It also established provincial branch organizations and set about championing the rights of labor. The party invited labor syndicates to affiliate with it and began organizing its own syndicates. An American labor observer noted, "The party itself was established by fiat from above and has no roots in the working class. Alam himself is one of the richest absentee landlords in Iran, and his party's declarations on behalf of labor are taken just about as seriously as those on land distribution and the division of huge estates."[65]

To critics of "democracy from above," the shah responded:

People sometimes criticize our new parties by saying that they have been imposed from the top rather than rising from the rank and file of the people. Some cynics even claim that the parties are mere puppets of the Government or the Crown. That, of course, misses the whole point about how you can foster parties in a newly developing country such as Iran. In a country where tradition still weighs heavily, nothing could be more unrealistic than to suppose that locally-based parties will spontaneously appear and flourish.[66]

Considering all that had been done by the government and the security forces to suppress every kind of spontaneous political movement, the shah's statement was disconcerting, to say the least. In his book, *Mission for My Country,* the shah had said: "If I were a dictator rather than a constitutional monarch, then I might be tempted to sponsor a single dominant party such as Hitler organized or such as you find today in Communist countries. As a symbol of the unity of my people, I can promote two or more parties without directly associating myself with any."[67] "The human values inherent in true political democracy," he continued, "merit whatever price we have to pay for it."[68] He then declared: "Fortunately, however, democracy is not without roots in Persia, and it is in harmony with the spirit of my country that we now have a planned programme of democratic development."[69] In 1975 the shah suddenly decided to eliminate all government-approved political parties and establish instead his single Rastakhiz (Resurrection) Party. It is not surprising that within a short time, an order was issued to remove his own autobiography from the bookshelves.

Having recruited a number of former Tudeh members, such as Dr. Mohammad Baheri and Parviz Rassouli, the Mardom Party presented itself as the champion of the workers. In the meantime, the ruling Melliyoun Party under Prime Minister Eghbal was taking the opposite tack. Agha-Khan Bakhtiar, Eghbal's minister of labor, made clear soon after taking office that in the government's view labor syndicates were an unnecessary nuisance. To drive this point home, the ineffectual ITUC was temporarily closed down in August 1957. No more labor syndicates were registered, and a proclamation was published warning leaders of the unregistered syndicates that they faced prosecution for their activities.[70]

American embassy officials continued to ignore the incompatibility between autocracy and autonomous labor unions, persisting in the hope that the two could coexist. Hence in 1958, R. C. Johnson reported: "The outlook for Iranian labor and for the effect which the labor situation will have on the political stabililty of the country is not, therefore, a promising one. Slow progress was to be expected, but unless some improvement in these conditions is achieved relatively soon the dissatisfaction which is already widespread will result in increasing strikes and disturbances in Iranian society."[71]

In September 1958, Dr. Jamshid Amouzegar, described by the American embassy as "young, aggressive, and capable" was promoted from the post of vice minister of health to that of minister of labor. The appointment was interpreted by optimistic American labor officials as a reflection of "the shah's concern with the lack of gains attained by the government in achieving the support and loyalty of the labor force during the period since the overthrow of the Mossadegh Regime."[72]

In his new role as minister of labor, Amouzegar promised American officials to encourage the formation of syndicates. By December, the ministry had registered twenty-five workers' syndicates and five employers' syndicates. However, unofficial workers' syndicates continued to be far more numerous than those recognized by the ministry. The American embassy thought it unlikely that many of the clandestine organizations would obtain official recognition. There were a number of reasons for this. While the Melliyoun Party was placed in charge of the executive branch by the shah, the Mardom Party had established close ties with a number of syndicates. "The Ministry of Labor was therefore reluctant to provide the opposition party with an officially recognized power base."[73] In this the ministry was supported by the shah, who said: "Trade unions should wisely be kept quite separate from political parties. Trade unions should concern themselves primarily with improving the economic situation of their members, while parties have a much broader role to play. Some of the members of a given trade union may prefer one political party, others another; and the union should not be weakened by internal political partisanship."[74]

10

Anglo-American Influence
over Labor

$\mathcal{F}$ROM 1953 TO 1963, both the British and American embassies continued to take a direct interest in Iranian labor affairs. The British embassy maintained a full-time labor attache in Iran. This official, who in the mid-1950s was Alan G. Read, "devoted most of his efforts to the rehabilitation of the Iranian Trade Union Congress (ITUC), although maintaining a strict air of neutrality toward all labor organizations as far as his overt operations [were] concerned."[1]

United States influence over labor affairs was exerted through the Labor Development Division of the United States Operations Mission to Iran (USOM/I), which was established in June 1954. A major reason for United States' interest in Iranian labor was the belief that "a strong labor movement would . . . contribute to political stability in Iran and in the Middle East generally. Such a movement would also reduce political tension by removing many of the causes of discontent among the working classes of the country."[2]

The Iranian autocracy, however, was not willing to establish political stability by this route, which would, in its view, lead to democracy; it preferred repression as the means of maintaining one-man rule.

The Labor Development Division had four major sections—Labor-Management Relations, Labor Training, Employment Security, and Labor Standards—which together corresponded to certain functions of the Ministry of Labor. The division was staffed by thirteen American specialists and seventeen Iranians, a majority of whom were also employees of the Ministry of Labor.

The Labor Development Division was engaged in two projects: labor training and labor services. The labor training project extended technical assistance and necessary material aid to the government for the purpose of instituting and improving job and supervisor training techniques, which would in turn improve the skills and understanding of the workers, apprentices, and supervisors. The labor services project gave technical assistance and necessary material aid to the government in the general field of labor law enforcement and labor-management relations.[3]

One way in which the division's program was implemented was to conduct labor seminars for workers and to send some of the graduates to the United States on what were called "observation-type training programs." In 1954, only one Iranian labor leader was sent to the United States; by 1961, about six hundred workers had participated in a variety of such programs conducted in Iran and the United States. This, it was hoped, would "counteract, at least in part, the attitude [held by many Iranians] that the United States [was] only interested in those on the top of the social and economic ladder."[4]

A major assumption of United States policy toward Iran was that economic development would lead to political gains, or, at a minimum, political stability. It was therefore assumed that economic development and political reform could be carried out sequentially rather than concurrently. Thus R. E. Cunningham reported that

> the lot of the Iranian worker, while it is a poor one, is infinitely better than it was fifty years ago. With his country again receiving a respectable income from its petroleum resources and about to embark on a widespread economic development program, there should be greater prosperity in the country. This should mean more jobs and increased income for the working classes. Once the working population feels the benefits of a small rise in its standard of living, it may go on to demand a proportionate share in the national income. These demands can be made effective if the workers can find effective leaders. It will be a difficult struggle, but it can be done.[5]

If one were to draw a single lesson from the Iranian upheaval, it would be that economic-social development must be carried out in concert with political reform.

1959 Labor Law

During Dr. Amouzegar's term as minister of labor, a new labor law was approved by the Majles, superseding the law passed in 1949. The new law was approved by the Joint Labor Committee of the Senate and the Majles on 18 March 1959, and was put into effect by Prime Minister Eghbal without being passed on the floor of the two houses. The new bill, like that of 1949, was to be enforced for a trial period of two years, beginning 6 April, and then to be reviewed by the Senate and Majles for confirmation as established law.

The 1959 labor law, which was extremely brief, contained only basic statements of principles and practices.[6] It was to be supplemented by implementing regulations which would need promulgation only by the High Labor Council, to be composed of three members each from government, management, and labor, but in fact to be controlled by the incumbent minister of labor.

The council was appointed in September and in the last four months of 1959 approved regulations concerning factory councils, settlement of disputes, and employment of foreign nationals. No action was taken, however, regarding the more sensitive issues, such as the formation and registration of syndicates and revision of the minimum wage scale. In helping to draw up the new law, as well as in drafting the implementing regulations, the United States labor advisers had assumed the role previously taken by the British labor attache.[7]

While the United States was attempting to promote "collective-bargaining-type unions," the Iranian government was busy discouraging them. As noted earlier, by the end of 1958 only some two dozen syndicates had been registered by the Ministry of Labor. The 1959 labor law suspended even this nominal activity. The law was so constituted that

> its implementation depended upon the promulgation of supporting regulations. Although the Law stated that syndicates could be formed and that they should be registered, nevertheless the necessary regulations specifying exactly how these things were to be accomplished were not drawn up and approved by the High Labor Council until well into 1960. Thus, the syndicates which were already registered at the time of the decree of the new law were, during the remainder of the year, unable to register and any

proposed syndicates were similarly stopped from achieving legal status.[8]

This suspension of registration was typical. The shah always enjoyed pointing out that Iran's social legislation was "more progressive" than even those of the Scandinavian countries. In practice, however, the status of trade unions was more like that in the totalitarian states; the government feared that if it permitted effective labor organizations to flourish, it would risk that such organizations would fall under the control of "irresponsible or subversive elements" such as former Tudeh members.[9]

Enactment of progressive labor laws was also intended as a public relations exercise for domestic and especially for international consumption. In the words of a U.S. Annual Labor Report for Iran: "The labor law offers a useful document of the forward-thinking of Iranian social legislation in international conferences—unless it is used in a situation in which delegates present know by experience of Iranian conditions and can prudently and in good taste refer to them."[10]

Labor Minister Amouzegar, according to the American embassy, failed for several reasons to achieve "any outstanding results" in his reform program during the first six months of his administration: political rivalry for control of labor organizations, opposition by management to any change in the status quo, and personnel shortcomings in the ministry.

In October 1959 Dr. Amouzegar moved over to become the minister of agriculture and was replaced by Hasan-Ali Mansour. Four months later, in February 1960, Mansour relinquished the post to Abdolreza Ansari.

Role of SAVAK in Labor Affairs

"The major problem in organizing and maintaining effective labor unions," wrote Emil G. Lindahl, chief of the Labor Division of the U.S. Mission to Iran, on 26 September 1961, "can be summed up in one word, SAVAK, otherwise known as the National Security Police." SAVAK, created in 1957 with the help of the American and Israeli intelligence services, was initially headed by General Teimour

Bakhtiar, military governor of Tehran from 1953 to 1957. The personnel of SAVAK were provided by the Office of the Tehran Military Governor and the Intelligence Department of the army, G-2. In describing SAVAK, Lindahl wrote:

> This organization, while being charged with protecting the country against internal subversion, a worthy cause, in practice is engaged in activities that in effect protect the landlord-employer from effective unions. During the year [1961] SAVAK arrested nine members of the board of directors of the Tehran Printers Syndicate. The victims were in jail for 7 months without charges being made, and released with the statement by the authorities that "we're sorry, we made a mistake."[11]

In the course of investigating the problems of organizing effective unions in Iran, Lindahl interviewed General Hasan Pakravan, the new chief of SAVAK (he replaced Teimour Bakhtiar on 15 March 1961), General Hossein Fardoust, the shah's most trusted friend and second in command of SAVAK; and Colonel Mowlavi, the director of the Tehran Department of SAVAK. All three officials were adamant in denying the role ascribed to SAVAK by the Ministry of Labor, wherein SAVAK was supposed to be the major obstacle to the formation of "proper collective-bargaining-type syndicates." Colonel Mowlavi had a staff in Tehran of fourteen colonels in plainclothes who were assigned districts of the city for which they were responsible in terms of contact with workers and workers' organizations, reported Lindahl, "the purpose being to guide the workers along constructive paths and to help them solve their problems. The strike of brick workers is a case in point."[12]

In June 1959 a week-long strike of Tehran brick workers had taken place. The strike involved thirty thousand brick kiln workers and thirty thousand additional personnel, including truck drivers.[13] The workers walked out because the employers had not paid them for seven months. Instead of cash, the employers had given chits that were good only in certain shops in the brick kiln area. "According to workers," reported the American embassy, "these shops were operated by the so-called worker representatives and the prices [were] higher than in regular shops where cash was necessary."[14] At the same time, the strikers were demanding a 35 percent increase in wages and an accounting of their wage deductions, which, according to U.S. sources, were ostensibly being deposited in the Workers' Social Insurance Organization but

> which allegedly—and more likely—were going into the pockets of the kiln owners or the work contractors who were responsible for bringing the workers to Tehran from rural areas. After severe coercion by police and military forces and by SAVAK, the strikers were worn down and forced to accept the kiln owners' offer of a 20 percent wage increase—which offer was supported by the Ministry of Labor as a reasonable basis for settlement. Additionally, the Ministry promised to look further into the workers' grievances.[15]

Colonel Mowlavi was proud of what he considered the "accomplishment" he and his staff at SAVAK had made in resolving the problem that brought about the strike.[16]

A common complaint against SAVAK was its practice of branding as Communists those who agitated for a better life. The reluctance of the government to permit workers "more freedom to organize in their own interest," wrote E. L. McGinnis, an American labor official, "creates pressures which could force workers into Communism."[17]

Challenge to Autocracy

The year 1960 was the first of three challenging years for the shah's autocratic government. The economic gains which were to compensate the population for the loss of their political freedoms had not materialized, and the promise by the shah of a two-party system was exposed as an empty gesture.

The previous year had brought to an end the economic "honeymoon" which had prevailed since the oil agreement with the consortium of oil companies in late 1954. This four-year period had been marked not only by boom conditions throughout all sectors of the economy, but also by freedom from foreign exchange restrictions. According to the Labor Report of 1959, "Consumer goods of all descriptions flooded into Iran, coinciding with successive years of good agriculture crops. . . . Although in the perspective of Iran's past economy, supply was plentiful, demand nevertheless overtook it."[18]

Cost-of-living indices rose sharply in the spring of 1959, and the increases for the year as a whole were far larger than in the immediately preceding years. The Bank Melli composite index for seven cities (base 1936–1937) averaged 1456 during 1959, or an increase of 10.1 percent over the 1958 average figure; the comparable increase of 1958 over 1957 had been only 0.2 percent.

It also became apparent in 1959 that Iran's foreign exchange reserves were being drawn down at an extravagant rate—with an annual loss of $50 million. This called for remedial action in the form of import restrictions, implemented mainly through a tightening of import credits.[19]

Following on the heels of this economic crisis, the autocracy faced its first political challenge since 1951–1953, when Dr. Mossadegh was prime minister. The problem first appeared in June 1960, as the nineteenth session of the Majles ended and the shah's promised two-party system was put to the test. The election campaign for the twentieth session of the Majles in the summer of 1960 illustrated the inconsistency of a two-party system in an autocracy. The shah could not insist on making all major decisions himself and at the same time create two political parties to compete for the people's votes.

There were, as usual, conflicting statements and inconsistencies between words and deeds. In his 1961 autobiography the shah wrote: "In a democracy the people must share in deciding their own destiny, and in most matters the best way to choose the wise path is through public discussion and argument."[20] At the same time Prime Minister Eghbal was setting a new standard for subservience to the monarch, pronouncing all government actions to be implementations of His Majesty's instructions. Moreover, he was the first prime minister to refuse publicly to answer an interpellation (*estizah*) about his government by a Majles deputy. This was done in the face of the shah's public statement that "the Prime Minister and all other ministers are individually and jointly responsible to both houses of Parliament."[21]

The constant identification of government actions with the will of the shah had placed leaders of the Mardom Party at a decided disadvantage in the campaign for the Twentieth Majles. How could they criticize the ruling party without appearing to criticize the monarch? The dilemma was explained by Dr. Mohammad Baheri, a Mardom Party leader:

Whatever plan the majority party brought forth, it stressed that it was in accordance with the wishes of His Imperial Majesty. Perhaps the previous governments had said the same thing in order to be respectful of the monarch, but not so much as the Eghbal Cabinet. In order to deal with this problem the opposition had found another formula. The Mardom Party would say, "yes, you are following the directives of His Majesty, but while we understand those directives correctly, you do not". Consequently the main discussion was over the correct meaning of His Majesty's orders.[22]

It did not take long for the politically sensitive Iranians to realize that the two-party system was inconsistent with Iran's autocracy—just as "nonpolitical" labor unions had proved to be earlier. Once again demonstrating their astuteness and political maturity, the workers referred to the Melliyoun and Mardom Parties as *Pepsi Bozorg va Pepsi kouchoulou,* "large Pepsi and small Pepsi."[23]

During the election campaign, the first secretary-general of the Melliyoun Party, Dr. Nosratollah Kassemi, was discharged on the personal order of the shah while he was campaigning for the party's candidates for the Twentieth Majles. Apparently he had been too critical of Asadollah Alam, leader of the Mardom Party.

In 1960 the election to the United States presidency of John F. Kennedy, who appeared to advocate political liberalization in Iran, unsettled the shah in the same way that the election of President Jimmy Carter, with his emphasis on human rights, would trouble him in 1976. The opposition to the shah, composed of the followers of Dr. Mossadegh and known as the National Front, was ready once again to challenge the supporters of autocratic government.

During the month of August 1960, people in the provinces protested the course the elections were taking and demanded their cancellation. On 1 August armed troops broke up pre-election demonstrations in the provinces outside of Tehran. On 13 August, when reports continued to indicate that the Melliyoun Party was winning, charges were made that the elections were rigged. In Tehran a week later, a thousand students and workers protested that the elections were unfair.

On 22 August 1960, Dr. Mozaffar Bagha'i, an early supporter of Dr. Mossadegh who had broken with the former prime minister in 1952, relaunched his Zahmat-Keshan (Toilers) Party, which had been inactive since 1953, and led a campaign of passive resistance against the government, calling Prime Minister Eghbal a traitor. On 27 August, the elections, which were scheduled separately for various provinces, ended in Tehran. On the same day, the shah was forced to admit publicly that he was not fully satisfied with the national elections, placing the blame on the "54-year-old electoral system" that he wished to see improved.

Sharif-Emami Cabinet: 1960–1961

With the economy failing and the election discredited, Premier Eghbal, on 28 August, submitted his resignation, and the shah appointed Engineer Ja'far Sharif-Emami, minister of industries and mines in the Eghbal cabinet, as prime minister. Sharif-Emami in turn appointed Dr. Ahmad-Ali Bahrami as minister of labor.

On 1 September, the shah "suggested" that all newly elected Majles deputies resign to pave the way for new elections. Everyone obliged except Amir Amirkeyvan, former secretary-general of the ITUC, who had been elected from Esfahan. He refused, asserting that his election was genuine and that he could not legally be forced to resign. In January 1961 new elections for two hundred seats in the Twentieth Majles opened with balloting in some towns, during which a number of clashes were reported. In Esfahan, the refusal to permit Amirkeyvan to be a candidate caused considerable unrest and demonstrations by the workers.[24]

On 26 January, members of the National Front, who considered Dr. Mossadegh to be their leader and who advocated constitutional monarchy for Iran, led ten thousand Tehran University students in a demonstration, charging that the elections for the Twentieth Majles were not free. Six days later, the shah responded by denouncing those in Iran and abroad who opposed his "program of gradual reform and progress." On 5 February Tehran University was closed because of student demonstrations in the bazaar district of Tehran. The next day students demonstrated in Tehran against the closing of the university and the Teachers' Training College. A week later the university was opened, after eighty students had been arrested for taking part in the demonstrations. On 20 February the twentieth session of the Majles was convened by the shah, who called for a new law to ensure "honest" elections.

In 1960 regulations concerning the formation and registration of syndicates were prepared and later approved by the High Labor Council. Within six months, fifty syndicates were legally registered in Tehran and seven in Esfahan. By the end of the year, the number had reached sixty. According to an American official, the process was halted the following year, when "despite interest in syndicates in every part of the country only two syndicates were registered." The two consisted of an association of dental technicians and a guild of tailors in Mashhad.[25]

Only a few of the Tehran syndicates were sufficiently well organized to merit special mention or had enough dues-paying members to afford salary and office rent for a full-time officer. Some of these "syndicates" would, in fact, have been better named as guilds, since their members were mostly self-employed tradesmen rather than employees of a firm. One such organization was that of the Tehran bakers; it had between two thousand and three thousand members, five separate offices in Tehran and its suburbs, and one full-time and one part-time paid official. Because the price of bread was a politically sensitive issue, it was important to maintain an association of bakers so that government control over the supply and price of bread could be better implemented.

The bakers' general secretary was Abbas Khorram, who had been a participant in U.S. labor programs. Khorram was reported by an American source to be "a target of much abuse by SAVAK and various Ministry of Labor officials who for the most part consider it a bother to deal with workers who won't take no for an answer."[26]

The Syndicate of Glass Workers, which more closely fitted the definition of a labor union, had 1,200 dues-paying members who contributed 1 percent of their wages in dues.[27] The syndicate was led by Akbar Amir-Ahmadi, also a participant in U.S. labor training programs.[28] Another syndicate that appeared impressive on paper, but whose effectiveness was not apparent, was that of government employees, led by Fatollah Ghaffari, who also published the union's weekly newspaper *Ettehadieh* (Union).[29]

Although a syndicate of the employees of the National Iranian Oil Company of Tehran, led by Heidar Rahmani, was allowed to register, no syndicate was permitted in the oil fields. Efforts to form an oil workers' syndicate "were frustrated by the Labor Ministry's refusal to accept registration in spite of provisions under the law permitting it."[30]

Amini Cabinet: 1961–1962

Prime Minister Sharif-Emami was unable to restore political calm in Tehran and other major cities. On 2 May 1961, teachers across the country went on strike to protest their low salaries. In Tehran, a teacher was shot to death by a police officer during a demonstration in front of the Majles building. Three days later, Prime Minister Sharif-Emami resigned, and the Shah appointed Dr. Ali Amini in his place. This appointment was made, according to the Shah, because of American pressure. A new minister of labor, Ataollah Khosrovani, was also appointed, remaining in office until November 1968.

Prime Minister Amini was a protege of his wife's uncle, former Prime Minister Ahmad Qavam, under whom he had served in various capacities. Like Qavam, Prime Minister Amini preferred to take bold steps without the inconvenience of an unrepresentative and uncooperative Majles. On 9 May the prime minister secured a royal decree bringing to an end the twentieth session of the Majles—then only 59 days old—enabling him to rule without legislative "obstruction."

According to the controversial 1949 amendment to the constitution,[31] the shah was given the power to dissolve both houses of parliament. However, as the monarch himself had written: "I must state my reason for doing so . . . and must immediately call for fresh elections so that the new chamber or chambers may convene within the space of three months."[32] Nevertheless, the Majles was kept closed for the next 2½ years, while the shah consolidated his hold on the political system of the country.

The appointment of Dr. Amini was interpreted as the beginning of a period of political liberalization by many opponents of autocracy. They felt that the economic and political failures of the shah, combined with American pressure for reform, had placed him on the defensive. They were further encouraged by democratic sentiments expressed by the shah, for example: "We now have achieved a situation comprising two active major parties [Melliyoun and Mardom] plus a number of minor ones. Anyone who desires can, without fear or hindrance, form additional parties so long as they do not serve foreign masters."[33]

A few days after Dr. Amini's appointment, the National Front convened its congress and then organized a rally of eighty thousand of its supporters at the Jalalieh Polo Grounds, demanding immediate elections. This was the first such mass meeting in Iran by an opposition group in nearly ten years. The shah, however, had no intention of returning the powers he had acquired since 1953. Hence, a second rally by the National Front, scheduled for 21 July to commemorate the Thirtieth of Tir 1331 (21 July 1952, when Dr. Mossadegh was returned to power) was disrupted by security forces. Two days later a number of its leaders were arrested.

On 19 August 1962 the shah presided over the gathering of a "half million" people at the Doshan Tapeh airfield to commemorate the overthrow of Dr. Mossadegh's government eight years earlier. This writer remembers hearing a rebroadcast of the shah's speech over Tehran Radio that evening. The shah's voice and his manner of delivery were totally new. In contrast to his past speeches, when he sounded timid and soft-spoken, on this and future occasions he was loud and tough.

Clearly the shah had decided to shed his role as reigning monarch and to become instead a "revolutionary monarch." A series of programs was launched, including land reform for the peasants and, later, profit-sharing for the workers, which became known successively as the "Sixth of Bahman Revolution," "The White Revolution," and finally "The Shah-People Revolution." The shah had decided to adopt these reforms not only to appease the Kennedy administration in the U.S. but also to take the wind out of the sails of the National Front. These programs together with others, such as stock ownership for the workers, price control, and administrative reform, were carried out with little success until the last days of the monarchy in 1979.

On 4 November 1961, the shah called for Iran, in partnership with the United States, to turn his country into a "showplace" of the non-Communist world, and ten days later asked Prime Minister Amini to tell the cabinet to develop legislation incorporating his reforms. Amini may have been the first to refer to the shah's proposed reforms as revolutionary: on 6 December he told a gathering of educators that "what we have done resembles a revolution." On 15 January 1962 the shah signed the land reform bill approved by the Council of Ministers and ordered its enforcement.

On 21 January, students of Tehran University, supporting the National Front, called a strike, demanding the reopening of the Majles through free elections (the legislature had been closed for eight months). They chanted "Reform, Yes. Dictatorship, No." The following day, government troops stormed the university for the first time in its history—hitherto it had been considered a sanctuary—assaulting students and damaging equipment. Two hundred people were reported injured. A number of National Front leaders and members of the university faculty, including Dr. Gholam-Hossein Sadighi, Dr. Karim Sanjabi, and Dr. Mehdi Azar—all former ministers in Mossadegh's cabinets—were arrested. The remaining leaders of the National Front urged all "Honorable patriots" to unite to fight the government and join the national strike set for the next day.

On the following day, security forces attacked the protesting demonstrators, and one student was killed. On the same day the government closed the university (until 3 April), and Dr. Ahmad Farhad, chancellor of the university, and members of the faculty resigned in protest against the government's actions. At the same time, three daily newspapers were suspended for "inciting unrest and student demonstrations." On 27 January the remaining National Front leaders, including Dr. Shapour Bakhtiar, Mohammad-Ali Khonji, and Mas'oud Hejazi, were arrested and joined their colleagues in prison. While the shah referred to the demonstrations as an "unholy alliance" between leftists and rightists, Prime Minister Amini, at a gathering of landlords on 10 February, called land reform the "White Revolution" and recommended that they cease their instigations against the program.

Having set his "reform program" in motion and his "house in order," the shah was ready to meet the new American president. On 11 April 1962 he and Empress Farah arrived in Washington and were received at the White House by President and Mrs. John F. Kennedy. In a subsequent meeting with members of Congress, the shah successfully wooed them by reassuring them that "Iran wouldn't surrender to Communism."

On his return from the United States, the tension between the shah and Prime Minister Amini reached the breaking point. The monarch had felt all along that the Kennedy administration had imposed Amini on him. More recently, the two had clashed over the size of the military budget and whether the Ministry of War ought to be exempt from the across-the-board budget reductions slated for all other ministries. At the same time, it was assumed by many of the Iranian elite that the shah had convinced Washington that he had yielded to their demands for reform, and that he should lead the reform program himself without the services of Prime Minister Amini. When the documents relating to these meetings between President Kennedy and the shah are available, it will be important

to find out whether these speculations were correct. More impor-
tantly, it will be useful to know whether the Kennedy administration's
conception of reform included political reform along with social and
economic reform, i.e., land reform and profit-sharing, or whether
socioeconomic gains were to be made at the expense of political
freedom, and the latter considered a luxury. Hindsight now tells us
that, without the discipline and structure provided by political reform,
plans for economic and social development can, and most likely will,
go astray. It is interesting to note that the shah himself, in 1961,
expressed support for this idea; unfortunately, he failed to heed his
own advice.

> Experience in the past few years has shown that political stability
> doesn't necessarily follow economic development. Paradoxically,
> static and undeveloped societies—some of the South Sea islands,
> for instance—may show much more political stability than do
> those which are achieving rapid economic advance. On the other
> hand we know of certain Middle Eastern countries that have shown
> remarkable economic progress in recent years, but nevertheless
> have experienced grave political difficulties. They have had no
> political programmes comparable with their plans for economic
> development. The lesson seems to be that planned political and
> economic evolution must go hand in hand, or serious trouble will
> ensue.[34]

Alam Cabinet: 1962–1964

On 19 July 1962 Asadollah Alam, one of the shah's most trusted
aides, was appointed prime minister following Dr. Amini's resignation. Dr. Amini left for Switzerland on 7 August when his opponents
demanded his arrest and trial on charges of violating the constitution
—a replay of the treatment given to Prime Minister Qavam when he
was forced out of office in 1947.[35]

On 25 August, U.S. Vice President Lyndon Johnson arrived for
a two-day goodwill tour of Tehran and declared that Iran's security
was critical to the United States. No public word was spoken
regarding Iran's unconstitutional government or its treatment of
Iranian citizens who were demanding the opening of the Majles,
which, by this time, had then been closed for sixteen months.

Although Vice President Johnson said nothing, articles were written about Iran's political situation, thanks to a free press in the United States. In 1962, two well-known labor reporters visited Iran and wrote articles about conditions they found there. Victor Reisel was one; the other was Arnold Beichman, who had accompanied Vice President Johnson to Iran. His critical articles appeared in the *Christian Science Monitor* and the *Federationist,* an AFL-CIO publication. These articles were characterized by the American embassy as "most accurate and a fair observation of things as they are in Iran from a labor point of view." On the other hand, the articles "incensed" Iran's minister of labor, Ataollah Khosrovani, who blamed the U.S. labor specialists in Iran for providing embarrassing information to the American reporters.[36]

There was no doubt that the American labor officials attached to the U.S. Mission in Iran had great sympathy for the Iranian workers and were just as critical as they of the government that was responsible for the existing state of affairs. As one official wrote: "When unemployed workers show up at Iran's Employment Service Office with bottles of kerosene in their pockets threatening suicide by fire unless a job is provided for them, desperation is certainly present. When teachers risk life and limb in demonstrations to win better than $40.00 a month in salary, Iran's intelligentsia can be considered frustrated. Conditions such as these provide a fertile basis for the spread of Communism."[37]

The contradictory behavior of the Iranian government puzzled U.S. labor officials, who wondered why it did not use its power to promote "collective-bargaining-type" syndicates. "Certainly with the police-state control the government has," wrote one, "if problems were sincerely dealt with in terms of resolving them, they could be and would be resolved."[38]

During 1962 the Ministry of Labor, under Khosrovani, continued to prevent the election of worker representatives, constantly referring, instead, to the need for "real workers" to assume the role of labor leaders.[39] An embassy official summed up the situation: "The eight textile syndicates that have made application two years ago for recognition by the authorities are still waiting for this recognition. MOL [Ministry of Labor] officials claim SAVAK is the problem. SAVAK, of course, claims that the Ministry blames them for everything."[40]

Officials of the U.S. embassy seemed perplexed by the discrepancy between the pro-labor statements made by the Shah and the anti-union actions of the Ministry of Labor: "The Government of Iran can be said to have double standards. Their public attitude is, 'we should have free democratic unions.' Privately through SAVAK they coerce and intimidate workers and their leaders to prohibit formation of effective trade unions."[41]

The confusion on the part of the American labor officials was understandable. In his book, the shah had given support to the principle of trade unionism. He had pointed out the connection between economic democracy, which he hoped to achieve, and trade unionism: "There is one final feature of economic democracy which people have now become mature enough to adopt in earnest. I am speaking of free trade unions—which are of course unknown in totalitarian countries. I firmly believe in such unions as instruments of democracy. They are necessary to ensure that economic democracy extends into the industrial system in the modern world."[42]

In recalling the past, he criticized the Tudeh unions of the 1940s because of "their preoccupation with personalities rather than policies."[43] At the same time he displayed a certain disdain—even disrespect—for the basic intelligence of common workers and seemed to view them as a herd of sheep with no judgment: "A union boss would become temporarily popular, and a union would grow around him. Later, when he became too weak or too powerful, or when the workers tired of his lack of programme, they would desert him and turn to somebody else who might deserve their faith no more than the previous man. Strong, responsible unions cannot grow in that fashion."[44]

Having expressed his disagreement with the earlier unions, the shah explained that, in his opinion, a union "should have clear-cut programmes known to all the members, reliable leaders democratically elected by the rank and file, and practice responsible democracy in their internal management."[45] Finally, the shah assured his readers that the Ministry of Labor "encourages the formation of trade unions."[46]

There is an air of genuine innocence in the report of an American labor adviser: "The Minister of Labor [Ataollah Khosrovani] has time and again reported His Majesty's wish that the Iranian year 1341 (1962) will go down in history as the year of syndicates."[47] And yet not only did registration of syndicates not proceed, but "with a handful of exceptions most of [the] registered syndicates [were] little more than paper organizations."[48] The labor adviser continued:

> Their leadership is exclusively from the group of government-approved "labor leaders" who have dominated Iranian labor affairs for the past twenty years. There is no single instance of workers in a given industry or factory being able to organize a syndicate or elect union leaders freely without the close supervision or at least full knowledge and approval of the authorities.

> Perhaps the security requirements of the regime dictated this policy. However, the non-representative character of labor organization in Iran must be included in the definition of worker conditions here.[49]

It was not surprising, therefore, that the American labor adviser in 1963 found "virtually no dialogue between labor and management in Iran." He added that "collective bargaining as such is non-existent." A review of labor relations as they had existed in Iran in the spring of 1946 would have shown that conditions had certainly deteriorated between those dates.[50]

The provisions of the labor law regarding the formation of syndicates were not the only features of the law not being implemented. Even its "nonpolitical" aspects, including provisions for overtime, elimination of child labor, severance pay, and working hours, remained unenforced. "In almost all industries," reported the American embassy, "use of child labor, excessive hours, neglect of industrial safety and hygiene continue to be ignored, or are 'forgiven' by the Ministry of Labor upon payment of the appropriate bribe to the labor inspectors."[51] Added to all this, the American labor expert, D. Levintow, reported that "any worker who petitions for enforcement of existing labor law provisions is liable to denunciation by his employer as a subversive agitator. Security officers seem impelled by the configuration of power here to support politically connected entrepreneurs rather than politically isolated (from the power nexus) workers."[52]

These security measures had, in fact, served to mask the mounting dissatisfaction of labor and had "caused resignation and despair among workers fearing the consequences of protest."[53]

The closing of all legal channels of protest led inevitably to sabotage, and later to armed struggle against the monarchy. One such act of sabotage occurred at the Jeep factory, when "handfuls of welding beads were dropped into the company's deep well where they were ingested by and destroyed a $27,000 pump." The sabotage was apparently related to a long-standing protest by the workers about poor food which was causing widespread intestinal disorders.[54]

Even in the area of worker training, which certainly had no security implications, little progress was made. It would have seemed logical, in view of the promised economic development, for the training of workers to carry a high priority. On the contrary, the Ministry of Labor failed to fulfill promises made to the ILO to expand the U.S.-assisted South Tehran Workers' Training Center into a facility for the training of foremen and instructors. An ILO official stationed in Iran "regretted that there was no way in which the ILO could withdraw discreetly from its agreement to provide $750,000 to finance the project."[55]

During 1963 the Ministry of Labor was reported by the U.S. embassy to be continuing its "halfhearted and irregular efforts to enforce the basic labor legislation."[56] This was not surprising, given the political system of Iran. There was in fact little reason why the ministry should enforce labor legislation vigorously. There were no unions to express the collective will of the workers or to push for the implementation of the labor law. There was no longer a free press to publish worker complaints. The Majles was more than ever under the total control of the court. The executive branch, led by members of the cabinet, had become the personal appointees of the shah. The minister of labor was not accountable to anyone except the monarch; to remain in his post, he had only to please him. And for the shah, the implementation of the labor law held a very low priority—especially since, in his view, its implementation could lead to ever-greater expectations on the part of the workers and the eventual reappearance of a force that could challenge his autocratic rule.

A noteworthy example of the failure of U.S. policy toward labor unions in Iran was Hasan Nabizadeh, considered by American labor officials to be the "most effective syndicate leader" in Esfahan. After participating in a workers' education program sponsored by the U.S. Agency for International Development (AID), Nabizadeh, in the capacity of labor representative, had worked with management to increase production in the Nakhtab mill by 70 to 100 percent. According to an American labor expert, "this was made possible because Nabizadeh had told the workers that if a noticeable increase in production could be achieved, he would persuade the employer to give the workers a share of the increased profit that resulted."[57] Instead, Nabizadeh and his fellow leaders of the Nakhtab mill workers' syndicate were fired.

Nabizadeh was paid 27,000 *tomans* ($4,000) as a combination of severance pay and a negotiated amount to encourage his peaceful resignation. This successful termination of employment was the result of a series of efforts on the part of the employer to get rid of Hasan Nabizadeh and his syndicate. All previous efforts had resulted in a strike by the employees of the Thread [Nakhtab] Mill in support of Nabizadeh.

According to the workers, Nabizadeh's termination was further coerced by the local SAVAK chief, who threatened to include his name on the list of Communists that was being compiled.[58]

Two points should be made here: First, the Nabizadeh case brought into focus the contradictory policy of the United States in promoting trade unions within an autocratic system. The U.S. government, through its AID program, spent time and effort instructing labor leaders in order to promote labor unions trained for collective bargaining. However, the autocracy that the United States supported and the SAVAK that it helped to create in 1957 were undermining the labor program. SAVAK even prevented American labor officials from showing a film proposed for use in their training classes because it portrayed a strike, in spite of the fact that the film clearly explained the strike as a procedure of last resort.[59] At the same time, three graduates of the course, "fresh from learning how to form a trade union, and presumably fired with zeal to put their new learning into practice, have had applications for syndicate registration rejected because, in the Ministry's view, this is not the right time for union activity."[60]

The second point is that unrelenting worker support for Nabizadeh provides further proof that Iranian workers had the maturity to judge, and the dedication to follow, genuine leaders and were not, as has been claimed by some observers, including the shah, a herd of sheep ready to follow the demagogue of the day. Before Nabizadeh and his followers were defeated, the entire working population of Esfahan was mobilized on their behalf. In the months of May and June 1961 the strike of Nakhtab mill workers spread to other mills in Esfahan and reached a climax in a parade of workers from the Nakhtab and adjoining mills, which was highlighted by the carrying of a "corpse," the alleged victim of police brutality in the Shahnaz mill. When the army was reported to be on its way, the "pallbearers" became excited and dropped the "corpse," who then rose from his "bier" and ran away. This event greatly affected E. L. McGinnis, a U.S. labor official, who wrote:

> For a government that has a modern labor law on its books it becomes revealing of the lack of enforcement when workers have to resort to trickery and public deception in order to have their problems heard or understood. Were the workers to seek a public forum, were they to attempt soap box oratory, they know they would be stopped. Since death is sacred in Iran the workers sought their forum under the only cover that could not be interfered with by the authorities. They failed only because they did not have a real corpse.[61]

Hasan Nabizadeh and Amir Amirkeyvan were tagged as the leaders of the demonstration and were exiled for six months to Rafsanjan, a city a few hundred miles south of Esfahan.[62] During the same period, the directors of the syndicates at the Zayandehroud and Shahnaz textile mills were fired. Observed a U.S. official: "This is in spite of the labor law provision that no one can interfere with the workers' right to have a syndicate."[63] The government obviously believed that a more permissive policy toward trade unions would threaten internal security.[64]

In a final note to his report dated 6 July 1963, the American labor adviser, Emil G. Lindahl, appealed to the top officials of his own government and those of its Western allies to help change the course Iran had taken toward its workers: "Certainly if the Western countries of the world are interested in a stable and secure Iran, a solution ought not be difficult to obtain in this very important field of activity." [65]

In a subsequent report, D. Levintow wrote: "Even a cursory examination of the present condition of most Iranian workers suggests that they now constitute a potential, albeit presently controlled, threat to the Iranian stability and the continued tenure of the regime."[66]

American labor officials were apparently not in a position to know that Iran's problem was more basic: it stemmed from the autocratic system of government that the United States had helped reimpose on Iran in October 1946, when Qavam was forced to submit to the will of the shah, and again in August 1953, when the Mossadegh government was overthrown with the aid of the CIA. The United States, in the 1940s and 1950s (but perhaps not in the 1960s), had the means to deal with the root of the problem—the unconstitutional nature of Iran's political system—by pressing the Shah to implement the Iranian constitution and hold free elections. However, any attempt to force the autocracy to tolerate and coexist with trade unions was futile. They were incompatible. If the government had been less autocratic, as in the 1920s and 1940s, then labor unions would have developed spontaneously on their own; they would not have needed a gardener to help them grow.

Continuing to hope for the best, U.S. labor officials even tried to "educate" the SAVAK officers regarding "the value of real [labor] organizations in terms of internal security."[67] This was done on the assumption, to quote the U.S. Labor Report of 1963, that "the Shah undoubtedly wishes to win broad popular support from industrial workers by improving their lot."[68] The "educational" meetings arranged with SAVAK were canceled without explanation but U.S. liaison officers in contact with SAVAK told labor officials that the atmosphere at that time was not conducive to further meetings on the subject.[69]

At about the same time, U.S. AID drivers and carpenters struck the AID Mission because of pending layoffs and their concern about severance. The strike had an ironic ending. According to Lindahl, "the incident of the striking drivers and carpenters was resolved by terminating their employment with the aid of SAVAK and the controlled press." As a result, "not much noise was made about the incident."[70]

Lindahl was obviously disturbed by the turn of events. The SAVAK he had been criticizing was now being used by the United States AID Mission, just as it was used by other employers, to facilitate the discharge of redundant workers and to suppress a strike. This event led to Lindahl's asking a poignant question: "In a country that is 80% illiterate, what kind of protection does a censored press offer an offender [employer] when a hundred or more highly vocal workers, with family trees spreading to all corners of the land, have some justification for a bitter [feeling toward] the U.S., developers of free democratic societies?"[71]

There should be little difficulty in understanding why, even as early as 1963, the seeds of contempt for the autocratic monarchy and its major foreign supporter, the United States, were sown in Iran.

An earlier warning by R. C. Johnson was also prophetic: "Labor in Iran, though docile and tractable, can be aroused, is quite capable of being violently led, and is hardly likely to wait forever for some definite signs of progress for the worker. Whether the long-term trend will move rapidly enough to avert an eventual (though not immediately likely) explosion is the question."[72]

Epilogue

*T*HIS WORK has focused on the interrelationship between labor unions and autocracy in Iran from 1906, the beginning of constitutional government, to 1963 when the Shah totally subjugated the legislative branch and personally took over the decision-making powers of the prime minister and the important ministries. I would like to conclude the book, however, with an overview of the 1963–1978 period, when autocracy was in full force, and then take a brief look at labor relations under the Islamic Republic of Iran.

In contrast to the main body of this book, which is based on primary sources, in this Epilogue I have drawn on my own recollections of the period from 1963 to 1976 when I lived and worked in Iran. This chapter is also based on published works of colleagues who have conducted their own in-depth research on the post-revolutionary period.

Years of Autocracy: 1963–1978

What follows may dismay some of my Iranian friends. Because, as a member of Iran's privileged class, I too benefited from some of the policies and practices that I deplore, my words may be

233

considered hypocritical. I cannot be an objective judge of such criticism, but I subject myself to it voluntarily because I believe that silence or the selective choice of materials will deny my children and their children the opportunity of learning from our mistakes. We must live with the hope that their Iran will be governed according to laws legislated by their representatives.

From 1963 to 1978 the government's official but unstated labor policy was that if workers remained silent and apolitical, then the government would protect the security of their jobs by pressuring employers to refrain from discharging their workers. At the same time, the government would endeavor to give workers a share in the rising prosperity enjoyed by their employers.

By 1978, the Iranian working class was no longer an insignificant proportion of the population. Their number had increased nearly fivefold between 1963 and 1978. While industrial workers totalled approximately 880,000, that number increased to 1,272,000 if one included wage earners employed by urban services and small manufacturing plants, workshop employees, shop assistants, and wage earners in banks, offices, and other agencies.[1]

Beginning in 1963, the year I completed my studies in the United States and returned to work in my father's manufacturing business in Tehran, the prosperity of Iran's growing privileged classes was gradually becoming visible. Public display of this new affluence by the entrepreneurs was kept in check during the 1960s due to a discernible sense of mission among them—many of whom were former merchants or sons of merchants turned industrialists. Their mission was to reinvest their retained earnings to expand their industrial enterprises. I remember vividly the pride exhibited by these pioneers as they personally conducted tours of their modern and relatively efficient factories for any and all visitors. They derived so much pleasure from the physical growth of their installations that they had little need to change the relatively simple lifestyle of the traditional merchant class in Iran.

The minister of economy from 1962 to 1969 was in many ways the right man in the right place at the right time, as he set a personal example for the industrialists to follow. For example, he had refused the new government automobile provided to the other ministers. Instead, throughout his term as minister, he rode in the vehicle used by his predecessors and continued to live in an unpretentious house. This style of leadership was effective; industrialists who wished to be seen in the best light knew that any ostentatious behavior on their part would jeopardize their next request for tariff protection and other favorable decisions by the Ministry of Economy. There was also the Ministry of Finance and its tax collectors to worry about in any decision to display new wealth.

Increasing oil income in the early 1970s brought many changes to Iran: a pretentious arrogance on the part of Iranian leaders and vulgar self-indulgence by the beneficiaries of oil revenues. This state of affairs reached its peak a year or two prior to the revolution of 1979. Although the gross national product grew dramatically between 1963 and 1977, and more and more people were drawn into the mainstream of society, Abrahamian writes in *Iran Between Two Revolutions,* "it was also evident that the growth did not benefit all equally. On the contrary, it benefited the rich more than the middle and the lower classes."[2] And, he continued, "the oil boom brought to the middle classes decent housing, small cars, and an annual tour of Europe." But to wealthy industrialists it brought business empires "unimagined by earlier entrepreneurs, palaces worthy of ancient kings, and scandals that far overshadowed those of the previous generation."[3]

An early sign of this opulence was the chauffeur-driven Mercedes used by factory owners to go to work, as well as by members of the cabinet, and later by the top executives of private and public corporations. In rapid succession, fabulous mansions, no longer affordable by their counterparts in Europe, were constructed in northern Tehran by members of this expanding club. Company drivers, cooks, and waiters, who were brought into the owners' homes to serve the guests, witnessed (and reported to their fellow workers in the factory) extravagant banquets with singers and musicians, given by their bosses for each other, for important foreign visitors, for members of the royal family, and for high government officials on whom the entrepreneur depended for permits and regulations. Men of newly found wealth and their ladies no longer had their clothes made by Iranian tailors; they were purchased abroad during frequent trips to Paris, London, and New York.

The shah and the empress encouraged this style of life. A series of celebrations for foreign and domestic dignitaries to mark the crowning of the shah in 1967 and to celebrate the twenty-fifth century of monarchy in 1971 resembled settings in a fairy tale and dramatically exceeded the upper limits of opulence. The royal family also initiated the custom of taking their winter vacations in Switzerland; they were followed by courtiers and the rich, who established their own practice of taking summer vacations in their apartments and villas in the south of France. In Iran the shah and the empress rarely traveled by automobile, which would have given them more personal contact with their own citizens; they began the practice of flying by helicopter from place to place within the city of Tehran.

Workers witnessed in less than a single generation changes in their city and among their fellow countrymen that were truly dramatic. My father, for example, lived until 1962 in the Amirieh district of central Tehran where his house was across the street from a grocery store, a butcher, a cobbler, and a bakery. The neighborhood was heterogeneous; rich and lower-middle class lived on the same street, frequented the same shops, used the same public bath house, and wore clothes of similar quality and style. This proximity of different economic classes, combined with the natural reluctance of members of the merchant class to engage in conspicuous consumption, resulted in a harmonious neighborhood. On Thursday evenings, I remember, a local mullah would come to our house, sit in the entrance hall, recite prayers, and then depart. On holy days, there were great religious processions, organized by the local mosque, going through our street. Although I did not participate in these myself, I watched with fascination.

I myself attended the Ghaza'eri School, the neighborhood public elementary school, from 1946 to 1948. Although my father was probably the wealthiest among the students' parents, this fact did not prevent my integration within the school. Students all wore the same uniform made of locally manufactured cloth, so there was little obvious distinction among us. We competed in the classroom and the schoolyard on the basis of ability rather than family background. There was a free flow of ideas among the students.

When I returned to Iran in 1963, my parents had moved to a new residential area in an enclosed compound, located at the foot of the Alborz mountains in Niavaran. In 1965, after another assassination attempt on his life, the shah abandoned his administrative and residential palaces in the center of Tehran and moved to the Niavaran Palace which backed onto the same mountains in the northeastern corner of Tehran as my parents' house. From 1963 to 1968, my daily drive from my house in Niavaran to my office on the edge of the Bazaar was a daily reminder of the great chasm developing between the northern and southern parts of Tehran—the one pseudo-modern, the other traditional.

As time went by, we, too, became totally integrated into the *shomal-e shahr*, "north of the city." We no longer had to mingle or even view from the windows of our cars the ordinary people of Tehran. From the mid-1960s, living in "our Tehran" was not very different from living in a European city; our homes, our offices, our clothes, our children's schools, our restaurants, and especially our mode of behavior, were pale carbon copies of the Western version. Henceforth, we rarely had the occasion or the desire to visit the southern part of the city.

Many Westerners and some Iranians have viewed these changes as an indication of progress, but in retrospect, I see them as a major factor contributing to the collapse of the former regime. As workers and the other underprivileged witnessed their nation being split into two societies, their government, by means of political repression, attempted to keep it as one. In 1971 the first series of executions of young leftists was announced. These bright and dedicated individuals, some of whom were students at Aryamehr University, Iran's M.I.T., had chosen the only path of protest against inequality and repression the autocracy had been unable to eliminate—armed revolt. A year later the shah told the International Labor Office conference in Geneva that Iran was ready to give financial aid to other developing countries. Meanwhile, a strike of only a few hours would bring SAVAK agents into a factory to suppress a protest by arresting the leaders.

Profit Sharing

On 9 May 1961, as noted earlier, Iranian autocracy entered a new stage. The shah closed the Majles and ruled by decree through the cabinet for the next 2½ years, after which a group of even more submissive deputies were selected and placed in the legislature.

In 1962 the shah launched a major campaign to forge an alliance between himself, the peasants, and the workers. Having already initiated a land reform program, he could no longer count on cooperation from the landowners. In order to win workers' support, he began to make a series of promises without regard to the government's ability to fulfill them.

The first grand scheme, that was to make Iranian workers as prosperous as those in the most advanced countries of Western Europe, was the "profit-sharing" law, which was to give the worker "a real feeling of the society's respect for his personality, endeavor, and hard work." In 1962, an American labor expert working in Iran reported that, during the year, the Ministry of Labor had surveyed profit-sharing programs in other countries and had prepared a similar law for Iran:

> While reported in the newspapers as [calling for] 20% of the profit, the profit-sharing law was not intended by the Minister of Labor to be a program that had as its primary purpose the sharing of profits through legislation. The real purpose was, and still is, to encourage the formation of collective-bargaining trade union organizations (syndicates). The profit-sharing aspect of the law was intended as a last resort if collective bargaining could not be implemented in a given workshop or industry. The Ministry of Labor, then, through a profit-sharing commission, would examine the economics of the situation and recommend a sharing of the profits of a given employer [that was] not to exceed 20%.[4]

Iranian workers did not need encouragement to establish labor unions. The only step the government needed to take was to *stop preventing* their formation. As for the profit-sharing law, it was typical of the government's intermittent public relation campaigns to give the regime a progressive image at home and, especially, abroad. The government would take an idea from abroad and attempt to implement part of it, but only halfheartedly. Moreover, many of these ideas had been tried and discarded as ineffective in other countries, and yet in Iran they would be presented as revolutionary innovations. In the case of profit-sharing, an old concept in American personnel management[5] was hailed as a fourth principle of the "Shah-People Revolution," while the government was actively preventing the formation of genuine labor unions and the election of workers' representatives. Thus, the profit-sharing law became whatever the Ministry of Labor wished it to be. It is not surprising, therefore, that the profit-sharing law failed to have its intended effect of drawing workers closer to the regime and so giving them a stake in the political system. The observation of the American labor official was prophetic: "This law becomes just another entry in the statute books of Iran, and will very probably be talked about; but little implementation or enforcement is expected, for a country that cannot enforce its minimum wage laws that have existed for many years, its tax laws, etc., offers little prospect of being able to enforce a very controversial workers' profit-sharing law."[6]

Although the profit-sharing law did mean additional income for the workers, it failed to achieve its intended purpose. Since the Ministry of Labor did not trust either the employers or the workers to implement the law correctly, it directed the program unilaterally. In the opinion of Livernash and Argheyd, who have made a detailed study of labor relations in Iran, this "unconcealed distrust was the reinforcement of an adversary attitude between employers and workers, the very thing the law was purportedly meant to rectify."[7]

Syndicates

Iran continued to be without independent labor unions after the overthrow of Prime Minister Mossadegh in 1953. On 9 February 1965, the last major revision of the labor law of 1959 was carried out by the monarchy. An important provision of this legislation was that neither workers' representatives nor union officers could be discharged or have their jobs changed in such a way as to hinder the performance of their duties as representatives or officers without prior approval of the Ministry of Labor. An equally important provision in the new law was a mechanism for the settlement of disputes "amounting to compulsory arbitration."[8]

Although the number of syndicates, or factory-based labor unions, rose from about 30 in the early 1960s to approximately 519 in 1972,[9] the workers continued to be inadequately represented. This is confirmed by Assef Bayat, who reports that "in five out of twelve factories investigated, the 'workers' representatives' had been officially employed by SAVAK. One factory lacked any syndicate leaders. In three, the syndicate leaders, though not SAVAK agents, had sold out their workers' interests. Three others were militant and loyal to their rank and file interests."[10]

Not only were syndicates unrepresentative, but they also failed to perform their official functions. Although one of the tasks of the syndicates was to conclude collective labor contracts, such agreements, according to Livernash and Arghayd, had been formulated generally "only in connection with the profit-sharing program and seldom with regard to conditions of employment."[11] A notable exception was the oil industry, where syndicates "played a much more active role and where formal collective bargaining has covered a much broader range of issues."[12]

Housing

In the early 1970s the infusion of oil revenues into the national economy sent prices sky-rocketing, particularly the cost of housing. So a campaign was begun to build company housing for workers. Subsequent to a declaration on television by the shah that all factory owners must build houses for their employees, workers in one plant went on strike demanding immediate implementation of the shah's directive. The factory personnel office telephoned the Ministry of Labor for help. Efforts by Ministry officials to quiet the workers were unsuccessful. Naively, the "worker deputies in the Majles" were brought in to explain that implementation of His Majesty's orders required time. This ploy also failed to satisfy the workers, who were rapidly learning to deal with government tactics and were in the process of innovating their own.

The strikers accused the visitors of lying and betraying the "shah-people revolution" and demanded that the shah himself appear on television once again to explain his real intention. The workers had discovered that by expressing their loyalty to the shah they could criticize those of his policies being implemented by Ministry officials. Some time earlier, it was reported that oil workers in Abadan had prevented their managers from leaving the refinery by pasting pictures of the shah on the doors of their automobiles as they chanted *"Javid Shah"* (long live the king). In order to open their car doors, the managers would have had to tear His Majesty's photograph. In 1976, striking workers of Chit-e Jahan textile factory in Karaj faced the shah's troops with pictures of the monarch in their hands. In a strike incident at the Iran National automobile factory, workers disrupted managers' speeches by chanting, "long live the king."[13]

During the housing incident, the official workers' representatives were as helpless as the managers. According to Bayat, "In the absence of a genuine workers' representative in any critical disputes with management during the Pahlavi period, a representative would be unofficially chosen from among the militant workers to conduct negotiations."[14] The strike over housing ended when the strike leaders were arrested.

Factory owners were willing to build worker housing provided the municipality revised its zoning regulations and issued building permits, the Ministry of Water and Power provided water and electricity, banks arranged financing, and the Ministry of Finance

granted tax incentives. But this would have required close coordina-
tion of duties among several government agencies—an act made
unlikely by the decision-making system initiated by the shah,
whereby he would deal with individual ministers directly without
coordinating the various ministerial functions through the prime
minister and the cabinet. By 1978 an insignificant number of workers
lived in company-built housing, and yet the shah stated from exile
in 1979 that as a result of the policies of his government the Iranian
worker "was inexpensively housed."[15]

Minimum Wage

Another set of unfulfilled promises involved the minimum wage.
Here again the Shah's directive was not in tune with his other policies.
On 2 March 1975 he stated: "At any rate, by the end of the Fifth Plan
(March 1978), there will not be a single working Iranian with a
monthly salary of less than 12,000 *rials* a month ($170), no matter
what his job. Certainly the workers' average earnings will far exceed
this floor level. Sharing 20 percent of factory profits nets workers
more than three months' worth of pay a year. As far as the welfare
of the workers is concerned, we will always be a few steps ahead
of them, giving them benefits they never thought of."[16]

A simple calculation indicated that implementation of this directive—to increase the 1975 minimum monthly wage of 3,600 *rials*
to 12,000 *rials* in three years—would have required an annual wage
increase of approximately 50 percent—something no economy could
afford. Once again the workers were left to wonder why the shah's
orders were not being followed. One explanation was that the
decision-making process was at fault. The shah would announce
decisions without prior study and without consulting the officials and
departments concerned. Another explanation was that in the hope
of holding their positions a day longer, ministers sometimes chose
to praise the shah's decisions rather than to point out their
weaknesses.

Wider Share Ownership Program

Finally, the shah decided to make all Iranian workers capitalists.
Through the Wider Share Ownership Program the workers were to

become part owners of the businesses in which they worked. Those
who are familiar with labor relations know that this idea, once
considered a panacea in United States industry, was later set aside
as another questionable item in a long list of employee benefits. Yet
in Iran this idea was presented as revolutionary and became the
thirteenth point of the "Shah-People Revolution." On 16 May 1972
the shah advised the industrialists to come forward and sell at least
one-third of their shares to the public. "Our primary view" he said,
"is that in the first stage [the shares] must be offered to the workers
and staff of the companies."[17] Predictably, a few weeks later, the
minister of economy announced that 86 industrial corporations had
"volunteered" to sell shares to their employees and the public.[18]

Dissatisfied with the slow pace of the "voluntary" stage of the
program, the shah decreed on 14 April 1975 that 49 percent of the
shares of certain private corporations had to be in the hands of the
general public by October 1978.[19] Shortly afterward, the minister of
economy announced that 320 firms would be obliged to participate
in the program and that a number of investment companies would
be established to buy and hold shares not bought by workers and
the general public. These shares would be gradually sold to the public.
Workers would be eligible for loans of up to 100,000 *rials* ($1,500)
granted to them over a three-year period. These loans were to be
repaid by the workers over a ten-year period and would carry a 4
percent interest rate. To be eligible, a worker must have been
employed by the firm for at least three years. The shah later said
that this program would "prevent the creation and growth of
industrial feudalism."[20] However, after all this fanfare, the government admitted in February 1976 that only 14,222 workers of 26
companies had become stockholders in their companies.[21]

With the failure of so many grandiose promises and so much
inequality and repression, it is not surprising that some of the younger
workers should become politicized and should be attracted by the
revolutionary doctrines of the Islamic Mojahedin-e Khalgh and the
Marxist Cherik-ha-ye Fada'i-e Khalgh, the two newly-founded
underground political organizations that took up arms against the
regime. Mohammad-Sadegh Fateh, senior partner of the Jahan
Industrial Group, was the first target of the revolutionary workers.
He was assassinated as he drove to work one summer morning in
1971 in revenge for the massacre earlier in the spring of his textile
workers at Caravan-Sara Sangi by the gendarmerie as they marched

from Karaj toward the Ministry of Labor in Tehran to present their grievances.

Even on the eve of the revolution, May Day 1978, the shah was repeating his oft-told tale that Iranian workers "were among the fortunate few in the world," that they were benefiting from "the most advanced and progressive laws" and that they enjoyed "an exceptional status." He specifically referred to the profit-sharing law and the Wider Share Ownership Law as examples of the benefits his rule had bestowed upon them.[22]

Gholam-Hossein Saedi, Iran's popular playwright, has often said that the intellectuals turned on the ignition key of the revolution, but once the movement gained momentum, the workers' strikes dealt a severe blow to the monarchy and brought about its downfall. In the words of Ervand Abrahamian:

> During the upheavals of early 1978, the urban wage earners had been conspicuous by their absence. The situation changed drastically after June, however, when the urban poor, especially construction laborers and factory workers, started to join the street demonstrations. Their participation not only swelled the demonstrations from tens of thousands of marchers to hundreds of thousands, and even millions, but also changed the class composition of the opposition and transformed the middle-class protest into a joint protest of the middle and working classes. Indeed the entry of the working class made possible the eventual triumph of the Islamic Revolution.[23]

Beginning in September 1978, workers in the Tehran oil refinery went on strike and were joined by the workers in the oil refineries of Esfahan, Shiraz, Tabriz, and Abadan. A few days later, cement workers in Tehran struck, calling for "better wages, removal of martial law, and freedom for all political prisoners."[24] The wave of strikes spread like wildfire. Soon, workers were making political as well as economic demands. As a result, not only were many of the oil refineries shut down, but most of the oil fields as well. The petrochemical complex in Bandar Shahpour, the National Bank, the copper mines near Kerman, and forty other large industrial plants were also shut down.[25] According to Abrahamian, by the third week of October "the working class had joined the middle classes to bring about a massive and unprecedented general strike."[26]

Alternating between a policy of carrot and stick, the government attempted to negotiate with the strike leaders. A quarter-century of repression, however, "had effectively destroyed all free labor unions, all independent professional associations, and all opposition parties with grass root organizations."[27] There were, in fact, no genuine leaders at the head of the pseudo-labor organizations to consider the government's pleas.

The monarchy collapsed in a way unanticipated by anyone. One friend, who, to my surprise, reappeared as a leader of the Tudeh Party after the revolution, told me in February 1978 that the shah faced no serious threat because the workers and the peasants had their heads in the "trough" (akhour). Other friends considered the army, with American support, to be a formidable force. "Who has ever heard of an armless populace overthrowing an army?" was considered a legitimate question. A member of the royal family told me in September 1978 that His Majesty had been through similar turmoil a number of times before and would come out victorious once again.

Up to his last days, the shah was puzzled by the behavior of the workers. In his final book, entitled The Shah's Story, the monarch expressed the belief that "certain legal advantages belonging to Iranian workers had no equivalent even in industrialized or socialist nations."[28] In referring to the Wider Share Ownership Program he wrote: "But it seems that such a scheme was destined to failure. Can anyone tell me why?" He continued, "In 1973, when I visited a sugar refinery near Quchan, 80% of the workers had cars and 50% had servants."[29] In seeking an explanation, the shah writes: "It is because we were reaching the end and a real democracy was coming into being that the forces of destruction united against me."[30]

Some members of the Iranian upper class have a more derogatory explanation: foreign conspiracy. The shah had become too independent for the West; Iran was becoming the Japan of the Middle East and had to be cut down to size.

Some American experts have pointed to the "rapid pace of modernization." The backward Iranians could not be dragged into the twentieth century as abruptly as His Majesty had attempted to do so. As for the workers, they turned against their benefactors because of their character, general ignorance, and ingratitude.

My own understanding of what happened is that the workers had become so totally fed up with the widening gulf between the words and deeds of the Iranian leadership that they joined the revolution as soon as it began to gather steam. As for an explanation of the causes of the revolution, my view concurs with that of Abrahamian:

> The revolution came because the Shah modernized on the socioeco-nomic level and thus expanded the ranks of the modern middle class and the industrial working class, but failed to modernize on another level—the political level; and that this failure inevitably strained the links between the government and the social structure, blocked the channels of communication between the political system and the general population, widened the gap between the ruling circles and the new social forces, and, most serious of all, cut down the few bridges that had in the past connected the political establishment with the traditional social forces, especially with the bazaars and the religious authorities. Thus by 1977 the gulf between the developing socioeconomic system and the underdeveloped political system was so wide that an economic crisis was able to bring down the whole regime. In short, the revolution took place neither because of overdevelopment nor be-cause of underdevelopment but because of uneven development.[31]

Because of the repressive nature of its government, the auto-cracy felt obliged to justify its means to the people by promising desirable ends. That is why the shah often told his ministers: "We shall always be a few steps ahead of them, giving them benefits they never thought of." Thus he was forced into a corner: he would make greater and greater promises—promises that were unrealistic given the country's economic, social, cultural, and administrative structure. These promises of better things to come would raise the level of people's expectations. The shah would then claim, with little evi-dence, that his promises had been fulfilled, thereby negating his modest accomplishment and focusing the public's attention on the wide gap between words and deeds. Progress on the socioeconomic front which could have been evaluated as modest-acceptable in comparison with that of other developing countries was seen as totally inadequate as long as the shah insisted on using the most advanced countries of the world as his points of reference. His attempts to present his modest progress as revolutionary opened him to charges of deception. No matter how much he insisted that Iran was on the verge of catching up with the West, it could not be denied that in terms of human resources Iran was an underdeveloped country. Iran in 1978 with 2,615 people per physician ranked seventh among its Middle Eastern counterparts, following Libya (899), Egypt (1,093), Turkey (1,773), Jordan (1,977), Iraq (2,208), and Syria (2,514). In terms of newspaper readership Iran ranked sixth among the seven nations. As for literacy, Iran with a 37 percent rate ranked fifth behind Turkey (60), Libya (50), Egypt (44), and Syria (40).[32] According to Iran's own statistics the total number of illiterates had actually increased to 15 million by 1978.[33] Even the majority of those considered literate knew little more than how to read and write. As for many of the university graduates, we had learned to be pseudo-Westerners rather than sophisticated Iranians.

Post-Revolutionary Iran

Assef Bayat, who has recently made an on-the-spot study of labor relations under the Islamic Republic of Iran, has divided the post-revolutionary era into three periods. In the first period, between February and August 1979, he finds "a power vacuum in the factories after the flight of the owners and senior managers." Bayat finds in the second period, from September 1979 to June-July 1981, a systematic return of "management from above." The third period began in June 1981 with the dismissal of President Banisadr, the mass execution of opposition forces, and the takeover of management and workers' organizations by the Islamic zealots.[34]

The revolution of February 1979 had many constituencies and each set out to achieve its own ends. A typical set of worker demands, as reported in the newspaper *Ettela'at*, was presented by representatives of a group of construction workers, accompanied by leftist students, on 3 March 1979, to Daryoush Forouhar, minister of labor in the provisional government of Mehdi Bazargan. These demands included reinstatement of discharged workers, establishment of an unemployment benefit scheme, intervention of workers in the administration of factories, utilization of student proposals in factory decisions and in formation of syndicates, and abolition of the previous labor law. Although the labor minister agreed to reinstate the discharged workers and to give them lost pay, he opposed student interference in factories. Otherwise, he said, the door would be opened for other groups such as the intellectuals and "the clergy" to step in. "The workers do not need the advice of others. They know their own problems and the necessary solutions." The meeting ended inconclusively as workers and leftist students chanted revolutionary slogans and demanded immediate decisions while the minister asked for more time to consider their demands.[35]

Extensive and unabated labor unrest brought the leader of the revolution to the fore to placate the workers. In an open letter to the minister of labor on 18 March 1979, the Ayatollah Khomeini reminded him of the critical role played by the workers in bringing down the monarchy and instructed him to resolve their problems as soon as possible. At the same time, the ayatollah urged the workers to practice the art of "revolutionary patience." The government needed time to investigate their demands, he said. Sooner or later they would receive their unpaid wages.

> I ask the courageous workers not to listen to the malicious propaganda of certain elements because under a just Islamic government their grievances will be heard and their rights protected. Wages must be raised as soon as the financial condition of factories has been determined so that they [the workers] will be saved from poverty and can live, like others, in an atmosphere of freedom and welfare.
>
> Mr. Forouhar, you are aware that Islam has special respect for workers. Islam wants to assist the underprivileged to take their destiny into their own hands."[36]

The sympathetic message of reassurance to the workers was taken a step further by the ayatollah on May Day 1979 when, for the first time in more than twenty-five years, workers, students, and politicians with different ideologies participated in Labor Day festivities. The major event of the day was organized by the Islamic Republican Party (IRP), formed a few weeks earlier by the clergy and soon to become Iran's only ruling party. After recitation of verses from the Koran, messages recorded by the Ayatollah Khomeini and the Ayatollah Shari'atmadari, the senior nonpolitical religious figure, were played over the public address system.[37]

In his message the Ayatollah Khomeini spoke in words the workers had never heard from their rulers before. One can imagine the feeling of hope and ecstasy among the workers as they were told that their turn at power had finally arrived. "Designation of one day for workers is perhaps a formality and a gesture of homage;

otherwise, every day is labor day. Our workers are the managers of our human society. The [responsibility for the] administration of countries is [placed] in their hands, in the hands of the peasants and factory workers. It is they who govern nations. Therefore, they are responsible for important affairs and deserve great respect."

He then assured the workers that Islam held them in high regard and warned them not to listen to the leftists, who wanted the wheels of the economy to remain at a standstill. "They do not care for you. It is dear Islam that grants you esteem and believes in your just claims and will deliver your rights to you. Let Islam be put in practice. Let the rotten roots of despotism and foreign domination be removed. Let those who serve others [foreigners] be incapacitated. You are our brothers. You are our loved ones. You must govern this country."[38]

All political parties and labor organizations participated in these Labor Day festivities. Those attending the ceremony organized by the IRP were addressed by a representative of the Palestine Liberation Organization, by future President Abolhasan Banisadr, and by the IRP leader, the Ayatollah Hossein Beheshti. The second major event was organized by the Tudeh Party, making its first public appearance in nearly twenty-five years. The third event was a procession organized by a coalition of independent Marxist organizations, including Cherik-ha-ye Fada'i-e Khalgh, which was led by unemployed workers. This procession was soon disrupted, however, by several hundred violent demonstrators shouting "Islam is victorious. Communism is doomed," who forced the marchers to listen to their speakers as they sat on the street pavement. This was the first appearance of the IRP goon squads, later called *Hezb Allahis*, who gradually eliminated all opposition groups from the political arena by the use of physical violence. The Islamic Mojahedin-e Khalgh organization held its celebration in the city of Karaj, less than an hour's ride west of Tehran.

Participants in each of these gatherings approved the texts of declarations prepared earlier by the organizers. The IRP called for the formation of "management councils" in factories, with the participation of worker representatives, "for the purpose of proper planning of production, distribution, pricing, and protecting the rights of workers and society." The leftist coalition demanded "participation" of workers in the management of industrial and agricultural establishments, and the Mojahedin urged that all factories be administered by "employee councils" (*showra-ye karkonan*), composed of genuine representatives of blue collar workers, white collar employees, and the employers. All three groups also called for equal pay for equal work by women.

The independent Left and the Mojahedin had a number of similar demands not shared by the IRP, including preparation of a new labor law with the participation of the workers—the Leftists adding that the workers must also take part in the drafting of the new constitution. The leftists and the Mojahedin also called for the expropriation of all industrial establishments and banks owned by foreigners. Finally, both the IRP and the leftists urged creation of work for the unemployed, while the Mojahedin went a step further, asking that the right to permanent employment be included in the new constitution.

The independent Left had a larger list of demands than the others; it called for provision of adequate housing for workers, prohibition of child labor, legalization of the right to strike, and freedom of activity by syndicates—demands first made by workers nearly sixty years earlier and still beyond the reach of Iranian workers.[39]

In charting an "Islamic" labor policy and as an indication of its opposition to "foreign" concepts of any kind, the Islamic Republican Party proposed that a day other than the internationally observed May Day be designated as labor day in Iran—"one that would be a reminder of the role played by the workers in the victory of the Islamic revolution."[40]

Showras

Even before May Day 1979, the minimum wage of workers was more than doubled by the Ministry of Labor, and employers were gradually forced to re-employ discharged workers and to place seasonal workers on the regular payroll. These economic decisions were without political implications. However, the promise that workers would take their destiny into their own hands and would live in an atmosphere of freedom remained as unfulfilled as during the shah's rule. It must have been difficult for workers, only a few months after the revolution, to doubt the words of their revolutionary and spiritual leader, even though his promises regarding freedom of association sounded similar to those of the shah. While the shah had stated that Iranian workers enjoyed the protection of the most progressive labor laws in the world, the Ayatollah Khomeini brought the glad tidings that Islamic government would allow workers to take their destiny into their own hands.

The workers went back to work, and many of them began to practice the new art of "revolutionary patience." In the meantime, other workers did not remain still. As a first step they moved against the SAVAK agents in the factories by forming commissions to identify and investigate these individuals.[41] This was the beginning of the movement to establish factory *showras,* or councils.

The term *showra,* which had seen common usage during the 1940s, when the Tudeh Party organized provincial councils, was once again used on the eve of the revolution, but this time by the Mojahedin-e Khalgh, Cherik-ha-ye Fada'i-e Khalgh, and others. Now, however, the word *showra* had a broader meaning that included worker participation in managing the firm. According to Bayat, the constitution of the *showra* of one factory stipulated that the *showra* had the duty "to intervene in [all] the affairs of the factory," including purchasing, sales, and pricing functions. "They indeed did intervene in all factory affairs."[42]

Bayat also reports that almost all workers he interviewed conceived of the *showra* "as the sole responsible body in the factory, the organ through which the workers could exert power and could question those who, until recently, ruled them in the factory."[43]

While the *showras* were being established at the factory level, more familiar provincial labor organizations were being formed across the country. One such union was the Central Council of the Workers of East Azerbaijan. Its chairman was Akbar Dizehji. Even six months after the revolution, the problems faced by organized labor had a familiar ring. In an interview with a Tehran newspaper, Dizehji accused the provincial authorities of intentionally ignoring worker grievances and preventing union activity by confiscating its assets.[44] "It seems that no official in our province is concerned about our problem," he said. "The voice of the workers is not being heard. For this reason I have come to Tehran. Perhaps in the capital city someone will hear the painful cry of us workers."[45]

Worker Takeovers

Even before the collapse of the monarchy, some workers and staff had begun to take over the management of their factories. During this period the workers managed some factories through their *showras.* According to Shaul Bakhash, author of *The Rule of the Ayatollahs,* "In dozens of instances, owners who hoped to hold on to their enterprises were driven away by worker militancy, the inability or unwillingness to meet payrolls, and by deteriorating financial conditions."[46] Workers at the Minoo Industrial Group, for example, imprisoned the owners in the plant for a number of days as they demanded the nationalization of the firm.[47] The Bazargan government expressed early and direct opposition to the *showras,* claiming that the "triumph of the revolution eliminated the need for them."[48] According to Bakhash, however, in some instances where employees seized control and ousted the former management, "officials were inclined to look the other way as long as the new management was able to pay its way and maintain order."[49]

The first period of post-revolutionary labor relations came to an end in August 1979, only six months after the revolution, when, according to Bayat, "the Left organizations were attacked, and their headquarters ransacked; the government banned progressive newspapers, and monopolized the official media." These events were followed by gradual attacks on independent and leftist *showras* and on individual workers.

Management from Above

The second period of labor relations, from September 1979 to June-July 1981, was marked by a systematic return of "management from above," reports Bayat, and increasing repression of "non-Islamic" elements.[50] Nevertheless a large cross section of trade unions had a limited participation in May Day celebrations in 1980. Although the initiative for the event was even more definitely in the hands of the IRP and its associated trade unions, called Anjoman-ha-ye Eslami-e Kargaran, or Islamic Associations of Workers, the trade union of oil workers and the Marxist Peikar Organization were able to publish their May Day programs in the newspapers.[51] The nine processions organized by the IRP commenced, as in the previous year, at different corners of Tehran, but this time converged in front of the former embassy of the United States, referred to as the "Den of Spies"—an indication that Labor Day had now become integrated into the ruling parties' political programs regardless of its relevance to labor.

At the former American embassy, the Ayatollah Khomeini's second May Day statement was a far cry from his message of the year before. There was no reference this time to workers' power or their role in the governance of the nation. Instead, the ayatollah attempted to bring the workers down from their pedestal by telling them that "everyone" labored. "With this in mind," he said, "Labor Day is the day of all the people of Iran and not of a particular segment of the population." He then once again attacked government critics—and the leftists in particular—for disrupting orderly work and for attempting to deceive the workers and peasants by telling them that they were their genuine supporters.[52]

At the conclusion of the celebration organized by the IRP and directed by Hojjat-ol-Eslam Mousavi-Kho'iniha, leader of the students who had seized the American embassy, a sixteen-point manifesto was approved. Only three of the sixteen points dealt directly with labor affairs. These were calls for resolution of the unemployment problem, issuance of regulations concerning the *showras,* and passage of a new labor law. The remaining items dealt with domestic and foreign policy issues.[53]

Banisadr, who was now keeping his distance from the IRP, spent May Day 1980 in Esfahan, which he called "Iran's Labor City," encouraging the workers to labor harder in order to strengthen the revolution. Workers affiliated with the National Front, led by some of the late Dr. Mossadegh's associates, celebrated May Day, not, as was their custom, in the streets, but in the safe haven of the front's headquarters.[54]

Within a year after the revolution, many workers had concluded that little of the power wrested from the former regime had accrued to them. A leader of the syndicate of the oil pipeline workers complained that the living conditions of the workers were still unsatisfactory. His grievances included: exorbitant prices, low wages, housing that absorbed much of the workers' income, prevention of the formation of labor unions by the Ministry of Labor, persistence of anti-labor laws legislated during the former regime, and lack of attention to the lawful demands of the workers.[55]

Trade union activity was, as always, a direct function of the country's political atmosphere. When Bazargan, an "Islamic liberal," was ousted by the clergy in November 1979, the clergy-dominated government supported Islamic associations which would equally represent the workers and management and include representatives of the Ministry of Labor. "The associations were a vehicle for the consolidation of the clergy's power, opposed to both 'liberal managers' and the independent *showras*," observes Bayat. In August 1980, the government formalized its plans for the *showras* as the Ministry of Labor approved regulations granting them only a consultative role. "Such regulations, however, could not regulate labor-management relations," observes Bayat. "When labor had the upper hand, it went far beyond the legal limits; when management could, it suppressed the [council], even preventing elections."[56] The actual practice of the *showras*, Bayat points out, "depended directly on the balance of forces within the production unit."[57]

At the same time, the government established special committees in the factories in order to "purify" them from "the conspiracies of the agents of the West, the East, and the overthrown Pahlavi regime." Since the workers had already ejected the remaining agents of the SAVAK, "this invariably referred to the self-activity of the rank-and-file workers and the purge of the militant elements." These "purging committees" (*Hey'at-ha-ye Paksazi*) consisted of a representative each of the provincial governor, the revolutionary prosecutor, the factory management, and the Ministry of Labor, and an elected employee.[58]

The third post-revolutionary Labor Day took place in 1981. Participation had now been limited to three groups: the ruling party of the clergy, the IRP; the Tudeh Party; and the majority faction of Cherik-ha-ye Fada'i, which had thrown in its lot with the Tudeh Party, the party it had for so long opposed. The IRP and the Tudeh Party maintained their uneasy alliance by holding separate demonstrations: the IRP in the morning and the Tudeh Party in the afternoon.[59]

It did not take long for the Tudeh Party, the last ally of the IRP, to be eliminated also. The party's leaders were soon arrested, and some were executed as spies for the Soviet Union.

Suppression of the Labor Movement

The third period of post-revolutionary labor relations began in June-July 1981 with the dismissal of President Banisadr and the mass execution of the opposition forces, especially the Mojahedin-e Khalgh. Bayat writes: "Features of this period in the factories included the hegemony of the *maktabi* [Islamic] management and the Islamic Associations, militarization of the factories, attacks on the formal wages of the workers (the real wages had already been lowered

by the mounting rate of inflation), and an official ban on the
formation of even pro-government *showras* for the time being."
Banisadr's minister of labor, Mohammad Mir Sadeghi, who had a
"liberal" attitude toward labor relations, was replaced by Tavakoli,
a follower of the hard-line Hojjatieh faction of the clergy. According
to Bayat, "Tavakoli rejected even the vague idea of 'Quranic showras.'"
Tavakoli added, "Islam does not recognize the *showra* system; in
Islam the government belongs to God, prophets and *imams*, and in
their absence, to the *na'ib* [deputy] *imam*"[60] —for the present, meaning
the Ayatollah Khomeini.

Iran had come full circle in less than three years, as all hope
that the revolution of 1979 would lead to a political system conducive
to the formation of independent trade unions was once again
disappointed. The workers and the people of Iran had lost another
battle, but their struggle would never end.

Appendix A
Biographical Notes

Amirkeyvan, Amir. An Esfahani labor leader, Amirkeyvan was born in the Takht-e Foulad district of Esfahan around 1920. His family was engaged in agriculture. Amirkeyvan was employed at the Nour textile mill where he soon became popular among his fellow workers. Initially he maintained good relations with two other Esfahani labor leaders, Taghi Fadakar and Shams Sadri, but later he broke away from both of them, forming his own union affiliated with EMKA.

Amir-Khizi, Ali. A prominent Tudeh Party leader, Amir-Khizi was born in Tabriz about 1900. At one time he was a teacher in Tabriz schools. Early in his political career he was a member of the opposition Mossavat (Equality) Party. Later he was imprisoned by Reza Shah for his membership in the Arani group, or "Fifty-three" Marxists. A founder of the Tudeh Party and a member of its first Central Committee, Amir-Khizi was re-elected by the Party Congress in 1944 and 1948. He was also a prolific contributor to the Tudeh press. On 18 May 1949, he was sentenced to death, *in absentia*, by the Tehran Military Tribunal. See U.S.G., Department of State, O.I.R. report no. 4940, U.S. National Archives.

Atighehchi, Ezatollah. A leader of the Tudeh union, the CUC, Atighehchi did not receive public notice prior to 1944, when he was listed as an engineer and a "courageous" writer for the *Giti* newspaper. In May 1945, he was a strike leader at the Kermanshah oil refinery. Shortly thereafter he left Iran to live in France. Using a Lyon carpet business as his base, he became allegedly engaged in espionage, maintaining contacts with Soviet agents, as well as with the shah, the Tudeh Party,

French military intelligence, and intelligence agents in Switzerland and North Africa. See *Salnameh-e Donya* :1323, 168; *Zafar*, 5 June 1945; and U.S. Government, Department of State, O.I.R. report no. 4940, U.S. National Archives.

Beriya, Mohammad. A poet and militant Communist, Beriya became a labor leader in Tabriz. "Beriya," meaning "without hypocrisy," was a pen name; his legal name was not used and is unknown. He was born in 1917 in Tabriz, the son of Esma'il, who worked as a carpenter. As a youth, Beriya spent a number of years in the Russian Caucasus and in Esfahan. He studied in Baku and wrote his first poem against a bookseller who overcharged him for a dictionary. This led to a student protest against the shop owner. He was first employed as a street sweeper, for which he was paid 6 *rials* a day. After performing his military service, which inspired him to write poems against army injustice, he later became a foreman, and then a musician at the park merry-go-round in Tabriz.

Beriya lived in the Soviet Union for two years, returning to Iran in 1943. He then set up a print shop in Tabriz where he published the bilingual newspaper *Beriya* in Persian and Azari. He wrote and published many poems in Azari, which were described as "rude, but with some literary merit," attacking Reza Shah, the fascists, and social injustice. He spoke Azari, Persian, and Russian, was said to have an excellent speaking voice, and was a formidable rabble-rouser. He was also described as "intelligent, energetic, and sincere." The British consul-general in Tabriz, rarely sympathetic to the Left, described him as "an unprincipled scavenger-lampoonist, whose Soviet connections have brought him to comparative affluence." Shortly after rising to power, he divorced his wife and, in February 1946, married a young school girl of the Borhani family. He was reportedly killed by a mob in Tabriz on 12 December 1947. See *Ra'd-e Emrouz*, no. 426; *Rahbar*, 10 January 1945; U.K.G., "Review of Events in Azerbaijan," 22 August 1944 (E5568/138/34) PRO; U.S. Government, Military Attache in Tehran, report no. R35–45, 31 March 1945, U.S. National Archives; and R. Rossow, "The Battle of Azerbaijan," 30.

Dehgan, Seyyed-Mohammad. A leader of the General Trade Union of Tehran in the 1920s, Dehgan was the son of Seyyed-Mohammad-Taghi, a resident of the village of Kalhor of Kashan and the nephew (*amouzadeh*) of Seyyed-Jalal Kashani, editor of the newspaper, *Habl-ol-Matin*. Dehgan studied under Abdol-Rahim Talebov in the Caucasus and later developed a good command of the Russian language and literature. He translated a number of Russian works into Persian, including the *Communist Manifesto*. After the closing down of his newspaper, *Haghighat*, and his return from Moscow, Dehgan moved to the town of Babol, where he became a cotton farmer. Using Russian books on cotton farming, Dehgan created a model farm, and other local farmers followed his practices. In 1925 he was arrested for his past political activities, but was later released on the occasion of Reza Shah's coronation in the spring of 1926. He was then employed at the State Cotton Monopoly in Khorramabad. He died there a few years later. See S. Mani, *Tarikhcheh-e Nehzat,* 14, 18, 31–3.

Eftekhari, Yousef. A veteran socialist labor leader, Eftekhari was born in 1903 in Azerbaijan, where he received his early education. He was involved in the 1929 AIOC strike in Abadan and was imprisoned as a Communist by Reza Shah during the 1930s. Upon his release in 1941, he became a labor organizer, first directing his attention to the Soviet-controlled areas in northern Iran. He later became active in the south. He was suspected by the Americans of having Communist leanings, an accusation he vigorously denied. See U.S. Government, Department of State, O.I.R., report no. 4940, U.S. National Archives.

Enghelab, Khalil. A lawyer and labor leader, Enghelab was born in Azerbaijan around 1907. During the rule of Reza Shah he was employed by the Tabriz Department of Justice until his imprisonment for three years for allegedly preaching revolution. Released in 1941, he remained in Tehran until the summer of 1942, when Governor-General Fahimi appointed him as advocate-general in the High Court of Tabriz. He was described by the British consul in Tabriz as

> unimpressive in appearance, vehement, and undisciplined by temperament, but possessed of a certain imitative cleverness which passes for ability here. It is related that even at school he wrote with red ink. It is also recorded that he quarrelled with and wounded his French teacher while yet a boy. It is said that if he encountered opposition, Enghelab was accustomed to shout: "Stop, you are speaking to your future prime minister." Also, he has recently been explaining where Hitler and Mussolini have gone astray and making it clear that he, Enghelab, will not commit the same mistakes.

See U.K. Government, "TD," 30 November 1942 (E80/80/34) PRO.

Eskandari, Soleiman-Mirza. A radical prince of the Qajar royal family, Eskandari fought on behalf of the constitutionalists in 1909 against Mohammad-Ali Shah. As a founder of the Democratic Party in that same year, he was reputed to be a Socialist. Subsequent to the Anglo-Russian invasion of 1911, Soleiman-Mirza directed the government of resistance of the Committee for National Defense in Kermanshah. After the Russian revolution divided the small Socialist movement in Iran into reformists and radicals, Soleiman-Mirza remained in the Democratic Party as a reformer and nationalist. In 1919, as a leader of the anti-British Democrats, he denounced the Anglo-Iranian agreement of 1919, and in 1921 he formed the Socialist Party. In 1923 he served briefly in Reza-Khan's first cabinet as minister of education. In 1927, when Reza Shah dissolved the Socialist Party, Soleiman-Mirza was forced into political retirement. Later, he returned to the political stage as the chairman of the newly founded Tudeh Party. See E. Abrahamian, "Social Bases," 181–87.

Fadakar, Taghi. The founder of the Esfahan labor unions, Fadakar was born in Esfahan in 1903. His father, Sheikh Mohammad Ansar Turk Hamedani, was a cleric who studied in Najaf and subsequently took up residence in Esfahan. From Hamedani's marriage to the cousin of Molla Bashi-e Esfahani issued two sons: Mirza Bagher Araghi Esfahani and Mirza (Sheikh) Taghi Fadakar, who was three years younger. Fadakar's father died at the age of forty when Fadakar was only two years old. After completing his studies, Fadakar's older brother, Bagher, took up a teaching position in Esfahan. He also wrote poetry. As a result of his friendship with Heidar-Khan, Bagher participated in the Jangali Movement. He was wounded in a skirmish at Talesh and subsequently died. Meanwhile, Fadakar worked his way through school in Esfahan, where he attended Golbahar primary school and Saremieh and Sadr high schools. He then attended the College of Political Science (Madreseh-e Siyasi) in Tehran.

While in the capital, Fadakar became acquainted with Hasan Modarres and Soleiman-Mirza Eskandari, then the leader of the Socialists. Moreover, as a result of his brother's influence, he spent a short time fighting in the Jangali Movement. Fadakar's first job was with the Soviet Commercial Office in Esfahan (Sherkat-e Panbeh-e Shargh), where he learned some Russian. Subsequently, he was employed in the Esfahan Department of Registry and placed in charge of census and statistics for the districts of Chahar Mahal-e Bakhtiari and Boir Ahmadi. Later, he took up the legal profession and represented the leaders of the Bakhtiari tribe.

After the abdication of Reza Shah in 1941, Fadakar organized the textile mill workers of Esfahan, then formed unions for handmade-textile workers, drivers of motor vehicles and carriages, and others. Because of his success in organizing the workers and his known sympathies toward Marxism, Fadakar was persuaded by A. S. Kambakhsh to join the Tudeh Party. Shortly thereafter, all union signboards in Esfahan were changed to indicate their association with the Tudeh Party. As a deputy in the Fourteenth Majles, Fadakar supported the acceptance of Pishevari's credentials. During this time he formed a bond of friendship and mutual respect with Dr. Mohammad Mossadegh. In the spring of 1946, the party instructed Fadakar to return to Esfahan and, together with a number of emigrants from the Russian Caucasus, build an arsenal in preparation for a possible armed uprising. Esfahan was to divert pressure from the Pishevari regime if the central government decided to attack Azerbaijan. In September 1946, Mozaffar Firouz, minister of labor and propaganda, arrived in Esfahan to arrest a number of individuals including Fadakar. Having received warning of Firouz's intentions, all ammunition produced and stored at the Nour factory was dumped in the river, and Fadakar escaped to Tehran.

After the unsuccessful attempt on the life of the shah in Tehran in February 1949, Fadakar was arrested, but was soon released through the intervention of Dr. Mossadegh, after promising to remain in Tehran. Once Dr. Mossadegh became prime minister, Fadakar was able to return to Esfahan. He then became a candidate for the Sixteenth Majles, but the elections were never held in Esfahan. After the August 1953 coup, in which Dr. Mossadegh was removed as prime minister, Fadakar once again came under surveillance. He spent the following years initially practicing law and then farming in Esfahan— both endeavors made difficult by SAVAK interference. In the early morning of 27 June 1971 Fadakar was run over by an automobile on his farm outside of Esfahan. He had gone to the site at 5:00 A.M. in order to negotiate the sale of part of his property. A week later, a policeman turned himself in and claimed the death was the result of an accident. Iraj, one of Fadakar's five children, strongly suspects foul play.

Jahani, Hossein. A founder of the Tudeh Party, Jahani was born in Tehran in 1904, the son of a skilled craftsman named Ostad-Ali. He left primary school after a few years because of the death of his father, becoming an apprentice to a carpenter. He continued to study at night. In 1925 he joined Soleiman-Mirza Eskandari's Socialist Party and in 1928 organized a union of wage-earning carpenters. Jahani, like Mahzari, was a founding member of the Tudeh Party. As a leader of the Central Council, he was elected secretary, while at the same time he represented the carpenters' union. As a joint candidate of the Tudeh Party and the Central Council for the Fourteenth Majles from Tehran, he finished forty-eighth. At the First Party Congress in August 1944, he represented the town of Saveh. In 1945 he was co-chairman of the party's propaganda commission. As late as June 1948, he was a member of the Executive Board of the Central United Council. See *Rahbar*, no. 351; *Zafar*, no. 118; J. A. Grant, 21 August 1944 (E5733/1905/34) PRO; *Razm*, 7 October 1943; *Mardom*, 19 October 1943; and U.S. Government, Department of State, O.I.R. report no. 4940, U.S. National Archives.

Mahzari, Ebrahim. The first leader of the Tudeh trade union, Mahzari was born in the Province of Azerbaijan around 1908. When he was only fifteen days old, his father, along with fifteen other constitutionalists, was executed by firing squad during the pro-constitutional uprising in Azerbaijan. His mother then took him to the Province of Gilan, which at the time was occupied by the Czarist Russian army, subsequent to the Anglo-Russian Treaty of 1907. By the time Mahzari was ten years old, his mother had died of starvation, according to the Tudeh newspaper *Mardom* of 16 October 1943. At the age of fifteen, Mahzari was employed in a factory and spent a good part of his wages on

educating himself. At seventeen, he organized a secret union, for which
he was detained in Qasr prison. After three years of detention, he was
exiled to Semnan, where he organized the workers of the local cotton
spinning factory. Once again he was put in jail—initially in Semnan
and later in Tehran. After being released, he spent two years in military
service and then was employed in a Tehran factory. After the
occupation of Iran by the Allies in 1941, Mahzari participated in the
organization of the Tudeh Party's Central Council and was elected
chairman while he was employed at the Ghaniabad copper smelting
factory as a lathe-operator. As a candidate to the Fourteenth Majles,
he received the joint support of the Tudeh Party and the Central
Council. He finished forty-fourth. Mahzari was a leading member of
the Tudeh Party from the start. In October 1942, at the First Provincial
Conference of the Tudeh Party in Tehran, he was elected to the Central
Committee. In August 1944, he represented Tehran at the First Party
Congress. See *Razm*, 28 September and 7 October 1943; J. A. Grant,
21 August 1944 (E5733/1905/34) PRO; *Mardom*, 20 October 1943; and
Rahbar, no. 351.

Ovanessian, Ardeshir (Ardashez). A veteran Communist leader, Ovanessian was the son of a carriage driver of Armenian extraction. He was
born around 1905 in the town of Rasht. His family, however, was
originally from Shapour (Salmas) in the province of Azerbaijan.
Ovanessian attended primary school in Rasht and later studied for two
years in Russia, allegedly at the Young Communist School in Moscow.
He then spent some time in France before returning to Iran. Ovanessian
was an active organizer of the Persian Communist Party and the trade
union of the time. His memoirs of this period are an important source
of information. He was first imprisoned at the age of seventeen and
spent eleven or more years in various prisons, including the Island of
Qeshm, to which he was banished after his arrest in 1934 for his
membership in the Communist underground. After his release in 1941,
he became a founding member of the Tudeh Party. The U.S. State
Department described him as a "veteran agitator, author of the treatises
on Tudeh party organization, and one of the outstanding Soviet trained
leaders in the party." In a U.S. military intelligence report, he was called
"intelligent; perhaps the best versed in Marxist theory of the Tudeh
leaders; an intense personality, is honest and quite sincere. His long
confinements have understandably embittered him. He likes to think
of himself as an Iranian rather than as champion of the distrusted
Armenian minority. . . . He is pro-Soviet and a fanatical Communist;
is one of the most important figures in the party, and is reliably reported
by two independent sources to lay down official doctrine for the entire
party." Ovanessian was elected to the Fourteenth Majles as an
Armenian representative in 1944 and in the same year was named to
the Tudeh Central Committee. In August 1945, he organized a peasant

rebellion in Azerbaijan. Later, after the Tehran police had found documents implicating him in a plot against the government, he abandoned his position in the Majles, fled to Rasht, and eventually became director-general of propaganda for the Azerbaijan regime. When that regime collapsed, he fled with Pishevari to the Soviet Union. He was wanted by the Iranian police once the roundup of Tudeh leaders in 1949 began and on 18 May was sentenced to death *in absentia* by the Tehran Military Court. Ovanessian spoke Persian, Armenian, Azari, Russian, and some English. See U.S. Government, "Who's Who in the Tudeh Party," 31 March 1945 (RG226/126793) U.S. National Archives.

Pishevari, Mir-Ja'far. Leader of the Azerbaijan autonomy movement, Pishevari was born in the village of Zavieh in the Khalkhal district of Azerbaijan in 1893. His father was a poor *seyyed* (descendant of the prophet) and his family was known for its liberal views. Pishevari had a difficult life as a child. He learned Persian, Azari, and Arabic (by reading the Koran). He was reportedly a voracious reader. Pishevari supported himself financially from the age of twelve. He moved to Baku, capital of Russian (later Soviet) Azerbaijan, where he was employed at the Iranian School. He worked during the day and studied at night. After passing his examinations, he was given a teaching position in which he taught Arabic and Islamic law. He joined the Adalat Party, later known as the Persian Communist Party, and became one of its leaders, editing the party newspaper *Horriyat* (Liberty). Upon his return to Iran and association with the Communist leader Heidar-Khan, Pishevari participated in the Jangali Movement. Subsequently, he moved to Tehran and helped organize the General Trade Union. He was also editor of *Haghighat*. In 1930 Pishevari was imprisoned. Freed along with other political prisoners in 1941, he became publisher of the newspaper *Ajir*. After his credentials were rejected by the Fourteenth Majles, Pishevari formed the Democratic Party of Azerbaijan and became a leader of the autonomy movement of the province. After the collapse of the regime in December 1946, he fled to Baku, where, in August 1947, he was mysteriously killed in an automobile accident. See U.S. Government, Tabriz Consulate, 21 June 1946 (891.00/6–2146) U.S. National Archives; and U.S. Government, Department of State, O.I.R. report no. 4940, U.S. National Archives.

Qavam, Ahmad (Qavam-os-Saltaneh). A prime minister under two shahs, Qavam was the son of Mo'tamed-os-Saltaneh and was born about 1872. He was appointed vice minister of the interior in December 1909, vice minister of war in April 1910, and minister of war in July of the same year. Between 1911 and 1921 he served as minister of the interior and finance a number of times. On 4 June 1921 he became prime minister. Among those serving on his first cabinet were Dr. Mohammad Mossadegh as minister of finance and Reza-Khan (later Reza Shah) as minister of war.

In 1923, Qavam was arrested for an alleged plot against the prime minister, Reza-Khan, and his estates were confiscated. Released shortly afterward, he left Iran and lived for several years in Paris. On his return to Iran in 1930, he built an estate at Jalalieh, near Tehran, where he lived in retirement until Reza Shah's abdication in 1941. In August 1942 he became prime minister once again and formed his first post-Reza Shah cabinet. Although he was considered to be pro-British early in his career, the British now found him to be too independent. He was, however, considered to favor increased American influence in Iran, believing that it was the only means of keeping Iran free of foreign domination. Qavam was described by the American military attache as wily, unscrupulous, strong, severe, capable, and tireless. His ruling passion was said to be a desire for power. He was, on the other hand, considered enlightened, progressive, and sincerely interested in effecting social reform in Iran.

Princess Ashraf Pahlavi has given the following description of Ahmad Qavam:

> Although Qavam [in 1947] was 70 years old, he was an extremely charismatic politician. An aristocrat through and through, Qavam was something of a martinet. He allowed no chairs in his office except his own, so that no one else, not even his own ministers, could sit in his presence. Nor would he allow members of Parliament to speak directly to him. Qavam insisted that remarks be addressed to his secretary, who in turn would relay the speech to "His Excellency." If anyone forgot this rule and spoke directly to the Prime Minister, he would turn to his secretary and ask, "What is this gentleman saying?"

See J. Zargham-Boroujeni, *Dowlat-ha-ye Asr-e Mashroutiyat*, 46–105; U.S. Government, Military Attache in Tehran, 29 March 1946 (RG–226/50148) U.S. National Archives; and Ashraf Pahlavi, *Faces in a Mirror* (New York, 1980), 81.

Rousta, Reza. The main founder of the CUC, Rousta was born to a peasant family in the village of Vishka (within several kilometers of Rasht) in 1903. After studying for a few years under the supervision of the village cleric (*akhound*),he moved to the city of Rasht, where he continued his education through high school with the aid of his uncle, a domestic servant. While in high school, he was involved in sociopolitical activities. In conjunction with his teacher, Hossein Jowdat, he organized literary and cultural meetings. They also formed adult literacy classes, published a magazine, and organized theatrical plays. He then left school and joined the revolutionaries under the leadership of Heidar-Khan, the founder of the Persian Communist Party, who made a great impact on Rousta's political development. In 1922, after the fall of the Jangali Movement (an effort led by Mirza-Kouchek-Khan to gain autonomy for Gilan), he left for the Soviet Union to pursue further studies, returning to Iran in 1923. In Tehran he joined Soleiman-Mirza Eskandari's Socialist Party and took part in the electoral campaign for the Fifth Majles working for the National Bloc. As a result of his participation in the electoral campaign, his clandestine publication of tracts, and his organization of a mass meeting at Masjed-e Shah, the police began to pursue him. Rousta, however, succeeded in escaping to Esfahan and then moved to Kerman. In Esfahan he worked together with Seyyed-Mohammad Tanha, known as Esma'ili, leader of the printers' union. He contracted typhus there and after recovering moved to Kerman, where he was employed at the Russian Commercial Office. In Kerman he also worked with the *Bidari* newspaper and organized meetings with workers. In 1931, however, he was arrested in Kerman and confined in the Qasr prison in Tehran. After serving five years in solitary confinement, he was exiled to Damghan, where he worked in a garage as a clerk for two *rials* a day and taught French in the evenings. In 1937, he was again arrested together with his father, sister, and younger brother—at the same time as the arrest of the "fifty-three" Marxists. After ten months of imprisonment he was exiled to Saveh, where he was again imprisoned, this time for a little over a month. After a few months in Saveh, he was arrested for the fourth time and spent another 2½ years in the local prison. He was again released but rearrested in 1941. In September he was released from prison, returned to Tehran and became a founding member of the Tudeh Party and a member of its first Central Committee. Weekly meetings of cell (*howzeh*) no. 52 were held at his house on Thursday afternoons. As a member of the Central Committee in charge of organizational affairs, he visited various cities in order to open party branches. Rousta was the prime mover in the creation of the Central United Council on 1 May 1944. He also served as editor of the union's organ *Zafar*. He was named to the Inspection Commission of the Tudeh Party in 1945 and in the same year to the Council of the World Federation of Trade Unions despite his brief imprisonment by Tehran authorities to prevent his attending the WFTU meeting in Paris.

Rousta's career came to a virtual end in April 1947 when he was arrested on charges of inciting revolution, embezzling 1 million *rials* in union funds, and committing other offenses. He remained in jail until November, when he was released on bail. He then dropped from sight, although he was named to the Tudeh Central Committee in 1948. It was reported that he had gone to Paris and then to the Soviet Union. Rousta was described by a U.S. official as "hard-working, ruthless, and given to Marxist cliches." His wife, Showkat, was said to have been a Soviet agent. On 18 May 1949 he was sentenced to death *in absentia* by the Tehran Military Court. He died in the Soviet Union. See G.

Lenczowski, *Russia and the West*, 105; U.S. Government, War Department, 15 September 1945 (RG226/32421) U.S. National Archives; *Rahbar*, 19 January 1944; *Ra'd-e Emrouz*, 31 August 1944; *Razm*, 8 October 1943; *Mardom*, 13 October 1943; and U.S. Government, Department of State, O.I.R. report no. 4940, U.S. National Archives.

Simonian, Ghazar. Reportedly a member of the secret committee of the Tudeh Party, Simonian was born in Tehran about 1908 of an Armenian family. After studying in the American (Alborz) College of Tehran, he taught in the Soviet School at Tehran, worked in a minor capacity for Kampsax, a Scandinavian engineering firm in Iran, and also engaged in political activity which resulted in his spending some seven years in jail. After joining the Tudeh Party, he ran unsuccessfully for the Fourteenth Majles as representative of the southern Armenian communities of Iran. He then became a translator for *Journal de Tehran* and a contributor to the Tudeh press. He was also active in the Central United Council and a member of its Executive Committee. In 1948 he was employed by the Czech Legation at Tehran as adviser and chief translator, and was reportedly the person in this legation through whom the Tudeh Party received subsidies from the Soviets. In 1949 he was sentenced to death *in absentia* following the attempted assassination of the shah. See U.S. Government, Department of State, O.I.R. report no. 4940, U.S. National Archives.

Appendix B
Comparison of Estimated Number of Employees in Various Industries and Members Claimed by the CUC

Industry	No. Firms*	No. Employees	No. Members Aug. 45	No. Members Aug. 46
Agriculture	71	4,580	–	5,000
Cotton Ginning	(60)	(2,000)†	–	–
Wool Processing	(10)	(180)	–	–
Fisheries	(1)	(2,400)†	–	(5,000)
Mining	N.A.	5,000	7,000	8,000
Food and Kindred Products	346	14,910	16,200	16,500
Canning	(5)	(500)†	–	–
Dried Fruit	(25)	(2,000)†	–	–
Flour Milling	(100)	(3,200)†	–	(3,500)‡
Rice Milling	(30)	(330)†	–	–
Sugar Refining	(35)	(5,500)†	(1,200)	(2,000)
Tea Processing	(54)	(2,000)†	–	–
Beverages	(65)	(730)	–	(3,000)
Fats and Oils	(2)	(200)	–	–
Ice Making	(30)	(450)	–	–
Other Unspecified Categories	–	–	(15,000)	(9,000)
Tobacco	1	2,000	2,000	2,200
Textile and Apparel	85	30,000	18,000	40,000
Lumber and Wood	40	750	–	–
Furniture	30	580	–	–
Paper and Allied Products	5	250	–	–
Printing and Publishing	40	1,000	1,100	2,150

265

Industry	No. Firms*	No. Employees	No. Members Aug. 45	No. Members Aug. 46
Chemical and Allied Products	**100**	**6,500**	**3,250**	**2,300**
Soap	(16)	(840)	(750)	–
Matches	(45)	(4,200)	(2,000)	–
Other	(39)	(1,460)	(500)	–
Petroleum	**1**	**62,000**	**–**	**45,000**
Rubber	**10**	**360**	**–**	**–**
Leather	**30**	**1,400**	**–**	**–**
Non-Metallic Mineral Products	**185**	**7,275**	**825**	**4,200**
Bricks	(80)	(2,500)	–	–
Refractories	(1)	(230)	(250)	–
Porcelain	(7)	(120)	–	–
Glass and Glassware	(40)	(2,400)	–	(3,000)
Cement	(3)	(1,400)	(600)	(1,200)
Concrete Products	(50)	(525)	–	–
Cut Stone and Stone	(4)	(100)	–	–
Primary Metal Products	**32**	**190**	**–**	**–**
Fabricated Metal Products	**95**	**1,220**	**–**	**–**
Machines	**8**	**625**	**–**	**–**
Electrical Power Generation	**100**	**5,000**	**–**	**–**
Misc. Manufacturing	**2**	**150**	**–**	**–**
Railroad Transportation	**1**	**18,000**	**32,000**	**20,000**
Warehousing	**7**	**1,000**	**–**	**–**
Automotive Repairs	**50**	**1,000**	**–**	**–**
Total	**1,239**	**163,790**	**80,375**	**143,350**
Unclassified Categories				
Munitions			2,000	3,000
Carpet and Silk Weaving			4,000	22,000
Transport			6,000	15,000
Road and Dock			34,000	56,000§
Public Places of Entertainment			2,000	–
Agricultural Workers			58,000	8,000
Various Guilds and Trades			7,000	9,000
Municipal and Governmental Departments			15,000	1,500
Teaching, Medical, Nursing, Engineering, and Technical Professions			1,100	6,700‖
Powerhouse and Post, Telegraph, and Telephone			250	600
Electrical Firms			–	–

Industry	No. Firms*	No. Employees	No. Members Aug. 45	No. Members Aug. 46
Slaughterhouses				3,000
Public Power				1,500
Cotton Pickers				2,000
War Ministry Works	_____	_____	_____	1,500
Grand Total	**1,239**	**163,790**	**209,750**	**276,150**

Sources: Figures for the estimated number of employees were drawn from the following: I. G., Vezarat-e Kar va Tablighat, "Amar-e Amal-kard-e Sanayeh-e Keshvar dar Sal-e 1326" (Tehran, 1948); ibid., "Amar-e Amal-kard-e Sanayeh-e Keshvar dar Sal-e 1328" (Tehran, 1949).

Figures for the number of members claimed by the CUC in August 1945 were drawn from W. J. Handley, "Labor in Iran," pp. 26–27. Figures for the number of members claimed by the CUC in August 1946 were drawn from W. J. Handley, "Labor in Iran—Update," 19 October, 1946 (RG-84/2260) Nat. Arch., pp. 15-16.

* Includes firms employing ten or more employees.
† Seasonal.
‡ Includes grain elevators.
§ Includes 11,000 "dock workers and others" plus 45,000 "builders."
‖ Includes 3,000 "educators," 2,700 "hospital workers," and 1,000 "engineers and technicians."

Notes

Chapter 1

1. M. T. Nasehi, "Tashkilat-e Kargari-e Iran," *Rahbar* (10 April 1944).

2. *Tarikhcheh-e Mokhtasar-e Showra-ye Mottahedeh-e Markazi-e Ettehadieh-ha-ye Kargaran va Zahmatkeshan-e Iran* (Tehran: 1953), 4.

3. S. Zabih, *The Communist Movement in Iran* (Berkeley, California: University of California Press, 1966), 65.

4. *The Times*, 28 June 1910.

5. E. G. Browne, *The Press and Poetry of Modern Persia* (Cambridge, England: Cambridge University Press, 1914), 35–6.

6. George Lenczowski, *Russia and the West in Iran 1918–1948: A Study in Big Power Rivalry* (Ithaca, N.Y.: Cornell University Press, 1949), 10.

7. T. T. Hammond, *Lenin on Trade Unions and Revolution 1893–1917* (New York: Columbia University Press, 1957), 3.

8. Ibid., 42.

9. Ibid., 124.

10. Abdossamad S. Kambakhsh, *A Short Survey of Worker's and Communist Movement in Iran*, 2 vols. (Stassfurt: Tudeh Press, 1972), 1: 17–18.

11. "Maram Nameh-e Jam'iat-e Mojahedin," *Asnad-e Tarikhi-e Jonbesh-e Kargari, Sosiyal Demokrasi, va Kommonisti-e Iran*, 2nd ed., 4 vols. (Florence: Mazdak, 1974), 1: 46. Hereafter: *Asnad-e Tarikhi*.

12. Saleh Aliyev, "Sanadi dar bareh-e Hezb-e Sosiyal Demokrat-e Iran," *Asnad-e Tarikhi*, 1: 38–41.

13. Kambakhsh, *A Short Survey*, 1: 24.

14. Z. Z. Abdullaev, "Promyshlennost i zarozhdenie rabochego klassa Irana," in *The Economic History of Iran, 1800–1914*, ed. Charles Issawi (Chicago: University of Chicago Press, 1971), 50–152. The magnitude of immigration becomes even more evident when we realize that in 1915 the total population of Iran was 11 million and the urban population only 2.3 million.

15. Kambakhsh, *A Short Survey*, 1: 14.

16. "Tarikhcheh-e Hezb-e Edalat," *Asnad-e Tarikhi*, 3: 129–130.

17. Ibid.

18. Ibid.

19. E. Abrahamian, "Social Bases of Iranian Politics: The Tudeh Party, 1941–53," Ph.D. thesis, Columbia University, 1969, 187.

20. "Maram Nameh-e Halieh-e Fergheh-e Kommonist (Bolshevik-e) Iran: Sho'beh-e (Iran) Beinolmelal-e Kommonist-e sevvom," *Asnad-e Tarikhi* 1: 57. By 1922, the PCP was reported to have fifteen hundred members. Lenczowski, *Russia and the West*, 101.

21. Lenczowski, *Russia and the West*, 99–100.

22. Ibid., 98.

23. For more details of Dehgan's background, see Appendix A.

24. S. M. Dehgan, "Gozaresh be Daftar-e Ejra'i-e Beinolmelal-e Sandika-ha-ye Sorkh," *Asnad-e Tarikhi*, 6: 105–106.

25. S. Mani, *Tarikhcheh-e Nehzat-e Kargari-e Iran* (Tehran: 1979), 8.

26. Dehgan, "Gozaresh," *Asnad-e Tarikhi* 6: 105–106.

27. Mani, *Tarikhcheh-e Nehzat*, 9.

28. Ibid.

29. *Haghighat*, 12 January 1922.

30. H. Jowdat, "Mobarezat-e Kargaran va Siyasat-e Zed-e Kargari-e Selseleh-e Pahlavi," *Donya* 12 (February 1976): 60.

31. Dehgan, "Gozaresh", *Asnad-e Tarikhi* 6: 105–106. The population of Tehran at this time was estimated as 200,000.

32. In 1920 a political party–labor union was established in Tabriz. Anyone whose livelihood did not depend on the "exploitation of others" could join. The union published a newspaper called *Takamol* and succeeded in reducing rents in the bazaar in 1921 (A. Soltanzadeh, "Jonbesh-e Sandika'i dar Iran," *Asnad-e Tarikhi* 4: 108–109).

33. Dehgan, "Gozaresh," *Asnad-e Tarikhi* 4: 105–106.

34. Lenczowski, *Russia and the West*, 103.

35. *Ra'd*, the newspaper for which Dehgan worked, was owned by Seyyed-Zia. Mani, *Tarikhcheh-e Nehzat*, 12. Seyyed-Zia became prime minister in February 1921 and then, having been exiled from Iran, returned after the outbreak of World War II.

36. Other individuals connected with this paper were Mirza-Seyyed-Ahmad Behbehani, the publisher, and Mir-Ja'far Pishevari, an editor of the paper.

37. *Haghighat*, 30 December 1922.

38. For a partial description of events leading to Reza-Khan's march on Tehran, see E. Ironside, ed., *High Road to Command: The Diaries of Major-General Sir Edmund Ironside 1920–22* (London: Leo Cooper, 1972).

39. G. Waterfield, *Professional Diplomat: 1880–1961* (London: Murray, 1973), 77.

40. Ibid., 63.

41. Ibid., 78.

42. Arthur C. Millspaugh, *The American Task in Persia* (New York: Arnos Press, 1973), 80.

43. Waterfield, *Professional Diplomat*, 79.

44. Ibid., 107.

45. Ibid., 74, based on Loraine to Curzon, dispatch no. 62, 31.1.22 F.O. 371/7804.

46. Iranian Government, *Mozakerat-e Majles: Dowreh-e Chaharom* (Tehran: Majles Press, 1944), 1161–62. Hereafter: Iranian Government, *Mozakerat IV*.

47. Ibid., 1162–63.

48. Hossein Makki, *Tarikh-e Bist Saleh-e Iran* (Tehran: Majles Press, 1946), 2: 118–34.

49. Ibid.

50. Reza Shah Pahlavi, *Safar Nameh-e Khouzestan* (Tehran, 1976), 27.

51. Ibid., 163.

52. N. S. Fatemi, *Diplomatic History of Iran 1917–1923* (New York: Russell F. Moore Co., 1951), 288–92.

53. Ibid. The British, too, were active in winning favor with the press by making payments through the APOC to friendly newspapers. G. Waterfield, *Professional Diplomat*, 71.

54. Fatemi, *Diplomatic History*, 293–94. A *toman* equals 10 *rials*.

55. Lenczowski, *Russia and the West*, 105.

56. For details of Soleiman-Mirza Eskandari's background, see Appendix A.

57. The Soviets, and the Tudeh Party and their affiliated trade unions offered similar support to Ahmad Qavam in 1946 only to be defeated by the man they had supported.

58. Reza-Khan's cabinet held office from 25 October 1923 to 13 April 1924.

59. *Haghighat*, 12 May 1922.

60. In response to the silence of Majles deputies, *Haghighat* (1 January 1922) protested: "Foreign personnel force the government to dissolve the union of postal workers, and the Majles, the same Majles for whose establishment these same workers gave thousands of sacrifices, does not raise a voice against the violation of one of the principles of the constitution."

61. For details of Qavam's background, see Appendix A.

62. Soltanzadeh, "Jonbesh," *Asnad-e Tarikhi*, 4: 107–110.

63. Dehgan, "Gozaresh," *Asnad-e Tarikhi*, 4: 105–106.

64. Jowdat, "Mobarezat-e Kargaran," *Donya* 12: 60.

65. Lenczowski, *Russia and the West*, 103.

66. L. P. Elwell-Sutton, *Persian Oil: A Study in Power Politics* (London: Lawrence and Wishart, 1955), 68.

67. Abrahamian, "Social Bases," 191.

68. Ibid., 15 June 1922.

69. Lenczowski, *Russia and the West*, 66.

70. Mani, *Tarikhcheh-e Nehzat*, 13–14; Lenczowski states that this trade union victory was cheered by the Soviet press which also expressed its support for the PCP's efforts in developing "the strike movement in the oil regions." Lenczowski, *Russia and the West*, 139.

71. Lenczowski, *Russia and the West*, 66.

72. Iranian Government, *Mozakerat IV*, 402.

73. Ibid., 403.

74. Iranian Government, *Mozakerat IV*, 424–25.

75. Mohammad Sadr-Hashemi, *Tarikh-e Jarayed va Majallat-e Iran* (Esfahan: 1948), 224–25.

76. Kambakhsh, *A Short Survey*, 1: 29–30.

77. Mani, *Tarikhcheh-e Nehzat*, 14–15.

78. Ibid., 18–19.

79. United States (U.S.) Government, Tehran Embassy, "Annual Labor Report:

1951," 10 May 1952 (Document no. 888.0615/1052), (United States National Archives [U.S.NA], Washington, D.C.).

80. Mossadegh fully appreciated that the elevation of the country's "strongman" to the throne was an ominous move against the country's constitution, which had stripped all responsibilities from the monarch. For a full discussion, see Hossein Makki, *Doktor Mossadegh va Notgh-ha-ye Tarikhi-e Ou* (Tehran, 1945), 29–33.

81. Lenczowski, *Russia and the West*, 105.

82. Kambakhsh, *A Short Survey*, 1: 32.

83. Mani, *Tarikhcheh-e Nehzat*, 21.

84. A. Ovanessian, "Khaterati dar bareh-e Tehran," *Asnad-e Tarikhi*, 1: 130–31.

85. "Program-e Amaliyat-e Hezb-e Kommonist-e Iran," *Asnad-e Tarikhi*, 1: 106.100, 107.

86. Ibid., 107.

87. Philip Hoffman, 28 June 1928 (891.00/1447) (U.S. NA).

88. Ibid., 30 August 1928 (891.00/1455) (U.S. NA). Modarres, the religious leader, for instance, was secretly seized and conducted to a small town in the province of Khorasan, where he was reportedly murdered. David Williamson, 2 May 1929 (891.00/1472) (U.S. NA).

89. Among the arrested was Ja'far Pishevari. Ovanessian, "Sazman-e Khorasan," *Asnad-e Tarikhi* 1: 114–15.

90. Mani, *Tarikhcheh-e Nehzat*, 23–24. May Day was also celebrated in Mashhad as late as 1930. Ardeshir Ovanessian had been sent there to organize the party and the carpet-makers. Ovanessian, "Sazman-e Khorasan," *Asnad-e Tarikhi*, 1: 114–15.

91. Lenczowski, *Russia and the West*, 116.

92. Williamson, 31 May 1929 (891.00/1475) (U.S. NA).

93. Ibid. 14 June 1929 (891.00/1480) (U.S. NA).

94. R. H. Clive, 23 July 1929 (891.00B/26) (U.S. NA).

95. Williamson, 14 June 1929 (891.00/1480) (U.S. NA).

96. Kambakhsh, *A Short Survey*, 1: 35.

97. Ibid. The same source reports that other segments of the population, particularly the unemployed workers, also joined the strike, bringing the total number to around twenty thousand. The workers of Masjed-e Soleiman also struck on that day.

98. Ibid.

99. Ibid.

100. U.S. Government, Tehran Legation, 1 June 1931 (891.00B/54) (U.S. NA).

101. Elwell-Sutton, *Persian Oil*, 68–69.

102. U.S. Government, Tehran Legation, 1 June 1931 (891.00B/54) (U.S. NA).

103. Kambakhsh, *A Short Survey*, 1: 36.

104. Elwell-Sutton, *Persian Oil*, 68–69.

105. Kambakhsh, *A Short Survey*, 1: 36.

106. "Action Committee," quoted in U.S. Government, Tehran Legation, 1 June 1931 (891.00B/54) (U.S. NA).

107. Williamson, 31 May 1929 (891.00/1475) (U.S. NA).

108. Charles E. Hart, 3 December 1930 (891.00B/29) (U.S. NA).

109. Iranian Government, *Majmou'eh-e Ghavanin-e Sal-e 1310* (Tehran: Rouznameh-e Rasmi, 1932), 38. Hereafter: Iranian Government, *Majmou'eh-e Ghavanin*.

110. Abrahamian, "Social Basis," 193.

111. Jowdat, "Mobarezat-e Kargaran," *Donya*, 12: 61.

112. James S. Moose, Jr., 23 November 1938 (891.00B/70) (U.S. NA).

113. Ibid. Reza Shah was even more ruthless with his own aides after they fell from his favor. For a description of the fate of such men as Teimourtash, Sardar As'ad, Ayrom, and Dadgar, see Paul H. Alling, 10 February 1937 (891.99/1650) (U.S. NA).

114. F. Mo'tamedi, *Tarikh va Hoghough-e Kar va Bimeh-e Ejtema'i dar Iran* (Tehran: 1975), 22–23.

115. C. Chaqueri, *The Conditions of the Working Class in Iran* (London: 1978), 142–43.

116. International Labor Office (ILO), "Agricultural and Industrial Activity and Manpower in Iran," *International Labor Review* 59, 5 (1949): 557. For a description of the prevailing working conditions in the Kerman carpet-making industry, see Soltanzadeh, "Iran-e Mo'aser," *Asnad-e Tarikhi* 4: 103–04.

117. Haj-Hasan Tafazzoli, interview with author, Kashan, 26 July 1977.

118. Raymond Hare, 15 October 1934 (891.655/30) (U.S. NA). The total number of persons employed directly in the carpet industry was estimated to be around 250,000. Ibid.

119. M. A. Djamalzadeh, "An Outline of the Social and Economic Structure of Iran," Part 2, *International Labor Review* 63, 2 (1951): 178–91.

120. Iranian Government, *Majmou'eh-e Ghavanin-e 1315*, 170–80.

121. Equal to seven to twenty days wages of an unskilled worker.

122. Iranian Government, *Majmou'eh-e Ghavanin-e 1315*, 170–80.

123. Moose, 20 July 1940 (891.1758) (U.S. NA).

124. Minor, 12 August 1941 (891.00/1816) (U.S. NA).

125. See M. Agah, "Some Aspects of Economic Development of Modern Iran," Ph.D. thesis, Oxford University, 1958.

Chapter 2

1. Minor, 12 August 1941 (891.00/1816) (U.S. NA).

2. See pages 44–45 of this book.

3. See page 23 of this book.

4. *Rahbar,* 30 January 1943.

5. Mikhail S. Ivanov, *Rabochii Klass Sovremennogo Iran* (Moscow: NAVK, 1969), 209–11.

6. Abrahamian, "Social Bases," 181–82.

7. Ibid., 203.

8. U.S. Government, "Political Parties of Iran—Tudeh Party," 25 June 1943 (RG-226/38055) (U.S. NA).

9. Ibid.

10. U.S. Government, "J.I.C.A. report no. R-35-45," 31 March 1945 (RG-226/126793) (U.S. NA).

11. Even in March 1945, Western observers were reporting that "there is no presently available evidence showing Soviet subsidizing [of Tudeh party affiliates]." Ibid.

12. The opinion of Fereidoun Keshavarz cited in W. J. Handley, "Labor in Iran," 31 January 1946 (RG-84/2260) (U.S. NA), 30.

13. This point is discussed further on page 37 of this book.

14. *Razm,* 11 August 1943.

15. Ibid.

16. Ibid., 12 August 1943.

17. Ibid., 13 August 1943.

18. Ibid.

19. Ibid.

20. Hammond, *Lenin on Trade Unions*, 35.

21. *Razm*, 13 August 1943.

22. *Rahbar*, 29 February 1943.

23. Zabih, *The Communist Movement*, 153.

24. *Razm*, 10 August 1943. For a discussion of Fadakar's union, see Chapter 8.

25. *Razm*, 19 August 1943.

26. For more background data on Jahani, Mahzari, and Ovanessian, see Appendix A.

27. For more background data on Rousta, see Appendix A.

28. *Rahbar*, 2 August 1943. The other presiding officers were Hasanzadeh and Marani, representing the railway workers.

29. Hammond, *Lenin on Trade Unions*, 39.

30. *Razm*, 22 August 1943.

31. *Zafar*, 29 June 1944.

32. *Razm*, 19 August 1943.

33. Ibid.

34. Ibid., 24 August 1943.

35. *Rahbar*, 29 February 1943.

36. *Razm*, 12 August 1943.

37. Ibid., 24 August 1943.

38. Ibid., 25 August 1943.

39. *Rahbar*, 14 April 1943.

40. *Razm*, 24 September 1943.

41. *Rahbar*, 29 June 1943.

42. Ibid., 4 August 1943.

43. Ibid., 14, 15, and 29 February 1943.

44. See below on same page of this book.

45. *Rahbar*, 4 August 1944.

46. Ibid., 6 August 1943.

47. Zabih, *The Communist Movement*, 152.

48. *Razm*, 22 August 1943, and *Rahbar*, 29 February and 2 March 1943.

49. Handley, "Labor in Iran," 31 January 1946 (RG-84/2260) (U.S. NA), 30.

50. *Rahbar*, 22 November 1943.

51. See pages 17–18 of this book.

52. *Rahbar*, 22 November 1943.

53. Ibid.

54. Ibid.

55. *Zafar*, 13 July 1944.

56. *Rahbar*, 4 August 1944.

57. Ivanov, *Rabochii Klass*, 211 and *Mardom*, 11 November 1942.

58. See Harold B. Minor's account of living conditions in 1941, quoted on pages 25–26 of this book.

59. Louis G. Dreyfus, Jr., 8 March 1943 (891.00/2003) (U.S. NA).

60. Arthur C. Millspaugh, "First Monthly Report of the Administer General of Finances," 19 February 1943 (U.S. NA).

61. See page 71 of this book.

62. *Rahbar*, 3 February 1943.

63. Ibid., 8 February 1943.

64. Ibid., 7 April 1943.

65. Ibid.

66. Dreyfus, 8 March 1943 (891.00/2003) (U.S. NA).

67. *Rahbar*, 12 February 1943.

68. *Razm*, 29 August 1943.

69. *Rahbar*, 3 August 1943.

70. Dreyfus, 12 December 1941 (891.00/1818) (U.S. NA).

71. Ibid., 19 March 1942 (891.00/1858) (U.S. NA).

72. For more detail on the bread riot of 8 December 1942, see ibid., 9 December 1942 (891.00/1961) (U.S. NA).

73. *Ettela'at*, 21 January 1943.

74. For a discussion of the establishment of the Ministry of Labor, see page 67 of this book.

75. *Rahbar*, 3 May 1943.

76. *Ajir*, 10 June 1943.

77. Iranian Government, *Majmou'eh-e Ghavanin: 1322*, 49–50.

78. *Assr-e Eghtesad*, 19th April 1944.

79. *Ra'd-e Emrouz*, 8 August 1944.

80. U.S. Government, "Basic Survey of Labor Affairs in Iran," 26 September 1955 (888.06/9-2655) (U.S. NA).

81. The Hamrahan Party, founded by Mostafa Fateh, Dr. Hasan Mosharaf-Naficy, and others, adopted a Socialistic ideology and attempted to offer competition to the Tudeh Party. However, since the key founder was an employee of the Anglo-Iranian Oil Company, the party was given a British label and became known as "Trottist," in reference to Alan Trott, oriental secretary of the British Legation. See U.S. Government, Military Intelligence Division W.D.G.S., "The Hamrahan (Socialist) Manifesto," 21 July 1943 (RG226/40452) (U.S. NA).

82. Ibid.

83. Ibid.

84. U.S. Government, "Basic Survey of Labor Affairs in Iran," 26 September 1955 (888.06/9-2655) (U.S. NA).

85. U.S. Government, Office of Strategic Services (OSS), 5 July 1943 (R. G.-226/40178) (U.S. NA).

86. *Rahbar*, 8 February 1943.

87. Ibid., 21 June 1943.

88. *Razm*, 24 September 1943.

89. *Mardom*, 31 October 1943.

90. Dreyfus, 2 July 1943 (891.00/2030) (U.S. NA).

91. United Kingdom (U.K.) Government, Ministry of Information, Overseas Planning Committee, "Plan for Propaganda for Persia Appreciation," 25 March 1942 (RG-226/64281) (U.S. NA).

92. Dreyfus, 2 July 1943 (891.00/2030) (U.S. NA).

93. Ibid., 24 August 1942 (891.00/1918) (U.S. NA).

94. Ibid., 2 July 1943 (891.00/2030) (U.S. NA).

95. Ibid.

96. *Rahbar*, 4 August 1944.

97. For details of elections in Esfahan, see pages 159–60 of this book.

98. *Ra'd-e Emrouz*, 5 March 1944. While the two Central Council candidates finished forty-fourth and forty-eighth, seven businessmen finished ahead of them, indicating the relative political power of the Tudeh Party and the business group in delivering votes in Tehran.

99. *Rahbar*, 7 August 1944.

100. Zabih, *The Communist Movement*, 151; S. M. Badi, *Rabochii Klass Irana* (Moscow: Nauka, 1965), 100, repeats the same assertion.

101. *Rahbar*, 26 April 1944.

102. For background data on Atighehchi, Eftekhari, and Enghelab, refer to Appendix A. For more details on Enghelab and his union activities in Tabriz, see Chapter 5, especially pages 99–100. Enghelab, later called Dr. Khalil Azar, became a candidate for the presidency of the Islamic Republic of Iran in 1979.

103. *Razm*, 8 August 1943.

104. Ivanov, *Rabochii Klass*, 212.

105. *Ra'd-e Emrouz*, 2 November 1943.

106. Ibid.

107. Initially the consolidated organization was called the General Union of the Workers of Iran (Ettehadieh-e Kolleh Kargaran-e Iran). As of June the name was changed to Showra-ye Mottahedeh-e Markazi-e Ettehadieh-ha-ye Kargaran va Zahmatkeshan-e Iran. *Mardom*, 16 May 1944 and *Rahbar*, 20 June 1944.

108. *Mardom*, 3 May 1944.

109. *Ra'd-e Emrouz*, 5 and 8 May 1944.

110. Ibid., 8 May 1944. The CUC later claimed that Eftekhari had disrupted their gathering.

111. *Neda-ye Haghighat*, 2 January 1946.

112. Ibid., 27 July, 1944.

113. Ibid., 22 June 1944 and J. A. Grant, 21 August 1944 (Document no. E5733/1905/34) (Public Record Office [PRO], London).

114. *Zafar*, 22 June 1944.

115. *Razm*, 22 August 1943.

116. Ivanov, *Rabochii Klass*, 219. For a discussion of the Esfahan trade union, see Chapter 7. See also Handley, "Labor in Iran," 31 January 1946 (RG-84/2260) (U.S. NA), 26.

117. Handley, "Labor in Iran," 31 January 1946 (RG-84/2260) (U.S. NA), 26.

118. Ivanov, *Rabochii Klass*, 213.

119. Ibid., 215.

120. Handley, "Labor in Iran," 31 January 1946 (RG-84/2260) (U.S. NA), 27.

121. See pages 265–67 of this book.

Chapter 3

1. The attitude of the Soviet Union regarding the need for close collaboration with the West had begun to change after the defeat of the Germans at Stalingrad a year earlier.

2. Elwell-Sutton, *Persian Oil*, 107.

3. *Zafar*, 6 July 1944.

4. U.S. Government, Department of State, Office of Intelligence Research (OIR) report no. 4940 (U.S. NA).

5. *Shahbaz*, 21 June 1945.

6. *Neda-ye Haghighat*, 2 January 1946.

7. *Zafar*, 22 June 1944.

8. Ibid., 19 June 1945.

9. Ibid., 22 June 1944.

10. Ivanov, *Rabochii Klass*, 216.

11. Zabih, *The Communist Movement*, 89–90.

12. Ivanov, *Rabochii Klass*, 215–16.

13. U.S. Government, OSS, 1 November 1944 (RG-226/48894) (U.S. NA).

14. Refer to page 107 of this book.

15. Iranian Government, *Majmou'eh-e Ghavanin-e Sal-e 1323* (Tehran: Rouz-nameh-e Rasmi, 1945), 33.

16. *Razm*, 17 November 1944.

17. U.S. Government, OSS, 26 November 1944 (RG-226/106312) (U.S. NA).

18. *Ajir*, 19 November 1944.

19. U.S. Government, OSS, 29 November 1944 (RG-226/106312) (U.S. NA).

20. *Rahbar*, 1 November 1944.

21. Zabih, *The Communist Movement*, 96.

22. Handley, "Labor in Iran," 31 January 1946 (RG-84/226) (U.S. NA), 30.

23. Formerly known as the Anglo-Persian Oil Company (APOC).

24. For details of this strike, see U.S. Government, "Monthly Labor Report," 1 November 1948 (RG 319/506663) (U.S. NA).

25. For details of this controversy, see discussion of the proceedings of the Fourteenth Majles, page 488.

26. Ivanov, *Rabochii Klass*, 217.

27. *Zafar*, 19 August 1945.

28. Ibid., 26 August 1945.

29. Ivanov, *Rabochii Klass*, 217.

30. Zabih, *The Communist Movement*, 97.

31. Ibid., 98.

32. Handley, "Labor in Iran," 46–47.

33. For details on this union, see pages 163–65 of this book.

34. Handley, "Labor in Iran," 47.

35. This was the first of a series of "surprises" confronting the CUC. For further examples, see pages 58 and 79–80 of this book.

36. Wallace Murray, 2 October 1945 (891/5043/10-245), (U.S. NA).

37. Ibid., 4 October 1945 (891.00/10-445), (U.S. NA).

38. U.S. Government, Strategic Services Unit, 9 October 1945 (RG-226/24874) (U.S. NA).

39. *Neda-ye Haghighat*, 10 February 1946.

40. Ibid.

41. For more details on Amirkeyvan, refer to Appendix A.

42. Handley, "Labor in Iran," 31 January 1946, (RG-84/2260) (U.S. NA), 48. According to one participant, becoming a member of the ILO delegation was a prize sought by many in the autumn of 1945. At that time, travelling to Europe was difficult by commercial means. ILO delegates, however, were flown from Iran to Paris on a

plane belonging to the French government. Aziz Farmanfarmiain, interview with author, Tehran, July 1978.

43. See page 110 of this book.

44. *Zafar*, 3 May 1946.

45. For background data on Qavam, refer to Appendix A.

46. See pages 14–15 of this book.

47. George Allen, 6 June 1946 (RG-84/2255) (U.S. NA).

48. See last paragraph of Appendix A.

49. *Neda-ye Haghighat*, 27 January 1946.

50. Ibid., 12 February 1946.

51. *Zafar*, 7 April 1946.

52. For additional discussion of these events, see "The Soviet Union and the Movement to Establish Autonomy in Iranian Azerbaijan," Manoucheh Vahdat, Ph. D. thesis, Indiana University, 1958 (109–30).

53. The Iranian year begins on 21 March.

54. *Zafar*, 1 April 1946.

55. U.S. Government, Tehran Embassy, "Monthly Labor Report," 3 June 1946 (RG-309/2159) (U.S. NA). Hereafter: "MLR"

56. *Zafar*, 20 and 25 April 1946.

57. Ibid., 18 April 1946. Also, U.S. Government, "MLR," 18 April 1946 (RG-319/2159) (U.S. NA).

58. See page 166 of this book.

59. *Zafar*, 10 April 1946.

60. U.S. Government, "MLR", 18 April 1946 (RG-319/2159) (U.S. NA).

61. *Zafar*, 23 April 1946.

62. Handley, "Labor in Iran," 31 January 1946 (RG-84/2260) (U.S. NA), 53. See also pages 23–24 of this book.

63. Handley, "Labor in Iran," 41.

64. Ibid., 42.

65. The first labor bill was presented by the Sa'ed government on 16 July 1944 and the second by Bayat on 15 February 1945.

66. Handley, "Labor in Iran," 31 January 1946 (RG-84/2260) (U.S. NA), 53.

67. U.K. Government, "Future of Trade Unions in Persia," 2 April 1947 (E 2815/41/34) (PRO).

68. L. F. L. Pyman, 20 January 1947 (E 497/41/34) (PRO).

69. The composition, duties, and procedure of the High Labor Council, too, were to be determined by the Council of Ministers.

70. U.K. Government, "Labor Law Approved by Council of Ministers," 6 June 1946 (E 5130/149/34) (PRO).

71. U.S. Government, "MLR," 3 June 1946 (RG-319/2159) (U.S. NA).

72. Ibid., 28 December 1946 (RG-84/2256) (U.S. NA).

73. U.K. Government, "Oil Workers' Strike in Persia," 17 July 1946 (E6878/401/34) (PRO).

74. *Zafar*, 7 May 1946.

75. Ibid., 26 April 1946.

76. See pages 124–25 of this book.

77. Ernest Bevin, 4 June 1946 (G543/57/46) (PRO).

78. Ibid.

79. See page 138 of this book.

80. U.K. Government, Foreign Office, 22 June 1946 (G543/99/46) (PRO).

81. George Allen, 21 May 1946 (891.00/5-2146) (U.S. NA).

82. H. T. Le Rougetel, 8 June 1946 (G543/61/46) (PRO).

83. *Rahbar*, 13 June 1946.

84. See Chapter 5, page 110 of this book.

85. *Zafar*, 19 May 1946.

86. U.S. Government, "MLR," 28 December 1946 (RG-84/2256) (U.S. NA).

87. See pages 129–36 of this book.

88. U.S. Government, "MLR," 28 December 1946 (RG-84/2256) (U.S. NA). There is some evidence to suggest that the Abadan general strike was instigated or at least intensified by the AIOC itself. See pages 132–33 of this book.

89. Allen, 6 August 1946 (RG-84/2255) (U.S. NA).

90. Le Rougetel, 4 June 1946 (G 543/55/46) (PRO).

91. In explaining his motive for this move, the shah told George Allen that he desired to show Qavam his willingness to collaborate if Qavam would reciprocate. According to Allen: "Shah added, with laugh, that an incidental benefit of title (which Qavam is understood to have received with pleasure) is that it will be more difficult for Qavam to continue to pose as rabble-rousing leader of masses when he affects such aristocratic trappings." Allen, 1 August 1946 [RG-84/2255] (U.S. NA).

92. In an interview with the writer in August 1977, Habib Naficy confirmed that denying Tudeh control over labor affairs was an important motive in the formation of the Ministry of Labor and Propaganda.

93. William J. Handley, 30 April 1947 (RG-84/2256) (U.S. NA).

94. Le Rougetel, 20 August 1946 (E8157/149/34) (PRO).

95. Ibid., 8 October 1946 (G575/54/46) (PRO). Compare the above with the view of the U.S. ambassador on page 75 of this book.

96. Allen, 7 January 1947 (891.00/1-747) (U.S. NA).

Chapter 4

1. Abrahamian, "Social Bases," 4.

2. Dreyfus, 9 December 1942 (891.00/1962) (U.S. NA).

3. U.S. Government, OSS, 30 June 1944 (RG-226-83820) (U.S. NA).

4. Ibid., 5 July 1943 (RG-226/30178) (U.S. NA).

5. Dreyfus, 23 July 1943 (891.000/2032) (U.S. NA).

6. U.S. Government, Tehran Military Attache, 28 August 1943 (RG-226/43824) (U.S. NA).

7. Leland Morris, 6 December 1944 (891.00/12-644) (U.S. NA).

8. It is not recorded that dignitaries such as Averell Harriman ever asked the youthful shah how many decades it would take for people to understand the principles of democratic government, when his father, Reza Shah, and then the shah himself, devoted only 3 to 6 percent of the national budget to education—while allocating 30 to 40 percent to the army and police.

9. James Sommerville, 21 December 1948 (RG-84/2257) (U.S. NA).

10. See page 65 of this book.

11. Colonel Harold B. Haskins, 19 February 1945 (RG-84/2244) (U.S. NA).

12. Alling, 4 September 1942 (891.00/1914) (U.S. NA).

13. Colonel H. Norman Schwarzkopf, 1 January 1945 (RG-84/2243/710) (U.S. NA).

14. F. D. Roosevelt, 12 January 1944 (891.00/3037) (U.S. NA).

15. Morris, 15 September 1944 (RG-84) (U.S. NA).

16. Ibid., 25 September 1944 (RG-84) (U.S. NA).

17. The "Iranians" referred to by Ambassador Allen in his reports certainly did not include nationalists such as Dr. Mossadegh who was urging a policy of "negative equilibrium," i.e., absence of foreign influence in Iran rather than its balance.

18. Allen, 6 June 1946 (RG-84/2255) (U.S. NA).

19. U.S. Government, Military Attache in Tehran, 1 May 1947 (RG-319/370805), (U.S. NA).

20. Allen, 6 June 1946 (RG-84/2255) (U.S. NA).

21. Ibid.

22. Ibid., 14 October 1946 (891.00/10-1446) (U.S. NA).

23. Ibid., 21 January 1948 (RG-84/2257/800) (U.S. NA). Allen was partially impelled into action by the possibility that the Qavam cabinet would form a joint aviation company with the Soviets on a 50–70 profit-sharing basis. Dean Acheson apparently disagreed with Allen's initiative in siding with the Shah against Qavam.

24. Ibid. Compare with the British report on page 68 of this book.

25. Ibid.

26. U.S. Government, "MLR," 28 December 1946 (RG-84/2256) (U.S. NA).

27. Le Rougetel, 14 November 1946 (G575/66/46) (PRO).

28. Ibid., 12 November 1946 (G575/62/46) (PRO).

29. U.S. Government, "MLR," 28 December 1946 (RG/84-2256) (U.S. NA).

30. *Zafar*, 12 November 1946.

31. Ibid.

32. U.S. Government, "MLR," 28 December 1946 (RG-84/2256) (U.S. NA).

33. Le Rougetel, 14 November 1946 (G575/66/46) (PRO).

34. U.S. Government, "MLR," 28 December 1946 (RG-84/2256) (U.S. NA).

35. See pages 113–14 of this book.

36. Ibid.

37. U.S. Government, "MLR," 28 December 1948 (RG-84/2256) (U.S. NA).

38. *Ettela'at*, 11 December 1946.

39. U.S. Government, "MLR," 28 December 1946 (RG-84/2256) (U.S. NA).

40. Le Rougetel, 18 December 1946 (G575/79/46) (PRO).

41. U.S. Government, Embassy in Tehran, "Memorandum of Conversation," 25 August 1948 (891.5043/8-3048) (U.S. NA).

42. See pages 173–75 of this book.

43. Aramesh considered it necessary to proceed with this plan, even though he had claimed the previous month that the CUC was "in a state of voluntary liquidation." U.S. Government, Embassy in Tehran, 8 January 1947 (RG-319/34833) (U.S. NA).

44. U.S. Government, "Memorandum of Conversation," 25 August 1948 (891.5043/8-3048) (U.S. NA).

45. See pages 151–52 of this book.

46. Le Rougetel, 19 February 1947 (E1689/41/34) (PRO). The previous members of the executive committee were: Reza Rousta, Hossein Jowdat, Ali Kobari, Hossein Jahani, Asadollah Sadeghian, Moharram Hashem, and Khalil Paravar. *Zafar*, 10 April 1946.

47. Le Rougetel, 19 February 1947 (E1689/41/34) (PRO).

48. The change in disembarkation points was "explained" as the pilot's error.

49. Handley, 30 April 1947 (U.S. NA); Habib Naficy, interview with author, in Tehran, 8 August 1977; Mohsen Khajehnour, interview with author, Tehran, 27 July 1978; Allen, 27 February 1947 (891.5043/2-2727) (U.S. NA); and British Embassy, Tehran, 5 March 1947 (E2173/41/34) (PRO).

50. British Embassy, Tehran, 5 March 1947 (E2173/41/34) (PRO).

51. Allen, 7 March 1947 (891.5043/3-747) (U.S. NA).

52. Handley, 30 April 1947 (RG-84/2256) (U.S. NA).

53. E. P. Harries, April 1947 (E4070/41/34) (PRO).

54. Harries' contention was based on Aramesh's assertion that those who were arrested "had mutinied against public security and all of them possessed arms." U.S. Embassy, Tehran, 8 January 1947 (RG-319/34844) (U.S. NA).

55. See pages 143–44 of this book.

56. U.K. Foreign Office, 7 May 1947 (E4268/41/34) (PRO).

57. Handley, 30 April 1947 (RG-84/2256) (U.S. NA). On 6 June 1947 the WFTU fully endorsed Al-Aris and Borrisov in their indictment of the activities of the government against the CUC. Chancery, Tehran, 26 June 1947 (E5527/41/34) (PRO). One major criticism of the CUC which is substantiated was that it never held a congress.

58. U.S. Government, "Memorandum of Conversations," 25 August 1948 (891.5043/8-3048) (U.S. NA).

59. In an interview on 3 August 1978, Mehdi Sharif-Emami admitted that he had recruited a pretty Armenian girl to become secretary to Rousta. Rousta's one main weakness, allegedly, was his susceptibility to feminine charms.

60. U.S. Government, "Memorandum of Conversations," 25 August 1948 (891.5043/8-3048) (U.S. NA).

61. Handley, 30 April 1947 (RG-84/2256) (U.S. NA).

62. Shortly thereafter, most of the non-Communist countries left the WFTU and formed a rival organization called the International Federation of Free Trade Unions. ESKI was a founding member of the new unit.

63. Handley, 30 April 1947 (RG-84/2256) (U.S. NA).

64. Le Rougetel, 15 April 1947 (E3216/41/34) (PRO).

65. Ibid.

66. Handley, 30 April 1947 (RG-84/2256) (U.S. NA).

67. Le Rougetel, 22 April 1947 (E3416/41/34) (PRO).

68. See pages 129–36 of this book.

69. Pyman, 28 May 1947 (E4513/41/34) (PRO).

70. Handley, 30 April 1947 (RG-84/2256) (U.S. NA).

71. U.K. Government, Tehran Chancery, 17 July 1947 (E6613/41/34) (PRO).

72. U.S. Government, "Basic Survey of Labor Affairs in Iran," 26 September 1955 (888.0619-2655) (U.S. NA).

73. U.S. Government, Military Attache, Tehran, 1 May 1947 (RG-319/370805) (U.S. NA).

74. For data on Simonian, refer to Appendix A.

75. U.S. Government, "MLR", 1 November 1947 (RG-84/2256) (U.S. NA).

76. The Majles had rejected the Soviet oil concession in late October 1947.

77. U.S. Government, "MLR," 1 November 1947 (RG-84/2256) (U.S. NA). Naficy saw no contradiction in his profession of democratic principles and his active role in keeping Rousta in jail without a trial.

78. U.S. Government, "MLR," 1 December 1947 (RG-84/2256) (U.S. NA).

79. Ibid.

80. Ibid.

81. George Allen, 18 November 1947 (891.00/11-1874) (U.S. NA).

82. See pages 113–14 of this book.

83. See page 84 of this book.

84. The Majles on 23 October 1947 voted to consider the Qavam-Sadchivkov agreement of April 1946 regarding the oil concession as null and void.

85. Le Rougetel, 8 December 1947 (E1200/40/34) (PRO).

86. *Ettela'at*, 11 December 1947.

87. U.K. Government, British Embassy in Tehran, "Report for the Quarter ended 31 December 1947" (E293/25/34) (PRO). The arrangements for Qavam's ouster had already been made. Princess Ashraf Pahlavi, the Shah's twin sister, has described her own critical role in organizing the anti-Qavam votes. See Ashraf Pahlavi, *Faces in a Mirror* (Englewood, N.J.: 1980), 90.

88. U.K. Government, "Political Situation in Iran," 13 November 1947 (E1069/40/34) (PRO).

89. Allen, 21 January 1948 (RG-84) (U.S. NA).

90. U.K. Government, British Embassy in Tehran, "Report for the Quarter ended 31 December 1947" (E293/25/34) (PRO).

91. John D. Jernegan, 4 December 1947 (891.00/12-447) (U.S. NA).

92. Ibid.

93. Allen, 26 December 1947 (891.00/12-2647) (U.S. NA).

94. Le Rougetel, 28 January 1948 (E1809/25/34) (PRO).

95. John Crumme, 8 January 1948 (891.00/1-1948) (U.S. NA).

96. By this time the army, under the direction of the shah and Chief of Staff General Razmara, had taken full charge of anti-CUC activities.

97. U.S. Government, "Annual Labor Report, 1947–48," 1 October 1948 (RG-84/148), (U.S. NA).

98. U.K. Government, "Monthly Report," May 1948 (E6218/2232/34) (PRO).

99. Ibid., "Monthly Report," 6 September 1948 (E11971/2232/34) (PRO).

100. U.S. Government, "ALR, 1947–48," 1 October 1948 (RG-84/148) (U.S. NA).

101. U.K. Government, "Monthly Report," 6 September 1948 (E11971/2232/34) (PRO).

102. U.S. Government, "MLR," 1 September 1948 (RG-84/148) (U.S. NA).

103. U.S. Government, "Memorandums of Conversations," 25 August 1948 (891.5043/8-3048) (U.S. NA).

104. U.S. Government, "ALR, 1947–48," 1 October 1948 (RG-84/148) (U.S. NA).

105. U.S. Government, "MLR," 1 September 1948 (RG-84/148) (U.S. NA).

106. U.K. Government, "Monthly Report," 7 December 1948 (E16951/2232/134) (PRO).

107. See pages 129–36 of this book.

108. U.K. Government, "Monthly Report," 7 December 1948 (E16951/2232/134) (PRO).

109. U.S. Embassy had confirmed this on 5 February 1949. See Sommerville, (RG-84/2259) (U.S. NA). Fereidoun Keshavarz confirms that the party's central committee had no prior knowledge of the assassination attempt; however, he alleges that another central committee member, N. Kianouri, had instigated the incident in order to eliminate his rivals within the Tudeh Party. F. Keshavarz, *Man Mottaham Mikonam* (Tehran: Ravagh Press, 1979), 65–8.

110. Sommerville, 13 February 1949 (RG-84/2259) (U.S. NA).

111. Ibid., 4 February 1949 (RG-319/406) (U.S. NA).

112. U.S. Government, "MLR," 28 February 1949 (RG-84/148) (U.S. NA).

113. Sommerville, 5 February 1949 (RG-319) (U.S. NA).

114. Ibid., 13 February 1949 (RG-84/2259) (U.S. NA).

115. U.S. Consulate, Tabriz, 26 February 1949 (RG-84/2259) (U.S. NA).

116. Sommerville, 5 February 1949 (RG-319/406) (U.S. NA).

117. The injury to the shah was slight. He said the next day that his condition was excellent. Ibid.

118. Ibid.

119. U.S. Government, "MLR," 28 February 1949 (RG-84/148) (U.S. NA).

120. Sommerville, 6 February 1949 (RG-3219/406) (U.S. NA).

121. U.S. Government, "Translation of Letter," 30 April 1949 (RG-84) (U.S. NA).

122. U.S. Government, "MLR," 1 June 1949 (RG-84/148) (U.S. NA).

123. Member of the executive board of the CUC.

124. Head of the union of the unemployed.

125. Member of the executive board of the CUC and head of the taxi-drivers' union.

126. Member of the executive board of the CUC and head of the union of the Jews.

127. U.S. Government, "MLR," 1 June 1949 (RG-84/148) (U.S. NA).

128. U.K. Government, "Political Situations in Iran," 13 November 1947 (E-10691/40/34) (PRO).

129. Le Rougetel, 6 January 1948 (E-446/10/34.FO371) (PRO)

130. For an important exchange of letters between the exiled Ahmad Qavam and the shah, see U.K. Government, "Copy of Letter from A. Qavam to the Shah of Persia criticizing the election procedure and the Persian Constitution," 11 April 1950 (E-P1016/36, F0371/82311) (PRO).

131. See pages 215–18 of this book.

132. U.S. Government, "MLR," 2 May 1949 (RG-84/146/560) (U.S. NA).

133. John C. Wiley, 12 May 1949 (RG-84/2259) (U.S. NA). Wiley succeeded Allen as ambassador in the winter of 1948.

134. Ibid.

135. Wiley, 23 June 1949 (RG-84/2259) (U.S. NA).

136. Subsequent to the increase in the power of the shah, he was hereafter referred to as "His Imperial Majesty" rather than the "shah."

137. Wiley, 17 September 1949 (RG-84/2259) (U.S. NA). Illiteracy of the masses was a convenient excuse for many of the repressive measures adopted by the government. The shah also cited illiteracy when preventing the formation of political parties.

138. See pages 180–88 of this book.

Chapter 5

1. S. G. Ebling, 28 November 1944 (RG-84/2243) (U.S. NA).

2. Ebling, 22 November 1944 (RG-84/2243) (U.S. NA).

3. Ibid., 1 June 1945 (891.00/6-145) (U.S. NA).

4. Ibid.

5. Ibid., 5 May 1944 (891.00/3053) (U.S. NA).

6. Ibid., 28 November 1944 (RG-2243) (U.S. NA).

7. Richard Ford, 2 October 1943 (891.00/2063) (U.S. NA).

8. In order to appreciate the sub-subsistence level of life, the price per kilo of the following items in February 1944 should be noted: bread, 8 *rials*; tea, 260; sugar, 150; and mutton, 30 *rials*. U.K. Government, "Tabriz Diary" (hereafter "TD"), 7 March 1944 (E1867/138/34) (PRO).

9. Ebling, 22 November 1944, (RG-84) (U.S. NA).

10. Ibid.

11. U.K. Government, "TD," 28 February 1943 (E2730/80/34) (PRO).

12. Ibid., "TD," 6 July 1942 (E4404/163/34) (PRO).

13. Ebling, 7 May 1943 (891.00/2021) (U.S. NA).

14. See, for instance, U.K. Government, "TD," 28 February 1943 (E2730/80/34) (PRO).

15. See pages 36–37 of this book.

16. U.K. Government, "TD," 31 December 1942 (E1023/80/34) (PRO).

17. For data on the Central Board, see pages 46–47 of this book.

18. U.K. Government, "TD," 31 October 1942 (E7307/163/34) (PRO).

19. By the time of his election to the Fifteenth Majles in 1944, he was disowned by the Tudeh and the Soviets as a "reactionary."

20. U.K. Government, "TD," 30 November 1942 (E80/80/34) (PRO).

21. See page 38 of this book.

22. U.K. Government, "TD," 30 September 1942 (E80/80/34) (PRO).

23. R. W. Hefti, 12 December 1942 (891.504/10) (U.S. NA).

24. U.K. Government, "TD," 30 November 1942 (E80/80/34) (PRO).

25. For more data regarding Ali Amir-Khizi, refer to Appendix A.

26. *Rahbar*, 24 November 1943.

27. Hefti, 12 December 1942 (891.504/10) (U.S. NA).

28. Ibid.

29. Ibid. This statement is identical to the argument used in Tehran by *Zafar*. See page 51 of this book.

30. U.K. Government, "TD," 15 February 1943 (E1673/880/34) (PRO).

31. Ibid.

32. For similar occurrences in Tehran, see pages 37–38 of this book.

33. *Rahbar*, 5 February 1943.

34. U.K. Government, "TD," 28 February 1943 (E2730/80/34) (PRO).

35. Ibid., 15 May 1943 (E3196/80/34) (PRO).

36. Ibid., 28 February 1943 (E2730/80/34) (PRO).

37. Quoted in ibid., 7 July 1943 (E4562/80/34) (PRO).

38. At the end of August 1943, Dr. Abolghasem Sheikh, an official of the Ministry of Commerce and Industry, also visited Tabriz. He made a number of recommendations for reducing industrial conflict that were never adopted. See ibid., 30 September 1943 (E6475/80/34) (PRO).

39. Ibid., 7 September 1943 (E5654/80/34) (PRO).

40. Ibid., 30 September 1943 (E6475/80/34) (PRO).

41. See page 46 of this book.

42. At this time the number of unionized workers in Tabriz was estimated to be 5,000. Ebling, 27 November 1943 (RG-84/2243) (U.S. NA).

43. Ibid.

44. U.K. Government, "TD," 15 October 1943 (E6656/80/34) (PRO).

45. See pages 46–48 of this book.

46. Ebling, papers 12 May 1944 (RG-84/2243) (U.S. NA).

47. *Rahbar*, 16 May 1944, *Ajir*, 28 May 1944, and *Mardom*, 18 May 1944.

48. U.K. Government, "TD," 1 June 1944 (E3512/187/34) (PRO).

49. See page 110 of this book.

50. U.K. Government, "TD," 27 July 1944 (E4888/138/34) (PRO). If the consul general is correct, then the Soviets were more interested in Pishevari than were the Tudeh leaders in Tehran, who had ruptured their relations with Enghelab.

51. Ibid.

52. Ebling, 15 July 1944 (891.00/7-1544) (U.S. NA).

53. U.K. Government, "TD," 27 July 1944 (E4888/138/34) (PRO), and Ebling, 15 July 1944 (891.00/7-1544) (U.S. NA).

54. U.K. Government, "TD," 27 July 1944 (E4888/138/34) (PRO).

55. See pages 52–54 of this book.

56. For data on Pishevari, refer to Appendix A.

57. *Zafar*, 10 August 1944.

58. Beriya was reported to have written a poem expressing regret that the Aras River separated Iranian Azarbaijan from that of the Soviet Union. Tehran Military Governate, *Seyreh Kommonism dar Iran* (Tehran: Military Governorship of Tehran, 1957), 20. For more data on Beriya, refer to Appendix A.

59. See page 51 of this book.

60. U.K. Government, "TD," 7 September 1944 (E5846/138/34) (PRO).

61. Ibid., 10 August 1944 (E5165/138/34) (PRO).

62. Ibid., 19 April 1945 (E3164/239/34) (PRO).

63. U.S. Government, OSS, Report G-7700, 25 May 1945 (RG-84) (U.S. NA). Nevertheless, when employers protested the action of the AUC, the Soviet officials pleaded ignorance. See U.K. Government, "TD," 19 April 1945 (E3164/239/34) (PRO).

64. U.K. Government, "TD," 10 August 1944 (E5165/138/34) (PRO).

65. U.K. Government, "TD," 7 September 1944 (E5846/138/34) (PRO).

66. Ibid., 25 August 1944 (E5584/138/34) (PRO).

67. U.K. Government, "TD," 7 September 1944 (E5846/138/34) (PRO).

68. U.K. Government, "TD," 13 October 1944 (E6819/138/34) (PRO).

69. Ebling, 29 October 1944 (891.00/10-2844) (U.S. NA).

70. Ibid.

71. U.K. Government, "TD," 2 November 1944 (E7102/318/34) (PRO).

72. Ibid.

73. U.K. Government, "TD," 14 December 1944 (E239/239/34) (PRO).

74. U.K. Government, "TD," 2 November 1944 (E7102/318/34) (PRO). The workers were not alone in their skepticism of the owners' inability to pay. Abdol-Aziz Kalantari, director of the Tabriz Chamber of Commerce, also discounted the employers' financial plight. He contended, for example, that the Calcatehchi factory was still making a 30 percent profit. "What owners call their losses, is, in fact, simply a reduction of the excessive profits they used to make." See U.K. Government, "TD," 16 November 1944 (E7498/138/34) (PRO). This line of argument between employers and the employees was repeated during labor disturbances following the Iranian revolution in the spring of 1979.

75. U.K. Government, "TD," 28 December 1944 (E391/239/34) (PRO).

76. U.K. Government, "TD," 28 February 1945 (E1940/239/34) (PRO).

77. U.S. Government, OSS, no. G-6843, 4 January 1945 (RG-226/110214) (U.S. NA).

78. U.K. Government, "Tabriz Six-month Report," 16 March 1945 (E2445/239/34) (PRO).

79. U.S. Government, OSS, no. G-7152, 20 February 1945 (RG-226/116460) (U.S. NA).

80. By September 1945, the membership had increased to eight to nine thousand. Tabriz Six Month Report, 18 September 1945 (E7384/239/34) (PRO).

81. Part of the blame for the vacancy of the two posts must be shared by the previous prime minister, Ebrahim Hakimi.

82. *Ajir*, 10 June 1945.

83. U.K. Government, "TD," 8 June 1945 (E4810/239/34) (PRO).

84. U.K. Government, "TD," 13 July 1945 (E5612/239/34) (PRO).

85. *Ajir*, 17 July 1945.

86. U.K. Government, "Tabriz Six Month Report," 18 September 1945 (E7384/239/34) (PRO).

87. Ibid., 16 March 1945 (E2445/239/34) (PRO).

88. Ibid., 18 September 1945 (E7384/239/34) (PRO).

89. *Ajir*, 10 April 1944.

90. Ibid.

91. *Ajir*, 13 June 1944.

92. Ibid., 16 July 1944.

93. U.K. Government, "TD," 30 November 1944 (E7777/138/34) (PRO).

94. U.K. Government, "TD," 16 August 1945 (E6973/239/34) (PRO).

95. Ibid.

96. U.K. Government, "TD," 21 September 1945 (E7359/239/34) (PRO).

97. U.K. Government, "TD," 21 November 1945 (E9804/239/34) (PRO).

98. Ibid.

99. U.K. Government, "TD," 21 November 1945 (E9804/239/34) (PRO).

100. U.K. Government, "TD," 31 December 1945 (E900/900/34) (PRO).

101. Ibid.

102. Ibid., 31 January 1946 (E1714/900/34) (PRO).

103. R. Rossow, papers, 21 May 1946 (RG-319/2159) (U.S. NA).

104. U.K. Government, "Azarbaijan Labour Law," 3 September 1946 (E19210/950/34), (PRO).

105. U.K. Government, "TD," 31 August 1946 (E9264/900/34) (PRO).

106. U.K. Government, "Azarbaijan Labour Law," 3 September 1946 (E19210/900/34) (PRO).

107. Qavam had delayed the elections for the Fifteenth Majles past the deadline he had agreed to with the Soviets. Subsequent to a strongly worded Soviet protest dated 6 October 1946, it was announced that preparation for elections would begin immediately. See Allen, 7 January 1947 (891.00/1-747) (U.S. NA).

108. Ibid.

109. Allen, 7 January 1947 (891.00/1–747) (U.S. NA).

110. Ibid. and Keshavarz, *Man Mottaham Mikonam* (Tehran, 1979) 33. Also refer to R. Rossow, "The Battle of Azarbaijan," *The Middle East Journal* 10 (Winter 1956) 31.

111. Keshavarz, who praises Pishevari for his bravery and loyalty to Iran, strongly believes that Pishevari was liquidated by the officials of Soviet Azerbaijan who were unhappy with his lack of subservience. "Pishevari was a friend of the U.S.S.R. not . . . its servant." Ibid.

112. F. Lester Sutton, 30 December 1946 (891.00/3046) (U.S. NA).

113. U.K. Government, "TD," 15 March 1948 (E4544/1736/34) (PRO).

114. U.K. Government, "TD," 27 June 1948 (E8786/1736/34) (PRO).

115. U.K. Government, "TD," 21 August 1948 (E11396/1736/34) (PRO).

116. U.S. Government, Tabriz Consulate, 16 February 1949 (RG-319/406) (U.S. NA).

117. Edward L. Waggoner, 30 December 1948 (RG-84/2257) (U.S. NA).

118. Leslie Pott, 6 December 1948 (E16063/1807/34) (PRO).

119. To the list of factors leading to the evacuation of Soviet troops from Iran must be added the ultimatum issued to Stalin by Truman and pressure applied by the Security Council of the United Nations. See Vahdat, "The Soviet Union and the Movement to Establish Autonomy," 116–17.

120. Keshavarz, *Man Mottaham Mikonam*, 36.

Chapter 6

1. See page 10 of this book.
2. See page 28 of this book.
3. See map, "Principal Towns of Iran."
4. ILO, *Labour Conditions in the Oil Industry in Iran* (Geneva, 1950), 5.
5. AIOC, *The Anglo-Iranian Oil Company in Iran* (London, 1947), 3.
6. ILO, *Labour Conditions*, 5.
7. The production figures are for the year 1945. They are taken from U.K. Government, "Memo on Policy of AIOC," 7 October 1946 (E10146/401/34) (PRO).
8. U.K. Government, "Labour and Industrial Development in Persia," 25 September 1944 (E6051/1905/34) (PRO).
9. K. J. Hird, 31 December 1946 (E495/35/34) (PRO).
10. U.K. Government, "Labour and Industrial Development in Persia," 25 September 1944 (E 6051/1905/34) (PRO).
11. Randall S. Williams, 3 September 1946 (RG-84/2256) (U.S. NA).
12. Ibid.
13. See page 54 of this book.
14. Sir Reader Bullard, 30 May 1945 (FO249/1453) (PRO).
15. Bullard, 12 August 1945 (FO248/1453) (PRO). In accordance with the tripartite agreement between the U.S., Great Britain, and the Soviet Union, British troops withdrew their forces from Iran prior to the deadline of March 1946.
16. Ibid., 16 February 1944 (E1519/139/34) (PRO).
17. The port city Khorramshahr is only a few miles away from Abadan. See map, "Principal Towns of Iran."
18. Colonel H. J. Underwood, formerly a British military attache in Tehran, was employed by the AIOC in 1945. As the company's chief security officer, his function was "to keep a watch on subversive activities among the company's employees." See Pyman, 20 July 1946 (E6895/401/34) (PRO).
19. U.K. Government, "Khoramshahr Diary" (hereafter "KD"), 7 May 1946 (G543/9/46) (PRO).
20. U.K. Government, "KD," 31 December 1943 (E139/139/34) (PRO).
21. See pages 14–15 of this book.

22. In May 1946 Mehdi Hashem-Najafi, an Iranian national originally from the holy city of Najaf in Iraq and deported to Iran in 1942–1943 by the British, told the visiting M.P., Jack Jones, that he had been sent by the Central Council to Abadan in secret in 1943 to organize the trade union movement in that area. See Jack Jones, 3 July 1946 (E6501/401/34) (PRO).

23. U.K. Government, "KD," 1 May 1944 (E3251/139/34) (PRO).

24. See pages 46–47 of this book.

25. See page 103 of this book.

26. Ibid., 16 May 1944 (E3555/139/34) (PRO).

27. U.K. Government, "KD," 1 September 1944 (E5736/139/34) (PRO). Ali Omid was also active in setting up a trade union in Ahwaz, *Zafar*, 9 April 1944.

28. U.K. Government, "KD," 1 December 1944 (E2381/238/34) (PRO).

29. *Zafar*, 9 April 1944.

30. Jones, 3 July 1946 (E6501/401/34) (PRO).

31. U.K. Government, "KD," 1 February 1945 (E1346/238/34) (PRO).

32. *Rahbar*, 26 April 1945.

33. See pages 54–57 of this book.

34. See pages 111–12 of this book.

35. E. H. O. Elkington, 13 May 1946 (E4391/401/34) (PRO).

36. See pages 57–58 of this book.

37. U.K. Government, "KD," 1 April 1946 (E3397/940/34) (PRO).

38. Elkington, 13 May 1946 (E4391/401/34) (PRO).

39. Jones, 3 July 1946 (E6501/401/34) (PRO).

40. Elkington, 13 May 1946 (E6501/401/34) (PRO).

41. Jones, 27 June 1946 (E6501/401/34) (PRO).

42. H. J. Underwood, 1 May 1946 (G543/6/46) (PRO).

43. Ibid.

44. Ibid.

45. Jones, 3 July 1946 (E6501/401/34) (PRO).

46. Elkington, 13 May 1946 (E4391/401/34) (PRO).

47. Ibid.

48. Ibid.

49. Le Rougetel, 13 May 1946 (G543/10/46) (PRO).

50. U.K. Government, Khoramshahr Consulate (hereafter KC), 13 May 1946 (G543/11/46) (PRO).

51. Le Rougetel, 13 May 1946 (G543/10/46) (PRO).

52. Williams, 6 June 1946 (RG319/283762) (U.S. NA).

53. Le Rougetel, 13 May 1946 (E4391/401/34) (PRO).

54. Jones, 3 July 1946 (E 6501/401/34) (PRO).

55. Williams, 6 June 1946 (RG319/283762) (U.S. NA).

56. *Zafar*, 16 May 1946.

57. Elwell-Sutton, *Persian Oil*, 143.

58. Williams, 6 June 1946 (RG319/383762) (U.S. NA).

59. Le Rougetel, 13 May 1946 (G543/10/46) (PRO).

60. Elkington, 13 May 1946 (G543/6/46) (PRO).

61. Le Rougetel, 21 May 1946 (E46621/401/34) (PRO).

62. Williams, 6 June 1946 (RG319/283762) (U.S. NA).

63. U.K. Government, "Note of Latest Information from Anglo-Iranian Oil Company, Ltd.," 14 May 1946 (E4391/401/34) (PRO).

64. Le Rougetel, 16 May 1946 (E4480/401/34) (PRO).

65. Ibid.

66. Ibid.

67. Le Rougetel, 18 May 1946 (E4571/401/34) (PRO).

68. AIOC, 22 May 1946 (G543/35/46) (PRO).

69. Le Rougetel, 23 May 1946 (E4733/401/34) (PRO).

70. Ibid.

71. A. C. Trott, 29 May 1946 (G543/47/46) (PRO).

72. See pages 61–64 of this book.

73. Williams, 6 June 1946 (RG319/283762) (U.S. NA).

74. Le Rougetel, 27 May 1946 (G543/44/46) (PRO). Jack Jones called this payment of strike pay "a thing unprecedented in trade union history." "Labour Troubles in Persia," *Manchester Guardian*, 18 July 1946.

75. In the future, the workers would be able to buy staple commodities including those mentioned above plus cheese, fats, beans and peas from company shops at cost price. See Le Rougetel, 28 May 1946 (E4821/401/34) (PRO).

76. Williams, 6 June 1946 (RG319/283762) (U.S. NA). The same position maintained a month later in Abadan led to the general strike of 14 July 1946.

77. U.S. Government, Military Attache in Tehran, 27 May 1946 (RG3291/274592) (U.S. NA).

78. U.S. Government, Military Attache in Tehran, 23 July 1946 (RG319/291706) (U.S. NA).

79. Underwood, 27 May 1946 (G543/83/46) (PRO).

80. M. Audsley, 29 July 1946 (E7822/401/34) (PRO).

81. Allen, 9 July 1946 (891.00/7-946) (U.S. NA).

82. U.K. Government, KC, 31 July 1946 (E6587/401/34) (PRO).

83. U.K. Government, KC, 3 July 1946 (E9621/401/34) (PRO).

84. U.K. Government, KC, 4 July 1946 (E9622/401/34) (PRO).

85. Ibid.

86. U.K. Government, KC, 8 July 1946 (E9623/401/34) (PRO).

87. Ibid.

88. Audsley, 19 July 1946 (E6981/401/34) (PRO).

89. Le Rougetel, 11 July 1946 (E6565/401/34) (PRO).

90. See pages 64–66 of this book.

91. U.K. Government, KC, 8 July 1946 (E9623/401/34) (PRO).

92. U.S. Government, Military Attache in Tehran, 23 July 1946 (RG319/291706) (U.S. NA).

93. Sutton, 31 July 1946 (891.00/8-646) (U.S. NA).

94. Allen, 9 July 1946 (891.00/7-946) (U.S. NA).

95. Underwood also confirmed that the Central Committee of the Tudeh Party (whose members were about to join the cabinet) had ordered the strike postponed. See: Sutton, 31 July 1946 (891.00/8-646) (U.S. NA).

96. U.S. Government, Military Attache in Tehran, 23 July 1946 (RG319/291706) (U.S. NA).

97. U.K. Government, Ahvaz Consulate General (hereafter ACG), 14 July 1946 (E6594/421/34) (PRO).

98. U.S. Government, Military Attache in Tehran, 23 July 1946 (RG319/291706), (U.S. NA).

99. Ibid.

100. U.K. Government, ACG, 15 July 1946 (E6659/401/34) (PRO).

101. Ibid., 14 July 1946 (E6594/4011/34) (PRO).

102. U.S. Government, Military Attache in Tehran, 23 July 1946 (RE319/291706), (U.S. NA).

103. Ibid.

104. Allen, 22 July 1946 (891.5045/7-2246) (U.S. NA).

105. Williams, 3 September 1946 (RG84/2256) (U.S. NA).

106. Le Rougetel, 15 July 1946 (E6662/401/34) (PRO).

107. U.S. Government, Military Attache in Tehran, 23 July 1946 (RG319/291706) (U.S. NA).

108. Even before the arrival of Firouz, the British officials in Khouzestan had anticipated at least one of his moves. Skrine cabled Le Rougetel from Khorramshahr that the governor, Willoughby, and he were all afraid that Firouz would release the KUC leaders from prison. See C. Skrine, 15 July 1946 (E6668/401/34) (PRO). Fifty-four others remained in jail. See C. P. Skrine, 16 July 1946 (E65871/401/34) (PRO).

109. U.S. Government, Military Attache in Tehran, 23 July 1946 (RG319/291706) (U.S. NA).

110. G. N. S. Gobey, 16 July 1946 (E7617/401/34) (PRO).

111. Trott, 16 July 1946 (E6748/401/34) (PRO).

112. Le Rougetel, 17 July 1946 (E6788/401/34) (PRO).

113. U.K. Government, KC, 17 July 1946 (E6760/401/34) (PRO).

114. U.S. Government, Military Attache in Tehran, 23 July 1946 (RG319/291706) (U.S. NA).

115. Allen, 22 July 1946 (RG-84/2255/800) (U.S. NA).

116. U.S. Government, Military Attache in Tehran, 23 July 1946 (RG319/291706) (U.S. NA).

117. F. Lee, 3 July 1946 (E6501/401/34) (PRO).

118. Jones, 3 July 1946 (E6501/401/34) (PRO).

119. Ibid.

120. The law to which Bevin refers was instituted by Reza Shah in 1931 (see page 22 of this book), probably partly as a result of the 1929 Abadan strike and at the request of the oil company. In the 1940s, the AIOC took the position that Iranian law did not allow them to recognize trade unions. And, of course, the company did not want to break Iranian law.

121. Bevin, 23 June 1946 (E5755/401/34) (PRO).

122. Compare for instance: U.K. Government, "Report Up to 21 May 1947" (G15/28/47) (PRO), with U.K. Government, "KD," 31 May 1947 (E6161/1067/34) (PRO).

123. E. A. Berthoud, 15 October 1946 (E10347/401/34) (PRO).

124. W. N. Cuthbert, 3 July 1946 (E6501/401/34) (PRO).

125. Berthoud, 10 July 1946 (E6798/401/34) (PRO).

126. Skrine, 5 June 1946 (G543/56/46) (PRO).

127. Le Rougetel, 16 July 1946 (E6744/401/34) (PRO).

128. U.K. Government, "Oil Workers' Strike," 17 July 1946 (E6878/401/34) (PRO).

129. U.S. Government, Military Attache in Tehran, 23 July 1946 (RG319/291706) (U.S. NA).

130. Williams, 3 September 1946 (RG84/2256) (U.S. NA).

131. Pyman, 18 July 1946 (E6788/401/34) (PRO).

132. Trott, 24 July 1946 (E7054/401/34) (PRO).

133. See page 67 of this book.

134. *Zafar*, 12 September 1946.

135. U.S. Government, Consul in Basra, 30 September 1946 (RG84/2255) (U.S. NA).

136. U.K. Government, "KD," 1 November 1946 (E11582/940/34) (PRO).

137. U.K. Government, "KD," 1 January 1947 (E1427/1067/34) (PRO).

138. See page 128 of this book.

139. Le Rougetel, 8 October 1946 (G575/54/46) (PRO).

140. Allen, 9 July 1946 (891.00/7-946) (U.S. NA).

141. Underwood, 26 May 1946 (G543/82/46) (PRO).

142. U.K. Government, "KD," 1 January 1947 (E1427/1067/34) (PRO).

143. Le Rougetel, 27 August 1947 (G15/39/47) (PRO).

144. AIOC, "Report Up to Noon," 15 September 1947 (G15/42/47) (PRO).

145. AIOC, "Report Up to Noon," 30 August 1947 (G15/41/47) (PRO).

146. Bevin, 3 November 1946 (G575/61/46) (PRO).

147. Skrine, 5 June 1946 (G543/56/46) (PRO).

148. U.K. Government, Foreign Office, 18 December 1946 (E11714/40/34) (PRO).

149. Ibid.

150. AIOC, "Report Up to Noon," 21 February 1947 (G15/11/47) (PRO).

151. AIOC, "Extracts from Speeches Made at Certain Secret Meetings," 10–20 January 1947 (G15/6/47) (PRO).

152. Fateh was also the principal founder of the Hamrahan Party.

153. AIOC, "Report Up to Noon," 25 July 1947 (G15/36a/47) (PRO). Refer to note 6, page 257 of this book.

154. U.K. Government, "KD," 1 March 1947 (E2937/401/34) (PRO).

155. AIOC, "Report Up to Noon," 26 January 1947 (G15/6/47) (PRO). Four of the signatories had been arrested a few days before the publication of the manifesto, then released as a result of Fateh's intervention—leading to the protest by their opponents that the above individuals had been intimidated. See: AIOC, "Report Up to Noon," 15 March 1947 (G15/16/47) (PRO).

156. U.K. Government, KC, 27 January 1947 (G15/4/47) (PRO).

157. Eftekhari and several of his colleagues had participated in the Abadan strikes of 1929. See pages 21–22 of this book.

158. AIOC, "Translated Extracts from Speeches at Secret Meetings", 1–10 February 1947 (G15/11/47) (PRO).

159. See page 46 of this book.

160. AIOC, "Report Up to Noon," 26 January 1947 (G15/6/47) (PRO). Moreover, the four other OWU leaders were accused of spying for the company. See AIOC, "Translated Extracts From Speeches at Secret Meetings," 22–30 January 1947 (G15/7/47) (PRO).

161. A. E. Watkinson, 10 February 1947 (G15/8/47) (PRO).

162. AIOC, "Translated Extracts from Speeches at Secret Meetings", 1–10 February 1947 (G15/11/47) (PRO). In February 1943 in Tabriz the reverse of this had happened when the governor-general turned the office of the non-Tudeh union over to the Tudeh Party. See page 101 of this book.

163. OWU membership was reported at 2,000 in mid-March 1947. U.K. Government, KC, 13 March 1947 (G15/13/47) (PRO), and 3,500 in May 1947—although as few as 200 attended union meetings. U.K. Government, "KD," 1 June 1947 (E6161/1067/34) (PRO).

164. U.K. Government, "KD," 1 March 1947 (E2937/1064/34) (PRO).

165. AIOC, "Report Up to Noon," 21 January 1947 (G15/34/47) (PRO).

166. AIOC, "Report Up to Noon," 19 August 1947 (G15/40/47) (PRO).

167. AIOC, "Report Up to Noon," 21 June 1947 (G15/34/47) (PRO).

168. Shapour Bakhtiar, 9 February 1947 (G15/42/47) (PRO).

169. Hird, 19 October 1948 (E14058/2006/34) (PRO).

170. AIOC, "Report Up to Noon," 15 September 1947 (G15/42/34) (PRO).

171. U.K. Government, "Workers in Khouzestan," 13 May 1948 (E6158/2006/34) (PRO).

172. Hird, 19 October 1948 (E14058/2006/34) (PRO).

Chapter 7

1. Charles Gault, "Report on the Isfahan Province," 25 June 1945 (E4969/222/34) (PRO).

2. Iranian Government, *Vezarat-e Kar va Tablighat*, "Amar-e Amalkard-e Sanaye'-e Keshvar dar Sal-e 1326" (Tehran, 1948).

3. Gault, "Report on the Isfahan Province," 25 June 1945 (E4969/222/34) (PRO).

4. For a description of the life of a Tabriz factory worker, see page 97 of this book.

5. U.S. Government, OSS, 23 December 1944 (RG-226/10245) (U.S. NA).

6. Gault, "Report on the Isfahan Province," 25 June 1945 (E4969/222/34) (PRO).

7. Gault, 31 December 1942 (E566/247/34) (PRO).

8. Shams Sadri, *Dar Rah-e Vazifeh: Yaddasht-ha-yeh Shams Sadri* (Esfahan, 1951), 6.

9. U.K. Government, Isfahan Consulate, "Copy of the Minute Signed in the Presence of Aghai Nasr (dated 16/6/21)" (F.O. 799/16) (PRO). Hereafter: U.K. Government, IC.

10. It is not clear why the date of the celebration preceded the date of the agreement.

11. For additional data on Fadakar, see Appendix A.

12. Sadri, *Dar Rah-e Vazifeh*, 7.

13. Other labor leaders who lost their fathers early in their life include: R. Mahzari, H. Jahani, and R. Rousta.

14. Shapour Ghane, "Interview with Iraj Fadakar" (son of Taghi), Esfahan, 30 May 1979 (unpublished).

15. Ghane, "Interview with Iraj Fadakar."

16. Reza Rousta also worked for the Soviet Commercial Office in Kerman. U.S. Government, War Department, 15 September 1945 (RG-226/32421) (U.S. NA).

17. Ghane, "Interview with Iraj Fadakar."

18. Interview with Amanollah Ghoreishi in Tehran, 11 September 1978.

19. Sadri, *Dar Rah-e Vazifeh*, 10.

20. For a discussion of CUC ideology, see pages 31–34 of this book.

21. Interview with Amir Amirkeyvan in Tehran, 24 and 25 July 1978.

22. Ibid. Also Sadri, *Dar Rah-e Vazifeh*, 15–16.

23. Sadri, *Dar Rah-e Vazifeh*, 6.

24. Ibid.

25. Ibid., 7.

26. U.K. Government, "Isfahan Diary" (hereafter "ID"), 15 January 1943 (E972/247/34) (PRO).

27. See pages 37–38 of this book.

28. U.K. Government, "ID," 31 March 1943 (E2518/247/34) (PRO).

29. Sadri, *Dar Rah-e Vazifeh*, 11.

30. U.S. Government, OSS, 23 December 1944 (RG-226/10245) (U.S. NA).

31. U.K. Government, "ID," 31 March 1943 (E2518/247/34) (PRO).

32. U.K. Government, "ID," 17 February 1943 (E1671/247/34) (PRO).

33. U.K. Government, "ID," 30 April 1943 (E3197/247/34) (PRO).

34. U.K. Government, "ID," 17 February 1943 (E1671/247/34) (PRO).

35. U.K. Government, "ID," 15 April 1943 (E2866/247/34) (PRO).

36. *Rahbar*, 8 April 1943.

37. U.K. Government, "ID," 15 April 1943 (E2866/247/34) (PRO). The employer's influence on the central government was similar to that of the British in Khouzestan. Kamal-Hedayat was the first of a series of officials to be ousted by the mill owners.

38. U.K. Government, IC, "Copy of the Minutes Signed in the Presence of Dr. Sheikh," 27 April 1943 (F.O. 799/16) (PRO).

39. See pages 24–25 of this book.

40. U.K. Government, IC, "Copy of the Minutes", 27 April 1943 (F.O. 799/16) (PRO).

41. *Rahbar*, 13 April 1943.

42. For details on the Hamrahan Party, see page 42 of this book.

43. Sadri, *Dar Rah-e Vazifeh*, 24–5. It is indicative of Fadakar's magnanimous character that he and a number of UWE members visited Hamrahan Party's offices and extended greetings to Fateh. Ibid.

44. Sadri, *Dar Rah-e Vazifeh*, 23, and U.K. Government, "ID," 30 June 1943 (E4260/247/34) (PRO).

45. Led by General Hasan Arfa.

46. *Rahbar*, 27 June 1943.

47. U.K. Government, "ID," 30 June 1943 (E4260/247/34) (PRO).

48. Ibid., 15 July 1943 (E4723/247/34) (PRO).

49. See Appendix A of this book.

50. Sarem-ed-Dowleh (Akbar Mas'oud) was the most influential private citizen in Esfahan, and a personal friend of the British consul, Gault. The ablest son of Zel-es-Soltan to survive the anti-Qajar campaign of Reza Shah, he derived his authority not only from his Qajar heritage, but also from his familial ties with the other men of wealth and power in the city as well as from his ownership of equity in most of the local textile mills.

51. Amir Amirkeyvan claims that the place of exile was changed to the more pleasant town of Damavand as a result of a bribe paid by the mill owners. Amir Amirkeyvan, interview with author, Tehran, 24–25 July 1978.

52. Ibid.

53. U.K. Government, IC, "Copy of Minutes" (F.O. 799/16) (PRO).

54. Another indication of the influence of the mill owners over the shah was given on 5 January 1946 when it was reported that the shah had stopped the order of Alahyar Saleh, minister of interior, for the dismissal of a governor-general unpopular with the EUC. Bullard, 5 January 1946 (E149/149/34) (PRO).

55. U.K. Government, IC, 31 July 1943 (E5009/247/34) (PRO).

56. Other members were: Ahmad Kaf'ami, Ne'mattollah Bahrampour, Mahmoud Boghrati, Hasan Asretala'i, Ahmad Keshavarz, Abdol-Hossein Bozorgzad, George Ghostanian, and Ali Shamideh. Sadri, *Dar Rah-e Vazifeh*, 17–8.

57. Ibid.

58. U.S. Government, Office of Intelligence and Research, no. 4940, 21 August 1950 (U.S. NA).

59. *Rahbar*, 13 April 1943.

60. *Razm*, 10 August 1943.

61. Sadri, *Dar Rah-e Vazifeh*, 29.

62. U.K. Government, "ID," 15 August 1943 (E5198/247/34) (PRO).

63. U.K. Government, "IC," 30 September 1943 (E5653/247/34) (PRO).

64. Although a number of merchants, artisans and landowners were against Fadakar's election, Gault and Sarem-ed-Dowleh succeeded in persuading them to give Fadakar their support. Sadri, *Dar Rah-e Vazifeh*, 29.

65. *Rahbar*, 26 November 1943.

66. Ibid.

67. U.K. Government, IC, 29 February 1944 (E1760/35/34) (PRO).

68. Mostafa Fateh was leader of the Hamrahan Party. The Vatan Party had opened an Esfahan branch in January 1944. Gault had worried that it would "concentrate on the oppression of the working class." U.K. Government, "ID," 15 February 1944 (E152/35/34) (PRO).

69. Ford, 10 April 1944 (RG-84/2243) (U.S. NA).

70. U.K. Government, IC, 15 April 1944 (E2788/35/34) (PRO).

71. Ford, 18 May 1944 (891.504/3) (U.S. NA).

72. Sadri, *Dar Rah-e Vazifeh*, 28. See also U.K. Government, IC, 15 March 1944 (E1968/35/34) (PRO). Mozaffar Firouz, writing in *Ra'd-e Emrouz* (22 April to 4 May 1944) and N. S. Fatemi, speaking in the Majles (Iranian Government, *Mozakerat-e Majles Chahardahom* [Tehran: 1945], 430) and Hajir (Ibid., 455–7) lent strong support to the mill owners.

73. See pages 157–58 of this book.

74. Ford, 18 May 1944 (891.541/13) (U.S. NA).

75. U.K. Government, IC, 30 April 1944 (E2960/35/34) (PRO).

76. Sadri, *Dar Rah-e Vazifeh*, 40–41.

77. U.K. Government, IC, 16 June 1944 (E3914/35/34) (PRO).

78. Sadri, *Dar Rah-e Vazifeh*, 50–52.

79. U.S. Government, OSS, 16 June 1944 (RG-226/79123) (U.S. NA).

80. Ford, 28 May 1944 (RG-84/2243) (U.S. NA). See also Iranian Government, *Mozakerat-e Majles-e Chahardahom* (Tehran, 1945), 457–564. In the second week of April, Keshavarz and Lankarani had attempted to discuss the situation in Esfahan on the floor of the Majles, but were prevented by the majority vote. *Ajir*, 15 April 1944.

81. U.S. Government, OSS, 8 July 1944 (RG-226/84161) (U.S. NA).

82. U.K. Government, IC, 15 July 1944 (E4893/35/34) (PRO).

83. Sadri, *Dar Rah-e Vazifeh*, 27.

84. U.K. Government, "ID," 30 September 1944 (E6442/35/34) (PRO).

85. Sadri, *Dar Rah-e Vazifeh*, 27.

86. Sadri, *Dar Rah-e Vazifeh*, 33.

87. *Rahbar*, 18 May 1944.

88. Sadri, *Dar Rah-e Vazifeh*, 44–8.

89. In May 1944, the U.S. embassy had reported that in an interview Fadakar

had indicated that he no longer considered himself a member of the Tudeh Party. Ford, 28 May 1944 (RG-84) (U.S. NA).

90. Sadri, *Dar Rah-e Vazifeh*, 56–8.

91. Ibid., 58–9.

92. Ibid., 58–62.

93. Ibid., 63.

94. Ibid., 67–71.

95. Ibid.

96. Ibid., 83–4.

97. Ibid., 86–90.

98. According to the British labour attache, K. J. Hird, Sadri received a monthly payment of 30,000 *rials* from the mill owners to promote their interests. Hird, 11 November 1947 (E10855/40/34) (PRO). Kambakhsh alleged that Majles Deputy Heidar-Ali Emami rented in his own name the office space used by Sadri's union. *Rahbar*, 22 January 1945.

99. According to Amirkeyvan, the articles of association was prepared by Dr. Hossein Fatemi and Ressa, former editor of *Ghanoun*.

100. U.K. Government, IC, 31 March 1945 (E2547/222/34) (PRO). Sadri, *Dar Rah-e Vazifeh*, 99–101; Amir Amirkeyvan, interview with author, Tehran, July 1978; *Dad*, 30 March 1945, and *Ajir*, 19 April 1945.

101. U.S. Government, OSS, 24 March 1945 (RG-226/54698) (U.S. NA).

102. Handley, "Labor in Iran," 31 January 1946 (RG-84/2260) (U.S. NA), 25.

103. *Ajir*, 24 April 1945.

104. U.K. Government, IC, 31 May 1945 (E4593/222/34) (PRO).

105. U.K. Government, "ID," 31 May 1945 (4593/222/34) (PRO). Also U.S. Government, OSS, 15 June 1945 (RG-226/135200) (U.S. NA), and *Bakhtar*, 27 May 1945. *Ajir* claimed that Sarrafian was killed by the employers because he intended to disclose their secret activities. *Ajir*, 29 May 1945.

106. U.K. Government, "ID," 30 June 1945 (E5391/222/34) (PRO).

107. U.S. Government, OSS, 15 April 1945 (RG-226/125113) (U.S. NA).

108. U.K. Government, "ID," 30 June 1945 (E5391/222/34) (PRO).

109. U.K. Government, "ID," 15 September 1945 (E7225/222/34) (PRO).

110. ILO, *Labour Conditions*, 46.

111. U.S. Government, "MLR," 18 April 1946 (RG-319/2159) (U.S. NA).

112. *Zafar*, 14 April 1946.

113. Fadakar's son, quoting his father, lends support to the above contention as he states that in the spring of 1946, the party instructed Fadakar to return to Esfahan with a number of emigrants from the Russian Caucasus to develop an arsenal in preparation for a possible armed uprising. Esfahan was to divert pressure from the Pishevari regime, if the central government decided to attack Azerbaijan. Ghane, "Interview with Iraj Fadakar".

114. U.K. Government, "ID," 3 May 1946 (E4669/585/34) (PRO).

115. As a measure of the reemergence of Tudeh influence in Esfahan, *Zafar* reported that 40,000 people attended the May Day rally at which Abdossamad Kambakhsh and Noureddin Kianouri spoke. *Zafar*, 15 May 1946.

116. Qavam was being more conciliatory toward labor in Tehran than in the provinces. See pages 59–60 of this book.

117. *Zafar*, 14 April 1946.

118. Ibid., 19 April 1946.

119. Ibid., 15 May 1946.

120. U.S. Government, "MLR," 28 December 1946 (RG-84/2256) (U.S. NA).

121. Ghane, "Interview with Iraj Fadakar." A thousand other Tudeh members, including Bahrampour, were arrested. U.K. Government, "ID," 30 September 1946 (E10499/585/34) (PRO).

122. See pages 57–60 of this book.

123. The same report adds: "This is the fourth occasion within a period of 3 years that the laborers in Isfahan have switched their allegiance." Nothing was said of the actions of the employers, the police, and the army in arresting and imprisoning those workers expressing "allegiance." (U.S. Government, "MLR," 28 December 1946 (RG-84/2256) (U.S. NA).

124. See page 173 of this book.

125. U.K. Government, "ID," 3 May 1946 (E46691/585/34) (PRO).

126. See pages 180–81 of this book.

127. U.S. Government, "MLR," 1 December 1947 (RG-84/2256) (U.S. NA).

128. U.K. Government, "ID," 28 February 1948 (E3470/3470/34) (PRO).

129. U.K. Government, "ID," 17 August 1948 (E11392/3470/34) (PRO).

130. Ibid., 28 February 1948 (E3470/3470/34) (PRO).

131. The employers had on their own initiative instituted a check-off system deducting 1 percent from all workers' wages. Thus, Amirkeyvan's followers were obliged to pay an additional sum to their own union.

132. U.K. Government, "ID," 17 August 1948 (E11392/3470/34) (PRO).

133. U.S. Government, "MLR," 1 October 1948 (RG-84/148) (U.S. NA).

134. U.S. Government, "MLR," 1 June 1948 (RG-84/148) (U.S. NA).

135. U.S. Government, "MLR," 1 December 1947 (RG-84/2256) (U.S. NA).

136. U.S. Government, "MLR," 1 June 1948 (RG-84/148) (U.S. NA).

137. U.K. Government, "ID," 17 August 1948 (E11392/3470/34) (PRO).

138. U.K. Government, Embassy in Tehran, "Monthly Political Report," 9 June 1948 (E8006/2252/34) (PRO).

139. U.S. Government, "MLR," 1 July 1949 (RG-84/146) (U.S. NA).

Chapter 8

1. See pages 65–66 of this book.

2. See pages 99–100 of this book.

3. See pages 164–65 of this book.

4. U.S. Government, Embassy in Tehran, "Memorandum of Conversation," 25 August 1948 (891.5043/8-3048) (U.S. NA).

5. U.S. Government, "MLR," 1 June 1948 (RG-84/148) (U.S. NA).

6. U.S. Government, "Labor Notes," 4 September 1947 (RG-84/2256) (U.S. NA).

7. U.S. Government, Embassy in Tehran, "Memorandum of a Conversation," 25 August 1948 (891.5043/8-3048) (U.S. NA).

8. Handley, 30 April 1947 (RG-84/2256) (U.S. NA).

9. Ibid.

10. Ibid.

11. U.S. Government, "Annual Labor Report, 1947–48," (hereafter, ALR) 1 October 1948 (RG-84/148) (U.S. NA).

12. Handley, 30 April 1947 (RG-84/2256) (U.S. NA).

13. U.S. Government, "ALR, 1947–48," 1 October 1948 (RG-84/148) (U.S. NA).

14. U.S. Government, "MLR," 1 June 1948 (RG-84/148) (U.S. NA).

15. U.S. Government, Military Attache in Tehran, 1 May 1947 (RG-319/370805) (U.S. NA).

16. See pages 83–84 of this book.

17. Mohammad Ali Mas'oudi informed Sharif-Emami that the shah desired his resignation. Mehdi Sharif-Emami, interview with author, Tehran, 3 August 1978.

18. U.S. Government, "Memorandum of Conversations," 25 August 1948 (891.5043/8-3048) (U.S. NA).

19. See pages 86–87 of this book.

20. U.S. Government, "ALR, 1947–48," 1 October 1948 (RG-84/148) (U.S. NA).

21. Ibid.

22. Handley, 30 April 1947 (RG-84/2256) (U.S. NA).

23. According to Handley, Naficy had surrounded himself with many of the best educated and qualified young Iranians. He himself was considered to be "one of the most sincere, able, hardworking, and honest men in Iran." Ibid.

24. Allen, 13 June 1947 (891.00/6-1347) (U.S. NA).

25. Hird, 17 June 1947 (E5527/41/34) (PRO).

26. See pages 80–81 of this book.

27. Foreign Office, 7 May 1947 (E4268/41/34) (PRO).

28. U.S. Government, "Labor Notes," 4 September 1947 (RG-84/2256) (U.S. NA).

29. U.S. Government, "Labor Notes," 1 October 1947 (RG-84/2256) (U.S. NA).

30. Ibid.

31. Le Rougetel, 31 December 1947 (E291/25/34) (PRO).

32. Le Rougetel, 8 January 1947 (E497/41/34) (PRO).

33. Handley, 30 April 1947 (RG-84/2256) (U.S. NA).

34. Hird, 17 June 1947 (E5527/41/34) (PRO).

35. U.S. Government, "Labor Notes," 4 September 1947 (RG-84/2256) (U.S. NA).

36. Hird, 11 November 1947 (E10855/40/34) (PRO).

37. U.S. Government, "Labor Notes," 1 October 1947 (RG-84/2256) (U.S. NA).

38. U.S. Government, "MLR," 1 November 1947 (RG-84/2256) (U.S. NA).

39. With the CUC affiliate in Khouzestan smashed and lack of worker support for government-controlled unions, there were no viable unions in Khouzestan.

40. Hird, 11 November 1947 (E10855/40/34) (PRO).

41. See pages 164–65 of this book.

42. EMKA claimed to represent some 28,000 industrial and 50,000 agricultural workers and peasants. Commenting on these figures, British Labor Attache Hird stated "these figures cannot be checked but they are probably a more honest assessment than the membership figures claimed by any other workers' organization in Persia." Hird, 11 November 1947 (E10855/40/35) (PRO). The American embassy, on the other hand, considered these figures to be "a fabulous exaggeration." The embassy estimated EMKA's membership to be "surely less than 10,000 and probably less than 5,000." U.S. Government, "MLR," 1 December 1947, (U.S. NA). ESKI claimed 75,000 members. Ibid.

43. Ibid.

44. Ibid.

45. See Appendix A.

46. Naficy had himself aided Shams Sadri's rise to power by electing him labor

delegate to the ILO conference of October 1945. See pages 55–57 of this book.

47. U.S. Government, "MLR," 1 December 1947 (RG-84/2256) (U.S. NA).

48. U.S. Government, "ALR, 1947–48," 1 October 1948 (RG-84/148) (U.S. NA).

49. U.S. Government, "MLR," 1 December 1947 (RG-84/2256) (U.S. NA).

50. Hird, 11 November 1947 (E10855/40/34) (PRO).

51. U.S. Government, "MLR," 1 December 1947 (RG-84/2256) (U.S. NA).

52. Hird, 11 November 1947 (E101855/40/34) (PRO).

53. Ibid.

54. U.S. Government, "MLR," 1 December 1947 (RG-84/2256) (U.S. NA).

55. Ibid.

56. Following the vote of no confidence against Qavam by the Majles, the chamber president, Sardar Fakher Hekmat, accompanied by Hedayat, led the seizure of the Democratic Party headquarters. U.S. Government, "MLR," 2 January 1948 (RG-84/148) (U.S. NA).

57. U.S. Government, "MLR," 2 February 1948 (RG-84/148) (U.S. NA).

58. Ibid.

59. See pages 78–79 of this book.

60. U.S. Government, "MLR," 2 February 1948 (RG-84/148) (U.S. NA).

61. Ibid.

62. Ibid.

63. U.S. Government, "MLR," 1 April 1948 (RG-84/148) (U.S. NA).

64. U.S. Government, "MLR," 2 February 1948 (RG-84/148) (U.S. NA).

65. Hird, 30 April 1948 (E6672/3313/34) (PRO).

66. Ibid.

67. U.S. Government, "MLR," 1 April 1948 (RG-84/148) (U.S. NA).

68. Other committee members were: Asadollah Sadeghiar, Sabou Hosseini, and Habibollah Bijar.

69. U.S. Government, "ALR, 1947–48," 1 October 1948 (RG-84/148) (U.S. NA).

70. Hird, 16 August 1948 (E11427/821/34) (PRO).

71. U.S. Government, "MLR," 1 October 1948 (RG-84/148) (U.S. NA).

72. U.S. Government, "MLR," 1 November 1948 (RE-319/506663) (U.S. NA).

73. U.S. Government, "MLR," 2 January 1948 (RG-84/148) (U.S. NA).

74. U.S. Government, "MLR," 1 October 1948 (RG-84/148) (U.S. NA).

75. U.S. Government, "MLR," 1 December 1948 (RG-84/2257) (U.S. NA).

76. Ibid.

77. U.K. Government, "Report on Economic Conditions," 21 December 1948 (E16246/10005/34) (PRO).

78. U.S. Government, "MLR," 1 December 1948 (RG-84/2257) (U.S. NA).

79. U.K. Government, "Report on Economic Conditions," 21 December 1948 (E16246/10005/34) (PRO).

80. U.S. Government, "MLR," 31 December 1948 (RG-84/148) (U.S. NA).

81. U.S. Government, "MLR," 1 December 1948 (RG-84/2257) (U.S. NA).

82. No condemnation or even criticism was ever made by the U.S. embassy of such activity by the army which was being actively developed and advised by the U.S. government.

83. U.S. Government, "MLR," 1 December 1948 (RG-84/2257) (U.S. NA).

84. U.S. Government, "MLR," 31 December 1948 (RG-84/148) (U.S. NA).

85. U.S. Government, "ALR, 1951," 10 May 1952 (888.06/5-1052) (U.S. NA).

86. See page 59 of this book.

87. See page 129 of this book.

88. U.S. Government, "ALR, 1951," 10 May 1952 (888.06/5-1052) (U.S. NA).

89. Ibid.

90. U.S. Government, "Annual Labor Report on Iran, 1952," 19 January 1953 (888.06/1-1953) (U.S. NA).

91. Ibid.

92. Ibid.

93. Ibid.

94. Ibid.

95. Ibid.

96. Ibid.

97. Ibid.

Chapter 9

1. U.S. Government, "Basic Survey of Labor Affairs in Iran," September 26, 1955 (888.06/9-2655) (U.S. NA), 28. Hereafter: U.S. Government, "Basic Survey of Labor."

2. Ibid., 29.

3. U.S. Government, "Labor Affairs in Iran: September 1955–January 1957," January 31, 1957 (888.06/1-3157) (U.S. NA), 7. Hereafter: U.S. Government, "Labor Affairs in Iran."

4. U.S. Government, "Basic Survey of Labor," 40.

5. U.S. Government, "Labor Affairs in Iran," 19.

6. U.S. Government, "Basic Survey of Labor," 30.

7. Ibid., 22.

8. Ibid., 21.

9. U.S. Government, "Labor Affairs in Iran," 15.

10. U.S. Government, "Basic Survey of Labor," 40.

11. See page 161 of this book.

12. Mohammad Reza Shah Pahlavi, *Mission for My Country* (London: Hutchinson, 1961) 183.

13. U.S. Government, "Labor Report–1960," 29 March 1961 (888.06/3-2961) (U.S. NA), 13.

14. Ibid., 43.

15. U.S. Government, "Labor Report–1963," 3 February 1964 (888.06/2-364) (U.S. NA), 15.

16. U.S. Government, "Basic Survey of Labor," 5.

17. U.S. Government, "Annual Report–1952," 13.

18. U.S. Government, "Basic Survey of Labor," 42.

19. Ibid.

20. U.S. Government, "Labor Affairs in Iran," 15.

21. Ibid., 4–5.

22. Ibid., 5.

23. Ibid.

24. U.S. Government, "Basic Survey of Labor," 28.

25. U.S. Government, "Labor Affairs in Iran," 5.

26. No evidence subject to public scrutiny was presented for this and similar allegations.

27. U.S. Government, "Basic Survey of Labor," 48.

28. U.S. Government, "Labor Affairs in Iran," 6.

29. U.S. Government, "Labor Affairs in Iran," 5.

30. U.S. Government, "Basic Survey of Labor," 28.

31. Ibid., 4.

32. Ibid., 28-9.

33. Ibid., 36.

34. See page 191 of this book.

35. U.S. Government, "Basic Survey of Labor," 46.

36. Amir Amirkeyvan attended the ILO conference for the last time in 1956. U.S. Government, "Labor Affairs in Iran," 46.

37. U.S. Government, "Basic Survey of Labor," 35.

38. Ibid., 44.

39. See pages 61-64 of this book for details of the previous law.

40. U.S. Government, "Basic Survey of Labor," 43.

41. This function was taken over by the SAVAK after 1957.

42. U.S. Government, "Basic Survey of Labor," 43-4.

43. Ibid.

44. Ibid., 40.

45. Ibid.

46. U.S. Government, "Basic Survey of Labor," 43.

47. U.S. Government, "Basic Report-1961," 26 September 1962 (888.06/9-2662) (U.S. NA), 15.

48. Ibid.

49. See page 135 of this book regarding setting of wages after the Abadan General Strike.

50. U.S. Government, "Labor Report-1960," 44.

51. U.S. Government, "Basic Report-1961," 7.

52. U.S. Government, "Basic Report-1962," 6 July 1963 (888.06/7-663) (U.S. NA), 4.

53. Ibid.

54. U.S. Government, "Labor Report-1959," 4 June 1960 (888.06/6-460) (U.S. NA), 44.

55. U.S. Government, "Basic Survey of Labor," 21.

56. U.S. Government, "Labor Report-1960," 44.

57. See page 178 of this book for previous brick kiln workers strike.

58. U.S. Government, "Basic Report-1961," 4.

59. U.S. Government, "Labor Report-1960," 7.

60. U.S. Government, "Labor Report-1959," 47.

61. See page 15 of this book.

62. U.S. Government, "Labor Affairs in Iran, 1957," 2-3.

63. Ibid.

64. Ibid., 3.

65. U.S. Government, "Labor Affairs in Iran, 1957," 2.

66. M. R. Shah Pahlavi, *Mission for My Country*, 173.

67. Ibid.

68. Ibid., 178.

69. Ibid., 164.

70. U.S. Government, "Labor Affairs in Iran, 1957," 5.

71. U.S. Government, "Labor Affairs in Iran, 1957," 9–10.

72. U.S. Government, "Semi-Annual Labor Report, July through December 1958," May 9, 1959 (888.06/5-959) (U.S. NA), 1.

73. Ibid., 4–5.

74. M. R. Shah Pahlavi, *Mission for My Country*, 184.

Chapter 10

1. U.S. Government, "Basic Survey of Labor," 36.

2. Ibid., 44.

3. Ibid., 37.

4. U.S. Government, "Basic Report–1961," 16.

5. U.S. Government, "Basic Survey of Labor," 50–51.

6. See pages 62–63 of this book.

7. U.S. Government, "Labor Report–1959," 2.

8. Ibid., 11.

9. U.S. Government, "Semi-Annual Labor Report, July through December 1958" (888.06/5-959), 7.

10. U.S. Government, "Annual Report–1952," 11.

11. U.S. Government, "Basic Report–1961," 11.

12. U.S. Government, "Basic Report–1962," 6–7.

13. U.S. Government, "Labor Report–1959," 1.

14. U.S. Government, "Basic Report–1962," 6–7.

15. Ibid., 13.

16. U.S. Government, "Basic Report–1962," 6–7.

17. U.S. Government, "Basic Report–1961," 15.

18. U.S. Government, "Labor Report–1959," 8.

19. Ibid.

20. M. R. Shah Pahlavi, *Mission for My Country*, 172.

21. Ibid., 170.

22. Dr. Mohammad Baheri, interview with author, Cannes, France, August 1982.

23. U.S. Government, "Basic Report–1961," 18.

24. U.S. Government, "Labor Report–1960," 8.

25. U.S. Government, "Basic Report–1961," 12.

26. Ibid.

27. U.S. Government, "Labor Report–1960," 16–17.

28. U.S. Government, "Basic Report–1961," 12.

29. Ibid., 13.

30. U.S. Government, "Labor Report–1960," 18a.

31. See pages 92–93 of this book.

32. M. R. Shah Pahlavi, *Mission for My Country*, 169.

33. Ibid., 172.

34. Ibid., 164.

35. See page 86 of this book.

36. U.S. Government, "Basic Report–1962," 8.

37. U.S. Government, "Basic Report–1961," 14.
38. U.S. Government, "Basic Report–1962," 8.
39. Ibid.
40. Ibid., 9.
41. U.S. Government, "Basic Report–1961," 17.
42. M. R. Shah Pahlavi, *Mission for My Country*, 183.
43. Ibid., 183–184.
44. Ibid.
45. Ibid., 184.
46. Ibid., 186.
47. U.S. Government, "Basic Report–1962," 9.
48. Ibid., 10.
49. U.S. Government, "Labor Report–1963," 4.
50. See pages 59–60 of this book.
51. U.S. Government, "Labor Report–1963," 2.
52. Ibid., 4.
53. Ibid.
54. Ibid., 3.
55. Ibid., 2.
56. Ibid., 2.
57. U.S. Government, "Basic Report–1961," 16.
58. Ibid., 11.
59. U.S. Government, "Labor Affairs in Iran, 1957," 6.
60. Ibid.
61. U.S. Government, "Basic Report–1961," 11.
62. Ibid.
63. Ibid., 12.
64. U.S. Government, "Labor Report–1963," 1.
65. U.S. Government, "Basic Report–1962," 9.
66. U.S. Government, "Labor Report–1963," 3.
67. U.S. Government, "Basic Report–1962," 9.
68. U.S. Government, "Labor Report–1963," 4.
69. U.S. Government, "Basic Report–1962," 9.
70. Ibid.
71. Ibid.
72. U.S. Government, "Labor Affairs in Iran, 1957," 26–27.

Epilogue

1. Ervand Abrahamian, *Iran Between Two Revolutions* (Princeton: Princeton University Press, 1982), 434.
2. Ibid., 448.
3. Ibid., 448–449.
4. U.S. Government, "Basic Labor Report 1962," 6 July 1963 (888.06/7-663) (U.S. NA), 5–6.
5. See for example J. C. Harper, *Profit Sharing in Practice and Law* (London: Sweet & Maxwell, 1955).

6. Ibid.

7. E. Robert Livernash and Kamal Argheyd, "Iran," in A. Blum, *International Handbook of Industrial Relations, Contemporary Development and Research* (Westport, CN: Greenwood Press, 1981), 274.

8. Ibid., 267.

9. Ibid.

10. Assef Bayat, "Workers' Control After the Revolution," Middle East Research and Information Project (Merip), *Reports*, No. 113, March–April 1983, 21.

11. Livernash and Arghayd, "Iran," 269.

12. Ibid.

13. Bayat, "Workers' Control," 22.

14. Ibid., 21.

15. M. R. Shah Pahlavi, *The Shah's Story* (London: Michael Joseph, 1980), 95.

16. Habib Ladjevardi, "The Minimum Wage" (Unpublished case study) (Tehran: Iran Center for Management Studies, 1975), 3.

17. Ladjevardi, "The Wider Share Ownership (A)" (Unpublished case study) (Tehran: Iran Center for Management Studies, 1975), 4.

18. Ibid.

19. Ladjevardi, "The Wider Share Ownership (B)" (Unpublished case study) (Tehran: Iran Center for Management Studies, 1975), 1.

20. Ladjevardi, "The Wider Share Ownership (C) (Unpublished case study) (Tehran: Iran Center for Management Studies, 1976), 4.

21. Ibid., 11. In a report to the shah the minister of industries and mines stated that 64 companies had transferred 20 percent of their shares for sale to workers, farmers, and the public to the Financial Organization. He also reported that applications for purchase of shares had been received from workers in 75 companies. Ibid. The shah states that by 1978, 153 industrial companies had sold their shares to 163,000 workers and peasants. M. R. Shah Pahlavi, *The Shah's Story*, 95.

22. *Ettela'at*, 1 May 1978.

23. Abrahamian, *Iran Between Two Revolutions*, 510.

24. Ibid., 517.

25. Ibid., 518.

26. Ibid., 518.

27. Ibid., 516.

28. M. R. Shah Pahlavi, *The Shah's Story*, 125.

29. Ibid., 95.

30. Ibid., 157.

31. Abrahamian, *Iran Between Two Revolutions*, 427.

32. *The World in Figures* (London: The Economist Newspaper, 1981), 18, 20, 21.

33. Abrahamian, *Iran Between Two Revolutions*, 427.

34. Bayat, "Workers' Control," 19–20.

35. *Ettela'at*, 4 March 1979.

36. Ibid., 19 March.

37. Ibid., 2 May 1979.

38. Ibid., 2 May 1979.

39. See Chapter 1 of this book.

40. *Ettela'at*, 2 May 1979.

41. Bayat, "Workers' Control," 20.

42. Ibid., 21.

43. Ibid., 22.

44. See Chapter 5, pages 100-101.

45. *Khalgh-e Mosalman,* no. 12, 28 October 1979.

46. Shaul Bakhash, *The Reign of the Ayatollahs: Iran and the Islamic Revolution* (New York: Basic Books, 1984), 183.

47. *Kar,* no. 48, 28 February 1979.

48. Bayat, "Workers' Control," 19.

49. Bakhash, *The Reign of the Ayatollahs,* 182.

50. Bayat, "Workers' Control," 19.

51. Ibid., 19.

52. *Ettela'at,* 30 April 1980.

53. Ibid., 3 May 1980.

54. Ibid.

55. Ibid.

56. Ibid.

57. Bayat, "Workers' Control," 21.

58. Ibid.

59. Ibid., 20.

60. *Nameh-e Mardom,* 2 May 1981.

61. Bayat, "Workers' Control," 20.

Bibliography

Unpublished Primary Sources

National Archives Building, Washington, D.C., U.S.A.

Record Group 59, General Records of the Department of State, Series: Document numbers 800.5041, 891.00/159 to 3064, 891.00/6-1344 to 12-3046, 891.5041/3 to 5045/1.
Record Group 226, Records of the Office of Strategic Services (Iran).
Record Group 319, Record of the Army Staff, boxed: 406, 2159, and 2160.
Reports of the Office of Intelligence & Research, Department of State, Nos. 4304, 4940, 5272, and 5714.15.

Washington National Records Center, Suitland, MD., U.S.A.

Record Group 84, Records of the Foreign Service Posts of the Department of State, boxes: 146, files 350, 350.3, 370, 500, 500.2, 560, 560.2, 850; 148, files 850.4 (Labor); 2243, files 700, 710, 800, 800.1, 800.2, 800.3, 801.A, 844, 846; 2244, files 800, 850; 2255, file 800; 2256, files 800, 850.4; 2257, file 800; 2258, file 850.4; 2259, file 950.4; 2260, files 350, 360.1, 850.4.
Record Group 319, Records of the Army Staff, boxes 460 (G-2 Message file), 2159 and 2160.
Handley, W. J. "Labor in Iran," 31 January 1946 (RG-84/2260/850.4).
_____. "Labor in Iran," 19 October 1946 (RG-84/2260/850.4).

——. "Visit of the W.F.T.U. Delegation to Iran," 30 April 1947 (RG-84/2256/850.40).
——. "Labor Conditions in A.I.O.C.," 3 July 1947 (RG-319/0407874).

Public Record Office, London, England

F.O. 248 (Tehran), Legation and Consular Correspondence, 1941–1948. Piece numbers: 1453, 1468, 1471–2, 1475, 1479, 1483, 1488, 3511, 45433–54, 52763, 52768, 52791, 52794, 61968–75, 61992, and 61995.
F.O. 371 (Persia), Political and General Correspondence, 1941–1948. Piece numbers: 137873–4, 27249, 31408, 31412, 31426, 31429, 31439, 35063–4, 35078, 35090–4, 35117, 35120–1, 40158–63, 40177–9, 40219, 40222, 40224, 40228, 45460–1, 45476–8, 45483, 45512, 52704–6, 52713–26, 52740–2, 61968–78, 61981–4, 61992–4, 62008, 62025, 62059, 68703–4, 68711, 68723B, 68725B, 68734, 68737–8, 68741, 68746–7, and 68750.
F.O. 799 (Isfahan), Consular Correspondence, 1941–1948. Piece numbers: 3, 6, 10, 11, 16, and 32.
LAB. 13, International Labour, 1941–1948. Piece numbers: 39, 123, and 164.

Doctoral Dissertations

Abrahamian, E. "Social Bases of Iranian Politics: The Tudeh Party, 1941–53." Ph.D. thesis, Columbia University, 1969.
Agah, M. "Some Aspects of Economic Development of Modern Iran." D. Phil. thesis, University of Oxford, 1958.
Ladjevardi, H. "Labour and Politics in Iran." D. Phil. thesis, University of Oxford, 1981.
Mohammadi-Nejad, H. "Elite-Counterelite Conflict and the Development of a Revolutionary Movement: The Case of Iranian National Front." Ph.D. thesis, Southern Illinois University, 1970.
Raji, S. "The Evolution and Modernization of Industrial Relations System in Iran." Ph.D. thesis, New York University, 1972.
Tabari, K. "Iran's Policies Toward the United States During the Anglo-Russian Occupation, 1941–1946." Ph.D. thesis, Columbia University, 1967.
Vahdat, M. "The Soviet Union and the Movement to Establish Autonomy in Iranian Azarbaijan." Ph.D. thesis, Indiana University, 1958.

Interviews

Amirkeyvan, Amir, a leader of EMKA and ITUC; 24–25 July 1978, Tehran and 8 March 1984, Ft. Lauderdale, FL.

Azar (Enghelab), Khalil, a leader of the Central Board; 20 July 1978, Tehran (by telephone).

Chisholm, R. A., former industrial relations officer, AIOC; October 1978, London.

Dahesh, Abbas-Gholi, owner of Nour Mill in Esfahan; 24 July 1978, Tehran.

Dowlatabadi, J., a leader of the CUC; 28 August 1978, Tehran.

Fadakar, Iraj, son of Taghi Fadakar, founder of the UWE; 30 May 1979, Esfahan (interview conducted by Shapour Ghane).

Farmanfarmaian, Aziz, member of the Iranian delegation to the 1945 ILO Conference; 16 July 1978, Tehran.

Farmanfarmaian, Mohammad-Vali, minister of labor and propaganda, October–December 1946; 16 July 1978, Tehran.

Gault, Charles, British consul in Esfahan; 13 February 1979, London.

Ghoreishi, Amanollah, a leader of the CUC; 11 September 1978, Tehran.

Handley, William J., former American labor attache in Cairo; 21 September 1977, Richmond, VA.

Kazerouni, Seyyed Khalil, former head of Labor Office, AIOC; 31 July 1977, Tehran.

Khajehnouri, Mohsen, host to the WFTU Delegation to Iran in 1947; 27 July 1978, Tehran.

Naficy, Habib, former vice minister of labor; 8 August 1977, Tehran and 1–2 February 1984, Cambridge, MA.

Tafazzoli, Haj Hasan, owner of the Kashan Spinning & Weaving Mill; 26 July 1977, Kashan.

Case Studies

Ladjevardi, Habib. "The Minimum Wage," Tehran: Iran Center for Management Studies, 1975.

_____. "The Wider Ownership Program (A)," Tehran: Iran Center for Management Studies, 1975.

_____. "The Wider Ownership Program (B)," Tehran: Iran Center for Management Studies, 1975.

_____. "The Wider Ownership Program (C)," Tehran: Iran Center for Management Studies, 1976.

Published Primary Sources

Books and Articles

AIOC. *The Anglo-Iranian Oil Company.* London: Anglo-Iranian Oil Company, 1947.

Alavi, Bozorg. *Panjah-o-Seh Nafar.* Tehran: [194?].

Arfa, H. *Under Five Shahs.* London: Murray, 1964.

Asnad-e Tarikhi-e Jonbesh-e Kargari Sosiyal Demokrasi va Kommonisti-e Iran, i–vi. Florence: Mazdak, 1972–1976.

Bahar, Mohammad Taghi. *Tarikh-e Mokhtasar-e Ahzab-e Siyasi-e Iran: Engheraz-e Qajar.* Tehran: Rangin Press, 1942.

Bakhash, S. *The Reign of the Ayatollahs: Iran and the Islamic Revolution.* New York: Basic Books, 1984.

Bayat, Assef. "Workers' Control After the Revolution." In *Merip Reports,* No. 113, March–April 1983.

Chaqueri, C. *The Conditions of the Working Class in Iran.* London: 1978.

Farhang-Ghahramani, A. *Assami-e Nemayandegan-e Majles-e Showra-ye Melli.* Tehran: Majles Press, 1977.

Fateh, Mostafa. *Panjah Sal Naft-e Iran.* Tehran: Chehr Press, 1956.

ILO. "Agricultural & Industrial Activity and Manpower in Iran." In *International Labour Review* 49 (1949).

————. *Labour Conditions in the Oil Industry in Iran.* Geneva: ILO, 1950.

————. *Record of Proceedings of 27th Session International Labour Conference.* Paris: ILO, 1945.

Iran Almanac and Book of Facts. Tehran: Echo of Iran. Published since 1970.

Iranian Government. *Majmou'eh-e Ghavanin.* Tehran: Rouznameh-e Rasmi. Published since 1907.

————. *Mozakerat-e Majles-e Showra-ye Melli.* Tehran: Majles Press. Published since 1907.

————. Vezarat-e Kar va Tablighat (Ministry of Labor). *Amar-e Amalkard-e Sanaye'-e Keshvar dar Sal-e 1326.* Tehran: Vezarat-e Kar, 1948.

————. Vezarat-e Kar. *Amar-e Amalkard-e Sal-e 1328.* Tehran: Vezarat-e Kar, 1949.

————. Vezarat-e Kar. *Eghdamat-e Gheir-e Ghanouni.* Tehran: Vezarat-e Kar, 1947.

Ironside, Lord E., ed. *High Road to Command: The Diaries of Major-General Sir Edmund Ironside, 1920–22.* London: Leo Cooper, 1972.

Keshavarz, Dr. F. *Man Mottaham Mikonam.* Tehran: Ravagh Press, 1979.

League of Nations, Commission on Inquiry into the Production of Opium in Persia. *Report to the Council.* Geneva: League of Nations, 1926.

Makki, H. *Doktor Mossadegh va Notgh-ha-ye Tarikhi-e Ou.* Tehran: Elmi Press, 1945[?].

Mani, S. *Tarikhcheh-e Nehzat-e Kargari-e Iran.* Tehran: 1979.

Millspaugh, A. C. *The American Task in Persia*. New York: Arnos Press, 1973.
Pahlavi, Ashraf. *Faces in a Mirror*. New York: Prentice Hall, 1980.
Pahlavi, Mohammad Reza Shah. *Mission for My Country*. London: Hutchinson & Co., 1961.
____. *The Shah's Story*. London: Michael Joseph, 1980.
Pahlavi, Reza Shah. *Safar Nameh-e Khouzestan*. Tehran: Ministry of Court, 1976.
Sadri, Shams. *Dar Rah-e Vazifeh: Yaddasht-ha-ye Shams Sadri*. Esfahan: 1951.
Shorayeh Mottahedeh[?]. *Tarikhcheh-e Mokhtasar-e Showra-ye Mottahedeh-e Markazi-e Ettehadieh-e Kargaran-e Iran*. Tehran: 1953[?].
Zarghami-Boroujeni, J. *Dowlat-ha-ye Asr-e Mashroutiyat*. Tehran: Majles Press, 1971.

Newspapers and Journals

Ajir. Tehran: 1943–1945.
Asr-e Eghtesad. Tehran: 1944.
Bakhtar. Tehran: 1943–1945.
Bakhtar-e Emrouz. Tehran: 1952–1953.
Dad. Tehran: 1945–1950.
Dariya. Tehran: 1944–1946.
Demokrat-e Iran. Tehran: 1946–1947.
Donya. Irregular.
Ettela'at. Tehran: 1941–1983.
Haghighat. Tehran: 1921–1922.
Jebheh. Tehran: 1946–1947.
Jebheh-e Azadi. Tehran: 1950–1951.
Kar (Journal of the Ministry of Labor). Tehran: 1947–1949.
Kar. Tehran: 1979.
Khalgh-e Mosalman. Tehran: 1979.
Mardom. Tehran: 1943–1949 and 1979–1982.
Neda-ye Haghighat. Tehran: 1945–1947.
Ra'd-e Emrouz. Tehran: 1943–1946.
Rahbar. Tehran: 1943–1946.
Razm. Tehran: 1944–1946.
Shahbaz. Tehran: 1945.
Zafar. Tehran: 1944–1946.
Zendegi. Tehran: 1948–1949.

Published Secondary Sources

Abdullaev, Z. Z. *Formirovanie rabochevo klassa Irana.* Baku: Izdanie Akad. Nauk, 1968.

Abrahamian, E. *Iran Between Two Revolutions.* Princeton: Princeton University Press, 1982.

Arasteh, R. *Education and Social Awakening in Iran, 1850–1968.* Leiden: Brill, 1969.

Badi, S. M. *Rabochii klass Irana.* Moscow: Nauka, Glav. Red. Vostochnoe Litry, 1965.

Banani, A. *The Modernization of Iran, 1921–1941.* Palo Alto: Stanford University Press, 1961.

Bartsch, W. H. & J. Bharier. *The Economy of Iran 1940–70: A Bibliography.* Durham: Durham, 1971.

Bharier, J. *Economic Development in Iran 1900–1970.* London: Oxford University Press, 1971.

Bill, J. *The Politics of Iran: Groups, Classes and Modernization.* Columbus, OH: Merrill, 1972.

Browne, E. G. *The Press and Poetry of Modern Iran.* Cambridge, England: Cambridge University Press, 1914.

Cottom, R. *Nationalism in Iran.* Pittsburgh: University of Pittsburgh Press, 1964.

Djamalzadeh, M. A. "An Outline of the Social and Economic Structure of Iran." In *International Labour Review,* LXIII, 2. Geneva: 1951.

Ducroq, G. "La Politique du Gouvernment des Soviet en Perse." In *Revue du Monde Musulman,* LII. Paris: December 1922.

Elwell-Sutton, L. P. *Modern Iran.* London: George Routledge & Sons, 1941.

——. *Persian Oil: A Study in Power Politics.* London: Lawrence and Wishart, 1955.

——. "Political Parties in Iran." In *The Middle East Journal.* Washington, D.C.: Winter 1949.

Fatemi, N. S. *Diplomatic History of Iran 1917–1923.* New York: Russell F. Moore Co., 1951.

Hammond, T. T. *Lenin on Trade Unions and Revolution 1893–1917.* New York: Columbia University Press, 1957.

Harper, J. C. *Profit Sharing in Practice and Law.* London: Sweet & Maxwell, 1955.

Issawi, C. ed. *The Economic History of Iran 1800–1914.* Chicago: University of Chicago Press, 1971.

Ivanov, M. S. *Rabochii klass sovremennogo Irana.* Moscow: Nauk, 1969.

Jowdat, Dr. H. "Mobarezat-e Kargaran va Siyasi-e Zed-e Kargari-e Selseleh-e Pahlavi." In *Donya,* XII. February 1976.

Kambakhsh, A. S. *A Short Survey of Worker's and Communist Movement in Iran.* Stockholm: Tudeh Press, 1975. 2 vols.

Ladjevardi, H. "The Origins of U.S. Support for an Autocratic Iran." In *International Journal of Middle Eastern Studies*, 15. New York: May, 1983.

Lenczowski, G. "The Communist Movement in Iran." In *The Middle East Journal*. Washington, D.C.: January, 1947.

____. *Russia and the West in Iran 1918–1948: A Study in Big Power Rivalry.* Ithaca, NY: Cornell University Press, 1949.

____, ed. *Iran Under the Pahlavis.* Stanford: Hoover Institution Press, 1978.

Livernash, E. R. and Argheyd, K. "Iran." In *International Handbook of Industrial Relations*, edited by A. Blum. Westport, Ct.: Greenwood Press, 1981.

Lodge, G. *Spearheads of Democracy, Labor in the Developing Countries.* New York: Harper & Row, 1962.

Makki, H. *Tarikh-e Bist Saleh-e Iran.* Tehran: Majles Press, 1944–1945. 3 vols.

Military Governorship of Tehran. *Seyreh Kommonism dar Iran az Shahrivar-e 1320 ta Farvardin 1336.* Tehran: Military Governorship of Tehran, 1958.

Millen, B. H. *The Political Role of Labor in Developing Countries.* Washington, D.C.: Brookings Institution, 1963.

Mo'tamedi, F. *Tarikh va Hoghough-e Kar va Bimeh-e Ejtema'i dar Iran.* Tehran: 1975.

Rossow, R., Jr. "The Battle of Azarbaijan, 1946." In *The Middle East Journal*, 10. Washington, D.C.: Winter, 1956.

Rubin, B. *Paved with Good Intentions.* New York: Oxford University Press, 1980.

Sadr-Hashemi, M. *Tarikh-e Jarayed va Majallat-e Iran.* Esfahan: 1949. 3 vols.

Saikal, A. *The Rise and the Fall of the Shah.* Princeton: Princeton University Press, 1980.

Skrine, C. *World War in Iran.* London: Constable, 1962.

United States Government, Bureau of Labor Statistics. *Labor Law and Practice in Iran.* Washington, D.C.: Government Printing Office, 1964.

Waterfield, G. *Professional Diplomat, Sir Percy Loraine 1880–1961.* London: Murray, 1973.

Wilbur, D. N. *Reza Shah Pahlavi.* Hicksville, NY: Exposition Press, 1975.

Zabih, S. *The Communist Movement in Iran.* Berkeley, Ca.: University of California Press, 1966.

Zonis, M. *The Political Elite of Iran.* Princeton: Princeton University Press, 1971.

Index

LABOR UNIONS AND AUTOCRACY IN IRAN

was composed in 10-point Harris Fototronic TxT Aster and leaded 2 points by
Skillful Means Press, with display type in Legend by Dix Typesetting Company, Inc.;
printed sheet-fed offset on 50-pound, acid-free Glatfelter Antique Cream,
Smyth sewn and bound over 80-point binder's boards in Joanna Arrestox B
by Maple-Vail Book Manufacturing Group, Inc.; with dust jackets printed in 2 colors by
Philips Offset Company, Inc.; and published by

SYRACUSE UNIVERSITY PRESS
SYRACUSE, NEW YORK 13210